THE ENTREPRENEUR'S LEGAL COMPANION

D0713978

Daniel V. Davidson, J.D.

Radford University

Lynn M. Forsythe, J.D.

Craig School of Business
California State University, Fresno

Prentice Hall
Boston   Columbus   Indianapolis   New York   San Francisco   Upper Saddle River
Amsterdam   Cape Town   Dubai   London   Madrid   Milan   Munich   Paris   Montreal   Toronto
Delhi   Mexico City   Sao Paulo   Sydney   Hong Kong   Seoul   Singapore   Taipei   Tokyo

Editorial Director: Sally Yagan
Editor in Chief: Eric Svendsen
Acquisitions Editor: Kim Norbuta
Editorial Project Manager: Claudia Fernandes
Editorial Assistant: Meg O'Rourke
Director of Marketing: Patrice Jones
Marketing Manager: Nikki Jones
Marketing Assistant: Ian Gold
Senior Managing Editor: Judy Leale

Project Manager: Debbie Ryan
Production Manager: Fran Russello
Art Director: Jayne Conte
Cover Designer: Karen Salzbach
Full-Service Project Management: Sadagoban Balaji/Integra
Composition: Integra Software Services Pvt. Ltd.
Printer/Binder: Courier Companies, Inc.
Text Font: 10/12, Times Ten Roman

Credits and acknowledgments borrowed from other sources and reproduced, with permission, in this textbook appear on appropriate page within text.

Many of the designations by manufacturers and sellers to distinguish their products are claimed as trademarks. Where those designations appear in this book, and the publisher was aware of a trademark claim, the designations have been printed in initial caps or all caps.

Library of Congress Cataloging-in-Publication Data
Davidson, Daniel V.
  The entrepreneur's legal companion / Daniel V. Davidson, Lynn M. Forsythe. —1st ed.
    p. cm.
Includes bibliographical references and index.
ISBN-13: 978-0-13-607723-7 (alk. paper)
ISBN-10: 0-13-607723-4 (alk. paper)
  1. Businesspeople—Legal status, laws, etc.—United States. 2. Business enterprises—Law and legislation—United States. I. Forsythe, Lynn M. II. Title.
KF390.B84D38 2001
346.73'065—dc22

2009029910

10 9 8 7 6 5 4 3 2 1

Prentice Hall
is an imprint of

www.pearsonhighered.com

ISBN 10:   0-13-607723-4
ISBN 13: 978-0-13-607723-7

To my family—
My father, Joseph Davidson, who has always been there for me
My wife, Dee Davidson, my best friend
My children, Jaime and Tara, the pride and the joy of my life
Thank each of you for what you have added to my life.

—*Daniel Davidson*

To my family for all their love, support, and encouragement, especially Jim, Mike, and Mary Helen Poptanich and Aileen and Robert Zollweg

To John S. Poptanich, who was so generous with his advice and recommendations, especially with Chapter 13

To my Law for Entrepreneurship students for their helpful suggestions and enthusiasm for the subject

Thank you all.

—*Lynn M. Forsythe*

BRIEF TABLE OF CONTENTS

CONTENTS

PART V AVOIDING PROBLEMS: AN OUNCE OF PREVENTION

CHAPTER 14   Identifying Legal Risks Before *they* Become Legal Problems   283

PREFACE

FOCUS OF THE BOOK

The focus of the book is to address what entrepreneurs need to know about a number of legal issues in order to protect their ideas and investments in their enterprises. The book provides practical information about how to manage and minimize legal risks.

INTRODUCTION

Entrepreneurs are risk takers. Whether a person has decided to provide a new product or a new service, or has decided to provide an existing good or service in a new manner, he or she is taking a risk that the public will like the idea and support the endeavor. This is beneficial to society, because the entrepreneurial spirit is a key ingredient of the U.S. economy.

Being a risk taker does not mean being a risk *seeker*. It is one thing for entrepreneurs to take the risk that their product or service will capture sufficient market share. It is another thing altogether to disregard the risks presented by being careless or rash. Successful ventures are led by entrepreneurs using the legal protections that are available to them when launching their ventures.

Taking a preventative law approach, the purpose of this legal companion is to assist entrepreneurs on their journeys to success. It is often said that the way to be a successful entrepreneur is to make fewer mistakes than the competition. One way to do this is to anticipate the problems and to use the law to avoid them. Successful businesses seek to maximize profits as a path to value creation. One way to increase profits is to reduce risks. To do this though, entrepreneurs need to recognize and understand the different risks associated with launching and operating ventures. As the authors explain in this companion, many of the risks entrepreneurs experience are in the legal domain. This companion facilitates entrepreneurs' efforts to recognize and avoid legal risks as a foundation for venture growth and success.

The legal risks may vary depending on the type of enterprise. For example, a retailer will face different risks than a firm providing services, and an Internet host will be exposed to different risks than a photography studio. The authors will discuss the legal risks common to nascent enterprises.

Law provides rules, protections, and even potential liabilities in such areas as contracts, employment law, intellectual property, choosing a business form, and a myriad of other areas. Many of these topics will be addressed in this book. Although a single book cannot provide a comprehensive and detailed listing of all the legal areas entrepreneurs are likely to encounter, the authors address many of the key topics which are critical in launching ventures.

The discussion will begin with the decision to hire a lawyer. The appropriate choice can help entrepreneurs avoid many legal problems. Lawyers can be "partners" in helping entrepreneurs navigate their way through the problems that arise. By recognizing when a potential legal problem is involved, entrepreneurs can contact their attorneys in a timely fashion to prevent serious financial harm. When entrepreneurs wait until small legal issues become large legal problems, the issues are more difficult and time-consuming for their attorneys to resolve. Entrepreneurs can assist their attorneys by collecting and maintaining appropriate records.

Contracts can provide protections for entrepreneurs, such as protections from unauthorized disclosures of trade secrets or practices and protections from having key employees leave the venture to open their own competing firms. Contracts can also create obligations and potential liabilities that are not expected. When people use legal terms in contracts, courts will give the terms the legal meaning even if the people did not know that meaning. Offhand comments that are made in discussing the possibility of doing business may be deemed offers that the other people can "accept." Entrepreneurs can be bound to contracts before they realize it. Entrepreneurs can be sued for fraud based on statements in their business plan. So, *now* is the time to start learning about the legal environment of entrepreneurs and entrepreneurial ventures.

DISTINGUISHING FEATURES

This book includes a number of charts and exhibits to aid the entrepreneur's comprehension. Each chapter includes several *application questions* near the end of the chapter. These are questions for the entrepreneur to consider when *making decisions* about the topics covered in the chapter. The questions are at the intersection of law and business decision making, highlighting the key points raised in the chapter and emphasizing the practical implications of the topical coverage. Each chapter concludes with several *suggested activities* which encourage the reader to personally investigate one or more areas that were discussed in the chapter in order to get a "feel" for some of the things that will need to be addressed when a venture is launched.

When this book refers to an organization, resource, or Web site, the reference does not mean that the authors or the publisher endorse the organization, resource, or Web site and the recommendations that they may make. Internet

Web sites may change or disappear between the date of writing this book and when entrepreneurs use it.

The authors recognize that there are men and women entrepreneurs. In fact, there is a growing body of research about how men and women approach their entrepreneurial ventures in different ways. In referring to entrepreneurs the authors have decided to use masculine in one chapter and feminine in the next.

SUPPLEMENTS

Supplements are available for adopting instructors to download at www. pearsonhighered.com/irc. The site also includes detailed descriptions of the supplements. Registration is simple and gives the instructor immediate access to new titles and new editions. Pearson's dedicated technical support team is ready to help instructors with the media supplements that accompany this text. The instructor should visit http://247.pearsoned.com/ for answers to frequently asked questions and for toll-free user support phone numbers. Supplements include:

- Instructor's Manual
- PowerPoint Slides

COMPANION WEB SITE A useful companion Web site, www.pearsonhighered. com/entrepreneurship, offers free access to teaching resources for all books in the Prentice Hall Entrepreneurship Series including additional activities, links to latest research, sample entrepreneurship curriculum and syllabi, teaching tips, and Web resource links.

CourseSmart textbooks online is an exciting new choice for students trying to economize. As an alternative to purchasing the print textbook, students can subscribe to the same content online and save up to 50% off the suggested list price of the print text. With a CourseSmart etextbook, students can search the text, make notes online, print out reading assignments that incorporate lecture notes, and bookmark important passages for later review. For additional information on this option visit www.coursesmart.com.

ACKNOWLEDGMENTS

We are indebted to a number of individuals in the development of this book. We would like to thank Integra Software Services for their efforts in getting the book into print. We are indebted to Michael H. Morris and R. Duane Ireland for inviting us to participate in the Entrepreneurship Series. Their constructive comments and suggestions have helped us focus on key issues of concern to entrepreneurs.

We are also indebted to John S. Poptanich for his assistance with Chapter 13. His practical experience in dealing with insurance claims and insurance litigation provided a valuable perspective. His willingness to read drafts on short notice and to do additional research is also appreciated. However, any errors in the chapter are our responsibility and not his.

We also appreciate the assistance of the Prentice Hall publication team, especially Kim Norbuta and Claudia Fernandes.

Daniel V. Davidson, J.D.
Radford University

Lynn M. Forsythe, J.D.
Craig School of Business
California State University, Fresno

ABOUT THE AUTHORS

Daniel Davidson

Daniel Davidson is an alumnus of the Indiana University—Bloomington College of Business and the Indiana University—Bloomington School of Law. Professor Davidson has been teaching business law and legal environment classes since 1974, with stops at five different campuses over his career. He is currently teaching and serving (for the second time) as Chair of the Department of Accounting, Finance & Business Law at Radford University in Radford, Virginia. Professor Davidson has previously served as a part of the author team on three other textbooks, and he has authored or co-authored numerous journal articles. Professor Davidson has been the recipient of numerous teaching awards and several advising awards during his career. He is married to Dee Davidson, a high school math teacher, and is the proud father of a son, Jaime, who is the marketing director for the Berkshire Theater Company, and a daughter, Tara, who is a high school English teacher.

Lynn M. Forsythe

Lynn M. Forsythe received her B.A. from the Pennsylvania State University and her J.D. from the University of Pittsburgh School of Law. She passed the bar examinations in the states of California and Pennsylvania. She is professor of business law at the Craig School of Business at California State University, Fresno. Professor Forsythe has received numerous Craig School of Business awards, including the research award in 2008 and the service award in 2003, and again in 2006. She held the Verna Mae and Wayne A. Brooks Professorship of Business Law. She is a Coleman Fellow at the California State University Fresno Lyles Center for Innovation and Entrepreneurship.

Professor Forsythe is the author or co-author of numerous articles on business law and business law pedagogy. She served as a part of the author team on two other textbooks. She has held the positions of advisory editor, editor-in-chief, staff editor, and reviewer for *The Journal of Legal Studies Education.* She received two recent best paper awards, the 2009 Western Academy of Legal Studies in Business Best Paper Award and the 2007 Allied Academies Conference Distinguished Research Paper Award.

Professor Forsythe is active in the Academy of Legal Studies in Business. She has served as the chair and vice-chair of the Business Ethics Section of the academy. She has served in the officer ranks of the Western Regional Academy of Legal Studies in Business first from 1983 to 1987 and then from 2006 to 2009. She has also served as the Delegate or Alternate Delegate from the Western Region on numerous occasions.

Professor Forsythe is currently the Secretary of the Craig School of Business Chapter of Beta Gamma Sigma. She is also a member of Alpha Kappa Psi.

HIRING A LAWYER TO HELP PROTECT THE ENTERPRISE

Being a smart legal consumer can be the best weapon against lawsuit abuse.[1]

INTRODUCTION

Entrepreneurs are, by definition, risk takers. However, this does not mean that an entrepreneur should be a risk enhancer or should act in a reckless manner. While risks are unavoidable in the business environment, the prudent business person, and certainly the prudent entrepreneur, takes steps to minimize some, if not all, of the risks being faced.

After the prudent entrepreneur decides that she can meet an unmet need, or meet a need better than competitors, she must make several crucial decisions. First, and most important, is deciding on the *nature* of the business being started. Will the enterprise sell goods to customers, as a retailer or wholesaler, or will it sell services to customers? This, in turn, will help the entrepreneur decide whether the business will initially be operated locally, regionally, nationally, or internationally. Of course, the entrepreneur should also have some idea about the future plans and objectives for the geographic scope of the business operation since this will directly impact the second decision.

Next, the entrepreneur needs to decide on the best *organizational form* for the business. (This topic is covered in detail in Chapter 3.) Does the entrepreneur want to form a sole proprietorship, a partnership, a limited partnership, a limited liability partnership (LLP), a limited liability company (LLC), or a corporation? If the corporate form is chosen, should it be an "S" corporation or a "C" corporation? Should it initially be closely held or publicly traded? What are the implications, the benefits, and the burdens of choosing one form over the others? The decision reached here will potentially have long-term and far-reaching effects on the enterprise and should not be made lightly or hastily.

The first two crucial decisions are rather obvious to anyone who is considering launching a business venture, and the entrepreneur has probably been considering them. The third crucial decision to be made, however, is much less likely to have been considered: who will provide legal representation to the venture? Once the entrepreneur has decided on the attorney that she wishes to hire, a decision should be made about *how* to hire the attorney. For example, should the attorney be on **retainer**, or consulted on a case-by-case basis as needed? Most entrepreneurs avoid hiring an attorney on retainer because doing so requires an expenditure of funds early in the relationship. This is potentially disadvantageous because new ventures are often strapped for cash.

Retainers usually take one of two forms: either the client pays a certain amount of money for legal work to be performed, with the attorney then deducting fees and expenses as they are incurred, or the client pays a "retainer fee" in order to have the attorney "on call," available to the client as needed—and with fees charged for each time that such services are needed in addition to the retainer fee initially paid.

CHOOSING AN ATTORNEY

GATHERING RECOMMENDATIONS

Choosing an attorney is easy, but choosing the right attorney is more difficult. It requires an investment of time and energy, and the right attorney for one purpose will not necessarily be the right attorney for another legal purpose at another time. Many people select an attorney based on references from family and friends or word of mouth, basing their decision on their general perception of the attorney's qualifications and reputation. While this method has some validity, it is also fraught with danger. Before following the recommendations of friends and family, entrepreneurs should be certain that these friends and family members have had similar legal issues. For these reasons, an entrepreneur might do better soliciting recommendations from other entrepreneurs or venture capitalists. An attorney who is very highly regarded for his or her ability in preparing wills or handling divorces may not be a good selection for handling negotiations with a union or in drafting a contract for the international sale of goods to a foreign customer.

Many ventures regularly deal in one or more specific legal areas as a part of the firm's normal business practices. In such circumstances, the firm should seek lawyers who specialize in these areas. The firm may find that one lawyer is excellent in one or more of the areas in which representation is needed but is not as well versed or qualified in other areas. In such a situation, the firm may need to have multiple attorneys, depending on the legal issue involved in any given situation. It is not necessary to rely exclusively on one attorney or even one law firm for all of one's legal needs, although it is much simpler if the entrepreneur can do so. Just as some people choose a general practitioner to handle and coordinate their medical care, many entrepreneurs hire a general business attorney to coordinate their legal affairs. The general business attorney can anticipate legal problems in many legal areas and coordinate the efforts of the specialists.

The National Federation of Independent Business (NFIB) and the Citizens Against Lawsuit Abuse (CALA) issued a guide that provides "Helpful Tips for Hiring a Lawyer."[2] According to this guide, a business person can find legal counsel through any of the following resources:

1. The State Bar Association, through the local bar association, which will provide names of attorneys in the locality who specialize in the type of legal issues involved, and also will inform the business person if any of these attorneys have been the subject of an ethical inquiry or complaint.

2. Lawyer referral services, which will refer the business person to an attorney who handles legal issues similar to those the business person is facing. There is normally a fee, frequently $30, associated with the use of a referral service. This fee is paid by the business person. Often the business person is entitled to a half hour consultation with the attorney to whom she is referred for no additional fee.

3. Recommendations, which were discussed above, especially those from fellow entrepreneurs who have faced similar situations, and from venture capitalists. Recommendations should also be sought from the entrepreneur's attorney, if that attorney does not specialize in the legal issues for which assistance is needed.

4. Advertisements, whether through the Yellow Pages, billboards, the Internet, or the media. The NFIB does point out that many lawyers do not advertise, and the entrepreneur should not believe everything that she sees in these advertisements. (The prudent entrepreneur would be well advised to cross-reference any attorney who has a particularly effective advertisement with the State Bar Association to see if the attorney's resume matches the advertising claims put forth.)

The recommendations of fellow entrepreneurs and the entrepreneur's attorney are probably the most relevant of these. Fellow entrepreneurs are likely to have faced similar situations and can call on their experience in making a recommendation, while the entrepreneur's attorney has a vested interest in the success of the venture and is also likely to have worked with—or against—any attorney he or she recommends, and has firsthand knowledge of the recommended attorney.

In addition, entrepreneurs may want to check *The Martindale-Hubbell Law Directory*, an excellent source of all-around information about attorneys. The directory is available on the Internet, through services such as Lexis. Martindale-Hubbell lists practicing attorneys by state and by city; it also lists areas of practice, backgrounds, honors, and publications. Perhaps the most important aspect of the listings in Martindale-Hubbell is a rating system under which attorneys are rated in three areas: legal skills, ethics, and professionalism. Ratings are voluntary, and not all attorneys choose to be rated. These ratings are derived from confidential surveys of local judges and attorneys, and provide a good indication of the respect with which any given attorney is held in his or her local legal community. These ratings are less important, but they do provide the entrepreneur with a measure of the respect of the local bar for the rated attorney, which should be a factor in selecting an attorney.

For those times that the entrepreneur needs a trial attorney, the National Board of Trial Advocacy publishes a membership directory that contains information on experienced trial attorneys. This is the only American Bar Association–approved directory of trial lawyers, and the board is the only national organization that certifies civil trial lawyers based on objective data.

Before the entrepreneur interviews the attorneys, she should think about the venture. Where is it now? Where will it be in three years or five years? What legal issues does she anticipate? Every venture will deal with contract law issues, an area in which virtually all attorneys are competent and comfortable, but many ventures will face legal issues in specialized areas. For example, if the venture will be manufacturing goods for export, an attorney who specializes in trade law will be needed. A venture that will be dealing with unionized employees will need an attorney who is familiar with labor law. An entrepreneur who is relying on a patent to gain access to an industry will need an attorney who regularly handles patent law issues. The entrepreneur should prepare a written document to help clarify the background needed in a lawyer.

INTERVIEWING THE ATTORNEYS

Once the entrepreneur has gathered the names of those attorneys who possess the desired background, it is time to make a selection. In order to do so, the entrepreneur should contact at least four or five of the lawyers on the list to arrange for interviews. (Some advise the entrepreneur to interview as many lawyers as possible. However, the entrepreneur wants to start the venture, not become an expert in hiring lawyers.) As one commentator noted, "There is no substitute for a face to face meeting when you are trying to select an attorney."[3] Before calling to schedule an appointment, the entrepreneur should be prepared to explain her situation and why an appointment is necessary. The entrepreneur should clarify whether the attorney will charge for the meeting and the information that should be brought. She should also be certain to find out what the attorney will expect from her as the client.

The entrepreneur may decide to invite the prospective lawyer to lunch, since a luncheon is less formal and it provides an opportunity to get to know the lawyer and his or her personality. If the lawyer is going to use junior associates or paralegals, it would be advantageous to invite them as well. The entrepreneur may find that she has more direct contact with these assistants than the attorney.

After interviewing each attorney, the entrepreneur should answer the following questions:

1. Am I comfortable enough with this individual to work with him or her?

2. Does this lawyer have the experience and the skill to adequately represent me and my business interests?

3. Do the lawyer's explanations seem clear and logical? For example, does he or she communicate in plain English or speak "legalese," making it difficult to follow the explanation? Is the lawyer condescending and aloof, or does he or she seem to be genuinely interested in working with the entrepreneur?

4. Do the lawyer's fees and expenses seem reasonable and justified?

5. Will the fee arrangement be in writing?

If the answer to each of these questions is "yes," the entrepreneur should consider hiring the attorney. If any question results in an answer of "no," the search for an attorney should continue.[4]

The final hiring decision may be affected by a few other questions that the entrepreneur will need to ask of the attorney(s) that she finds acceptable. Many of these questions can also be answered with a simple "yes" or "no."

1. Can the entrepreneur pay over time? Larger law firms are more likely to offer payment plans. The entrepreneur should ask for monthly billings even if she is spreading the payments over time, thus allowing the entrepreneur to better manage the legal fees and her cash flow.

2. Does the law firm use the Internet? This may provide an effective communication technique for the parties, and a good way to avoid "phone tag."

3. Does the law firm use secure Internet connections so that email communications are relatively safe?

4. How long does it normally take the attorney to reply to messages?

5. How much does the lawyer know about the industry that the entrepreneur is entering?

6. Does the lawyer have much experience dealing with entrepreneurs or handling their legal issues and problems?

7. Is the lawyer acquainted with other business people, including venture capitalists and bankers?

HIRING THE ATTORNEY

Once the entrepreneur has decided which attorney to hire, she will need to decide on what basis the attorney will be hired. There are a number of standard fee arrangements that are likely to be available, and the entrepreneur-as-client and

TABLE 1.1 Standard Fee Arrangements
Flat Fee—Payment of a set dollar amount for a particular service. Normally a flat fee arrangement is used for simple, straightforward activities.
Hourly Rate—Payment at a set dollar amount per hour (or portion thereof) devoted to the case or the legal issue involved. The hourly rate is likely to increase for time spent in hearings or in court. An hourly rate is likely to be used in those situations where the work is more complicated.
Contingency Fee—The attorney will receive a percentage of any amount the entrepreneur recovers as a result of the legal action. The percentage may vary, and often can be negotiated by the entrepreneur, perhaps in the form of a sliding scale based on the size of the recovery. The entrepreneur will still be liable for expenses incurred by the attorney in handling the matter. Normally used in civil suits involving a tort, especially if the attorney expects to be able to prevail in the cause of action. An attorney generally declines to accept the case on a contingent fee basis if he or she does not expect to prevail.
Retainer—A fee paid in advance by the entrepreneur to secure the services of the attorney for work to be performed in the future. Some retainers are "down payments" for services to be rendered; as the work is performed funds are deducted from the original fee; the amount may need to be replenished from time to time to assure adequate funds. Other retainer agreements ensure that the attorney will represent the entrepreneur, and the fee is for the assurance of representation. Any work actually performed will be billed at either a flat fee or an hourly rate, depending on the type of legal services provided. The prepayment requirement may be a "deal breaker" for nascent entrepreneurs.

the attorney will need to discuss which arrangement is best for their situation. As with any contractual relationship, it is important that the entrepreneur understand how she will be billed and what services will be provided. The standard fee arrangements are listed in Table 1.1. The entrepreneur will have to determine which fee arrangement is best in her particular situation. There is no "best" fee arrangement for entrepreneurs, consequently each individual entrepreneur should determine which fee arrangement works best in her particular situation. Even then, as the venture grows and matures, the best fee arrangement for that venture is likely to change. Thus, the entrepreneur will need to decide how to proceed based on her particular circumstances and the financial wherewithal of the venture at the time. If the venture is in its start-up phase, an hourly fee arrangement is likely to be most appropriate since it only requires the commitment of funds on an as-needed basis. A more stable venture may be better served by a retainer with the attorney, especially if the entrepreneur has confidence in the attorney or the law firm based on prior transactions.

If the attorney is being hired for a particular purpose or to handle a specific case, he or she is likely to be hired on either a *flat fee* basis or on an *hourly* basis. With a flat fee arrangement, the attorney is paid a specified dollar amount to provide a specific service. This arrangement is most likely to be used for something relatively standard and straightforward, such as incorporating a business or filing for bankruptcy.

If the legal situation is not so simple and straightforward, the lawyer is more likely to insist on being hired on an hourly basis. In this arrangement the lawyer charges a set fee per hour for each hour devoted to the legal issue or case. The hourly rate will also vary if the lawyer has to go to court, as opposed to handling the case less formally outside the courtroom. There is no set hourly rate for all lawyers, and lawyers with more experience and expertise will normally charge more per hour than lawyers with less experience or expertise. The experienced lawyer may still cost less because he or she may complete the task in fewer hours. It also increases the total costs to the business if a lawyer makes a mistake handling the venture's affairs. There are also regional differences in the hourly rates that attorneys charge.

When an attorney is hired on an hourly rate, the entrepreneur should ask for a written estimate of the number of hours likely to be needed. This provides an estimate of the expected total cost so the entrepreneur does not suffer from "sticker shock" when the bill is received. Also, if it actually takes much longer than estimated, the attorney may feel obligated to bill for the number of hours on the estimate. The entrepreneur should also ask whether junior associates or paralegals will be doing any of the work and what the hourly rate is for their services.

If the entrepreneur would like to use the attorney for more general representation, she should discuss hiring the attorney on a *retainer* basis. When an attorney accepts a retainer, he or she is paid a set amount "up front" in exchange for agreeing to represent the client for some specific time. The attorney is agreeing to be "on call" for the client, and has guaranteed to be available during the retainer period. Depending on the terms of the retainer agreement, the client may have to pay the retainer first in order to assure that the attorney is "on call" and available, and then the client will have to pay an hourly rate when the attorney is actually used. One of the assurances that the attorney is generally providing is that he or she will not accept another client who wants to sue or negotiate with the entrepreneur. The retainer agreement may also be viewed as a form of prepayment for legal services to be rendered, with any actual legal expenses being deducted from the balance in the retainer account as work is performed. Remember, however, that this up-front payment may be a financial strain on a new venture, perhaps with severe cash flow consequences. As a result, the entrepreneur will likely be better served, at least initially, by hiring the attorney on an hourly basis.

The attorney and the entrepreneur may also agree to a **contingency fee** arrangement, an arrangement in which the lawyer agrees to accept a percentage of any settlement acquired on behalf of the entrepreneur rather than being paid on the basis of either an hourly rate or a flat fee. Contingency fees are most often used when the entrepreneur is the plaintiff in a tort action and the attorney expects to recover a significant verdict. The contingency fee agreement often calls for one percentage rate if the case is settled out of court, with a second and higher percentage if the case goes to trial. The agreement might, for example, call for the attorney to receive one third of the settlement if the case is settled and one half if the case is decided at trial. Even if the parties agree to a contingency fee arrangement, the client will be expected to pay the litigation expenses incurred by the attorney. Sometimes the lawyer is willing to pay these expenses initially and then bill the entrepreneur for them. It is also important for the entrepreneur to find out if the contingency percentage is taken from the recovery before such expenses are deducted or after the deduction of expenses.

LARGE LAW FIRMS OR SMALLER FIRMS

Large law firms with many lawyers also have many clients. When entrepreneurs choose such a firm, they may discover that the firm cannot represent them in a particular matter because the "opponent" is also a client of the firm.

Large firms often charge a higher hourly rate, although they may be more efficient resulting in a lower overall cost. This may be attributable to the use of lower-cost junior associates and paralegals.

Large firms often have specialists in a variety of areas. If the entrepreneur chooses a large firm, she may not need to search for other counsel when a new legal issue arises. It is likely that the firm will have attorneys who specialize in areas such as trial work and patent law. It is probable that the entrepreneur did not meet these attorneys during the interview process. The entrepreneur may discover that she does not care for the personality of other attorneys in the firm.

One of the most important aspects of the large firm/small firm decision is how important will the entrepreneur be to the firm. If the entrepreneur hires a small firm, she may be one of the firm's most important clients. If the entrepreneur selects a large firm, she may be one of the smallest clients. This may influence how quickly the lawyer responds to the entrepreneur's urgent needs.

USING A LAWYER EFFECTIVELY

Selecting and hiring an attorney with whom the entrepreneur is comfortable and in whom she has confidence is only the first step in obtaining adequate legal representation. The entrepreneur needs to utilize this lawyer effectively to generate the greatest benefit with the least expense possible. An attorney's time is precious—and expensive—and the entrepreneur should take care to not waste her own time or the attorney's time when legal services are needed. In order to use her lawyer effectively, the entrepreneur should make every reasonable effort to be prepared before contacting the lawyer and to communicate clearly and concisely during the contact. The entrepreneur should also realize that the mere fact that an attorney has been hired or is available does not mean that the attorney needs to be consulted on every matter. Since entrepreneurs are generally proactive, they are less likely to take the time to consult with their attorney on every matter. They may be more likely to underuse than to overuse their attorney.

Obviously, there will be times when the entrepreneur needs to contact her attorney promptly because legal services are needed right away. If the entrepreneur receives service of process because she is being sued, the entre-preneur needs to contact the attorney as quickly as possible. Similarly, if the entrepreneur determines that she needs to file suit against another party, the entrepreneur should contact her attorney in a timely manner to discuss the matter and to ensure that the necessary steps are taken before the statute of limitations expires. However, many of these situations will arise owing to the commission of a tort, a civil wrong, most commonly in a non-business setting. An entrepreneur who has legal issues that arise in the normal course of her business will usually have the time to review the situation, to consider options, and to decide whether the attorney needs to be brought into the process. Of course, if there is any doubt about the advisability of bringing the lawyer into the process, the lawyer should be asked. If the entrepreneur has chosen the attorney wisely, the entrepreneur will be able to trust that the attorney will become involved only if his or her involvement is appropriate.

Before contacting the lawyer, the entrepreneur should formulate a brief statement that summarizes the issue, so that when the lawyer is called the entre-preneur can recount the problem succinctly. A 20- to 30-word summary of the issue is ideal. The entrepreneur then calls the attorney to make an appointment and provides the prepared statement summarizing the reason for the appoint-ment; the attorney will be able to estimate the amount of time likely to be needed and can schedule the appointment accordingly. The attorney can then request the necessary background information from the entrepreneur. Since the entrepre-neur lacks specific legal expertise, she may be surprised about what information is relevant to the legal matter.

Prior to the appointment itself, the entrepreneur should prepare a summary of the relevant information, together with a listing of dates, times, names, and addresses.[5] The summary of the relevant information should, ideally, be reduced to one or two pages, with the names and addresses and any other information appended. If there are any documents that are germane to the issues, a copy of these documents should also be appended. By providing the attorney with a con-cise summary and copies of the relevant documents, the attorney can more quickly and easily determine the best course of action for the entrepreneur. The attorney will also be able to determine if the situation will require the services of another attorney, one who specializes in the legal area that is involved in the particular case. In addition, by providing the information in an organized man-ner, the entrepreneur can minimize the time that the attorney needs to make an informed decision and provide a recommendation. The old adage "Time is money" should be amended slightly in these situations; when meeting with one's attorney, the saying should be "His time is my money."

When the entrepreneur is entering into contracts, she may find it cost effec-tive to write up the contract terms and then have the attorney write the actual contract. These documents are sometimes called term sheets. Obviously, the entrepreneur should avoid inserting terms that she does not understand. In the alternative, the entrepreneur may obtain a standard form contract and mark what should be changed and what she does not understand. The entrepreneur can then review the draft with the lawyer. (These ideas will be addressed in more detail in Chapter 12.)

For example, suppose an entrepreneur is planning to hire a person in an executive position. This newly hired individual will have access to propriety information that is being treated confidentially within the enterprise, possibly even treated as a trade secret. If the entrepreneur intends to include a non-disclosure statement, or a covenant not to compete in the employment contract, she should prepare some appropriate guidelines and then consult with her attorney to have the contract drawn up. The attorney will be able to ensure that these restrictions are likely to be upheld by the courts if a dispute should arise, being neither too restrictive, and thus possibly thrown out, nor too lax, thus failing to provide the protections initially sought.

The entrepreneur may also want to send the lawyer news clippings and articles that relate to the venture, and to ask the lawyer to send her articles. When the entrepreneur and lawyer have an ongoing relationship, this helps remind the lawyer about the entrepreneur and her venture. The attorney is more likely to think of the impact on the entrepreneur's venture when he or she reads about a new statute or court case.

The entrepreneur should also consider having the attorney periodically attend meetings with the venture's board of directors or management team. Often the entrepreneur will not realize that a planned action may have potentially negative legal implications. By having the attorney attend some of these meetings, the attorney will be able to recognize the potential problems and warn the entrepreneur in advance, thus possibly averting a misstep. The attorney will also be available if the entrepreneur, her management team, or the board of directors have questions about potential legal implications of an action or the best way to address a particular issue from a legal perspective. Some lawyers specializing in small businesses may agree to attend a certain number of meetings without an additional charge. However, even if there is an hourly fee charged for the attorney's attendance and participation, the savings from avoiding legal problems may make the expenditure a wise "investment."

USING LEGAL SPECIALISTS

Many attorneys develop a specialty in some area of law, whether through interest, experience, or serendipity. "Entrepreneurial law" is not recognized as a legal specialty at this time. However, the current business trends and practices that form the impetus for many entrepreneurial ventures also tend to drive the development of some of these legal specialties as attorneys recognize a growing demand for a particular specialization that coincides with their interests. There are attorneys and law firms that seek out entrepreneurships and small businesses as clients, thereby developing an expertise in the area even though it is not recognized as a "legal specialty" yet. The use of such a specialist, when appropriate, can be of tremendous benefit to the client, even though such a specialist is likely to charge more per hour than the client's regular attorney. However, the specialist may still be more cost effective because he or she can perform the service more quickly and accurately. For an entrepreneur the use of attorneys who specialize in different areas of the law may, on occasion, be essential for the betterment of the enterprise.

If an entrepreneur is launching a business on the basis of an invention, she will be well advised to seek the advice and guidance of a patent attorney. Patent law falls into the category of intellectual property law, a complicated field, and the lawyers who specialize in this area are apt to have a significant advantage over an attorney who has a more broad-based practice. Patents, copyrights, licensing, and trademarks involve very specific laws domestically and somewhat complex treaties in the international environment. Unless the attorney is familiar with these statutes and treaties, he or she is not likely to provide the same quality of advice and guidance as the specialist, and the time that it will take for the attorney to acquire even a portion of that expertise will be billed to the client. Thus, the added expenses of the specialist may be offset by the reduced number of hours needed to resolve the issue.

An entrepreneur who will be involved in a technology-related endeavor is likely to need a lawyer who possesses special technical expertise. Technical knowledge, whether involving computers and software or e-commerce, is a relatively new specialization, but one that is growing in importance and popularity.

If the entrepreneur will be dealing with unions, she may be better served by procuring the services of a labor law specialist than by relying on her regular attorney. While the regular attorney is likely to be very qualified and efficient when it comes to drafting a contract, he or she may be much less qualified to draft a collective bargaining agreement. Familiarity with the various federal and state labor and employment laws and knowledge of "hot button" issues that regularly arise in these areas will more than offset the extra expense of retaining the specialist, while also allowing the entrepreneur to take preventative steps to avoid the problem areas.

In a similar vein, employment law is an area in which an entrepreneur would be wise to rely on specialists because of the ever-changing scope of such areas as the Americans with Disabilities Act, the Family and Medical Leave Act, and the various equal employment opportunity topics that fall within the jurisdiction of the Equal Employment Opportunity Commission (EEOC).

Environmental law is another legal topic that is likely to require the use of a lawyer with special expertise. Compliance with the various environmental laws, both federal and state, is essential, and violations can be extremely expensive. The entrepreneur who will be operating a manufacturing facility, or who will be generating wastes and by-products that may pose an environmental hazard, will need the guidance of an environmental specialist.

Immigration law is a specialization that is increasingly in demand, especially for entrepreneurs engaging in any of a number of service industries. For example, the construction industry in many parts of the country has a significant number of immigrant employees, and the entrepreneur employer needs to ensure that she is in compliance with the immigration laws and that all of the employees are legally able to be employed. The increasing concern about illegal immigrants across the country makes this a specialization that is quite likely to grow significantly in the near future.

Entrepreneurs need to remember that lawyers are licensed by the individual states, and most U.S. lawyers are not licensed to practice outside their home state. They are generally not licensed to practice in foreign countries either. In addition, lawyers who are involved in international trade tend to specialize in certain countries. They are commonly used to assist in negotiations and review documents. Establishing a factory in China involves different issues and nuances than establishing a factory in Mexico. An attorney or law firm with experience dealing with a particular country or region can help the entrepreneur avoid some of the pitfalls that often arise in dealings with that country or region.

If an entrepreneur plans to establish the business as a partnership, a limited partnership, an LLP, an LLC, or a corporation, she will need to comply with federal and state securities regulations. While many attorneys are quite competent to handle the legal issues involved with securities at the state level in a particular state, a significant number will be less prepared to address the same or similar issues when the Securities and Exchange Commission's (SEC) rules and regulations are potentially at issue. In fact, a number of attorneys will recommend that the entrepreneur either consult with a specialist in securities law or allow the attorney to do so. Of course, the entrepreneur will be paying for this consultation in either case.

Recognizing when a legal specialist should be consulted, and then finding the correct specialist for the situation, will likely carry a higher initial expenditure, but the benefits over time will more than offset this additional initial cost, especially when the specialist helps the entrepreneur to avoid problems that might otherwise have occurred.

Table 1.2 lists the current "top five" areas of legal specialization, as determined by LawCrossing, a Web site listing jobs in law.

Other specialization topics listed as potential growth areas include environmental law, commercial real estate, and corporate compliance, especially with the new regulations imposed under Sarbanes-Oxley. Sarbanes-Oxley will be covered in more detail in Chapters 3 and 6.

TABLE 1.2 Today's Top Legal Specialties
1. Intellectual Property Law
2. Technical Expertise
3. Corporate Transactions
4. Private Equity
5. Immigration

Source: Maheu, Karen, "What's Hot? Today's Legal Specialities," *LawCrossing*, found at http://www.lawcrossing.com/article/index.php?id-3767.

HOW MUCH WILL THE ATTORNEY COST?

While the entrepreneur wants to work with an attorney or a law firm with whom she is comfortable, the attorney or law firm needs to be one that she can afford. Given the fact that cash is often tight, especially in the initial days of the venture, costs must be reasonable for the venture and must fit within the overall budget of the operation. Thus, the entrepreneur needs to understand how much the legal representation will cost, and how the expenses will be billed.

BILLING PRACTICES OF LAW FIRMS

The entrepreneur should ask the lawyer to provide a sample bill of the sort that she is likely to receive. This will give the entrepreneur a good idea of how readable the bill is and what types of things will be included. For example, law firms generally charge for things like making copies, courier service, and even for returning phone messages or taking phone calls. For business advice most lawyers charge by the hour or by the job. If the lawyer is charging by the hour, what increments does the firm use for billing? Does the attorney bill for 30-minute increments or 6-minute increments? A lawyer generally bills each time he or she gets the file out and speaks to the entrepreneur. Some lawyers charge for responding to emails, and some do not. Some lawyers may agree to attend one board meeting a month without charging for the time. The entrepreneur may want to negotiate for this. It is extremely valuable because the lawyer can alert the board and the chief executive officer to potential legal problems implicit in certain decisions. It will also keep the enterprise in the mind of the lawyer, who may know about opportunities or have valuable contacts.

One issue that may arise involves "hidden head counts." The lawyer may request that junior associates and paralegals attend meetings. This can result in being billed for two or three legal representatives from the law firm at the same meeting. The entrepreneur should ask that only one legal representative attend meetings unless she expressly approves more than one. Before approving the additional people, the entrepreneur should ask whether she will be billed for these additional people and how their attendance at the meeting will benefit the entrepreneur. The entrepreneur does not want to pay for the legal training of junior associates and paralegals.

It is not only permissible but also advisable to ask questions about bills and billing that the entrepreneur does not understand. The entrepreneur should also keep track of her contacts with the law firm, with whom she spoke, and the issue that was discussed. Such a record may prove valuable if there is ever a billing dispute.

ATTORNEY–CLIENT PRIVILEGE

Entrepreneurs tend to be somewhat reluctant to discuss the details of their enterprises, fearing that someone may take what one learns in the discussion to launch his own competing business, potentially to the entrepreneur's detriment. This is especially true for entrepreneurs involved in a business that concerns intellectual property. This reticence makes perfect sense when talking with most people, but it will be a detriment to the entrepreneur and her interests when talking with her lawyer. In order for a lawyer to provide the best advice and guidance possible, the lawyer needs access to all of the relevant information. Without full disclosure by the client, the lawyer cannot properly provide the services for which he or she was hired.

Fortunately for all involved, these communications between the client and the attorney can be open, candid, and unfiltered, thanks to the existence of the **attorney–client privilege**. "Attorney–client privilege protects confidential communications between an attorney and his or her client 'made for the purpose of furnishing or obtaining professional legal advice and assistance.'"[6] This privilege prohibits an attorney from revealing any communications between the attorney and the client without the client's permission except when the client informs the attorney of the client's intention to commit a crime in the future. The privilege belongs to the client, not to the attorney, and only the client can waive this privilege. The privilege is considered to be a fundamental right, preserving the constitutional right to having the assistance of counsel.[7] However, once the entrepreneur officially begins the business, for example, by forming it as a corporation, LLP, or LLC, the business itself may become the client. The entrepreneur should make it clear in her relationship with the attorney as to who is the client.

In a similar vein, the **attorney's work product** is privileged, although this privilege is not an absolute one. The attorney's work product refers to those tangible items the attorney has prepared in preparation for a trial, or in anticipation of a possible trial at some later date. The work product privilege is not a complete protection since a court may compel the disclosure of "factual" work product if the opposing counsel can show a substantial need for the information sought.[8] By contrast, the protection afforded to "opinion" work product, work reflecting the attorney's subjective beliefs and strategies, is nearly absolute.[9]

In applying this chapter, the entrepreneur should consider the application questions set out in the box below:

Application Questions

1. When an entrepreneur is considering hiring an attorney, what is the single most important thing that she should consider in making the selection?

2. What sort of fee arrangement should an entrepreneur seek when hiring an attorney, and does the maturity of the venture affect the fee arrangement that she is seeking?

3. What should an entrepreneur look for in her legal representation if the venture will be involved in international trade? How does this differ from what the entrepreneur would look for if the venture has no current international trade aspirations?

4. What legal specialties are likely to be involved in a given entrepreneurial venture, and how can these specialty topics best be addressed?

5. Why is attorney–client privilege important to an entrepreneur, and how does the existence of this privilege help to protect the entrepreneur in dealing with her attorney?

Summary

Choosing an attorney is one of the three most important decisions an entrepreneur makes when launching a venture, following the nature of the business and the organization of the business. The attorney will provide advice and guidance through the potential legal "minefields" that the entrepreneur may face in the venture. The process of choosing an attorney should not be taken in haste. The entrepreneur should use a careful and thoughtful approach to this decision.

The entrepreneur should seek recommendations from a variety of sources, including other entrepreneurs, venture capitalists, the State Bar Association, and the Martindale-Hubbell directory. Once a list of recommended attorneys has been developed, the entrepreneur should narrow the list down, based on what she perceives as the legal needs of the venture at the time, and interviews should be arranged with four or five of the attorneys at the top of the "short" list.

When the entrepreneur finds an attorney with whom she feels comfortable, and in whom she has confidence, that attorney should be hired. The entrepreneur will need to discuss the various fee arrangement possibilities and reach an agreement with the attorney on the type of arrangement they will be entering.

It is essential that the entrepreneur utilizes the attorney's time and expertise efficiently, taking advantage of the attorney's knowledge without misusing his or her time. The entrepreneur should make certain that, whenever possible, her discussions with the attorney are confidential, and made for the purpose of obtaining legal advice or assistance so that the communication is protected by the attorney–client privilege.

Key Terms

attorney–client privilege

attorney's work product

contingency fee

retainer

End-of-Chapter Questions

1. What sources should an entrepreneur use in developing a list of attorneys who might be appropriate legal representatives of the venture?
2. What sorts of questions should an entrepreneur ask of an attorney during the interviewing process in order to determine which attorney she should hire? Explain why these questions are appropriate.

3. When should an attorney who specializes in a particular area be selected as the primary counsel for the venture? Explain your reasoning.
4. An entrepreneur reached an agreement with a law firm for the firm to represent her venture, with the fee based on an hourly rate. One morning the entrepreneur called the law firm to obtain its fax number. When the receptionist answered the call, the entrepreneur asked to speak to the lawyer who normally represented her venture. The call was put through to the attorney, who talked with the entrepreneur for a few minutes, gave her the fax number, and ended the call. A few weeks later the law firm sent the entrepreneur a bill, including a charge for 10 minutes of the lawyer's time for the phone call. What could/should the entrepreneur have done in order to get the requested information while possibly avoiding this charge for "legal services"? Explain your reasoning.
5. What can the entrepreneur do to assure that a communication will be covered by the attorney–client privilege?

Suggested Activity

Find out what the hourly rates are for lawyers who specialize in business-related legal issues in the community where the venture will be located. Discuss the variations in the hourly fees and possible reasons or justifications for these variations.

Notes

1. "Helpful Tips for Hiring a Lawyer," National Federation of Independent Business (NFIB) (June 25, 2003), found at http://www.nfib.com
2. *Id.*
3. Richard, Alexander, "Mistakes to Avoid Before You Hire a Lawyer," *The Consumer Law Page*, found at http://consumerlawpage.com/article/howhire.shtml
4. "How to Hire a Lawyer," LawInfo.com, LawTips, found at http://www.lawinfo.com/index.cfm/fuseaction/client.lawtips
5. Alexander, note 3, *supra.*
6. *In re LTV Securities Litigation*, 89 F.R.D. 595, 600 (N.D. Tex. 1981).
7. "Answers to Questions About the Attorney–Client Privilege," American Bar Association, found at http://www.abanet.org/media/issues/acprivilegeqa
8. "Protection from Discovery — A Little About Work Product, Attorney–Client and Common Law Privileges," Lectric Law Library, found at http://www.lectlaw.com/files/lit16.htm
9. *Id.*

CHAPTER 2

AVOIDING LITIGATION

Litigation is bloodless war played by rules—expensive, exhausting, and generally out of control. It should be avoided whenever possible.[1]

INTRODUCTION

An entrepreneur usually has a simple objective: he wants to operate his venture in a profitable manner. He began the venture because he believed that he could provide a good or service that either was not being provided in the region or that he could provide more efficiently and less expensively than his competition in the region. It is highly unlikely that when he decided to initiate the venture he was thinking about filing suit against anyone or contemplating the likelihood of being sued by someone else. However, disputes *will* arise during the life of the venture, whether with customers, suppliers, or employees. When such disputes arise, they will need to be resolved, preferably in a manner that avoids undue expenditures of money, time, and energy. The resolution needs to be timely, appropriate, and hopefully advantageous to the entrepreneur.

The entrepreneur may want to address dispute resolution in the contracts that he enters, especially those with suppliers, retail customers, and employees. For example, the contract may specify that any disputes will be settled by means of **arbitration**, or that the parties must seek resolution through **mediation** before any other method for resolving the dispute can be utilized. There are also circumstances in which the contract will contain a **liquidated damages clause**. Under many circumstances, it is obvious that there has been a breach of the contract and it is evident which party is in breach. The only real point of contention is the amount of damages that have occurred. With a liquidated damages clause, the parties specify that if a party breaches the contract, that party will pay a preset and agreed upon amount for damages, and that this amount will fully satisfy the breaching party's obligation for the breach. The amount of damages can even be specified by formula; for example, the contractor will owe the landowner $100 for every day the contractor is late in completing the structure. Penalties for late payment are another form of liquidated damage clauses.

Liquidated damage clauses will be enforced by the courts if they meet two conditions:

1. The amount agreed upon is reasonable and not out of proportion to the expected damages.
2. Calculating the actual damages would be difficult if not impossible.

Dispute resolution can occur in a number of ways, ranging from informal to very formal. There is no single manner of dispute resolution that is the best alternative in every situation, nor should any method for resolving the dispute be rejected out of hand as an unacceptable alternative. Rather, the entrepreneur should evaluate the situation, discuss the legal ramifications with his attorney, and then attempt to settle the dispute with the other party in a manner that is mutually acceptable and, hopefully, mutually beneficial—or at least *not* mutually harmful. The remainder of this chapter will discuss the most common methods of dispute resolution, and also address some of the benefits and some of the drawbacks to each alternative. By examining these alternatives and by weighing the particular situation or dispute in which he is involved, the entrepreneur will have a basis for devising a strategy to resolve his disputes. The discussion will begin with the more formal alternatives.

LITIGATION

Many people think that legal controversies are likely to entail lawsuits, with all of the related expenses and time commitments that a lawsuit requires. While it is true that a legal controversy may entail a lawsuit, it is not inevitable that the parties will end up in court. In fact, most legal disputes involving civil law matters (tort cases, contract cases, employment law cases, etc.) do *not* end up being resolved in court. "Researchers have noted that: 'the very fact that a dispute has reached the court and has not been settled without litigation makes it unusual. Viewed against the baseline of potential lawsuits, litigation is not frequent, since for every dispute in the court records there are nine others that never even reached the filing stage.'"[2]

While litigation may be relatively unusual, lawsuits do happen, and the entrepreneur needs to be aware of the likelihood of being sued or of being forced to sue in order to settle a dispute. There are also certain factors that he should take into consideration before proceeding with a lawsuit rather than seeking some other method of resolving the controversy:

- Litigation consumes time and energy, often taking the entrepreneur away from his business for somewhat lengthy periods.
- Litigation distracts the principals and investors from business-related activities even if they are not physically away from the business.

- Litigation is adversarial, which may negatively affect future interaction with the other party, thus creating the possibility of a "lose-lose" situation.
- Litigation occurs in the public eye and is often reported in the media. An entrepreneur's reputation may be harmed by the publicity from a lawsuit even if he eventually prevails in the case.
- Litigation does not carry any guarantee of success, even for a party with a very strong case. In fact, it is often referred to as the hazards of litigation.

In the United States, a trial has three distinct stages, and each stage requires an investment of time, energy, and money. Table 2.1 shows the stages of a lawsuit. The first stage is the *pre-trial* stage, which includes the pleadings, discovery, and pre-trial conferences. The pleadings establish the basis for the lawsuit: the plaintiff files a complaint in which the cause of action is described and initial parameters of the case are established. Process is served on the defendant, informing him of the fact that the lawsuit has been filed and providing him with a time in which to respond to the complaint and its allegations or to admit fault and accept liability. The defendant files an answer in which he admits or denies any and/or all of the allegations in the complaint. At this point the issue has been joined, each party is aware of his or her position and of what the case will involve, and the proceedings are now in the hands of the attorneys unless and until the parties reach a resolution of the issues before the case goes to trial.

The attorneys will now enter into the *discovery* portion of the pre-trial stage. Discovery involves various legal maneuvers intended to gather information and evidence for use at trial, while also finding areas of agreement that will not need to

TABLE 2.1 The Stages of a Civil Trial	
Stage	*Activities*
Stage 1—Pre-Trial	*Pleadings*: Complaint, service of process, answer.
	Discovery: Depositions, interrogatories, requests for admissions, requests for production of documents.
	Conferences: Conferences between the parties to try to settle, pre-trial conference with the judge.
Stage 2—The Trial	Selection of the jury, plaintiff's case, defendant's case, motions, charge to the jury, **verdict**, judgment.
Stage 3—Post-Trial	*Motions:* A motion for a judgment N.O.V. (non obstante veredicto—notwithstanding the verdict, asking the judge to overrule the jury's verdict); a motion for a new trial; a motion for additur asking the judge to increase the size of the award; a motion for remittitur asking the judge to decrease the size of the award.
	Appeals: Possible reversals or remands for new trials.
	Enforcing the Judgment: Successful plaintiff may need to seek writs (attachment, execution), may need to use garnishment.

be argued at trial. Thus, discovery serves two purposes: it allows the parties to narrow the issues to only those matters that are in controversy, thus shortening the trial itself; and it allows each party to gather and evaluate the evidence that he or she will have available at the trial, and thus to evaluate his or her likelihood of success if the issue proceeds to trial. The entrepreneur and his employees will probably spend a significant amount of time collecting information and evidence during the discovery stage.

It is common for the parties to have conferences during the pre-trial stage, either informal conferences between the parties and their attorneys, or more formal conferences where the parties, their attorneys, and the judge confer in an effort to reach a resolution prior to going to court. It is not uncommon for the parties to reach an agreement and settle the dispute during this phase of the pre-trial stage, negating the need for a trial and ending the matter amicably. If the attorney was hired on a contingent fee basis, the agreement may provide for a lower percentage if the trial is settled at this stage.

If the matter is not resolved during the pre-trial stage, the parties move to stage two, the *trial*. The trial stage involves the ritualized and formal proceedings in the courtroom. During this stage the entrepreneur will be somewhat disconnected from the proceedings, although intensely interested in the outcome. He will be more of a spectator than a participant, and he may be very uncomfortable in this passive role.

Even if the entrepreneur prevails in the lawsuit, the matter is not yet resolved. The third stage of the proceeding is the *post-trial* stage. This third stage may well prove to be the most time-consuming, expensive, and frustrating stage for the entrepreneur. In this post-trial stage the losing party may file an appeal to a higher court, which may, in turn, reverse and remand the proceedings for a new trial or reverse the trial court and enter **judgment** for the appellant. Even if the entrepreneur prevails on appeal, there is the matter of collecting the judgment (assuming that the entrepreneur was the plaintiff). It is not unheard of for the plaintiff to get a judgment from the trial court but be unable to collect from the defendant for any number of reasons. It is the responsibility of the plaintiff to enforce the judgment, albeit with the right to seek some post-judgment assistance from the court in the form of writs of attachment and execution, garnishments, and so forth. Therefore, it should not come as a surprise that many people consider litigation to be a last resort, a final method of resolving a dispute rather than a starting point for settling a controversy.

ALTERNATE DISPUTE RESOLUTION

Alternate dispute resolution, normally referred to as ADR, involves methods for resolving disputes that are alternatives to trials. ADR is generally viewed as being faster, less expensive, less adversarial, and less distracting than a trial would be, and less likely to have a negative affect on future interactions or business dealings between the parties. Some forms of ADR involve the parties themselves working out a solution to their dispute, while other forms call for the intervention of a third party who becomes actively involved in the resolution. Regardless of the type of ADR used, the resolution of the dispute is likely to be easier than reaching a resolution through litigation. "A 1997 Deloitt & Touche survey of in-house counsel and private attorneys practicing primarily as outside corporate counsel found that 71% of all respondents believe that ADR makes the resolution of claims and disputes easier than traditional litigation."[3] Table 2.2, which follows the discussion of ADR, shows the various ADR methods. **Negotiation** is the most likely to be used since it is the fastest, the least expensive, and the least adversarial. However, negotiation—a discussion between the parties aimed at reaching an agreement that resolves the dispute— is also the least formal approach, and it requires a willingness to compromise on the part of both sides to the dispute. Most ventures will at least try negotiation first, and then move on to mediation or arbitration if the negotiation fails to result in a resolution.

Before entering into negotiation, mediation, or arbitration, the entrepreneur should request—or even require—an agreement that any offers or statements made during the process will not be admissible in court if the efforts to resolve the dispute by ADR fail and the parties end up in litigation. Failure to have such agreement may result in providing the opponent with ammunition to be used

TABLE 2.2 Alternate Dispute Resolution Methods	
Type of ADR	*Procedure*
Negotiation	Very informal, unstructured.
	The parties meet without a third party/facilitator, discuss, seek compromise and, ultimately, reach agreement.
Mediation	Informal, somewhat structured.
	The parties meet with a third party/facilitator who seeks to assist the parties in reaching a resolution. Mediator helps the parties to focus on the issues, to improve communications, and to find a common ground for resolving the issues.
Arbitration	Somewhat formal and structured procedure.
	The arbitrator serves as a decision maker. The arbitrator listens to the evidence, decides the outcome in the form of an opinion, and makes an award, where appropriate.
	The award is not appealable under most circumstances; the opinion is generally binding on the parties.
Online Dispute Resolution	Very flexible method of ADR. The parties enter into either mediation or arbitration, but do so online, using technology to speed up and streamline the process, while minimizing the costs and the potential inconveniences of traditional ADR. This is especially helpful when the parties are widely separated geographically.

in the court of law. In the alternative, the parties may be so cautious in their discussions in an effort to avoid making any damaging offers or statements that the ADR is not successful.

NEGOTIATION

"Litigation is expensive. An attorney will typically spend an average of two or three hours preparing for every hour in court. In addition, pre-trial discovery . . . add[s] to the expense. It is in your financial interest to resolve cases through negotiation when a high quality result can be obtained in this way."[4]

Negotiation is probably the most common method of dispute resolution, and it is the least structured and least formal method. Simply put, negotiation involves the parties meeting to discuss the controversy, discussing alternatives, and reaching an agreement as to how to settle the controversy in a mutually satisfactory manner. Most of the time negotiation will not involve the presence or participation of any third parties, although it is also somewhat common for each party to have his or her attorney present to help in the negotiation, especially if the goal of the negotiation is to achieve some compromise such as the revision of a contract or settlement of a claim. Negotiation is consensual; it is non-adversarial, it is informal, and it is a method of dispute resolution that virtually everyone has experienced at various times in his or her life. Whether it involves two people discussing where to go for dinner or which movie to rent, or determining rights and obligations in a contract, if the parties are discussing the options, looking at the alternatives, and striving to reach consensus, they are involved in a negotiation. Negotiation is likely to be the quickest method of resolving a dispute. In negotiation, the entrepreneur maintains some control over the result. Because a negotiation is only successful if each side agrees, it requires cooperation, which in turn helps to ensure the likelihood of future interactions—a very important factor for an entrepreneur who would prefer to be able to conduct more business with the other party in the future. However, because third parties are not involved and there are no set rules or procedures for negotiations, there is also a significant risk that the parties either will not be able to resolve the matter or that one of the parties may be able to dominate the negotiation, forcing an agreement by strength of will or force of personality. Further, a successful negotiation will lead to an agreement, and if one party later decides not to adhere to the terms of the negotiated agreement or settlement, the parties are back where they started, but with more time elapsed, and with each party now feeling less cooperative and flexible.

There are situations in which a party to a negotiation will feel a *need* to win the negotiation, and as a result decide to play "hardball" in the negotiating process. In such a situation, the party sees the negotiation as a "zero sum" game in which one party will finish the process positively while the other will finish the process negatively. Buying an office building may present such a situation. The buyer does not expect to buy another office building in the near future, and even if he does he is not likely to buy his next office building from the same seller; so the buyer feels a need to "win" the "game" of buying the building. He will not be concerned with any hard feelings or desires to "get even" that the seller may feel after the negotiation has concluded.

By contrast, many of an entrepreneur's negotiations will be with customers or suppliers, parties with whom he is likely to want to do business in the future. In order to enhance the likelihood of doing business with these parties in the future, the entrepreneur should make an effort to engage in *win-win negotiations.* There is a growing emphasis on win-win negotiations in a number of areas, and numerous of articles have been written addressing this topic. According to advocates of win-win negotiation, every negotiation has four possible outcomes, only one of which is mutually satisfying and beneficial:

I win, you lose.	I win, you win.
I lose, you win.	I lose, you lose.

If the entrepreneur wants to maintain a good working relationship with the other party, he will need to strive to reach an "I win, you win" result in the negotiation. In mathematical gaming theory this is referred to as a "non-zero sum game," a game where all parties finish the process positively. Such a result is likely to require more preparation prior to the negotiation, and the entrepreneur must negotiate openly and honestly. A person should consider at least the following points prior to a negotiation if that person is seeking a win-win outcome:

1. *Goals.* What do you want to get from the negotiation, and what is the other person likely to want?

2. *Trades.* What can you give the other person, and what can the other person give you?

3. *Alternatives.* If you cannot reach an agreement, what alternatives will you have? Is failure to reach an agreement an acceptable result?

4. *Relationships.* What is the expected outcome of the negotiation?

5. *Consequences.* What are the consequences if you win the negotiation? What are the consequences if you lose the negotiation? What are the consequences for the other person?

6. *Power.* Who has the power in the negotiation? Who stands to lose the most if no agreement is reached?

7. *Possible Solutions.* What solutions are available? What compromises might be made to reach an agreement?[5]

MEDIATION

"Mediation is a process in which a third-party neutral assists in resolving a dispute between two or more other parties. It is a non-adversarial approach to conflict resolution."[6] Mediation is a slightly more formal variation of a negotiation. "The role of the mediator is to facilitate communication between the parties, assist them in focusing on the real issues of the dispute, and generate options that meet the interests or needs of all relevant parties in an effort to resolve the conflict."[7] A mediator is expected to help the parties resolve their dispute themselves by helping them *focus* on the issues, possibly *reframe* the issue, *communicate* more effectively, *negotiate* more fairly, and, ultimately, reach an agreement. An entrepreneur will normally prefer mediation to arbitration or litigation because of the reduced cost relative to the other alternatives, as well as the likelihood of a quicker—and more amicable—resolution of the dispute. Mediation is also much more likely to result in a win-win resolution than is arbitration or litigation, and win-win resolutions encourage future business dealings between the entrepreneur and the other party to the dispute. In mediation the entrepreneur maintains a degree of control because he will not have a result forced upon him.

While mediation is more structured than negotiation, it is still an informal process in which there are few rules or procedures to follow; however the parties may agree to some rules or procedures, either in advance or with the mediator. The parties may decide to sit down in a conference-like setting with the mediator and work toward resolution of the dispute, or they may prefer to use "shuttle mediation," in which each of the parties is in a separate room or location and the mediator meets first with one and then with the other, communicating questions, concerns, and offers back and forth until a resolution is attained. In fact, as will be discussed in more detail later, mediation can even be conducted online, with the parties widely separated geographically, thus saving travel time and expense.

Mediation is nonbinding, and either party is free to withdraw from the process at any time prior to reaching an agreement. Despite this basic weakness in mediation as a method of resolving disputes, mediation is frequently very effective. A survey conducted by Deloitte & Touche reported that mediation was the preferred method of ADR of in-house attorneys, with 65% of the attorneys surveyed preferring mediation to arbitration.[8] Perhaps this preference for mediation is due to the confidential nature of mediation, coupled with the fact that mediation is an interest-based procedure that strives to provide a framework within which each party feels that he or she has achieved a successful result.

ARBITRATION

If negotiation has not led to a resolution of the dispute, the parties may choose to proceed to arbitration instead of or after mediation. Because the negotiation did not lead to an agreement, the parties may feel that reaching a voluntary agreement is unlikely, but proceeding to trial is not the preferred option. When such an impasse is encountered, having a private third party decide the matter may be the better alternative to a trial. "Arbitration is the most traditional form of private dispute resolution. Arbitration is [normally] a binding procedure."[9] Arbitration, like litigation, normally results in a "win-lose" resolution of the dispute. As a result, an entrepreneur is less likely to want to resort to arbitration in disputes involving business associates, unless it is obvious that each party is committed to his or her position and a compromise solution is highly unlikely.

Arbitration can be nonbinding or advisory. In these situations, each party presents his or her "case" to the arbitrator, and the parties then receive the arbitrator's "ruling." The parties then decide whether to accept the ruling and settle the dispute or reject it and continue seeking a resolution. This option may appeal to parties who are unwilling to concede control; however, it extends the length of time the dispute lasts. Obviously, the parties should decide whether the arbitration will be binding or nonbinding before they start the process.

The parties normally agree that when a dispute is submitted to arbitration, the finding of the arbitrator will be *binding*. Thus, the arbitrator is serving in an adjudicatory role unlike a mediator. The parties will normally contact an organization that conducts arbitrations such as the American Arbitration Association (AAA) or JAMS.[10] These organizations will provide a list of arbitrators, provide the rules under which the arbitration will be conducted, and supply any other procedures or guidelines needed to properly hold the arbitration hearing. They also normally rent conference rooms so that the arbitration can occur at a neutral site.

The arbitrator will conduct the arbitration hearing under the provisions of the Federal Arbitration Act, any applicable state arbitration statutes, and the rules and procedures of the organization (e.g., AAA or JAMS) conducting the arbitration hearing. These rules and procedures are similar to those for a civil trial, although less formal and less restrictive in regard to issues such as admissibility of evidence, hearsay, and so forth. Following the hearing the arbitrator will render an **opinion** on the issues, and make an **award**, if appropriate. As a rule, the opinion of the arbitrator and the award granted are final, and the losing party may not appeal, nor will he or she be allowed to then take the issue to court in an effort to obtain a different (more favorable) result. The decision of the arbitrator can only be reviewed by a court under very limited circumstances, such as an allegation of bias on the part of the arbitrator, or a showing of fraud or collusion by the arbitrator. On occasion an agreement to arbitrate will be set aside because of fraud or bias.

ONLINE DISPUTE RESOLUTION

Business persons prefer ADR to litigation owing to the efficiency, flexibility, and lower costs and expenses associated with ADR. Entrepreneurs are likely to be more amenable to ADR than others because ADR is so often handled by the entrepreneur personally, and entrepreneurs are, as a rule, proactive. By addressing the issue personally and directly entrepreneurs can achieve resolution quickly and get on with the business of operating the venture. However, as business becomes more global, and as more and more business is conducted online over the Internet and in cyberspace, ADR presents certain drawbacks. Mediation and arbitration have traditionally been conducted in a face-to-face environment, with the parties having the dispute and their third-party intermediary being in the same place at the same time. Contemporary business practices increase the likelihood that the parties will be widely separated geographically and in different time zones. When this is true, it becomes more difficult, more expensive, and less efficient to use the traditional styles of mediation or arbitration. Rather than abandoning either of these methods of dispute resolution, the parties may want to consider using **online dispute resolution** (ODR).

ODR is merely a new method of applying the practices of either mediation or arbitration. Rather than operating in a face-to-face environment, the parties are "meeting" in cyberspace through either synchronous or non-synchronous communication. Synchronous communications will involve the parties being online or linked at the same time, whether through the use of a teleconference or a chat room, or in some other manner. Asynchronous communications allow the parties to communicate with one another or with the mediator or arbitrator at different times, often by the use of email or fax communications. In fact, ODR provides greater flexibility than the traditional forms of ADR. Since each party can participate in the process from his or her office, there is no disruption for travel, nor are there any travel expenses. ODR is the preferred method of dispute resolution for consumer complaints under the North American Free Trade Agreement (NAFTA). There are a number of organizations that provide ODR, such as Cybersettle, SettlementOnline, ClickNsettle, and OneAccord; and the expenses associated with ODR tend to be lower than with the more traditional methods of dispute resolution. An entrepreneur would be well advised to consider using ODR to resolve disputes, especially if he is involved in a technology-based venture and is therefore comfortable with computing technology and usage.

AVOIDING LITIGATION

A number of commentators suggest that litigation is much more expensive than alternative forms of dispute resolution, and that business people—especially entrepreneurs—should avoid litigation if at all possible. One of the major reasons for these opinions is the cost of litigation, both in time and energy, as well as in money. The entrepreneur who is devoting his time to meetings with his lawyer, attending depositions, or answering interrogatories will not be able to devote his time to operating the venture. Time spent in preparation for a trial, and then in court, is time that could have, and perhaps should have, been spent furthering the entrepreneurial venture.

While it may be obvious that an entrepreneur should avoid litigation whenever possible, *how* to avoid litigation is not so clear. What should an entrepreneur do to avoid litigation? The best way to avoid litigation is to plan for the likelihood of disputes and take steps to preempt the dispute resolution process. Many sources of possible litigation will be addressed in this book. One method for such a preemptive action is the inclusion of an arbitration clause and/or a mediation clause in the venture's contracts. "A contractual arbitration clause is one of the most powerful ways that a business has to try to control its exposure to costly and dangerous lawsuits."[11]

An entrepreneur is well advised to include a clause calling for the use of ADR in employment contracts, as well as in contracts with suppliers, vendors, and even with customers. By specifying that the parties *must* resort to mediation or arbitration rather than litigation as an initial step in resolving disputes, the entrepreneur will have an excellent opportunity to reach a mutually acceptable result without resorting to a lawsuit. The clause may even call for an initial good-faith effort to resolve any disputes through negotiation or mediation, and then for the use of binding arbitration if the negotiation or mediation fails to settle the matter.

A well-drafted arbitration clause may specify a streamlined procedure, can shorten the time period in which a complaint can be filed, can limit discovery, or can otherwise tailor the process to reduce both the time and expense of the procedure. However, care must be taken to ensure that the procedures called for in the clause are fair and equitable to both sides, and also that the procedures do not run afoul of federal or state law. For example, California law imposes some limitations on the process for mandatory arbitration of employee disputes, and such clauses will be more strictly scrutinized than most other types of arbitration clauses.[12]

An entrepreneur who is operating a relatively small venture should consider specifying some form of ODR in his mediation and/or arbitration contract clauses. Having the mediation or arbitration take place online virtually eliminates the need to travel to the site of the proceedings; conducting the mediation or arbitration online permits asynchronous responses, so that the entrepreneur can submit information at times that are convenient to him and his attorney, allowing him to focus on the venture when necessary, and to address the dispute at times during which the venture needs less attention. However, care should be used so that the process does not languish.

Although the parties can agree to enter into arbitration at any stage of a dispute, the parties are more likely to agree to arbitrate when they are negotiating their initial contract. It is more difficult to reach an agreement to arbitrate *after* the dispute arises.

THINGS TO DO

The fact that the contract contains a clause that will preempt litigation is just a starting point. The entrepreneur and his attorney will also need to develop a strategy for when a dispute arises. Perhaps the best advice that can be given is to decide on an acceptable settlement proposal that will resolve the dispute, and then attempt to settle as early as possible. The sooner a settlement is reached the sooner the settlement meter stops ticking! In order to determine what will constitute an acceptable settlement, if the entrepreneur is the complainant/plaintiff, he must decide what the controversy is worth, and if the entrepreneur is the subject of the complaint, the defendant, he must decide how much he is willing to pay to settle the dispute.

When the entrepreneur is the complainant, he should ask the following questions:

1. How much can you realistically expect to receive as an award (arbitration) or judgment (litigation) if you prevail?
2. What is the likelihood that you will prevail?
3. Assuming you do prevail, how likely are you to be able to collect from the other party? (Some parties are "judgment proof," meaning that although you are able to sue and prevail, you are not able to recover the judgment because the person does not have the means to pay the judgment.)
4. How much is the proceeding going to cost?

For example, assume that the most the entrepreneur can reasonably expect to receive as an award is $40,000, his likelihood of prevailing is 50%, his chances of collecting from the other party if he prevails is 80%, and cost of the proceedings will be $10,000. The value to the entrepreneur if he goes through the procedure will be $6000:

$$(\text{award} \times \text{likelihood of prevailing} \times \text{chance of collecting}) - \text{cost; or}$$
$$(\$40,000 \times .5 \times .8) - \$10,000 = \$6000.$$

On the other hand, the settlement value will be $22,000:

$$(\text{the expected award or judgment} \times \text{likelihood of collecting}) - \text{cost; or}$$
$$(\$40,000 \times .8) - 10,000 = \$22,000.$$

Based on this, an offer by the entrepreneur to settle for $22,000 (the settlement value) would make sense, and any offer from the other party for more than $6000 would need to be considered since that offer would be higher than the predicted value after completing the procedure.

THINGS TO AVOID

If a dispute arises in which the entrepreneur is the party against whom a complaint is lodged, he is well advised to avoid doing any of the following, at least until the dispute is resolved:

APOLOGIES

An apology is likely to be viewed as an admission of fault, and thus an admission of liability, which is admissible in a court of law in the United States. While public opinion often favors an apology, the entrepreneur should discuss the implications with his attorney before making any sort of apology to the other party.

In many countries an immediate, sincere apology is expected. In some countries the citizens even expect a company official to visit the homes of the injured parties and apologize in person. In cases of international disputes, the entrepreneur may need the advice of both his U.S. attorney and an attorney in the other country.

Note that the entrepreneur may not know initially whether the litigation will occur in the United States or in a foreign country with different **rules of evidence**.

ADMISSIONS OF RESPONSIBILITY

While an apology is likely to be viewed as an admission of fault or liability, an admission of responsibility removes all doubt. Such an admission is an acknowledgment that the complaining party is entitled to a recovery. Not only will such an admission make it virtually impossible to prevail in any proceedings that may follow, it will also make it more difficult to settle for something close to the amount that the entrepreneur would otherwise expect to pay to the complaining party. The wisdom of admitting responsibility will also be affected by whether this is, or may also be, a criminal proceeding. Under the U.S. sentencing guidelines accepting responsibility may reduce the sentence. The entrepreneur should consult with an attorney with expertise in this area before making any statement.

HASTE

While reaching closure on the issue in some manner is desirable, and while it is normally advisable to settle quickly, acting with too much haste is often a mistake, and quite often an overly expensive mistake. The entrepreneur and his attorney should be relatively confident that all significant information has been gathered and analyzed and that the "settlement math" has been worked out before agreeing to any settlement. Realizing after the fact that there were extenuating circumstances, or that a claim has been exaggerated, will be detrimental to the entrepreneur; this may well occur if a settlement or resolution is reached without adequate efforts to gather facts and examine all of the circumstances surrounding the dispute.

In applying this chapter, the entrepreneur should consider the application questions set out in the box below:

Application Questions

1. What are the three main methods of alternate dispute resolution, and what are the benefits of each?
2. What is online dispute resolution, and how has its use affected dispute resolution for parties that are remote from one another?
3. Should the entrepreneur try to avoid litigation with this particular dispute? Why?
4. What are the benefits an entrepreneur can expect from litigating a dispute? The drawbacks?
5. Should the entrepreneur include a mandatory meditation clause in his contracts? Would a mandatory arbitration clause be preferable?
6. Does the entrepreneur want a continuing relationship with this party?

Summary

Disputes will arise at some point, despite the degree of care exercised by the entrepreneur. Resolution of these disputes can be very expensive in terms of time and energy, and in terms of financial costs. These disputes can result in the death of the entrepreneurial venture. Ideally, an entrepreneur will be able to resolve disputes in a timely manner and in a manner that is least costly in all of these terms.

Many people think of litigation first as a means to solve their disputes. However, lawsuits are expensive and time consuming, and they may also have a negative effect on reputations as well as future interactions between the disputants. If litigation becomes inevitable, the entrepreneur will be prepared since he has already retained an attorney, in part, for just this sort of situation. However, if an alternative method of dispute resolution can be used, this alternative will often prove beneficial to both sides.

Alternate dispute resolution is a less formal and less adversarial method of resolving disputes. There are three main methods of ADR: negotiation, mediation, and arbitration. Each of the three can be used in the traditional face-to-face method or in an online method of resolving the dispute. Negotiation involves the parties sitting down, discussing the dispute, and reaching an agreement about how to compromise so that both parties are content with the final outcome. Negotiation is the least formal and least structured method of ADR, but it is not final until both parties reach agreement *and* each party then performs as agreed. Mediation is somewhat more formal, with a neutral third person brought into the discussions as a facilitator to help the parties remain focused on the issues and the objections, enhance communications, and help the parties to reach an agreement on a resolution that is mutually acceptable. Arbitration is the most formal of the methods of ADR. In arbitration a third person is brought into the dispute to serve as a decider. The arbitrator will listen to each party, often in a trial-like atmosphere, examine the evidence, and then render an opinion. Most arbitrations are binding, with the disputants agreeing to accept the arbitrator's decision as the final word on the matter. This opinion will often involve an award if the complaining party prevails in the arbitration hearing.

Online dispute resolution involves the same methods of resolving the dispute, but is done without requiring the parties to meet face-to-face. ODR can also be done synchronously (at the same time, i.e., through a teleconference, a chat room, or some similar setting) or asynchronously (not at the same time, i.e., often through emails and faxes). ODR is especially attractive as a method of settling a dispute when the parties are widely separated geographically or the entrepreneur cannot afford to be tied up in meetings and hearings to the detriment of his venture.

Including mandatory mediation and/or arbitration clauses in contracts allows an entrepreneur to ensure that disputes will not be litigated. These clauses need to be carefully structured so that they do not appear to favor either party, thus prejudicing the proceedings and probably allowing a successful appeal to the courts by the losing party.

Key Terms

alternate dispute resolution
arbitration
award
judgment
liquidated damages clause

mediation
negotiation
online dispute resolution
opinion
rules of evidence

Resources

There are a number of classic resources that are likely to prove helpful in gaining a better understanding of this area, including:

Roger Fisher, William Ury, and Bruce Patton (1991). *Getting to Yes: Negotiating Agreement Without Giving In.* New York: Penguin Books.
Jenna Glatzer (2004, September 1). "Those Magic Phrases—How to Negotiate Like a Pro." *Home Business.*

End-of-Chapter Questions

1. What benefits should an entrepreneur expect to receive if he chooses to resolve a dispute by means of one of the forms of alternative dispute resolution (ADR) as opposed to settling that same dispute by means of litigation?
2. Why might an entrepreneur decide to eschew ADR and instead choose to use litigation to resolve a dispute with one of his suppliers? Would the same reasoning apply if the dispute was with one of the entrepreneur's customers or an employee? Explain.
3. How is mediation different from negotiation as a method of ADR? How are these two methods similar?
4. How is arbitration different from mediation? How is arbitration similar to mediation?
5. How is arbitration different from litigation? How is arbitration similar to litigation?
6. Assume that an entrepreneur is operating his venture in Ohio and he has a dispute with one of his customers who resides in New Mexico. Both the entrepreneur and customer agree that the dispute should be settled without resort to litigation. In your opinion, how should the parties resolve this dispute, and why do you prefer the method you have recommended?
7. Would your answer to the previous question be different if the entrepreneur and the customer resided in the same state or in adjoining states? Would it differ if the entrepreneur's dispute was with a supplier rather than a customer? Explain your reasoning.

Suggested Activities

1. Examine the likely costs of submitting a controversy to mediation and to arbitration. Which is more expensive? Compare these costs to the fees and procedures likely to be involved in a lawsuit. Which seems most advantageous to an entrepreneurial venture during its start-up phase?
2. Contact the local office of the American Arbitration Association. Obtain a fee schedule and a copy of the rules for a normal business dispute.

Notes

1. Vincent, DeCarlo, "How to Reduce the High Cost of Litigation," found at http://www.dicarlolaw.com/NetscapeHTRHCL.htm
2. Than N., Luu, "Reducing the Costs of Civil Litigation," Public Law Research Institute (PLRI), found at http://w3.uchastings.edu/plri/fal95tex/cstslit/html
3. Thomas D. Cavanaugh, *Business Dispute Resolution* (West Legal Studies in Business, 2000), "Briefing Point 1.1," p. 6.
4. Roy N., Martin, "The Cost of Litigation," found at http://www.roymartinpc.com/costoflitigation.html
5. http://www.mindtools.com/commskll/NegotiationSkills.htm
6. Christopher, Honeyman, and Nita Yawanarajah, "Mediation," *Beyond Intractability* (September 2003), found at http://www.beyondintractability.org/essay/mediation/
7. *Id.*
8. Thomas D. Cavanaugh, *Business Dispute Resolution* (West Legal Studies in Business, 2000), "Briefing Point 1.2," p. 8.
9. "Arbitration Defined," JAMS—The Resolution Experts, found at http://www.jamsadr.com/arbitration/defined_print.asp
10. JAMS, Inc. was originally an acronym for Judicial Arbitration and Mediation Services, Inc. Today it is known simply as "JAMS, the Resolution Experts."
11. DeCarlo, note 1, *supra.*
12. *Id.*

CHAPTER 3

SELECTING THE PROPER BUSINESS FORM

Because of its utility, the law of limited liability companies is very dynamic. New ideas and features seem to appear yearly with the objective of enhancing this form of business organization.[1]

INTRODUCTION

No one form of business entity is right for every entrepreneur and every venture. The entrepreneur needs to consider a number of factors before she makes a decision about what type of business form she should select. The entrepreneur's decision will be influenced by a number of factors, including the type of funding she expects to obtain, how much she plans to grow, and how she plans to exit the venture. In choosing a type of entity, the entrepreneur will also need to consider the degree of risk (legal liability) involved in the venture; the probable tax consequences of the various forms; the time and expense necessary to comply with legal rules; and the degree of flexibility that will be advantageous to the venture. The selection of a business form is not static: there are times in the life of a venture when it becomes necessary to change the business form. For example, a technology firm may start out as a **sole proprietorship** or partnership while the founders are working to create a viable technology. The business's potential liability may increase when it hires employees and/or locates customers, so the firm may incorporate at this point. Many entrepreneurs plan to change the type of business form as the entity grows and matures. This is an appropriate strategy; however, the entrepreneur should be aware that there may be tax consequences to changes in business form. The entrepreneur should consult with her tax specialists before committing to a change.

This Legal Companion will only focus on the types of business organizations commonly used in the United States. There is a trend to increase the choices available to the entrepreneur.[2] The authors will occasionally use the term "company" in later chapters. This is not to imply that the business is necessarily incorporated: the term is used as a synonym for venture or enterprise.

Many reference books on business organizations include a CD-ROM with sample **articles of incorporation, bylaws**, and other forms necessary to create a business. The entrepreneur should not blindly adopt these forms. If she wants to use the forms provided, she should complete the forms and have her attorney review them. The practice of preparing drafts and having her attorney review them is a common way for an entrepreneur to reduce her legal fees.

This chapter is organized around the major types of business forms commonly used by entrepreneurs: proprietorships (also called sole proprietorships), partnerships, limited partnerships, limited liability partnerships (LLPs), corporations, and limited liability companies (LLCs). Table 3.1 provides a comparison of these business forms. By necessity, the table summarizes some very complex rules and provides the framework for the chapter. The authors will elaborate on many of the rules. Depending on the business form chosen, the business may be able to provide attractive incentives to employees.[3] This complex area is outside the scope of this Legal Companion. The entrepreneur should be aware that there may be some exceptions and that state laws may vary. Also, traits that may be advantageous to entrepreneurs in some situations or stages of growth may be disadvantageous in other situations or stages of growth.

STEPS TO FORMING MOST BUSINESS ENTITIES

Much of this chapter will contain information that is specific to the type of business structure the entrepreneur is using. However, there is some information that applies to multiple types of business entities. This Legal Companion will address these general steps first. See Table 3.2 for a summary of the important steps that apply to most if not all business enterprises. The steps may not necessarily follow in this particular order, and some steps may overlap other steps in the formation process. Many of the steps are interrelated and some of them may be ongoing. These steps are really the initial plan for the venture. As with any plan, it may be necessary to modify the plan as the venture develops.

STEP 1

The entrepreneur should consider whether there are any forgotten founders who were involved at an earlier stage in the evolution and development of the idea. The forgotten founder might be someone who suggested the idea or who participated in the early conceptualization. These founders may not be currently involved in the effort to establish an operating company. If the entrepreneur does not seek out the forgotten founder and negotiate a solution, the forgotten founder might come forward at a later stage and claim an equal share in the successful

TABLE 3.1   A Comparison of Different Types of Business Organizations

Attribute	Proprietorship	Partnership	Limited Partnership (LP)*
Creation	Proprietor opens the business, subject to state and local licensing laws and regulations.	Partners enter into an agreement, either orally or in writing; no formalities are required.	Partners enter into a partnership agreement and file a written form designating the limited partners and the general partners.
Termination	Proprietor closes the business; death, insanity, or bankruptcy of the owner also terminates the business.	Partners agree to dissolve the partnership; death, bankruptcy, or withdrawal of any partner also dissolves the partnership.[†] The terms of the agreement or a court order may dissolve the partnership. If there is a liquidation of the assets after a dissolution, the business will wind up.	Partners follow same procedure as for a partnership, except the assets will be distributed in a different priority in case of a dissolution and liquidation of the business. The death, bankruptcy, or withdrawal of a limited partner does not dissolve the partnership.
Taxation[‡]	All business profits are taxed as the regular income of the owner; there are no federal income taxes on the business itself.	The business must file a federal tax return, but it is for information only. The income of the business is taxed as regular income to the partners.	The same tax procedure is followed as for a regular, general partnership.
Liability[§]	Proprietor has unlimited personal liability. First, business assets will be used, and then the personal assets of the owner will be used.	Partners have unlimited personal liability. First, business assets will be used, and then the personal assets of the partners. The partners are jointly and severally liable for the debts.	General partners have unlimited personal liability. First, business assets will be used, and then the personal assets of the general partners. The general partners are jointly and severally liable for the debts. Limited partners are only liable to the extent of their capital contribution. Suit can be brought against any partner to enforce his or her promise to make a contribution.**

(continued)

TABLE 3.1 (continued)

Attribute	Proprietorship	Partnership	Limited Partnership (LP)*
Advantages	Simplicity of creation; complete ownership and control of the firm.	Informality of creation; greater potential for expertise and capital in management (because there is more than one manager).	Somewhat greater flexibility than a general partnership; increased opportunities to raise capital.
Disadvantages	Limited capital; limited expertise; limited existence (when the owner dies, the business terminates).	Limited existence; lack of flexibility; potential liability.	Some rigidity in ownership and decision making; personal liability for general partners; limited existence.
Capital††	Angels and venture capitalists generally will not invest in a sole proprietorship unless the proprietor is willing to incorporate.	Capital can be obtained by selling a partnership interest. Angels and venture capitalists generally will not invest in a partnership.	Capital can be obtained by selling a limited partnership interest. Selling of limited partnership interests may be subject to securities laws. Angels and venture capitalists generally will not invest in a partnership.

Attribute	Limited Liability Partnership (LLP)	Corporation (Inc.) (Subchapter C or Subchapter S)	Limited Liability Company (LLC)
Creation	Partners enter into a partnership agreement and the partnership files a copy or some other notice with the state.	Parties prepare and file formal legal documents known as articles of incorporation with the state of incorporation; the entity must comply with any relevant state or federal security statutes or regulations.	LLCs may be formed by one or more members. Some states require at least two members. LLCs must file articles of organization with the state government.
Termination	Partners follow same procedure as for a general partnership.	Parties close the business, liquidate all business assets, surrender the corporate charter, and distribute the assets in accordance with state law; termination may also be due to the state revoking the charter.	Statute and/or agreement may limit the term of the LLC. The trend is to allow an LLC to have a perpetual existence. In many states the LLC will be at will unless it is designated a term LLC and the term is set. The LLC may dissolve when a member dies or withdraws depending on state law and the operating agreement.

Taxation§	The same tax procedure is followed as for a regular, general partnership.	A normal corporation (Subchapter C corporation) is treated as a separate taxable entity and pays taxes on its profits. Any dividends are also taxed to the stock-holders. This is called "double taxation." A Subchapter S corporation, regulated by the IRS, is taxed as if it were a general partnership despite its corporate status. A Subchapter S corporation is treated differently only for federal tax purposes. States may also tax them as partnerships.	Most LLCs can make an election to be taxed as either a corporation or a partnership. The LLC may have different taxation for state and federal purposes.
Liability†	Partner is liable without limit for his or her own wrongs and wrongs of people he or she directly supervises; the partner's liability for the wrongs of others is limited to his or her contribution to the firm.	Stockholders are *not* personally liable for debts of the corporation, so there is limited liability. Stockholders may lose their investment in the corporation if it fails.	All members are liable for association debts only to the extent of their capital contribution(s). A member can be required to pay any capital contribution contractually promised but not paid.
Advantages	Limited liability except for a partner's own wrongs and the wrongs of people the partner directly supervises.	Longevity, including the potential for perpetual existence; potentially unlimited access to capital and to expertise; freely transferrable ownership; limited personal liability of the owners.	Limited liability for all the members.
Disadvantages	Unlimited liability for partner's own wrongs; only permitted in some states. State law often restricts LLPs to professional groups, such as accountants, dentists, doctors, and lawyers.	Double taxation (except for a Subchapter S corporation); much more federal regulation; considerably more state regulation; formality and rigidity of the organization.	LLC statutes vary from state to state. Professionals may not be permitted to form an LLC in some states. There may be limitations on the transferability of shares.‡‡ Selling interests in an LLC may be subject to state and federal securities regulations. LLCs may have a limited term of existence.

(*continued*)

TABLE 3.1 (continued)

Attribute	Proprietorship	Partnership	Limited Partnership (LP)*
Capital††	Capital can be obtained by selling a partnership interest. Generally partnership interests are sold to junior associates in the profession. Angels and venture capitalists generally will not invest in an LLP.	Capital can be obtained by selling shares as long as the sale conforms to the corporation's rules and securities laws. It is easier to raise capital with corporations. Angels and venture capitalists are more comfortable investing in C corporations than most other forms. C corporations can be used for Initial Public Offerings (IPOs).§§ An S corporation would have to change to a C corporation for an IPO or if it seeks venture capital.	Capital can be obtained by selling memberships in the LLC as long as the sale conforms to the LLC's rules and securities laws. Angels and venture capitalists are becoming more comfortable with LLCs though some would not invest in an entity with pass-through taxation. Some venture capitalists and angel investor groups are organized as LLCs. The LLC would have to change to a corporation for an IPO.

Source: Courtesy of Lynn M. Forsythe, © Lynn M. Forsythe 2009.

* This column describes limited partnerships under the Revised Uniform Limited Partnership Act (RULPA) after the 1985 amendments.

† This applies to partnerships under the Uniform Partnership Act (UPA).

‡ Any change in the business form may result in tax consequences for the business and its owners.

§ The entrepreneur will be liable on any contract she guarantees for the entity regardless of whether the entity would normally protect her personal assets.

** RULPA §502 (a).

†† Chapter 6 includes a more detailed discussion on obtaining capital. Banks are willing to loan funds to any of these entities if the venture is financially sound and has good prospects for the future. Banks may require a security interest in the venture's assets and/or a loan guarantee from the venture's participants. Angels and venture capitalists only contribute advice and funds if they believe the venture can be successful.

‡‡ This may also be an advantage.

§§ IPO offerings are influenced by the economy. For example, there were no IPOs in the United States for the last quarter of 2008 and the first quarter of 2009. These are defined as IPOs with at least one U.S. venture capital investor that trades on a U.S. stock exchange. News Release from Thomson Reuters and the National Venture Capital Association, New York, April 1, 2009, "Venture-Backed Exit Market Remains a Concern in the First Quarter; No IPO Activity for Two Consecutive Quarters; First Time on Record," available at the National Venture Capital Association Web site at http://www.nvca.org/.

TABLE 3.2 Key Steps for Forming Business Entities
Step 1. Decide on the initial relationship of the owners. What is going to be the ownership interest of each person? Who is going to have a voice in how the enterprise is run? What is the relationship among the founders?
Step 2. Consider the venture's future and how it will grow. Will employees and founders be added to the enterprise?
Step 3. Select a name for the business entity.
Step 4. Choose a state in which to operate. This is where the entrepreneur will actually locate the business enterprise.
Step 5. Choose a state to be the legal home of the venture. This is the state where the venture will be incorporated or formed.
Step 6. Decide how much funding the enterprise will need and the probable sources of this funding.
Step 7. Decide how many investors the enterprise will need. Should the investors have different rights or will they require different rights before they are willing to invest?
Step 8. Decide how long the venture is expected to operate and the anticipated exit or harvest strategy.
Step 9. Consider the advantages and disadvantages of different types of business entities and make a selection.
Step 10. Follow the proper steps for forming the selected type of business entity.
Step 11. Convene the appropriate meetings to conduct business. Send agendas prior to the meetings and prepare minutes afterwards.
Step 12. Keep important papers together.

Source: Courtesy of Lynn M. Forsythe, © Lynn M. Forsythe 2009.

enterprise. Consequently, it is helpful to resolve any issues with forgotten founders or potential forgotten founders early in the process. For example, three PayPal employees, Chad Hurley, Jawed Karim, and Steve Chen, developed YouTube. However, many accounts of the development identify only Chad Hurley and Steve Chen.[4] Jawed Karim would be a forgotten founder if Hurley and Chen had not resolved the issues pertaining to his participation in YouTube.[5]

The entrepreneur should be aware that her financial future can be affected by the financial situation of her co-founders and co-owners. For example, assume that the entrepreneur forms a general partnership with Alex, who has the technical background necessary for the enterprise. She does not investigate Alex's financial position and subsequently Alex becomes insolvent. Alex's personal creditors will first have a claim against his personal assets. Then, to the extent that his bills are unpaid, his creditors will have a claim against the partnership and its assets. If the partnership is solvent, the creditors will usually receive a charging order, whereby the creditors will receive Alex's share of the profits. This problem is more acute in partnerships, but the insolvency of one of the owners can put strains on many business enterprises.[6]

STEP 2

The entrepreneur should consider the projected growth of her venture. When will she need to add the employees or co-owners necessary to take her venture to the next step?

STEP 3

The entrepreneur should conduct a search to make sure the name and Web site name she wants are available. She should search state[7] and local files of fictitious names, phone books, city directories, domain name registries, and state and federal trademark and/or service mark registries. Note that registering a name is not the same thing as registering a trademark or a service mark. The entrepreneur will probably want to do both. Trademarks are discussed in more detail in Chapter 11. Once the business entity is formed, the entrepreneur will add the appropriate designation to the end of the business name, for example, "Inc." If the entrepreneur is trying to avoid personal liability and is choosing a form to help protect her individual assets, she should avoid using her personal name, initials, or other reference to herself unless there is an important business reason to do so. In these cases, she would want to appear as distinct and separate from the entity as possible to help assure that she is insulated from liability.

STEP 4

The entrepreneur needs to decide where the physical facilities, such as the office, factory, or warehouse, will be located. Some businesses or entrepreneurs will not have as much flexibility in choosing a state in which to operate; for example, it is more efficient to make and can tomato sauce close to where the tomatoes are being cultivated. This decision will affect what laws and regulations the venture will have to follow. For example, if the venture is going to operate in California, it will have to comply with California environmental and labor laws.

STEP 5

The entrepreneur should consider a number of issues in choosing a legal home for the enterprise. These include the state or states from which it will operate, as mentioned in the prior step. Most of the law concerning business ventures is state law, and the state-specific rules may be advantageous or disadvantageous. For example, if the venture is incorporated in the state of Delaware, it will have to comply with Delaware law concerning how a corporation does business. The entrepreneur should also consider the initial filing fees to "create" the business and the annual filing fees. For example, see http://www.incorporateabusiness.com/state.htm for a state-by-state comparison chart of corporation and LLC filing fees.[8] The state may also require annual reports.

STEP 6

The entrepreneur should consider how she will grow the venture, including the speed of growth and the amount of capital required. She should think about long-term growth and not just her immediate needs. Angel investors, venture capitalists, and lenders will inquire about the entrepreneur's future plans, and not just her immediate needs.

Step 7

It may be difficult for the entrepreneur to obtain all the funds she needs from one or two sources. How many investors and/or lenders will she need to fuel the growth of her venture? How much control is she willing to give up? Some sources of capital will require an ownership interest in the venture and/or some degree of control over the venture in exchange for their investment. Some sources only invest in a particular industry, size of venture, and current stage of development.

Step 8

The entrepreneur and her co-founders may decide that they want to operate this venture until they become disabled or want to retire. If so, a buy–sell agreement between the owners would be appropriate. On the other hand, their model may be to grow the business quickly and then sell out to a larger company.

Step 9

The entrepreneur should consider the many factors involved in choosing a business form for the initial phase of her venture. She should anticipate the need to reevaluate the choice and possibly change the structure as the business grows.

Step 10

States often require a business entity to designate a **registered agent** in the state. A registered agent may be called an agent for service of process, local agent, or resident agent. A registered agent is the person designated to receive legal papers on behalf of the business entity. It can be a natural person or a legal person, such as a corporation. An officer of the entity can serve as the registered agent. The name and address of the registered agent is public information; so if the entrepreneur wishes to have a degree of anonymity, she should hire a professional to perform these services. Registered agents typically charge $50–$150 per year. It is helpful to have a registered agent with a stable address to receive these important legal documents. If a business is formed in one state and starts doing business in another state, it will generally need to register as a "foreign business" in the second state. It is a domestic business in the first state. When it registers as a foreign business in the second state, it will generally be required to appoint a registered agent, pay a filing fee, and pay other taxes.

Step 11

State law may require certain meetings, depending on the business form chosen. For example, a corporation may be required to have meetings of the board of directors. If a vote is taken or required, the entrepreneur should make sure that there are adequate votes in favor of a position before going forward.

For example, if the corporation requires a simple majority vote of the share-holders, that is, more than half, the entrepreneur needs to pay attention as to whether it is a simple majority of the shareholders at the meeting or of all the shareholders. Many times it is the latter.

STEP 12

There are a number of regulations and laws that require good systems for keeping and filing records so that they can be easily retrieved. Businesses commonly purchase a corporation kit or an LLC kit, but it is not necessary. The kits often include stock certificates and a corporate/organization seal for official documents. If a kit is not used, it is customary to use a 3-ring notebook to collect and organize agendas, minutes, and shareholder information. The entrepreneur should create a backup system for her records in case of loss, such as a loss caused by fires. The entrepreneur may be tempted to keep only electronic files. However, computers and travel drives can fail and document retrieval can be expensive and time consuming.

There are a number of options for business forms available to the entrepreneur. This guide will explore these options in the following sections.

BEING ALONE IN A SOLE PROPRIETORSHIP

An entrepreneur may be tempted to "go it alone" and form a sole proprietorship. Many entrepreneurial ventures start out this way. Sole proprietorships are quick and inexpensive to form and easy to operate: they do not have to follow the procedures imposed on corporations or LLCs. A sole proprietorship would be more suitable for a venture that can be started on a small scale and does not require an infusion of capital. Since the owner's personal assets are at risk, it is more suitable where there is low risk or where reasonably priced insurance will adequately address the issue of risk. An example would be a pet grooming business or a card shop franchise. In a sole proprietorship, the entrepreneur is in charge and she is not accountable to other owners and investors. Many entrepreneurs are independent and like the idea of working on their own and not having to answer to a co-owner or investor. One problem with this business form is that the entre-preneur does not have a "sounding board" for her ideas; however, she can form an advisory group or solicit advice from mentors. Other disadvantages include:

- Sole proprietorships have limited access to funds, making it more difficult to grow the venture.
- Access to human capital is more limited.
- The sole proprietor will be personally liable for any debts and obligations of the venture.
- The business is dependent on the sole proprietor.

- A sole proprietorship rarely survives the illness, injury, death, or mental incapacity of the entrepreneur, so the venture does not retain value if something happens to the sole proprietor.
- The sole proprietor will not receive unemployment compensation if the business fails.

Because of these disadvantages, the entrepreneur *may* want to change the business form at some point in her entrepreneurial journey.

FORMING A PARTNERSHIP WITH OTHERS

Entrepreneurs may decide to do business as a partnership because a partnership can be formed quickly and cheaply. The entrepreneur may need other people, so a sole proprietorship would not be effective. Consequently, she decides to pool her talents and capital with other owners. Partnerships are especially prevalent when one individual does not have the skills and traits necessary to start and operate the business by herself; for example, a business where one partner is better at sales and promoting the business and the other is better at writing software or the creative side of the venture. Consequently, two friends may decide to form a partnership to develop a new computer application.

Disadvantages to partnerships include:

- Regular partnerships are limited in their ability to raise funds.
- The entrepreneur will probably be liable for the acts of her partners, such as torts, if the torts are committed in the course and scope of the partnership.
- The authority to make decisions generally rests in each partner, so the authority to make decisions is divided. This can be an advantage, but when the partners do not agree on the goals and vision for the future, it is a disadvantage.
- One partner's business contracts generally can bind the partnership.
- The partners have unlimited liability for partnership expenses.
- It is more difficult for partners to enter and exit the business.

Businesses frequently form partnerships with other businesses for particular projects; for example, a research and development (R&D) partnership where an entrepreneur shares the risks (and potential rewards) of an R&D project with another firm, university, or governmental entity.

Partnerships are agreements subject to the general laws about contracts. As such, most partnership agreements can be oral unless they are established for a set number of years. However, the wisdom of having a written partnership agreement cannot be stressed too much. The advantages of having written partnership agreements include:

- In the writing process, the partners can discover possible points that are ambiguous or where the partners are not in complete agreement, and the partners have the opportunity to work out these issues.
- The written agreement provides a reference document when one or more of the partners cannot remember the initial agreement.
- The written agreement may reduce the likelihood that the partners may need litigation to resolve conflicts.
- The written agreement and its terms are easier to prove in court.

The following example illustrates what can happen to entrepreneurs who are enthused about the idea but fail to write down their respective rights and obligations.[9] Sandra Kruger Lerner is a successful entrepreneur: she and her husband were the original founders of Cisco Systems. When they sold their interest in Cisco Systems, she invested some of her funds in a venture capital limited partnership called "& Capital Partners." Lerner was a friend with Patricia Holmes. Holmes developed a unique color for nail polish while they were both in England. Lerner and Holmes returned to the United States and further developed the concept, including a name. Lerner said, "This seems like a good [thing], it's something that we both like, and isn't out there. Do you think we should start a company?" Holmes said, "Yes, I think it's a great idea."[10] Lerner asked her business consultant to secure the name "Urban Decay" for them, and she eventually convinced & Capital Partners to provide funding. Neither woman had experience in the cosmetics business, but they set about to make this venture successful. Their business model was to grow the business and then sell it. Lerner hoped to sell it to Estee Lauder. Both women worked in furtherance of the enterprise. Holmes was not paid for her work, but she did receive mileage. Eventually it became obvious that Holmes was being excluded and frozen out of the enterprise; so she sued. The jury and trial court ruled in favor of Holmes, concluding that the women were operating this venture as a partnership, and the appellate court confirmed that decision.[11]

PARTNERS ARE AGENTS

General partners are agents of the partnership. As such, they have broad authority to bind both the partnership and the other partners without the specific express consent of those partners. This authority derives from the applicable state law and the partnership agreement. There are certain things a general partner cannot do by herself under the Uniform Partnership Act. They include:

- Transferring partnership property to a trust for the benefit of the partnership.
- Selling the goodwill of the partnership. Goodwill is the good name and reputation of the business.
- Performing any act that will make it impossible for the partnership to carry on its business.

- Confessing a judgment against the partnership. Confessing a judgment is an acknowledgment in court that the partnership is legally responsible.
- Submitting a partnership claim or liability to arbitration.

The legal rules about agents will be discussed in more detail in Chapter 5.

LIMITED PARTNERSHIPS

A **limited partnership** is like a regular partnership, except that there are two types of partners: general (regular) partners and limited partners. A limited partner is one who provides cash, property, or services to the partnership and whose liability is limited to the value of what he or she provides to the business. Limited partnerships are often used to obtain investors for an enterprise. A limited partnership must have at least one general partner and at least one limited partner. Any legal person, including an association, a corporation, a natural person, a partnership, or a limited partnership can be a partner. General partners have the same rights and liabilities as regular partners in the regular partnerships previously discussed. Limited partners are often treated as investors by both the general partners and the courts. Investors may feel more comfortable investing in a limited partnership because their other assets are not at risk. Limited partnerships are used where one individual has a concept or idea and has most of the knowledge and skill necessary to implement the idea; she just lacks the capital necessary for the implementation. Limited partnerships may be subject to federal and state securities laws, and the entrepreneur will need to discuss her plans to solicit funds with her lawyer. A common example of a limited partnership is the restaurant business, where the general partner operates the restaurant and the limited partners are investors in the restaurant. Limited partnerships are also common in real estate development where a contractor is the general partner and the investors are limited partners. Limited partnerships have the same advantages as regular partnerships except that it is easier to raise capital. Limited partnerships have the same disadvantages, with the additional disadvantages of being more expensive to establish because most states require a written agreement and a limited partnership agreement is a little more sophisticated than a regular partnership agreement.

Limited partners give up something in exchange for their limited liability—they give up the right to manage the enterprise. A limited partner who starts taking part in the management will lose his or her status as a limited partner if a third party who is aware of this management sues him or her. The limited partner retains his or her protected status as far as the other partners are concerned. Frequently, there is litigation about whether a limited partner participated in management. A limited partner can act as an agent or an employee of the general partner or the partnership without being involved in management. The limited partner can also advise the general partners without being involved in management.[12]

A limited partner can also lose his or her protection if the partnership uses his or her surname (last name or family name). A limited partner who knowingly allows his or her name to be used in the business name will be liable as a general partner to creditors who do not know his or her true status.[13] The Revised Uniform Limited Partnership Act (RULPA) provides two exceptions: one is if the limited partner's surname is also the surname of a general partner and the other is if the partnership conducted business under that name before the entry of the limited partner.[14]

Limited partnerships are more formal than regular partnerships. They are required to complete a written document specifying the details of the partnership agreement and file it with the appropriate state official. Large limited partnerships can elect to be master limited partnerships (MLPs), whose shares are traded on the stock exchanges.

LIMITED LIABILITY PARTNERSHIPS

Limited liability partnerships are a particular type of partnership for professionals, such as accountants, dentists, doctors, and lawyers. Each partner is licensed in the profession and allowed and expected to participate in the management of the partnership. The partner has limited liability as to the mistakes of the other partners: she will be liable for their mistakes only up to her share of the partnership assets. However, she will be personally liable for her own errors and the errors of the people she directly supervises. Like other partnerships, these entities are relatively quick to establish and provide some protection for the entrepreneur's assets. There are economies in sharing the business as opposed to each professional establishing his or her own business entity, with separate staff, conference room, equipment, and library. Accountants might join together and form an LLP for their accounting practice. LLPs have the same advantages as regular partnerships, except there is reduced liability for the acts, such as malpractice, of the other partners. LLPs have the same disadvantages as regular partnerships. In addition, it is a relatively new legal entity, so there are less legal precedents to help define it.

CORPORATIONS

Entrepreneurs who wanted to protect their personal assets used to form corporations, and many of them still do. Investors understand corporations, and there are many advantages to the corporate business form for investors. In fact, many investors, such as many venture capital funds, are corporations themselves. Corporations provide limited liability for the owners of the corporation. If the legal rules are being followed, the most an owner can lose is her investment in the corporation. Because of this "protection," it may be easier for the entrepreneur to raise funds from potential investors. Corporations can potentially last forever; they will not terminate if a person dies or withdraws from the business entity. Of course, a corporation can be acquired by another business or it may become insolvent and stop operating. One problem with the corporate form is the potential for **double taxation** when the corporation pays out profits in the form of dividends. This will be addressed more fully in the Federal Income Taxation section later in this chapter. Other disadvantages to the corporate form are:

- Corporations are relatively expensive to form.
- Corporations are subject to more state and federal regulation than most other legal forms.
- The corporate form is more complex and subject to a number of formalities. (Some of these are listed in Table 3.4: Corporate Formalities.)
- The entrepreneur can lose control of her venture as other shareholders invest in her firm.

Corporations are well suited for businesses that will need substantial capital and/or carry a significant risk. Examples of the latter might include high-technology ventures and oil drilling.

The Model Statutory Close Corporation Supplement to the Revised Model Business Corporation Act (RMBCA)[15] allows corporations with 50 or fewer shareholders to elect to be close corporations. This election requires approval by two thirds of each class or series of shares of the corporation.[16] Once the election is made, the articles of incorporation and the share certificates must state that the corporation is a statutory close corporation.[17] This status allows the corporation to dispense with many of the formalities of governance, such as annual share-holder meetings. Section 25 says that the close corporation's failure to observe "the usual corporate formalities or requirements" is not a basis for imposing liability on the shareholders for the corporation's obligations.[18] The limited liabil-ity feature will remain intact.[19]

Under many circumstances, the fact that shares in the corporation can be easily transferred is an advantage. In other circumstances, free transferability of owner-ship may be a problem; for example, in a family business where the entrepreneur does not want interests transferred outside the family unit. These corporations with a few shareholders, frequently relatives and/or friends, are commonly called closely held corporations.[20]

What can the entrepreneur do to maintain the closely held nature of her corporation? If the entrepreneur perceives that the easy transfer of shares is a dis-advantage, she can establish restrictions on the transfer of stock. For example, these restrictions may permit the shareholder to only transfer shares to the shareholder's spouse, children, and grandchildren. Generally, the courts will favor transferability, often called the right of alienation, since it is an important right of property owners. The entrepreneur will want the restrictions to be fair, both because she wants the courts to enforce them and she or her heirs may be the ones who actually want to transfer the shares. Generally, to be enforceable, the restrictions should be (1) agreed to by the founders, (2) included in the bylaws, and (3) written on the stock certificates. Restrictions that are commonly accepted are those that limit shareholders' rights to encumber or sell their shares except by (1) offering the shares for sale first to the corporation or other shareholders on the same terms as the shareholder can sell to a bona fide prospective purchaser and (2) transfers by gift, bequest, intestate descent, or in trust for named family members, like spouse and children. In the alternative, the entrepreneur may enter into mandatory buy–sell agreements where either the other shareholders or the corporation must purchase the interest. Buy–sell agreements generally specify one or the other as the purchaser. In addition to the steps discussed in Table 3.2, corporations also need to comply with the steps to forming a corporation listed in Table 3.3.

Corporations must follow the appropriate formalities set forth by state law and the corporations' articles of incorporation[21] and bylaws.[22] Common formalities are set out in Table 3.4.

Regular corporations are commonly called C corporations because they are taxed under Subchapter C of the Internal Revenue Code. Some entrepreneurs

---

TABLE 3.3 Steps to Forming a Corporation

- Prepare the articles of incorporation. Generally, the articles need to include:
  - The corporation's name.
  - The corporation's purpose.
  - The corporation's duration.
  - The location of the principal office or registered agent.
  - The powers of the corporation and what type(s) of business it will operate.
  - The classes of stock, the number of shares of each class, and the amount of consideration received for all shares.
  - The initial directors. The initial directors are usually the promoters (incorporators).
  - The signatures of the promoters.
- Deliver the articles of incorporation to the secretary of state with any required fees. The secretary's office will check the articles and if they are in the proper form, the secretary will file them. The corporation officially exists when the articles are filed.
- Prepare the bylaws which specify how the corporation will be governed.
- Hold the organizational meeting of the board of directors and have someone take detailed minutes, which should be typed, signed, and filed in the corporate offices. It is preferable to have all the initial directors at the meeting, but only a quorum of the initial directors is required.

Source: Courtesy of Lynn M. Forsythe, © Lynn M. Forsythe 2009.

TABLE 3.4 Corporate Formalities

- Pay an annual fee to the state.
- File an annual report with the state.
- Provide proper notification for regular and special meetings. Participants can generally sign waivers for the notice.
- Hold annual meetings of the shareholders.
- Hold meetings of the directors at least annually.
- Prepare written minutes for all corporate meetings.
- Be sure that the required quorum is present for meetings.
- Be sure that the required number vote in favor of a proposal before going forward.
- Votes to remove directors and officers need a specified number or percentage of votes
- Respect the boundaries between the personal and corporate roles of officers, directors, and shareholders to avoid potential conflicts of interest.

want the limited liability of the corporate form but prefer pass-through taxation where the pro rata share of the income and deductions pass through to the actual owners. These entrepreneurs form S corporations under Subchapter S of Chapter 1 (§§1361–1379) of the Internal Revenue Code.

S CORPORATIONS

The number of S corporations has increased dramatically. For example, there were 724,749 S corporations in 1985 and 3,154,377 in 2002. The growth rate was especially high in S corporations with more than $10 million in assets. In 2002, 59% of all corporate tax returns were for S corporations.[23]

To form an S corporation, the entrepreneur would form a regular corporation by complying with the state law and then make an S corporation election with the Internal Revenue Service (IRS). S corporations must follow all the state rules for regular C corporations— they are just taxed in a different way. S corporations provide the advantages of limited liability like regular corporations, but they are taxed more like partnerships. It is more difficult to raise funds in an S corporation because of the restrictions on shareholders. There are a number of requirements before a corporation can make the Subchapter S election. The requirements include:

- The firm must be a domestic (United States) corporation.
- The corporation can have no more than 100 shareholders.
- All the shareholders must be U.S. citizens or residents. There can be no nonresident alien shareholders.
- Generally, all the shareholders must be human beings, certain tax-exempt organizations,[24] and/or qualifying trusts or estates. Other corporations cannot be shareholders.
- The corporation can have only one class of stock. Generally, the corporation can have different options or voting rights within that one class.

If a corporation ceases to meet the requirements, it will revert to a C corporation. In order to be an S corporation, the venture would make the S election by filing Form 2553 with the IRS. IRS forms and publications are available at www.irs.gov/ formspubs. The election must also include the written consent of the shareholders. The effect of the election is to have special tax treatment under §1362 of the Internal Revenue Code, where the profits and losses will be allocated to all the owners on the basis of their proportional ownership in the corporation.[25]

As with other business forms, there are disadvantages to Subchapter S corporations. In addition to the restrictions on who can be a shareholder, other potential disadvantages include:

- An S corporation cannot raise funds by recruiting corporate investors, including venture capital funds or institutional investors.
- An S corporation cannot issue founders' stock to key employees at low prices.

- An S corporation cannot create convertible preferred stock to sell to investors.
- Shareholders in S corporations must pay taxes on profits that are retained by the corporation.

Many entrepreneurs who would have chosen the S corporation form in the past will now choose the LLC form owing to the restrictions on S corporations.

LIMITED LIABILITY COMPANIES

The **limited liability company** is a relatively new form of business organization in the United States. With the passage of the first enabling statute for LLCs in Wyoming in 1977 and the subsequent passage of enabling statutes in the other states, each state has created its own variation of an LLC. Originally, most states required two or more owners in order to form an LLC; now, however, an entrepreneur can form a one-person LLC in most states. As with other state statutes, there are state-by-state variations. The National Conference of Commissioners on Uniform State Laws (NCCUSL) issued a uniform LLC statute called the Uniform Limited Liability Company Act (ULLCA) in 1995. This uniform act was not adopted widely, and the NCCUSL issued the Revised ULLCA in 2006.[26] Some of the major changes in the revised act are to provide for perpetual duration of the LLC, expand the members' freedom to decide the nature of their relationship, and generally allow the members to contractually establish the rights of members who want to leave the LLC.[27] As with other NCCUSL projects, this uniform act does not become law until it is adopted by the state legislature in a particular state.[28]

Owners who contribute funds to the LLC are called members, and members are not personally liable for the debts, liabilities, and obligations of the LLC. They can lose their capital contribution however. If the member has not paid the full amount promised, he or she can be forced to pay any remaining obligation. An LLC is managed by the members unless it is designated as a manager-managed LLC. In a member-managed LLC, the members have the right to manage the venture much like general partners would. In a manager-managed LLC, the members give up the right to manage the venture and they "transfer" that right to the manager(s), who may or may not also be a member(s). Generally, managers of LLCs are not personally liable either. Members and managers who commit torts will be liable for their own torts even if the tort was committed in conjunction with LLC activity. Some angel funds are organized as LLCs, such as the Boise Angel Fund, LLC.[29] In most states nonprofit organizations can form LLCs.

Most entrepreneurs who form LLCs are seeking the pass-through taxation of partnerships. Under the IRS code and regulations, an LLC will be taxed as a partnership unless it elects to be taxed as a corporation. To make this election, the entrepreneur would prepare and file IRS Form 8832, Entity Classification Election.[30] State governments do not necessarily follow the federal tax election or rules. LLCs do not have many of the limitations of S corporations. For example, the LLC can allocate losses specifically to certain members: in an S corporation the losses would have to be allocated pro rata.

As with other business forms, there are some disadvantages to LLCs in certain situations. Part of the problem is the fact that LLCs are a relatively new form of business organization and the governing law is in a state of flux. In addition, there are not many court cases and regulations to help clarify the rules. Other potential disadvantages include:

- Ownership interests in LLCs are generally not freely transferrable, making LLCs an undesirable choice where a large number of investors are anticipated.[31]
- The law is still developing over whether the selling of interests in LLCs is subject to state and/or federal securities laws. This seems to be more of an issue for the regulators when there are a large number of investors.
- There has not been extensive litigation to define the limits of liability.
- If the LLC is going to do business in multiple states with varying LLC statutes, it may be difficult to determine which state's law should apply.[32]
- Similar problems may exist if the venture is conducting business internationally.
- Professionals, such as accountants, may not form LLCs in many states.

See Table 3.5 for the steps to forming an LLC.

TABLE 3.5 Steps to Forming a Limited Liability Company

- Prepare the articles of organization. Most states have printed forms that are suitable for many typical small businesses. Generally, the venture needs to specify:
  - The name of the LLC.
  - The address of the LLC's office.
  - Name and address of the registered agent.
  - Name and address of each organizer.
  - The purpose of the LLC.
  - Whether the LLC is for a specified term and if so, what that term is.
  - Whether the LLC is to be managed by a manager and if so, the name and address of each manager.
  - Whether any of the members are to be personally liable for LLC debts and if so, who.
- The articles of organization need to be delivered to the secretary of state with any required fees. The secretary's office will check the articles and if they are in the proper form, the secretary will file them. The LLC officially begins when the articles are filed. The articles of organization can be changed by filing articles of amendment with the secretary of state.
- Prepare the operating agreement. Boilerplate documents should be avoided or used with extreme caution. The operating agreement specifies:
  - How it will be governed.
  - The financial obligations of members.
  - How profits, losses, and distributions will be shared.

TABLE 3.6 Distinctions Between Corporations and Limited Liability Companies

Attribute	Corporation	LLC
Title used for owner	Shareholder	Member
Title for what is owned	Stocks or shares	Membership
Document that creates the business entity	Articles of incorporation	Articles of organization (called certificate of formation or certificate of organization depending on the state)
Document that specifies how the business will operate	Bylaws	Operating agreement
Length of operation	Perpetual	Set term or at will. May be perpetual in some states

Source: Courtesy of Lynn M. Forsythe, © Lynn M. Forsythe 2009.

One of the things the members will need to address is their obligation to contribute additional capital. For example, will additional capital calls be forbidden or allowed? If they *are* allowed, will these contributions be voluntary or mandatory?

Some states do not permit professional LLCs, which are sometimes called PLLCs. These are LLCs where the members perform professional services, such as the practice of accounting, dentistry, medicine, or law. PLLCs are more sophisticated than standard LLCs.

Some of the main differences between corporations and LLCs are indicated in Table 3.6. As Table 3.6 illustrates, there are many differences in terminology. The entrepreneur should be aware that courts are borrowing many concepts and doctrines from corporation law, such as piercing the corporate veil, which is discussed below, and are applying them to LLCs.[33]

PIERCING THE CORPORATE VEIL

As the previous discussion indicates, one of the important factors in selecting a business form may be to insulate the entrepreneur's personal assets in case of a liability or failure of the business. There is a caveat however. The entrepreneur *can* be held liable even though she chose a business form that normally provides protection and she has followed the rules to properly form the business. When the court looks behind the business entity to the owners, it is commonly called piercing the corporate veil. The courts often use this term even though the entity that is being "pierced" is really an LLC. It is also called the "alter ego" doctrine, that is, the entity is the alter ego of the entrepreneur. Certain circumstances make it more likely that the court will pierce the corporate veil. The court will be more likely to pierce the corporate veil if the venture was created to defraud others or for other illegitimate purposes. The likelihood will also increase if the venture has inadequate capitalization. Courts will look at the venture's legal obligations and commitments and the amount of funds normally necessary to operate this type of business. "If capital is illusory or trifling compared with the business to be done and the risk of loss, this is a ground for denying the separate entity privilege."[34] The risk also increases if the entrepreneur is draining off business assets for personal use. For example, an entrepreneur may be tempted to do this if she sees that the venture is failing and heading toward insolvency. In one court case, the judge described the factors to be considered in deciding whether to pierce the corporate veil noting that no one factor is determinative.[35] In piercing the veil of multiple entities, he considered these factors:

- absence of corporate records
- commingling of funds and assets
- common ownership of stock for multiple corporations
- concealing and misrepresenting the ownership and management
- disregarding legal formalities
- diversion of assets to other businesses or personal accounts
- draining off funds by the dominant owner
- entering into a contract with others to avoid payment
- failure to observe corporate formalities
- failure of officers and directors to function in their roles
- failure to pay dividends
- failure to maintain an arm's length relationship in transactions between entities
- failure to maintain minutes for meetings or corporate records for the different businesses
- formation of a corporation with the intent to transfer liabilities to it
- identical people serving as officers and directors of multiple corporations
- insolvency at the time of the transaction
- lack of corporate assets
- manipulation of assets and liabilities so that assets would be in one entity and liabilities would be in another
- use of the corporate entity to obtain services and property to the detriment of creditors
- use of the corporation as a mere shell
- use of the same office or business location by the corporations and their owners

These then are behaviors to avoid.

For the entrepreneur to best protect herself and her assets, she should pay attention to details, especially the details required for the form of business entity she chose; she should use common sense; and she should maintain good records. A failure to follow formalities weakens the corporate shield. The entrepreneur should:

- keep the entity's affairs and transactions separate from personal transactions and other entities she owns
- obtain adequate capitalization when she forms the business
- avoid draining off assets from the venture
- maintain standard business records
- form the business for legitimate business reasons, such as the reduction of taxes and limitation of liability
- direct the entity's actions so that they advance the entity's interests, and not the personal interests of the entrepreneur

In other words, "Don't use your LLC as your personal playground."[36] The same holds true for a corporation.

As noted above, piercing the corporate veil can also occur between related business entities, such as parent companies and their subsidiaries. In these cases, the courts also use agency law principles to hold the parent company liable.

DECLARING ILLEGAL DIVIDENDS

In the structure of a corporation, the directors are the ones who declare dividends. The law imposes some requirements on dividends. For example, a corporation must pay cash dividends from a lawful source of funds. The dividend will be illegal if it will impair or weaken the capital structure of the corporation, in other words, if its payment will make it more difficult for the corporation to continue to do business. For example, owners may be tempted to take money in the form of dividends if they perceive that the business is about to fail and they want to recoup some of their losses to the detriment of corporate creditors. In the case of illegal dividends, the directors are personally liable for declaring the illegal dividend. If the corporation is insolvent when the dividend is paid, all shareholders who receive the illegal dividends will be required to return them. If the corporation is solvent when the illegal dividend is paid, and remains solvent, only those shareholders who know that the dividend is illegal will be required to repay it. Innocent shareholders can retain the dividend. Consequently, the shareholders and directors can share liability in the case of illegal dividends.

FEDERAL INCOME TAXATION

The entrepreneur will need to consider a number of attributes in selecting a business entity. One of the important considerations is how the venture and entrepreneur will be taxed. There are two basic types of business entities for federal income taxation. One type is called a "pass-through" entity, because the owners pay tax on their individual tax returns. In reality the income, losses, deductions, and credits pass through to the owners. When using pass-through taxation, the investors have to include the income on their individual tax returns whether or not the income is actually distributed to them.[37] Consequently, pass-through taxation is not an attractive feature if the entrepreneur wants to retain earnings to grow the venture, diversify it, or sell it to a large corporation. The other type of entity is recognized as a separate taxpayer that must pay its own taxes. In deciding among the forms, the entrepreneur will also want to consider the effective tax rates of the entity and the owners. Table 3.7 shows the types of tax and the necessary tax forms. The table does not distinguish between the various types of partnerships—general, limited, and limited liability—because all three types are basically taxed in the same manner under Subchapter K of the Internal Revenue Code. The LLCs shown in the table are passing through the income under Subchapter K. However, as previously mentioned, LLCs can elect to be taxed like C corporations.

TABLE 3.7 Income Tax Treatment of Business Entities		
Taxpayer	*Type of Taxation*	*Federal Tax Form*
Sole proprietors	Pass through	Schedule C of Form 1040
Partners	Pass through	Schedule E of Form 1040
Partnerships	These entities do the passing through.	Form 1065 is an informational return. The partnership provides each partner with a Schedule K-1, indicating each partner's share of income and expenses.
Shareholders in S corporations	Pass through	Schedule C of Form 1040
S Corporations	These entities do the passing through.	Form 1120S is an informational return.
LLC Members in one-member LLCs	Pass through	Schedule C of Form 1040
LLC Members in multimember LLCs	Pass through	Schedule E of Form 1040
Multimember LLCs	These entities do the passing through.	Form 1065 is an informational return. The LLC provides each member with a Schedule K-1, indicating each member's share of income and expenses.
Shareholders in C corporations	Taxes on dividends actually paid by corporation	Schedule B of Form 1040
C Corporations	Separate taxpayer	Form 1120

Source: Courtesy of Lynn M. Forsythe, © Lynn M. Forsythe 2009.

C corporations are often criticized for their double taxation. When a C corporation is formed, in effect another taxpayer is formed which must pay taxes on its taxable income. When it pays dividends to its shareholders, they must include the dividends on their own tax returns and pay tax. In this sense, there is double taxation. Often, the entrepreneur is an employee or officer of the company. When the corporation pays her a salary, the corporation is allowed a tax deduction for her salary as long as the amount is reasonable. In this situation, the company pays no taxes on this amount and she includes the salary on her own Form 1040. This amount is then subject to only one tax. Often the entrepreneur can choose to reduce her salary and/or not declare dividends, thereby leaving the funds in the C corporation. In many cases the C corporation may be the taxpayer with the lowest tax rate. Some states have limits on how much money can be left in the corporation if there is no valid business purpose for retaining the funds.

The income tax consequences can be an important consideration for potential investors. Some entrepreneurships are in industries where there is typically a long start-up period of significant losses before the ventures become profitable, for example, biotechnology companies. It is advantageous for the investors to be able to use these losses on their individual tax returns. Venture capital funds will not generally invest in pass-through entities because of tax restrictions on the tax-exempt partners of the venture capital fund. Many venture capital funds raise money from tax-exempt entities such as charities, pension funds, profit-sharing trusts, and universities. These investors would suffer negative tax consequences if the venture capital fund is invested in an entity with pass-through taxation.

There are, frequently, tax consequences to changing business forms, so the entrepreneur should discuss any changes she contemplates with her tax advisors.

The entrepreneur should also pay attention to timing.[38] In most situations she would not want to officially form the business in the last few weeks of the year, because if she does so she will have to file tax returns for the partial year if the business is a calendar year taxpayer. She also may have to complete annual filings that the state requires. Generally, it would be to the entrepreneur's advantage to wait until after the new year begins on January 1. Timing can be important in tax situations, and the entity may wish to pay bills early or delay billing a client if the entity is a cash basis taxpayer.

In applying this chapter, the entrepreneur should consider the application questions set out in the box below:

Application Questions

1. What business structure would be most appropriate?
2. Can the founder(s) assume personal liability for the venture?
3. How will the ownership interests be distributed?
4. Who will be the decision maker(s)?

5. How will disputes be resolved?

6. How much cash and property will be contributed to the business?

7. Do the founders have sufficient capital or do they need to acquire capital by obtaining loans or selling equity?

8. Do the founders need funds for living expenses during the initial start-up period?

9. How much control or ownership is the entrepreneur willing to give up?

10. Does the entrepreneur need others with business acumen or technical skills to assist in steering the business?

11. How much time and effort will each owner be expected to contribute?

12. Will there be incentives for the founders to stay with the company?

13. What if a founder leaves?

14. What if the other owners want a founder to leave?

15. Is there a forgotten founder who was involved at an earlier stage but is no longer actively involved?

16. Is the business expected to generate profits or losses? If it is expected to create losses, how long will it generate losses? (Pass-through losses may be an advantage.)

17. What are the income tax rates of the business and the principals?

18. Does the venture have to comply with local, state, and federal statutes and regulations? If so, what do the statutes and regulations require?

19. What documents must be filed initially?

20. What documents must be filed on a regular basis?

21. What is the exit strategy for the venture?

Summary

The entrepreneur can operate her venture using one of these business forms: sole proprietorship, partnership, limited partnership, limited liability partnership, C corporation, S corporation, or limited liability company. There is no one perfect business form, so the entrepreneur needs to weigh the advantages and disadvantages to select the best form for her particular situation. State law sets forth the rules of formation, operation, and closure of these business forms, with the exception of the S corporation. S corporations are named for Subchapter S of the Internal Revenue Code, which establishes the requirements for these corporations. S corporations are formed like regular corporations, except they have pass-through taxation.

In a sole proprietorship, the entrepreneur runs the business and makes the decisions concerning it. The business is not a separate taxpayer, and the entrepreneur puts all the income and deductions from the business on her individual tax return. She is personally liable for the debts and liabilities of the business. In a partnership, the entrepreneur joins with other partners to operate the business. All the partners are agents for each other and for the partnership. The partnership passes through income and deductions to the partners. Each partner is liable if the partnership does not have sufficient funds to pay its debts and liabilities. In a limited partnership, there is at least one general partner who is individually liable for partnership debts. There is also at least one limited partner. Limited partners are not personally liable for partnership debts unless they help manage the partnership. In a limited liability partnership, professionals join together to form the partnership. Each professional has unlimited liability for his or her own actions and the actions of the people he or she directly supervises. Each professional has limited liability for others in the partnership. All these types of partnerships have pass-through taxation.

A regular corporation is often called a C corporation because it is taxed under Subchapter C of the Internal Revenue Code. It is taxed as a separate entity, which results in double taxation of dividends. Dividends are taxed as part of the taxable income of the corporation and then again as part of the income of the recipient. In the usual case, the entrepreneur receives a salary from the corporation, which is only taxed once as long as the amount of the salary is reasonable. One of the largest advantages of all types of corporations is the limited liability afforded the owners of the corporation. Because of the limited liability feature, C corporations may be more attractive to potential investors.

Limited liability companies can be viewed as hybrids between corporations and partnerships, because LLCs have the limited liability of owners of corporations and they *can* have the federal tax treatment of partnerships. Since LLCs are a relatively new business form in the United States, the state laws governing them are in a state of flux.

Key Terms

articles of incorporation	limited liability partnership
bylaws	limited partnership
double taxation	registered agent
limited liability company	sole proprietorship

End-of-Chapter Questions

1. Consider the attributes listed on Table 3.1. What other attributes might be important to an entrepreneur, and why?
2. Why do most statutes indicate that a business operating under a particular form must designate the form in its business name, for example, DreamWorks SKG, LLC?
3. What are the differences between general partnerships, limited partnerships, and limited liability partnerships?

4. Under what circumstances might an entrepreneur want to form her LLC (or corporation) toward the end of the calendar year instead of waiting until after January 1? Why?
5. When might an entrepreneur be tempted to declare an illegal dividend? Why?

Suggested Activities

1. Select a hypothetical name and location for the entrepreneur's venture. Check to see if the name is available for use in that location and on the Internet. Are there any names that may be confusingly similar to the hypothetical name?
2. Visit the Web site(s) for the state where the entrepreneur wants to form her business. What are the comparative advantages of an LLC over a corporation in this state? What are the comparative advantages of a corporation over an LLC? In what respects are they the same?
3. Visit the Web site for the National Conference of Commissioners on Uniform State Laws. Locate the list of which states have adopted the Revised Uniform Limited Liability Company Act (2006) and the text of the act.
4. Search the Internet for the bylaws of a corporation, association, or organization. Analyze the bylaws. Which provisions should the entrepreneur include in her own bylaws? Why?
5. Visit the IRS Web site and obtain the Subchapter S corporation election form. Complete the form for a hypothetical venture.

Notes

1. The National Conference of Commissioners on Uniform State Laws (NCCUSL) Web Page entitled "Revised Uniform Limited Liability Company Act (2006)," found at http://www.nccusl.org/Update/uniformact_summaries/uniformacts-s-ullca06.asp
2. For example, the Uniform Limited Partnership Act (2001) recognizes limited liability limited partnerships (LLLP) under which the general partner is also protected from debts and obligations of the partnership. The NCCUSL Web Page entitled "Why States Should Adopt the Uniform Limited Partnership Act (2001)," found at http://www.nccusl.org/Update/uniformact_why/uniformacts-why-ulpa.asp
3. For example, C corporations can provide incentive stock options, and most other forms cannot.
4. For example, Chen and Hurley received Webby online achievement awards, but Karim did not. Anick Jesdanun (2007), "YouTube Co-founders Among Webby Winners: Steve Chen and Chad Hurley Were Named People of the Year," *The Associated Press* updated 5:35 p.m. PT, (May 1, 2007), found at http://www.msnbc.msn.com/id/18422701/
5. See *The Founding of YouTube*, The Utube Blog copied David Greising's story from the Chicago Tribune on the founding of YouTube, found at

http://theutubeblog.com/2006/10/15/the-founding-of-youtube/ The Chicago Tribune is not cited. For a more detailed account of Karim's involvement with YouTube, see Jim Hopkins (2006), "Surprise! There's a Third YouTube Co-founder," USA TODAY, Posted (October 11, 2006) 10:41 p.m. ET, found at http://www.usatoday.com/tech/news/2006-10-11-youtube-karim_x.htm Karim is given credit on YouTube's Web site. For additional examples, Bill Gates was a co-founder of Microsoft and Sam Walton was a co-founder of Wal-Mart. *Id.*

6. For more detailed information about the termination and wrapping up of business entities, see Daniel V. Davidson, Brenda E. Knowles, and Lynn M. Forsythe (2004), *Business Law Principles and Cases in the Legal Environment*, 8th edition, Thomson/South-Western, Mason, Ohio, Chapter 34, pp. 819–843. Reprinted by the publisher with a 2007 copyright.

7. Some states maintain files of all the domestic and foreign businesses registered in the state.

8. Many publications have tables that indicate the fees, contact information, and other information helpful in forming a business. For example, see Michael Spadaccini (2007), *Entrepreneur Magazine's Legal Guide – Business Structures*, Entrepreneur Media, Inc., Appendix D, State Reference Tables, pp. 359–427.

9. The facts provided in this example are obtained from the court cases.

10. *Holmes v. Lerner*, 88 Cal.Rptr.2d 130, 133 (Ca. App. 1st Dist. Div. 1, 1999), Opinion certified for partial publication, Rehearing denied September 7, 1999.

11. *Holmes v. Lerner*, 88 Cal.Rptr.2d 130 (Ca. App. 1st Dist. Div. 1, 1999).

12. The partnership agreement can grant voting rights to limited partners without them being involved in management. The Revised Uniform Limited Partnership Act (RULPA) specifically addresses what types of activities by themselves will not be considered control. The 1916 and 1976 versions of the Uniform Limited Partnership Act were adopted in 49 states, the District of Columbia, and the U.S. Virgin Islands. The 2001 version has been adopted by Arkansas, California, Florida, Hawaii, Idaho, Illinois, Iowa, Kentucky, Maine, Minnesota, Nevada, New Mexico, North Dakota, Virginia, and Washington. NCCUSL Web page, "A Few Facts About the Uniform Limited Partnership Act (2001)", found at http://www.nccusl.org/Update/uniformact_factsheets/uniformacts-fs-ulpa.asp (last visited May 22, 2009). More information about The Uniform Limited Partnership Act (2001) is found at the NCCUSL Web site at http://www.nccusl.org/

13. RULPA §303 (d). The Revised Uniform Limited Partnership Act (1967) with 1985 Amendments is commonly called RULPA.

14. RULPA §102 (2). However, the Uniform Limited Partnership Act (2001) permits the use of a limited partner's name. NCCUSL Web page, "Summary Uniform Limited Partnership Act (2001)," found at http://www.nccusl.org/Update/uniformact_summaries/uniformacts-s-ulpa.asp

15. The text of the Model Business Corporations Act (2002) version is found at http://www.abanet.org/buslaw/library/onlinepublications/mbca2002.pdf

16. Model Statutory Close Corporation Supplement §3. Definition and Election of Statutory Close Corporation Status, reprinted in footnote 1 of George J. Siedel (1987), "Close Corporation Law: Michigan, Delaware and the Model Act", 11 DEL. J. CORP. L. 383, (Winter 1987). A shareholder who votes against the amendment is entitled to dissenter's rights under MBCA Ch. 13.
17. Model Statutory Close Corporation Supplement §10. Notice of Statutory Close Corporation Status on Issued Shares, reprinted in note 16 of Siedel, (1987).
18. Note 16 of Siedel, (1987).
19. Locating the close corporation statute for a particular state may be difficult. Some states have an integrated statute where all the rules pertaining to close corporations are located in a distinct chapter of the corporation code. However, in other states the rules are dispersed throughout the corporation code.
20. Under the tax law, a closely held corporation has a technical definition. It is a corporation in which more than 50% of the value of the outstanding stock is owned directly or indirectly by 5 or fewer individuals in the last half of the tax year. It has additional restrictions on its tax treatment of passive activity losses, at-risk rules, and officer compensation. IRS Web page entitled "Entities: Sole Proprietor, Partnership, Limited Liability Company/Partnership (LLC/LLP), Corporation, Subchapter S Corporation," found at http://www.irs.gov/faqs/faq/0,id=199635,00.html
21. California Corporations Code §204 includes a number of optional provisions that may be included in the articles of incorporation.
22. California Corporations Code §212 lists a number of things that the corporation may include in its bylaws.
23. IRS Web page entitled "IRS Launches Study of S Corporation Reporting Compliance," found at http://www.irs.gov/newsroom/article/0,id=141441,00.html In July 2005, the IRS announced that it was going to begin a research study on the degree to which S corporations were complying with the tax code.
24. For example, §501(c) (3) corporations are permitted to be shareholders of S corporations.
25. Some states require a separate election at the state level, for example, New York and New Jersey.
26. The revised act is also called RULLCA. It has been adopted by Idaho and Iowa. NCCUSL Web Page entitled "A Few Facts About the Uniform Limited Liability Company Act (2006)," found at http://www.nccusl.org/Update/uniformact_factsheets/uniformacts-fs-ullca06.asp (last visited May 22, 2009).
28. *Id.*
28. For additional information see the NCCUSL Web Page entitled "Revised Uniform Limited Liability Company Act (2006)," found at http://www.nccusl.org/Update/uniformact_summaries/uniformacts-s-ullca06.asp and Larry E. Ribstein (2008), "An Analysis of the Revised Uniform Limited Liability Company Act," 3 VA. L. & BUS. REV. 35, (Spring 2008).
29. "Local Investors, RAIN Source Capital Form Boise Angel Fund to Invest in Local Companies; Kevin Learned, Boise Businessman, Named RAIN Source Capital's Idaho Field Agent," *Business Wire*, May 17, 2007, Boise, Idaho.

30. This form is available from the IRS Forms and Publications found at http://www.irs.gov/formspubs/index.html
31. For example, under the Revised ULLCA, a member may not transfer his or her interest unless the operating agreement permits it. The NCCUSL Web Page entitled, note 28, *Supra.*
32. Many LLC statutes state that other states should honor the law under which the LLC was officially formed, but there is no guarantee that this is what will happen. For illustration purposes, this would be a New York statute stating that other states should apply New York law to New York LLCs. This is generally what occurs with corporations.
33. For an example of a case applying the concept of piercing the veil to an LLC, see *Kaycee Land and Livestock v. Flahive*, 2002 Wyo. LEXIS 78 (2002).
34. *Briggs Transportation Co., Inc. v. Starr Sales Co., Inc.*, 262 N.W.2d 805, 810 (Iowa 1978), citing Ballantine, Corporations, §129, pp. 302–303 (rev. ed. 1946).
35. *Securities and Exchange Commission v. Elmas Trading Corp.*, 620 F. Supp. 231, 1985 U.S. Dist. LEXIS 16307 (Dist. of NV 1985), pp. 233–234, referencing W. Fletcher, 1 *Cyclopedia of the Law of Private Corporations* §41 (rev. perm. ed. 1980) and other precedents. In this case there were a number of instances where checks were written between the entities and individuals or obligations were noted on the entities' books but it was not clear what goods or services, if any, were provided in exchange for the funds.
36. Michael Spadaccini (2007), *Entrepreneur Magazine's Legal Guide—Forming an LLC in Any State,* Entrepreneur Media, Inc., p. 100. Also see the LLC Do's and Don'ts Checklist, p. 101.
37. The entrepreneur should discuss the consequences with her tax advisor. For example, one consequence with "pass through" taxation is the entrepreneur will have to calculate and possibly pay self-employment tax.
38. Timing of the venture itself and its relationship to the potential market and the economy are also important.

C H A P T E R

ESTABLISHING AND SERVING ON BOARDS OF DIRECTORS

A best-in-class board is a bulwark against questionable practices and a necessity for any corporation that aims to increase accountability and enhance shareholder value.[1]

INTRODUCTION

Most of this chapter focuses on establishing a board of directors based on the assumption that the entrepreneur has chosen to operate his business as a corporation. Many of the concepts, however, can apply to other business forms as well. When the entrepreneur incorporates his venture, the state of incorporation will require a board of directors. The state law will also impose a number of other formalities. Now the corporation will have to have board meetings and shareholders' meetings, with agendas distributed before the meeting and minutes prepared and distributed after the meeting. At this point the entrepreneur may begin to feel as if he is losing some control of his venture. If he has outside investors or shareholders, he is losing some control. This is a natural consequence of taking on investors or co-owners. In addition, many of those who have supplied financial capital to the firm will require some degree of control or some say in the company management as a condition of making an investment or loan. The entrepreneur should be aware of the type of control he is giving up when he selects various options. If he is not sure he understands the terms and their consequences, he should review the options with his lawyer.

Even if a formal board of directors is not required, the entrepreneur may still want to assemble a board of advisors. Or the entrepreneur may seek out mentors for advice. There are a number of advantages to having a board of directors, including (1) the potential for networking, (2) consultation, (3) the experience and expertise of the board members, (4) the additional prestige created by having certain individuals on the board, and (5) the board's ability to help resolve conflict among the officers and/or shareholders. Whether the entrepreneur has a board of directors or a group of advisors there are advantages to having them meet as a group. One advantage is the interchange of ideas between the members. For example, one member may make a suggestion and a second member may disagree. After the pros and cons have been discussed, generally, the full board will come to a decision or recommendation. Even if the ultimate decision is left to the entrepreneur, he will have the advantage of a full exploration of the issues. On the other hand, if the entrepreneur speaks to the mentors individually, the second mentor may merely disagree without a full comprehension of the first person's position and the reasoning behind it.

The term **corporate governance** is commonly used to describe the rules of a corporation and how it operates. Exhibit 4.1 illustrates how a corporation is governed from a legal perspective.

The founder may be surprised when the board of directors acts contrary to his wishes and desires. Once the business is incorporated the board of directors owes its primary duty of loyalty to the corporation itself, and not to the founders or shareholders.[2]

FIDUCIARY DUTIES

Directors and officers owe fiduciary duties to the corporation and the shareholders as a whole. The person who owes the **fiduciary duty** has the obligation to look out for the other person(s) to whom the duty is owed. The law commonly defines fiduciary duty as "a duty of utmost good faith, trust, confidence, and candor owed by a fiduciary . . . to the beneficiary . . . ; a duty to act with the highest degree of honesty and loyalty toward another person and in the best interests of the other person."[3] There has been some recent development in this legal area; generally however, the fiduciary duties are not owed to the founder, or to any

---

EXHIBIT 4.1 The Legal Model of Corporate Governance

Shareholders
|
elect
|
\|/
Board of directors
|
hire and fire
|
\|/
Officers and other top managers

Source: Courtesy of Lynn M. Forsythe, © Lynn M. Forsythe 2009.

specific shareholder, unless the corporate documents provide otherwise. Some aspects of fiduciary duties will be discussed in further detail in Chapter 5.

There can be an inherent conflict between these fiduciary duties of the board of directors and the desires of the entrepreneur-turned chief executive officer (CEO). Recently, the health of Steve Jobs, CEO of Apple, has been an issue and it has caused fluctuations in Apple stock prices.[4] There are allegations that the board of directors had information about Jobs' health but kept the information secret to the detriment of Apple shareholders.[5]

DUTIES AND RESPONSIBILITIES OF THE BOARD OF DIRECTORS

ESTABLISHING THE BOARD OF DIRECTORS

The officers of the company manage the day-to-day operations. However, the board of directors reviews the company's long-term strategies. The board needs to be small enough to serve as a deliberative and consultative body, but large enough to perform the job. The board typically consists of 7–11 directors. The state corporation code may specify a minimum number of directors. In some states corporations with a small number of shareholders may be permitted to operate with one or two directors. For example, in California, generally, a corporation is required to have at least three directors. However, a corporation with less than three shareholders may have fewer directors as long as there is at least one director for every shareholder.[6] The actual number of directors is specified in the articles or bylaws of the company.[7] It is helpful to have an uneven number of directors to reduce the likelihood of voting deadlocks.

SELECTING MEMBERS TO SERVE ON THE BOARD OF DIRECTORS

When the entrepreneur is looking for individuals to serve on the initial board of directors, or subsequent boards, he should take a long honest look at his strengths and weaknesses. (Even though the shareholders will vote on subsequent directors, the entrepreneur will be making recommendations to the nominating committee discussed below and voting on the directors in his role as a shareholder.) The entrepreneur can select board members that complement his skill set and assist in areas where he is weak. He should look for attributes that will help the company. Is the prospective board member honest, ethical, and organized? Does she have a positive reputation? If her reputation is very poor, the poor reputation may rub off on the entrepreneur's company. For example, having Bernard (Bernie) Madoff on the board might have been beneficial a few years ago, but his presence on the same board today would negatively impact the company's reputation and its ability to raise funds. How committed is the board member to this venture? Will she be available for phone calls and board meetings? Does she have the time to serve on the board? Does she have valuable contacts in the business community? Does she have practical expertise? Can she think strategically? Each person who joins the board is "a reason for others to stay or stay away."[8]

An entrepreneur sometimes selects a director with high visibility and a good reputation, even though he does not realistically expect much work from that director. In other words, the entrepreneur is selecting a "show horse" over a "work horse." For example, assume the entrepreneur convinced Bill Gates or a former U.S. president to be on the board even though he did not expect much actual work from that board member. There are a few potential problems with the decision to select a director who will only be a show horse. If there are too many show horses, it will be difficult for the board to complete its work. Because of other commitments, the show horse may not attend meetings or be available for phone calls. Resentment may build among the other board members if the show horse is being treated in a preferential manner and not assisting with board duties and responsibilities.

The entrepreneur should consider whether the potential member has enough time. Susan Shultz recommends that a person who is employed should not serve on more than two boards in addition to the company where he works. Boards of nonprofits should also be counted. She says that a person who is not employed can effectively serve on three or four boards.[9]

The entrepreneur should also consider the diversity of the board. Is there diversity in gender, race, religion, and national origin? If the board is relatively homogenous and lacking in diversity, the entrepreneur and the firm may miss out on an important perspective, for example, how Hispanics might view the company's position on a topic or the company's advertising campaign. The entrepreneur should also seek out diversity in age, education, expertise, geography, and industry. Additional information on forming a board is summarized in Table 4.1.

TABLE 4.1 How to Structure a Board and Recruit Members

- Write a charter for the board. Include how the board will be structured. The entrepreneur should know what he wants from the board and how he will measure if the board is successful. He should keep in mind the company's strategic plan.*
- Write down the critical needs of the company and create a needs matrix. Where is the venture headed and what skills and knowledge will be needed? For example, if the venture is going to expand into South America, a board member with knowledge about doing business in South America can be helpful. At least one board member should be a financial expert. SOX will require this for some companies. (This will be addressed in Chapter 5.)
- Develop a profile for each position on the board. How will each director be measured? What will constitute a successful director in this slot? Expertise is not sufficient. Each director should be able to contribute to the strategic planning process.
- Actively recruit directors that meet the profile for the position. The directors can provide expertise the company does not have in its CEO, employees, or consultants. Consider officers at companies with outstanding reputations in related fields where there may be synergies.
- Interview the potential board member. Pose tough questions and ask the potential member's advice. Ask her questions about strategy. This is an opportunity to consult with the potential board member and obtain her advice. Always look for individuals who will improve the quality of the board.

(continued)

TABLE 4.1 (*continued*)

- Conduct extensive reference checks on the potential board member. Check her performance both on other boards and at her place of employment. Ask the reference whether he would work with her again or whether he would hire her again. Does she see the larger picture? Can she think strategically?
- Recruit continuously. Refer to the needs matrix and maintain a list of potential board members for the different slots. This will allow the entrepreneur to respond quickly and effectively if there is an unexpected vacancy.

---

*One author suggests that the entrepreneur envision the board and its directors, because a person needs to imagine something before he can build it. Greg Warnock, "Building a Board from Scratch," Entrepreneurship.org, the Ewing Marion Kauffman Foundation Web site, found at http://www. entrepreneurship.org/ Resources/Detail/Default.aspx?id=10534.

TABLE 4.2   What Types of Decisions Do Boards Typically Make?

Boards
- Establish the long-term goals of the company and set overall policies.
- Hire a CEO to operate the company. Fire the CEO if necessary.
- Hire and fire other officers. In some companies, the CEO is the one with this authority.
- Determine the salaries for the CEO and other officers.
- Appoint interim directors to the board when a vacancy occurs.
- Declare dividends.
- Decide about mergers, acquisitions, and dispositions of corporate assets. These decisions may be subject to the approval of the shareholders, depending on the type of change and/or the provisions in the bylaws.
- Decide whether to begin new lines of business.
- Decide whether to exit a line of business.
- Decide whether to borrow money on behalf of the company.
- Direct corporate reorganizations.
- Decide whether to issue new classes of stock.
- Handle litigation.

Table 4.2 illustrates the types of decisions boards typically make. The entrepreneur may be tempted to reduce the authority of the board and the scope of its decision making; however, the authors advise against such a course of action. The entrepreneur should use the board to build and grow his company and to avoid problems. It is all too easy for the entrepreneur to lose track of the big picture and strategic plan and to focus only on the day-to-day operations of the venture. The board should focus on the big picture, and it will remind the entrepreneur to attend to the strategic plan.

Directors do not need to be shareholders of the corporation or residents of the state of incorporation unless the corporation code, articles of incorporation, or bylaws impose this requirement. Exhibit 4.2 illustrates the documents that govern the operation of the entrepreneurial venture.[10]

EXHIBIT 4.2 Governance Documents

State	Articles	
Corporation +	of +	Bylaws
Code	Incorporation	

Source: Courtesy of Lynn M. Forsythe, © Lynn M. Forsythe 2009.

The articles of incorporation and the bylaws may not conflict with mandatory provisions of the state corporation code. In some states, like California, the bylaws do not have to be filed with the state. Some boards and corporations also may have charters, operations manuals, and/or procedures manuals. They may also decide that they will use Robert's Rules of Order to conduct their business. Robert's Rules of Order is the standard for conducting business at meetings and assemblies. One of the advantages is that many individuals are already familiar with the rules in Robert's Rules of Order.[11]

RIGHTS OF THE DIRECTORS

Once they are elected (or appointed if it is a new company) to the board of directors, directors have certain rights, including the right to inspect the venture's financial documents. Courts and lawyers refer to the venture's financial documents and records as the books. It is difficult for the directors to make intelligent decisions if they do not have all the key information and there are situations where the CEO and other officers may keep information from the board. On occasion the corporation (and the courts) may decide to deny a director access to the venture's financial documents if the director is using the access for an improper purpose, such as stealing trade secrets.

Board members will serve for the length of time specified in the state statute, articles, or bylaws. The entrepreneur should give serious consideration to the length of time board members will serve. Does he really want them to serve for only one year at a time? In making a decision, he should consider the learning curve involved in learning about his venture and the industry.[12] The entrepreneur should also avoid the other extreme of an indefinite term. Term limits provide a more graceful termination of service than removing the director with or without cause. Despite the entrepreneur's careful selection, some directors may not work out. When directors who are not contributing are removed, it makes room for new directors who can provide enthusiasm, expertise, and new ideas. Of course, directors who are adding value to the corporation can be reelected to the board.

Many corporations use a classified board, where directors serve staggered terms; for example, with the exception of the initial board, each member will have a three-year term, and each year the shareholders will elect one third of the directors.[13] This has advantages because the learning curve may be very sharp. With a staggered term the corporation will not have a brand new board: there will be some continuity and some institutional memory. Directors do not automatically "retire" when their terms are over, they continue on the board until their replacements take over.

Traditionally, directors could be removed by shareholders "for cause," which means for a good reason. Many states now permit shareholders to remove directors by a majority vote even without cause.[14] In most jurisdictions, the board members are entitled to judicial review if they are removed from the board prior to the end of their terms.

RESPONSIBILITIES OF THE DIRECTORS

Traditionally, the corporation codes emphasized collective decision making by the board instead of decisions by individual directors or groups of directors. One of the advantages of collective decision making has already been addressed. Statutes set out that the board could only act when it was formally convened after proper notice and that directors could not send proxies to deliberate and vote in their place. The rules about advance notice of meetings have been relaxed in most states; however, if the corporation did not give proper notice the directors must generally agree in writing to waive the notice requirement.[15] A majority of the directors can make decisions without a meeting if this is permitted by the articles or bylaws. Technology is also making it easier to convene directors' meetings, and in many states directors' meetings can be held using chat rooms, teleconferencing, and videoconferencing.[16] The entrepreneur will probably want to provide in the articles or bylaws that these technologies can be used for directors' meetings.

Unless otherwise specified, a simple majority of the directors will constitute a quorum for transacting business[17] and actions taken by a majority of the quorum will be binding on the board of directors. The articles and/or bylaws can increase the number necessary for a quorum and/or the number required to approve certain actions.[18] If a director is a show horse, or otherwise not committed to the venture, she may often be absent, causing problems, including the potential lack of a quorum. Likewise, if she does not feel appreciated and respected, she may decide that attendance at the board meetings is not a priority for her. Generally, directors cannot enter into a valid agreement about how they are going to vote in advance of the actual vote. Directors are obligated to exercise independent, disinterested judgment. When the courts use the term disinterested in this context, they mean unbiased. It is difficult for directors to remain unbiased when they are also officers or shareholders in the company, or they want to do business with the company. Many of these **conflict of interest** problems will be addressed in the next chapter.

Board members can be held responsible to shareholders and creditors who rely on the financial records if they are not accurate. To entice members to agree to serve on the board of directors, the company may offer to purchase director's and officer's liability insurance (D&O insurance), which will be discussed in Chapter 13. Some state statutes allow the shareholders to amend the articles of incorporation to reduce the directors' liability for a breach of their duty of care,[19] thus reducing the need for D&O insurance. Normally, the articles state that the directors and officers will still be liable for acting in bad faith, for fraudulent acts, and for willful misconduct.

THE SARBANES-OXLEY ACT

> Dear Ms. Sarbox: The SEC estimates that it will cost $91,000 annually in order to be in compliance with just Sec. 404 [of SOX]. Is it really worth it?
> *Cheap in Charleston*
>
> Dear Cheap: Try looking at it from another angle. Cost of compliance: $91,000. Not being a convicted felon: Priceless.[20]

The authors do not want to scare the entrepreneur, but he may not want to add "convicted felon" to his resume. Initially, the entrepreneur will not be required to comply with §404 of the **Sarbanes-Oxley Act of 2002 (SOX)**[21] mentioned above; however, the downside is real.[22] As is typical with many statutes, various provisions of SOX apply to different types of business. For example, §404 applies to **reporting companies**, which are defined as companies that are subject to the public reporting requirements of the Securities Exchange Act of 1934. Companies that are not publicly traded and nonprofit corporations are currently exempt from the SOX requirements for boards of directors and SOX's other corporate governance provisions. In addition, both of the major stock exchanges exempt certain types of companies.[23] The stock exchanges are involved because the board governance provisions of SOX are implemented by the stock exchange(s) where a company is listed.

SOX is a federal statute intended to improve the corporate governance process and change the landscape of U.S. businesses. The goals included improving corporate governance, removing conflicts of interest, and restoring the confidence of investors and members of the public. SOX greatly expanded liability and reporting requirements. As with most corrective legislation, it is thorough and strict with a long list of requirements. What is SOX trying to correct? In 2001 and 2002, the following companies suffered financially due to questionable behavior by executives and board members: Adelphia, Enron, Global Crossing, Tyco, Xerox, and WorldCom. Fortunately for the entrepreneur, many of the SOX requirements do not directly apply to him at the early stages of his venture because the venture is not publicly traded.[24] However, SOX is affecting many aspects of business life for businesses of all sizes.[25]

Before SOX was enacted, in many corporations directors were primarily advisors to the CEO. They were frequently recruited because they had business or personal relationships with the CEO and/or other board members. Sometimes they were chosen because of their high public profile. Now, no matter why they were chosen originally, they need to actively monitor the corporation's management, especially in publicly traded corporations.

Even when compliance with SOX is not required, SOX rules are becoming the *new* standards for appropriate board behavior and corporate governance whether or not a business, technically, is subject to the rules of SOX.[26] As previously mentioned, board members in all companies owe fiduciary duties to the shareholders. Future litigation over whether these duties were breached is likely to be interpreted in light of SOX requirements (even for entities that are not required to comply with SOX). In other words, courts and juries may decide that the SOX requirements are the standard for reasonable and prudent behavior for business people. It may be advantageous for the entrepreneur to comply with other parts of SOX. Many authors predict a trend toward requiring compliance with additional sections of the act.[27] If the company is already complying with SOX, it will be easier for it to obtain investors like venture capitalists, because its financial records are perceived as being more reliable.[28]

Some of the SOX rules may not apply to the venture at the very beginning, but the entrepreneur may quickly find himself in the mire of SOX compliance. Compliance with SOX can help the entrepreneur in the long term. Banks and other financial institutions use SOX compliance in deciding whether to extend credit to an enterprise. Publicly traded financial institutions are expected to make sure that their clients are SOX compliant.[29] If the entrepreneur is in compliance and has integrated SOX best practices, he will be better able to negotiate favorable loan terms. Insurance underwriters are also more willing to accept a new client and negotiate competitive rates if the entrepreneur is compliant with SOX. He is considered a better risk. The entrepreneur will be required to prove that he is complying with all the SOX provisions before he can launch an initial public offering (IPO).[30] If or when the entrepreneur's enterprise becomes publicly traded, he will need to comply with the following provisions of SOX:

- The CEO *and* the chief financial officer (CFO) must each attach certifications to annual and quarterly reports certifying that they have reviewed the report and based on their knowledge it does not contain any untrue statements about material facts or does not omit a material fact. If a CEO or CFO knowingly and willfully violates this rule, he can be punished by up to 20 years in prison and a fine of up to $5 million.[31]

- The CEO and CFO will have to return to the company any bonuses or incentive pay they received from the company, or profits from trading in the company securities, if they were due to the company's material noncompliance with reporting requirements.

- Public companies cannot make personal loans to directors or executive officers.

SOX, in §307, requires the Securities and Exchange Commission (SEC) to establish standards for attorneys representing public companies. If the venture is a public company, its attorney is required to report evidence of material violations of securities law, breaches of fiduciary duties, or similar violations to the CEO or general counsel. If the CEO or the general counsel does not respond in an appropriate manner, the attorney must provide the information to the **audit committee** or the entire board. Consequently, the CEO cannot "brush off" the attorney's concerns. Table 4.3 provides some recommendations for avoiding problems under SOX.

TABLE 4.3 How to Avoid Problems under Sarbanes-Oxley Act (SOX)

What Should the Entrepreneur and Venture Do?
- Archive documents in a manner that lends itself to quick retrieval of documents.
- Be sensitive to corporate culture. If the culture is inappropriate, correct it.
- Create an audit committee.
- Establish a policy about gifts and loans to managers and employees.
- Integrate company databases and computer software to reduce the opportunities for manipulation of data.
- Use care in the destruction of documents. Err on the side of maintaining the records.
- Listen to concerns of the company's attorneys and accountants.
- Listen to concerns raised by the board of directors.
- Listen to concerns of employees.
- Provide good quality legal counsel to the CEO and CFO.
- Talk to the management team and employees about fraud and falsification of records.
- Create a thorough code of ethics and implement it. Everyone must follow the code.
- Model ethical behavior.
- Develop a policy on conflicts of interest and make sure that everyone follows it.
- Create and implement a policy on whistle-blowing.*
- Establish transparency in corporate dealings.
- Create an opportunity for managers and employees to speak freely without fear of reprisal.

*A whistle-blowing policy is discussed in more detail in Chapter 9. It is recommended that the entrepreneur reward his whistle-blowers. If he catches the problem early, he can save significant amounts. He may find it advantageous to establish a hotline for whistle-blowers to use.

A 1999 Commission of Sponsoring Organizations (COSO) study showed that many cases of fraud actually started with the CEO and/or the CFO.[32] For a "manual" on what to avoid, the entrepreneur can read about what caused the collapse of companies like Enron[33] and WorldCom.

Currently, most small businesses that are not publicly traded have to comply with SOX's whistle-blower protection and document preservation provisions.[34] The whistle-blower protection provisions are addressed in Chapter 9. The preservation of documents includes:

- Archiving and keeping documents so that they can be retrieved in a timely manner.
- Prohibiting the destruction and falsification of documents. It is illegal to destroy/falsify not only records pertinent to an ongoing federal investigation but also those that *might* be pertinent to contemplated investigations.

Under SOX it is a crime for any person to knowingly alter, conceal, create, or destroy any document to impede or impair any federal investigation. This crime can be punished by up to 20 years in prison and a fine.

The purpose of SAS 70 report is to certify that the corporation has instituted appropriate control systems. Even entrepreneurs that do not technically have to comply with SOX §404 may find that they need to complete the report because it is requested by their clients who are required to comply with §404.

The entrepreneur can purchase software to assist him in complying with SOX if the venture is governed by SOX or the entrepreneur is using SOX as the standard for good business practices.[35] There is even software customized for certain industries.[36] Some provisions of SOX will be addressed in other chapters of this Legal Companion, including Chapters 5 and 9.

WHO SHOULD SERVE ON THE BOARD OF DIRECTORS FOR THE VENTURE?

Ideal board members are pragmatic, strategic and tough-minded. They are willing and able to offer critical review, and are adept at giving direct guidance and feedback. Strong directors speak their minds, but they also have a real sense of partnership and of working together toward a common goal.[37]

Businesses commonly seek CEOs from other companies, but the entrepreneur can also consider presidents, chief operating officers, chief financial officers, heads of large operating units, venture capitalists, and other successful entrepreneurs. Venture capitalists and successful entrepreneurs often have the knowledge and experience that the entrepreneur needs, and these individuals are often passionate about helping other entrepreneurs during the early stages of the venture.[38] The entrepreneur can choose people who do not already serve on boards. Some entrepreneurs select board members with critical technical expertise. The first board member is especially important; her reputation and competence can play a key role in attracting others to serve on the board.

Entrepreneurs use different processes for selecting board members. The entrepreneur should solicit recommendations from numerous sources including his accountants, bankers, consultants, lawyers, and other advisors. Other CEOs can provide advice on who he might ask and who he might want to avoid. He should also speak with the potential board members. There are companies, such as Heidrick & Struggles International, Korn/Ferry International, and SpencerStuart, that help recruit board members and other top managers. The entrepreneur should consider the following issues when selecting board members:

- Is the potential member qualified to perform the critical oversight functions?
- Is the potential member knowledgeable about the business and the current economic climate?
- Does the potential member have sufficient time to be an effective board member or is she "spread too thin"? Is she willing to make a commitment to attend all the board meetings, committee meetings, site visits, and training? Is she willing to spend the time necessary for adequate preparation?

- Does the potential member's skills and expertise meet the needs of the corporation?
- Does the potential member have a good track record in business?
- Has the potential member successfully navigated through challenges similar to the ones the venture is facing or will be facing?
- What is the potential member's reputation and character?
- How does the potential member fit in with other board members? Will the potential member be able to work collegially with others on the board?
- Would this potential member be seriously interested in making a meaningful contribution to the success of the venture? Does she share a passion for the venture?

The entrepreneur can obtain preliminary information about the potential member from his contacts, business directories, and public sources.

The entrepreneur should consider the board as a whole. Is there a complementary blend of skills and personalities? If there is a mismatch of personalities the board may become dysfunctional and board meetings can be ineffectual.

In putting together the board of directors, obviously the entrepreneur should avoid individuals with questionable pasts. These individuals will taint the company and may even make it difficult for the company to secure loans and obtain investors. Under SOX, the SEC has authority to issue an order preventing a person who committed security fraud from acting as an officer or director of a public company.[39] Obviously, the entrepreneur should not select such a person even if he were not prohibited from doing so by the SEC. In a lesson learned from politics, the entrepreneur should carefully check the backgrounds of the people he is considering.

ADVANTAGES AND DISADVANTAGES OF OUTSIDE DIRECTORS

The trend is to include **outside directors** on the board. (Outside directors is another way of saying independent directors.) This trend may be more pronounced in large companies, but it is also the trend for entrepreneurial ventures. For example, for family businesses Ernesto Poza recommends a board of five to nine directors.[40] He recommends that the majority of the board be independent outsiders and that friends of the family not be included on the board because they may tend to rubber-stamp the CEOs decisions.[41] He recommends that the CEO be the only company manager on the board.[42] Poza cites a research project on the use of outside board members in family businesses, where the respondents most commonly reported the following benefits:

- "Outsiders provide unbiased objective views.
- They bring a fresher and broader perspective to issues of concern to the firm.
- They bring with them a network of contact.
- They make top managers accountable for their actions."[43]

The authors believe other entrepreneurial ventures would experience similar advantages from including outside board members. Susan Shultz reports on a Boardroom Consultants' study of 360 early-stage companies, where success "moved from 20% to 70% when independent boards" were used.[44]

Under SOX, a person is not an independent director if she serves "either directly or indirectly as a partner, shareholder, or officer of an organization that has a relationship with the company."[45] In making a decision about independence, both the National Association of Securities Dealers Automated Quotations (NASDAQ) and the New York Stock Exchange (NYSE) consider not only what the potential director is currently doing but also whether she or immediate members of her family were employees or executive officers for these other companies for the last three years.[46] Directors who also manage the company are called management directors. Obviously, they are not independent directors if they also hold the position of CFO or another management position. An independent board is one where a majority of the directors are independent from the founders and CEO and not subservient to them. Companies listed on the NYSE must have a majority of independent directors. Furthermore, the companies must report on which directors are independent and why the company came to that conclusion.[47] The NYSE also instituted rules for boards that have both management directors and non-management directors, requiring separate executive session meetings of only the non-management directors.[48]

In the past, both Adelphia[49] and Archer Daniels Midland (ADM) had boards that consisted primarily of family members and/or close friends. ADM provides an example of how a dependent board can fail to provide adequate supervision. ADM, the self-proclaimed "supermarket to the world," had a very dependent board. There were 17 members on the board, 10 of whom were relatives of the CEO, Dwayne Andreas, or current or former executives of ADM. A number of the other directors were also extremely loyal to Andreas. Just prior to the October 1996 shareholder meeting, ADM pled guilty to federal price-fixing charges and agreed to pay a $100 million criminal fine. It also owed substantial amounts in related civil settlements. Many of the shareholders claimed the board failed to provide adequate supervision because of the unusually close relationship between Andreas and the board.[50]

Whether or not an independent board is required, there are a number of advantages to an independent board, which are summarized in Table 4.4.

TABLE 4.4 Advantages of an Independent Board of Directors

1. The board will hold the founders, the CEO, and top managers accountable.
2. The board will challenge the founders' and managers' assumptions.
3. The board will bring in outside experience.
4. The board will have a fresh and broader perspective.
5. The board will have contacts the firm can use.
6. The board will provide a framework for control and add discipline.
7. The board can reduce bias.
8. The board can help resolve conflicts.

Venture capitalists and lenders will have some concerns about the interrelationship of the board members even in family businesses.

ATTRACTING PEOPLE TO THE BOARD OF DIRECTORS

When the entrepreneur is establishing the board of directors, he must consider the costs. There are both tangible and intangible compensations that entice potential directors to agree to serve on the board. Whether the entrepreneur is using a formal board of directors or an informal one, he should address the issue of compensation with the board members or advisors as early as possible. This will prevent a misunderstanding whereby the entrepreneur thinks that the advisors are volunteering their time but the advisors are expecting compensation. It can be a rude shock when the two sides become aware that they have different expectations.

Traditionally, directors were not compensated for their service to the corporation. However, there has been an increase in the amount of work the position entails and also in the potential liability associated with it.[51] Most corporations now pay directors for their service. However, if the directors are also shareholders, they may not expect compensation. They may be willing to serve in this role to protect their investment. The entrepreneur will need to decide how much he can afford to pay the directors and what compensation will be necessary to attract the people he wants to the board. Large corporations often pay each director's expenses to attend meetings, plus an annual fee (often called a retainer) and an attendance fee for each meeting. The Revised Model Business Corporation Act (RMBCA) permits the board of directors to establish their own compensation unless the articles of incorporation include a contrary provision.[52] Obviously, this can create some conflicts of interest, and the entrepreneur may want to provide that the directors cannot set their own pay.

Smaller companies generally pay (1) a monetary amount as a token of their appreciation and (2) some or all of the expenses of attending meetings, including travel expenses, hotel bills, and meals. Generally, the entrepreneur cannot really afford the going rate for the person's time. For example, if the entrepreneur were to calculate the number of days the director works on the board and compare it to the director's regular salary, the amount would probably be too great for the new venture to pay.[53] Executive search firms[54] publish data about trends in director compensation: this data is generally organized by company size and the structure of the board. The entrepreneur can use this data to gauge what might be appropriate compensation. Some entrepreneurships offer the directors stock options[55] or restricted stock grants as compensation. The advantage of such an arrangement is that the director will have a personal stake in the company. The disadvantage is that this personal stake can create a conflict of interest between the person as a director and the same person as a shareholder. The entrepreneur may have some other creative ideas for director compensation, but he should check with his attorney before using them. Some of them, such as interest-free or low-interest loans to the directors, may be illegal or pose other problems.

There is a trend toward suing directors. The corporation can purchase D&O insurance to protect directors (and officers) who are being sued in their corporate capacity.[56] Like most insurance policies, D&O insurance commonly has deductibles, upper limits on coverage, and certain events that are excluded. If the event is covered under the policy, the insurance company will pay the costs of defending against the litigation and any judgments or settlements that are due.[57]

The corporation can agree to indemnify directors that are sued in their corporate capacity. In other words, the corporation can promise to reimburse the directors for the amounts that they personally pay.[58] In this instance, the corporation is acting like a self-insurer.

Intangible compensation to board members includes the following: members

- enjoy the advisory process
- keep current in the industry
- learn new ideas that may be helpful in the board member's own company
- are exposed to how other corporations do things
- have the opportunity to network
- share their knowledge and experience
- shape the direction of the company, especially in the early stages
- obtain prestige

It is also critical to pay attention to what board members have to say, even if the board is a board of mentors. If these individuals feel ignored or that they are not valued, they are likely to stop actively participating, that is, preparing for and attending meetings will not be a priority in their lives.

BOARD MEETINGS

Boards of companies in the early stages often meet monthly. Boards of companies under stress also tend to meet monthly. Boards of more established companies tend to meet every other month or once a quarter. Board meetings typically last three to four hours. Meetings are generally scheduled after key reports are prepared so that the information can be shared with the board while it is timely.[59] The board members should have adequate time to review these reports prior to the meeting, however.

One way to help the board members feel that their advice and time are being valued is to run the board meetings efficiently. Technically, the chairman of the board runs the meeting, but the entrepreneur and company employees play an important role in preparing for the meeting even when the entrepreneur is not on the board. The company should send out an advance notice of the meeting as early as possible to help the board members schedule it. The company should provide an agenda for the meeting. It may become necessary to add items to the agenda, and it is possible to even add items at the board meeting. However, there may be certain agenda items that require advance notice under the bylaws or operating documents. The directors will also need background information. This should be sent to them early so that they can read it and reflect on it. The information should be organized in a way to make it accessible. The entrepreneur may need to have summaries prepared of longer documents. It is important not to overload the directors with information, or they are unlikely to study all of the information provided. Burying people with paperwork and data is a technique sometimes used to hide negative or damaging information. One of the advantages of holding the board meetings at the corporate offices is that company staff can obtain additional information if the board decides that it wants the data. This general advice is also applicable to the shareholders' meetings, although the items on the agenda for the shareholder's meetings will be different.

COMMITTEES

Historically, boards of directors made decisions as a whole group. Because the duties of the board are increasing and becoming more sophisticated, the trend is to divide the board of directors into committees. The board can establish committees and delegate duties to the committees unless the articles or bylaws provide otherwise. All members of the committee must be directors. The following powers must be exercised by the whole board and cannot be delegated to a committee:

- amending the bylaws
- appointing replacements for vacant seats on the board
- approving mergers that do not require a vote of the shareholders[60]
- authorizing the issuance of stock
- declaring dividends
- initiating actions for shareholder approval[61]

Other than these exceptions, the board can delegate powers to a committee to act on behalf of the entire board.

The common committees include the audit committee, the compensation committee, the executive committee, the investment committee, the litigation committee, and the nominating committee. In order for the committee structure to operate effectively, it is important to appoint the proper board members to each committee, that is, board members with an interest, knowledge, and appropriate expertise.

AUDIT COMMITTEE

The audit committee is responsible for evaluating company management and company auditors: it is distinct from company management. It does not complete the actual audit, but it should facilitate the audit. It hires and supervises the independent public accountants who audit the financial records. It should make sure that effective internal controls exist and are fully implemented by managers and employees. The audit committee should also ensure that all managers and employees involved in financial reporting and internal controls understand and properly fulfill their roles. It should work closely with the independent public accountants to identify and analyze reporting difficulties, and it should make recommendations to the rest of the board and corporate management as to how to improve reporting and internal controls.

Even "over-the-counter" traded companies that are not traded on a public stock exchange are required to disclose in their **proxy statements**[62] to shareholders (1) whether they have an audit committee and (2) whether the members of the audit committee are independent under the rules of the public stock exchanges. If the business grows to the point where it is traded on the stock exchange, the stock exchange may impose more stringent rules.

In publicly traded companies, NYSE and NASDAQ require the audit committee to adopt a written charter.[63] At least one person on the audit committee should be a financial expert. The SEC does not consider current and former CEOs to be financial experts. If the company is publicly traded, the company must disclose if none of its audit committee members are financial experts. If no member is a financial expert, the SEC requires an explanation as to why it is so. If SOX applies, the members of the audit committee must be "financially literate" and independent of management.

COMPENSATION COMMITTEE

One of the duties of the board is to establish the compensation, including salaries, bonuses, fringe benefits, and stock option plans, for the CEO and other executives of the company. A compensation committee can be created to perform this function, or the board as a whole can do this. Compensation for officers can be a tricky situation for board members who may have been invited to join the board by the officers and may have worked with the officers over a number of years. Board members may feel a loyalty to the CEO and other officers. Compensation packages may also be particularly difficult in family businesses.

Recently, lucrative compensation packages have been the source of much negative press, especially in companies that are failing or requesting government bailouts. Shareholders and members of the public query why the CEO of a company facing bankruptcy should be paid so well. This may be less of a problem in entrepreneurial ventures; however, lenders, venture capitalists, and other creditors will be concerned if the venture is struggling and the entrepreneur is being well paid.[64]

The board should use care in how the compensation package is structured. A poorly structured package may increase the likelihood that the CEO or another officer may be more concerned about his personal financial gain than that of the enterprise. In other words, the package may incentivize "wrong" behavior. For example, the CEO might make a decision that favors short-term gain over long-term gain on the belief that his compensation is based on short-term profitability rather than long-term profitability. He might also believe that he will not be staying with the company for the long term. In addition, some

CEOs and other executives are provided with a hefty compensation package when their employment is terminated. Entrepreneurs may be tempted to negotiate a lucrative severance package, which can also spawn dissatisfaction among the shareholders.

EXECUTIVE COMMITTEE

Most or all of the members of the executive committee are often **inside directors**, because it is easy for them to meet. An inside director is a director who is also an officer, major shareholder, or employee. The committee generally has power to act on specified matters between board meetings. It also generally conducts preliminary investigations of proposals. In the future the role of the executive committee may decline because of concerns about the board's independence. In many contexts there should be no inside directors or the CEO should be the only inside director.

INVESTMENT COMMITTEE

This committee makes the decisions about investing and reinvesting corporate funds.

LITIGATION COMMITTEE

This committee makes decisions about whether the corporation should initiate legal action. For example, if the shareholders or a group of shareholders want to sue the former board of directors, this committee would investigate and make a decision about initiating or joining a lawsuit. The potential conflict of interest concerns may be obvious, especially if members of the litigation committee served on the board with the potential defendants in the litigation.

NOMINATING COMMITTEE

This committee prepares the slate of directors for the vote at the shareholder meeting. The nominating committee may choose to use an executive search firm to increase the pool of possible directors and assist in the selection process. SEC rules require that nominating committees disclose how they identified and evaluated potential directors.[65] Note that other people including the entrepreneur and shareholders can also nominate directors.

SHOULD THE ENTREPRENEUR SERVE ON THE BOARDS OF OTHER COMPANIES?

When the entrepreneur is invited to serve on the boards of other companies, his initial reaction is probably to be flattered. The CEO, officers, or board members of another company think that he has something valuable to contribute. However, the entrepreneur should give the request careful consideration before he gives an answer. Table 4.5 lists some of the things the entrepreneur should consider. Being on a board of directors is a serious commitment that will take time and energy

TABLE 4.5	When the Entrepreneur Is Invited to Be on Another Company's Board, What Should He Ask?

The entrepreneur should ask:

- Why is the entrepreneur being invited to join the board? He should consider the degree of honesty and candor in the answer.
- Will there be compensation? How much will it be?
- What type of business is it?
- Are there likely to be conflicting interests? Are the interests complementary?
- What is the time commitment? Does the entrepreneur have the time to do a quality job?
- Is anything happening (or about to happen) with the company or industry that is likely to make the position more time consuming or risky?
- How many will be on the board of directors? Who will they be?
- Is insurance going to be provided? What are the policy limits?
- Is the company going to provide indemnification if the entrepreneur is sued in his official capacity?
- What is the length of the term?

away from the entrepreneur's own business. There may be a conflict of interest between the entrepreneur's company and the other company.[66] If the entrepreneur does not do a good job as director, it may negatively effect his business reputation and create potential legal liability. In addition, some CEOs do not make efficient use of the directors' time. Some of the advantages of serving on the boards of other companies include:

- prominence in the business community
- contacts and networking with other key players who are on the board or who are otherwise associated with the company
- learning from others about the economy and how to manage businesses
- career development

In considering his board and the board of other companies, the entrepreneur should reflect on the application questions set out in the box below:

Application Questions

1. What are the entrepreneur's strengths and weaknesses?
2. Is the entrepreneur required to have a board of directors?
3. Does the entrepreneur need a board of directors or board of advisors?
4. Where can the entrepreneur find potential board members? How should the entrepreneur approach the potential members?
5. Will board members complement the founder's temperament and knowledge?

6. What is the company's strategic plan?

7. Will the board members each bring different areas of expertise to the venture?

8. Will board members be able to provide contacts for the fledgling enterprise?

9. Does the entrepreneur plan to compensate the board members? If he does, how does he plan to compensate them?

10. How often should the board meet? Should the entrepreneur meet with them individually or as a group?

11. What type of information will the entrepreneur need to prepare for board members to keep them up to date on the company?

12. Is the company a U.S. public company or a non-U.S. company listed in the United States under SOX?

Summary

If the entrepreneur chooses to incorporate, he will need to establish a board of directors. Even if he is not required to have a board, he may want to organize a group of advisors to serve similar purposes. If he does incorporate, the corporation code of the state of incorporation will dictate how many directors are required. The minimum number may be reduced if the corporation has only a few shareholders. In a corporation, shareholders elect the directors who then have the right to hire and fire the CEO and other officers and top managers. The directors should leave the daily management to the officers, and the directors should work on strategic planning and the long-term goals of the corporation. The directors have the right to access the information necessary to make decisions, including the right to inspect the corporate books. The learning curve for directors is generally significant even for directors with business expertise, so it is common to stagger the terms of the directors. The directors generally act as group; however, there is a trend toward establishing committees. The committees may make recommendations to the board as a whole or the shareholders, or the committees may make independent decisions about matters under their authority.

SOX is a relatively new federal statute with significant potential impact on the entrepreneur and his venture. Some of the provisions will only apply at later stages of the venture's development, such as when corporate shares are sold to the public. Other provisions will apply to the nascent venture. Even requirements that are not mandatory for the venture at this stage of growth may be treated as best practices that are followed by prudent ventures. Consequently, courts, juries, lenders, and insurers may treat SOX requirements as a minimum standard. Many provisions of SOX apply to the formation of the board and behavior of the directors. These include defining and choosing independent directors and establishing compensation for directors and officers.

SOX also requires (1) that the CEO and CFO attach certifications to annual and quarterly reports and (2) that publicly traded companies do not make personal loans to directors or executive officers.

Once the entrepreneur establishes a reputation for being an astute business person, he may be invited to serve on the boards of other businesses. Although it is an honor to be asked, the entrepreneur should give the matter careful consideration because serving on the board of another company may create conflicts of interests and take the entrepreneur away from the core objectives of his business enterprise.

Key Terms

audit committee
conflict of interest
corporate governance
fiduciary duty
inside directors

outside directors
proxy statements
reporting companies
Sarbanes-Oxley Act of 2002 (SOX)

End-of-Chapter Questions

1. Table 4.2 summarizes the normal responsibilities of the board of directors. Which ones might cause the most concern to the entrepreneur/founder? Why?
2. What are the advantages and disadvantages of compensating the board members with company stock? Why?
3. What are the special challenges for the board of directors in family businesses? How can the members attempt to overcome these challenges?
4. When is an entrepreneur required to comply with SOX? What are the advantages of complying with SOX even when compliance is not required?

Suggested Activities

1. Prepare an analysis of the strengths and weaknesses of the founder(s). Considering this analysis, what traits should the founder(s) look for in members of the board of directors?
2. Create a process for selecting board members at the initial stage of the venture. What steps should the entrepreneur take and in what order? How will board members be screened? As the venture matures, what changes should the entrepreneur make in this proposed process?
3. Select three people to invite onto the initial board of directors. Why are these individuals being selected?
4. Research director's compensation in the community where the venture will be started. What is the range for compensation?
5. Create a checklist for when the entrepreneur might need to complete a SAS 70 report under SOX.[67]

Notes

1. *How to Select a Board Member,* Heidrick & Struggles International, found at http://www.heidrick.com/NR/rdonlyres/B90C383B-EB23-475E-A68F-4256BB8 F26F6/0/BW_HowToSelectBOD.pdf, p. 2.
2. For a study of the composition of boards in small private firms, see Mark K. Fiegener, Bonnie M. Brown, Dirk R. Dreux IV, and William J. Dennis, Jr. "CEO Stakes and Board Composition in Small Private Firms," *Entrepreneurship: Theory and Practice,* Vol. 24, Issue 4 (Summer 2000).
3. Bryan A. Garner, Editor in Chief, *Black's Law Dictionary*, 7th edition, West Group, St. Paul, MN, 1999, p. 523.
4. This appears to be partly attributable to the market's uncertainty as to who will follow Jobs as CEO and this individual's ability to lead Apple.
5. Adam Lashinsky, "Steve's Leave, What Does It Really Mean?" *Fortune,* February 2, 2009, pp. 97–102, and Roger Parloff, "The Right to Information vs. the Right to Privacy, Who Should Prevail, Investors or CEOs?" *Fortune,* February 2, 2009, p. 100. The second article suggests that commentators have indicated that the privacy approach may be illegal and/or should be made illegal.
6. California Corporation Code §212 (2009).
7. The articles of incorporation usually specify the initial directors.
8. Susan F. Shultz, "Developing Strategic Boards of Directors," *Strategic Finance* 1–5 (November 2003), p. 3.
9. *Id.*
10. As discussed in Chapter 3, other business entities have similar documents to specify how the entity operates.
11. The most recent version is Henry M. Robert III et al.(2000), *Robert's Rules of Order Newly Revised*, 10th edition, Perseus Publishing, Cambridge, MA. The official Web site for Robert's Rules of Order is http://www.robertsrules.com/
12. Many companies use a three-year term, but the entrepreneur could use a four or five year term if he wishes. Of course, the shareholders can elect the directors for multiple terms. The directors may not feel as great a commitment to the company if it is only a "one year gig."
13. RMBCA §8.06 specifically allows staggered terms on the board if there are nine or more board members. The Model Business Corporations Act (2002 version) is found at http://www.abanet.org/buslaw/library/onlinepublications/mbca2002.pdf
14. California Corporations Code §303 (2009) addresses the removal of directors without cause.
15. This is especially true of directors who did not attend the meeting.
16. RMBCA §8.20(b) authorizes board meetings by conference calls.
17. There is often litigation surrounding the quorum of the directors, such as whether a director who has a personal interest in the transaction can count in determining whether there is a quorum.

18. Often the number necessary is higher for important decisions, such as whether to approve a merger. RMBCA §8.24 permits a corporation to increase the number necessary for a quorum or approval.
19. The duty of care is discussed in Chapter 5.
20. Jill Gilbert Welytok (2006), *Sarbanes-Oxley for Dummies*, Wiley Publishing, Inc., Hoboken, NJ, p. 280.
21. Pub. L. No. 107–204, 116 Stat. 747 (2002). SOX is available on the internet at the SEC Web site at www.sec.gov/about/laws/soa2002.pdf
22. One common complaint about SOX, especially §404, is the cost of compliance. The indication is that compliance costs do go down significantly after the first year. Many politicians and business people are unhappy with compliance costs and the inaccuracy of the initial cost estimates. Welytok (2006), pp. 159–162. The primary purpose of §404 is to improve the accuracy of financial disclosure by requiring reporting companies to take greater responsibility for their own internal control over financial reporting (ICFR). "[T]here is no consensus on the cost-effectiveness of Section 404." John L. Orcutt, "The Case Against Exempting Smaller Reporting Companies from Sarbanes-Oxley Section 404: Why Market-Based Solutions Are Likely to Harm Ordinary Investors," 14 *FORDHAM J. CORP. & FIN. L.* 325 (2009), p. 330. In June 2003, the SEC estimated that the annual cost for §404 compliance would run $91,000 per company. It is actually significantly greater than that amount. Orcutt, p. 329. William J. Carney also discusses the costs associated with SOX compliance in William J. Carney, "The Costs of Being Public After Sarbanes-Oxley: The Irony of Going Private," 55 *EMORY L.J.* 141 (2006).
23. Under the NYSE rules, the following companies are exempt: companies in which more than 50 percent of the voting power is held by an individual, group, or another company; limited partnerships; and companies involved in bankruptcy proceedings. Under the NASDAQ rules, the following are exempt: limited partnerships, issuers who have certain levels of assets to back the stock; and certain registered management investment companies.
24. For a more detailed discussion of SOX, refer to Welytok (2006), and Peggy M. Jackson (2006), *Sarbanes-Oxley for Small Businesses, Leveraging Compliance for Maximum Advantage*, John Wiley & Sons, Inc., Hoboken, NJ, Chapter 5 of the Jackson book is particularly helpful with advice on implementation. In light of the recent Madoff scandal, additional government regulation is likely.
25. See Houman B. Shadab, "Innovation and Corporate Governance: The Impact of Sarbanes-Oxley," 10 *U. PA. J. BUS. & EMP. L.* 955 (Summer 2008). Lynn Stephens and Robert G. Schwartz, "The Chilling Effect of Sarbanes-Oxley: Myth or Reality?" *CPA J* (June 2006) studied the impact of SOX on entrepreneurial technology firms and the future plans of the firms.
26. For a discussion of the trend of private companies to comply with SOX, see Sophia Yen, "Developments in Banking and Financial Law: 2004: XI. Corporate Governance: C. Sarbanes-Oxley: Following the Private Company Trend of Voluntary Compliance," 24 *ANN. REV. BANKING & FIN. L.* 233 (2005).

27. Jackson (2006), p. 14.
28. Venture capitalists and other investors have become more cautious since the dot-com bust. Jackson (2006), p. 20. Other economic conditions, such as a recession, will also make venture capitalists more cautious.
29. Jackson (2006), p. 19.
30. While IPOs are used to obtain capital or liquidity, the entrepreneur should use care in deciding whether to have an IPO. IPOs are sophisticated transactions that require conforming to many rules and regulations. There is no guarantee that the IPO will be successful.
31. One consequence of this rule is that CEOs and CFOs are requiring certifications from the managers who supervised the preparation, and the managers are requiring certifications from those who prepared the reports.
32. Study reported in Jackson (2006), p. 33.
33. Interestingly the Enron board included many very competent and successful members. Shortly before its collapse, it was ranked as having one the five best boards in the U.S. in 2000 by *Chief Executive* magazine. Mark S. Schwartz, Thomas W. Dunfee, and Michael J. Kline, "Tone at the Top: An Ethics Code for Directors?" *Journal of Business Ethics* 58 (2005), pp.79–100, p. 80, citing NACS: 2002, "The Rise and Fall of Enron: Principles for Director Focus," *DM Extra*, p. 4. For an interesting article on the Enron board and common mistakes made in forming boards, see Susan F. Shultz, "Developing Strategic Boards of Directors." *Strategic Finance* 1–5, (November 2003).
34. Protection for whistleblowers is discussed in more detail in Chapter 9.
35. For good practical advice, see Jackson (2006).
36. SOX has created opportunities for small businesses that manufacture products that assist customers in complying with SOX and in consulting on SOX.
37. Joie Gregor, a Vice Chairman and member of the Board Practice at Heidrick & Struggles, quoted at *How to Select a Board Member,* Heidrick & Struggles International, found at http://www.heidrick.com/NR/rdonlyres/B90C383B-EB23-475E-A68F-4256BB8F26F6/0/BW_HowToSelectBOD.pdf Gregor also recommends that the board complete a "thorough and objective" assessment of how it is performing as a board and how it can improve.
38. The entrepreneur should arrange for education and mentoring for members who are first-time directors.
39. SOX §1105. The section includes a more specific definition of what is a public company.
40. Family enterprises may be especially reluctant to share information with outsiders. They should work to overcome that reluctance. Family enterprises have some unique problems with independence. For example, it may be difficult for a daughter to stand up to her father when she disagrees with his recommendations and family dynamics, such as sibling rivalry, may be accentuated in the business setting. For a discussion of how outside board members are helpful in getting a family business to participate in estate and succession

planning, see Ernesto J. Poza, *Family Business*, © 2004, South-Westtern, a division of Thomson Learning, Mason, Ohio, pp. 98–99.

41. *Id.*, pp. 140–148.
42. Other company officers may make reports to the board.
43. M. Schwartz and L. Barnes "Outside Boards and Family Businesses: Another Look," *Family Business Review*, 4 (3), (1991), pp. 269–285, cited in Poza (2004), p. 148.
44. Shultz (2003), p. 2. For other authors who recommend independent boards for entrepreneurs, see Joe Hadzima, "Outside Directors Do You Need Them and Where to Find Them," reprint from the Monthly Column in the Boston Business Journal at http://web.mit.edu/e-club/hadzima/outside-directors. html and Greg Warnock, "Building a Board from Scratch," Entrepreneurship. org, the Ewing Marion Kauffman Foundation Web site, at http://www. entrepreneurship.org/Resources/Detail/Default.aspx?id=10534
45. Welytok (2006), p. 115. The reader can see that the environment of boards of directors in undergoing significant change.
46. *Id.*, p. 115.
47. *Id.*, pp. 115–116.
48. *Id.*, p. 117.
49. Adelphia Communications Corporation was founded by John Rigas, who was the CEO. His son Timothy Rigas was the CFO and his other son, Michael Rigas was vice-president for operations. More than 40 lawsuits were filed against the Rigases for hiding debt, looting the company, and using the company as their "personal piggy bank." — Francie Grace, "Adelphia Execs Indicted," New York, September 23, 2002, http://www.cbsnews.com/stories/2002/11/14/national/main 529375.shtml and Francie Grace, "Bail Set for Adelphia Execs," New York, July 24, 2002, http://www.cbsnews.com/stories/2002/09/23/national/main522992. shtml See also "Former Adelphia VP Pleads Guilty to Fraud Charges," *CNN. com*, http://archives.cnn.com/2002/LAW/11/14/adelphia.plea/index.html (November 14, 2002). The flaws in the cash management system set up by the Rigases is analyzed in Leigh Redd Johnson and Holly R. Rudolph, "The Lessons of Adelphia's Cash Fraud," *The Journal of Corporate Accounting & Finance*, November/December 2007, pp. 19–24.
50. Kurt Eichenwald, "The Tale of the Secret Tapes," *The New York Times* (November 16, 1997), pp. B1 and B10; Nancy Millman, "ADM's New CEO: Allen Andreas," *Chicago Tribune* (April 18, 1997), p. 1; Richard A. Melcher, Greg Burns, and Douglas Harbrecht, "It Isn't Dwayne's World Anymore," *Business Week* (November 18, 1996), p. 82; Sharon Walsh, "Andreas Creates Executive 'Team'," *Washington Post* (November 1, 1996), p. F3; and Kurt Eichenwald, "Archer Daniels Midland Agrees to Big Fine for Price Fixing," *The New York Times* (October 15, 1996), pp. A1, C3. For more information about the price-fixing scandal, see Ronald Henkoff, "Behind the ADM Scandal: Betrayal," *Fortune* (February 3, 1997), pp. 82–87, and Mark

Whitacre's interview with Ronald Henkoff, "I Thought I Was Going to Be a Hero," *Fortune* (February 3, 1997), pp. 87–91.

51. Because of the increase in legal liability, qualified director candidates are becoming more selective about which board positions they are willing to consider.

52. RMBCA §8.11.

53. For example, the board members attend meetings, attend committee meetings, talk with the CEO, and spend time preparing for the meetings. If the board meets quarterly, the board member might spend 7–9 days a year working for the entrepreneur's corporation.

54. For example, Heidrick & Struggles International (http://www.heidrick.com/default.aspx), Korn/Ferry International (http://www.kornferry.com/), and SpencerStuart (International at http://www.spencerstuart.com//global and United States at http://www.spencerstuart.com/home/) all publish research on executive searches, including searches for board members. In their 34th Annual Board of Directors Study, Korn/Ferry noted that it is increasingly difficult to recruit high-quality directors; directors are serving on fewer boards but are working twice as many hours per board; and board size has decreased to an average of 10 members. Korn/Ferry Institute Announces 34th Annual Board Study Findings Press Release, found at http://www.kornferry.com/PressRelease/9964

55. In this context, a stock option allows the directors to purchase shares at a fixed price and/or for a fixed period of time.

56. It is estimated that D&O insurance costs $8000 to $20,000 per year for smaller companies. William H. (Bill) Payne, "Using the Board for Company Growth," Entrepreneurship.org, the Ewing Marion Kauffman Foundation Web site, found at http://www.entrepreneurship.org/Resources/Detail/Default.aspx?id=10270

57. D&O insurance is addressed in RMBCA §8.57.

58. Indemnification is addressed in RMBCA §§8.54 and 8.56 (1).

59. Joe Hadzima, "Don't Bore the Board of Directors (How to Use a Board Effectively)," reprint from the Monthly Column in the Boston Business Journal found at http://web.mit.edu/e-club/hadzima/dont-bore-the-board.html.

60. Short form mergers generally do not require a vote of the shareholders. Short form mergers are usually permitted when a subsidiary corporation merges into its parent corporation that owns most of its shares. In a short form merger the parent corporation adopts a merger resolution, mails the merger plan to the subsidiary's shareholders of record, and files the articles of merger with the state; the state then issues a certificate of merger.

61. Henry R. Cheesman (2009), *Contemporary Business and Online Commerce Law*, 6th edition, Pearson Education, Inc., Upper Saddle River, NJ, p. 788.

62. Proxy statements are documents that describe the matter for which the proxy is being requested, who is soliciting the proxy, and other relevant information.
63. For a Sample Audit Committee Charter, see Appendix C of Welytok (2006).
64. If during an audit the Internal Revenue Service feels that the compensation package is excessive, it may recharacterize the payment as dividends or some other type of payment.
65. These rules apply to corporations governed by SEC rules.
66. The entrepreneur may think that the company inviting him will have already considered conflicts of interests, but he should still look at it from his perspective. He may see conflicts of interests that they did not see.
67. One potential source of information on a SAS 70 report is the NDB firm, which provides accounting and consulting services. Its Web site is found at http://www.sas70.us.com/. The text of the SAS 70 standard is found at http://umiss.lib.olemiss.edu:82/record=b1038093

CHAPTER 5

OPERATING THROUGH AGENTS AND OFFICERS

The right people don't need to be managed. The moment you feel the need to tightly manage someone, you've made a hiring mistake.[1]

INTRODUCTION

Agents are the "actors" in most business activity. They perform many essential functions, including signing the lease for the office, agreeing to pay the utilities, ordering business cards, purchasing computers and software, buying or renting office furniture, hiring employees and consultants, and selling goods and services. The entrepreneur will be an agent for her business entity. The agency relationship is an arrangement where an agent may act for and bind the principal. The relationship can be created by an express contract, an implied contract, or by the law. This chapter will address many of the issues that occur when an agent enters into contracts for the venture.

Most businesses operate through the acts of their agents, including businesses that are not incorporated. For example, agents act for the benefit of limited liability companies (LLCs) and partners act as agents for the partnership. Partnerships often have other agents in addition to the partners. If the entrepreneur enters into a strategic partnership, the strategic partners can act as agents for this partnership. The entrepreneur needs to use care to accurately describe and limit the strategic partnership in discussions within the partnership and representations with the outside world. Otherwise it may be perceived by outsiders that the strategic partner is an agent for the entrepreneur and her entire business endeavor.

There are many "levels" of agents, some with very broad authority, like the chief executive officer (CEO), and some with relatively narrow authority, like the sales staff who sell the company's products. Common agents in a venture may include members of the board of directors, who are called directors. Members of advisory committees are generally not agents, but serve in the role of advisors and consultants. Officers of the venture are also high-level agents, including the CEO, vice-president, chief financial officer (CFO), and secretary. Independent contractors, discussed in Chapter 8, can also be agents. Employees, including part-time and temporary employees, can be agents.[2] As discussed later in this chapter, the question will be whether the person actually had the authority to act for the venture in this manner or whether the outsider reasonably believed the person had this authority. However, the entrepreneur will contract with many other firms and individuals without making them her agents. For example, if the entrepreneur hires a firm in Thailand to produce her clothes, generally, that firm is not her agent nor is it going to be perceived to be her agent. She may have some legal liability to the firm, but that liability will be based on the law of contracts. The firm will not be her agent when it purchases materials to use in fulfilling its contract with the entrepreneur.

The entrepreneur needs to use care in her selection of agents because they are representing her business and their actions can affect the finances and the reputation of her business. Oftentimes the business will be liable to outsiders, called third parties, for the actions of its agents, even if the agents disobey their instructions. (The law uses the term "third person" or "third party" to indicate anyone with whom the agent interacts and who is not a party to the principal–agent relationship.) Agents owe the business enterprise a number of important fiduciary duties, including the duties of care, obedience, and loyalty.

USING AGENTS TO ACT ON BEHALF OF THE VENTURE

An employee or independent contractor can act as an agent for the entrepreneur and her venture. The agent enters into contracts or performs functions similar to contracts on behalf of the entrepreneur; for example, the agent may sign company checks. This is in contrast to an employee who is performing physical acts on behalf of the entrepreneur/employer. The entrepreneur/employer is called the principal.

When a third person, like a customer, enters into a contract with the agent, the third person would generally prefer to sue the principal instead of the agent if there is a problem. The third person may want to sue the agent and principal together; however, the third party can generally be forced to make a choice or election to sue just one of them. The principal–agent relationship is a concern to the entrepreneur both because she is going to hire agents and also because she is going to act as an agent for her own firm. Exhibit 5.1 illustrates the relationship.

At different times the entrepreneur will be on all three sides of this triangle—agent, principal, and third party. For example, she will be the third party when she negotiates with an agent to have her goods produced by a manufacturing concern in Australia. When she is the third party dealing with someone else's agent, she should remember that she can always check with the principal if she is unsure whether the agent has authority to enter into this agreement. When the transaction in less common, say she is actually purchasing the manufacturing facility itself, she can ask the principal for a written statement confirming the agent's authority, such

EXHIBIT 5.1   The Agent–Principal Relationship

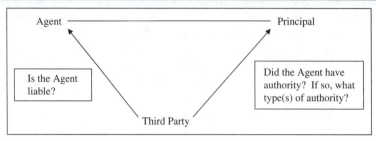

Source: Courtesy of Lynn M. Forsythe, © Lynn M. Forsythe 2009.

as a copy of the board of director's resolution authorizing the particular transaction and granting authority to the agent.

If there is a dispute, the court will analyze both whether there was an agency relationship and whether the agent had authority to act in this manner for the entrepreneur. In other words, did the entrepreneur delegate power to the agent to do this act? There are a number of different types of authority. In many factual situations, there will be more than one type of authority. See Table 5.1 for a summary of the most common types of authority.

TABLE 5.1   Types of Authority for Agents

Type of Authority	Description	Example
Express	Principal gives the agent the authority by spoken and/or written words. A writing is required in some circumstances because of the Statute of Frauds.* This authority is given prior to the agent's actions.	Pablo tells Aaron to purchase a restaurant franchise on Pablo's behalf.
Ratification	Agent did not have authority at the time of her acts. The principal approves the action after the fact using words or actions. A writing may be required in some circumstances because of the Statute of Frauds.	Penny tells Ann to research potential restaurant franchises that might be available. Ann is to report back with her findings. Instead Ann purchases a franchise on Penny's behalf. Penny approves the contract in writing.
Emergency	Agent will have emergency authority to enter into a contract as a response to an emergency if (1) an emergency occurs that requires a quick response, (2) the principal cannot be contacted in a timely manner, and (3) the agent's conduct was reasonable, and reasonably expected to benefit the principal.	Prudence hires Andrea to manage her gift shop. The weather service has announced that a hurricane is headed toward their community. Andrea goes to the hardware store and purchases lumber and nails to board up the store. She has the bill sent to Prudence.

(continued)

TABLE 5.1 *(continued)*		
Type of Authority	*Description*	*Example*
Implied	Agent can acquire implied authority through a series of transactions where she enters into agreements with the third party on the principal's behalf. The agent can also acquire implied authority due to her position or job title.	Pauline hires Angela to work in her office. Angela was told not to order office supplies for the company. Angela repeatedly orders office supplies and Pauline pays the bills.
Incidental (also called incidental powers)	Agent will have incidental authority to carry out transactions within her actual or apparent authority.	Alissa is given actual authority to obtain a loan for the business. Consequently, Alissa will have incidental authority to sign the loan documents and any other necessary paperwork.
Apparent[†]	This authority exists when a third party reasonably believes that an agent has authority to act in this manner because of the third party's dealings with the principal and the surrounding facts. The third party must be reasonable in believing the agent has this authority. Apparent authority will exist even if the principal did not intend to create the authority.	Paul fires Adam, who had worked as his sales agent for three years. After being fired Adam continues to call on his clients and take new orders and collect payments. Note that the court could also use implied authority in this situation.
Agency by estoppel (also called ostensible agency)[†]	The principal can be held liable for the contracts of a purported agent who is holding himself out as an agent for the principal. The principal will be estopped or prevented from denying the agency relationship if she knows that the purported agent is representing himself as her agent and she does not speak up to prevent the third party's loss.	Able is not an agent for Patty's Pie Company, Inc. However, Able is calling on businesses in town and representing himself as an agent for Patty's. Patty's becomes aware of Able's activities but Patty's does not take any action to protect the public from Able.

Notes: *The Statute of Frauds requires some contracts to be evidenced by a writing in order to be enforceable. The Statute of Frauds is discussed in more detail in Chapter 12.

[†]An actual agency relationship is not required for apparent authority or agency by estoppel. The person can be a purported (reputed) agent.

Source: Courtesy of Lynn M. Forsythe, © Lynn M. Forsythe 2009.

The entrepreneur can reduce the likelihood of litigation if she is careful in stating her agent's authority to the agent. She can ask the agent if he has any questions about what he is supposed to do and encourage him to contact her if questions arise later. She can also confirm the authority in writing to the agent, for example, by an email or text message. She should also be careful not to give third parties the impression that an agent has more authority than he actually does.

LIABILITY OF THE AGENT

Generally, the third party would prefer to hold the venture or principal liable instead of the agent. In many cases the principal has more assets. However, there are situations where the principal is unlikely to be held liable in court because of specific facts or the agent actually has more assets than the principal. An example of the latter would be if the agent is a successful serial entrepreneur and the principal is a start-up venture without much capital. In these situations, the third party may seek recovery from the agent.[3] An agent will be liable for any damages if he fails to represent his capacity. An example would be if the entrepreneur is acting on behalf of her new enterprise but does not make that clear to the third party. The third party may think the entrepreneur is acting in her own business interests. The entrepreneur and the other agents should be careful to represent their agency relationship when they sign documents. This can be accomplished by signing either the person's name followed by "for XYZ Company" or "XYZ Company by" followed by the person's name. Both styles clearly indicate the principal's name and the agency relationship.

An agent will also be liable if he intends to be bound on the contract. This is common when the agent is trading on his personal relationships with the third party; for example, the agent and the third party have a long-term friendship or business relationship and in order to "close the deal" the agent says, "I will personally guarantee the product." The agent may also be liable if he breaches his warranties of authority, which are discussed in the next section.

WARRANTIES OF AUTHORITY

When the entrepreneur and other agents act for the business entity, they are creating implied **warranties of authority**. These warranties exist merely because the agent has indicated to the third party that he works for a principal and he has named the principal. These are implied warranties, which means that the warranties arise from the transaction without any express statement by the agent. The agent is warranting that (1) the principal exists and is mentally competent, (2) the agent is an agent for the principal, and (3) the agent has authority to enter into this transaction on the principal's behalf. When the agent breaches his warranties of authority, the third party can sue him for any damages that result. An agent who is concerned that he may not have the necessary authority can negate the warranties by either expressly stating that there is no warranty or expressly informing the third party about the limits on his authority. In either case it would be advisable from the agent's position to put the statements in writing. (If the third party is willing to deal with the agent anyway, the third party is accepting the risk that the transaction may not be authorized.)

PROMOTERS

Promoters are the people who organize and start the corporation: they facilitate its creation by bringing the interested parties together. Before the corporation even exists and is recognized by the state government, the promoter works to obtain a location for the offices, establish utility service, hire some staff, obtain financing, etc. Promoters are also called preincorporators. Often, the entrepreneur is also the promoter; she is the agent for the corporation during the initial phase of operation and as such will have fiduciary duties to the corporation. Who is liable for these initial contracts? Generally, the promoter is liable for them. She should inform the other party that the corporation does not exist yet to avoid problems with any potential breach of warranty of authority. The contracts entered into by the promoter are generally discussed and approved at the first meeting of the board of directors. After this approval, the corporation will probably be liable based on the concept of ratification, thus making the corporation and the promoter jointly liable. The promoter will continue to be liable unless she is expressly released by the third party. The promoter may want to limit her personal liability at this initial stage. There are two basic techniques to do so: one is to ask the third party not to hold her personally liable, and the other is to seek a novation once the corporation has been formed. Novations are described below and illustrated in Exhibit 5.2. The entrepreneur should be aware that the third party may not be willing to release the promoter from her liability. Releasing the promoter may seem too risky to the third party who would like as many entities as possible liable on the agreement. At the preincorporation stage the corporation does not even exist and the third party will be unsure whether the corporation will have adequate funding. After the initial stages the third party *may* be willing to enter into a novation, whereby the third party agrees to release the promoter and hold only the corporation liable and the corporation agrees to be held liable. This novation is illustrated in Exhibit 5.2. Novations can occur with other types of contracts as well.

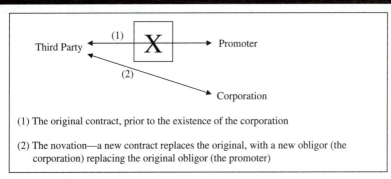

EXHIBIT 5.2 Novation of the Promoter's Contracts

(1) The original contract, prior to the existence of the corporation

(2) The novation—a new contract replaces the original, with a new obligor (the corporation) replacing the original obligor (the promoter)

Source: Courtesy of Lynn M. Forsythe, © Lynn M. Forsythe 2009.

FIDUCIARY DUTIES

As Justice Benjamin Cardozo stated in describing fiduciary duties, "Many forms of conduct permissible in a workaday world for those acting at arm's length, are forbidden to those bound by fiduciary ties. . . . Not honesty alone, but the punctilio of an honor the most sensitive, is then the standard of behavior."[4] The concept of fiduciary duties was introduced in Chapter 4. The discussion here focuses on officers and directors, however, the same duties will generally apply to other agents as well. The fiduciary duties of officers and directors are often explained as having three components: the duties of care, loyalty, and obedience. These components are summarized in Table 5.2. Courts will decide whether the officer or director is liable on a case-by-case basis. Even when the company has purchased director's and officer's liability insurance (D&O insurance), officers and directors can be held liable for amounts in excess of the policy limits.[5]

WHO IS OWED FIDUCIARY DUTIES?

The traditional rule is that directors of a corporation owe their fiduciary duties to the company and its shareholders. For example, in one classic case,[6] the court held that Henry Ford breached his fiduciary duty to the shareholders when he decided to withhold dividends so that he could sell cars more cheaply to the public at large.[7] Under the traditional rule, duties to any other groups exist only because there is a contractual obligation to them. However, the traditional rule has been evolving; for example, courts have recognized a fiduciary duty to the corporation's creditors if the corporation is nearing bankruptcy. In the United States, 31 states have enacted **constituency statutes,**[8] which either require or permit directors to consider the interests of other constituents of the corporation, including the corporation's employees, customers, suppliers, and creditors.[9] When the directors consider these other constituents, they may make decisions that favor these constituents over the shareholders. Some statutes even permit the directors to consider the economy of the state and the country.[10] For example, the directors could decide against closing a plant in a depressed U.S. community and moving the manufacturing operation to a foreign country. The directors might make this decision even though the cost of producing the goods in the foreign country and transporting them back to the United States would result in significant savings to the corporation over the next 10 years. Most of these state constituency statutes do not *require* the directors to consider the interests of these other constituents, the statutes merely permit it. Courts have not yet provided a detailed analysis of the legal effect of these statutes, although it appears that directors can use the statutes as a defense when they make a decision to benefit long-term non-shareholder interests such as employees or the environment, at the expense of short-term shareholder interests, such as dividends for the stockholders.

TABLE 5.2	**Fiduciary Duties**		
Duty	*Definition*	*Example*	*Consequences*
Care	Officers and directors must use care and diligence when acting for the venture. This duty encompasses the duty to (1) act in good faith, (2) use the care that an ordinary prudent person would use under similar circumstances, and (3) act in a manner they reasonably believe to be in the best interests of the corporation.	Jesse was a member of the board of directors. He missed three board meetings in a row and failed to study the materials for those meetings. Jesse attended the following meeting and voted on an important issue without adequate preparation.	Officers and directors are liable for losses that occur when they fail to exercise case.
Loyalty	Officers and directors must give priority to the interests of the corporation over their own interests. A number of activities will violate the duty of loyalty including (1) competing with the corporation without full disclosure to the corporation, (2) self-dealing in an agreement with the corporation, (3) making a secret profit on a transaction with the corporation, and (4) usurping a corporate opportunity. Self-dealing with the corporation will generally be permitted if there is full and fair disclosure of the personal interest and the transaction has been approved by disinterested directors or shareholders.	Janet is responsible for product development for the Z-Bot Electronic Toy Company. Melody approaches Janet with an idea for a partnership to create a new handheld game. Janet invests her personal funds in the partnership and does not tell the corporation or the board of directors about the opportunity.	Officers and directors who violate the duty of loyalty and make a secret profit are liable for the amount of the secret profit. The corporation may also be permitted to set aside the transaction.

(continued)

TABLE 5.2 (*continued*)			
Duty	*Definition*	*Example*	*Consequences*
Obedience	Officers and directors must act within the authority granted by the state corporation code, the articles of incorporation, the bylaws, operating procedures, and resolutions adopted by the board. If the venture is not a corporation, it will have similar documents that control its activities.	Jake was directed to deposit corporate funds into a money market account in the bank. Instead he opened a mutual funds account in the corporation's name with the funds.	Officers and directors are liable for any damages caused by their "unauthorized" acts.

Source: Courtesy of Lynn M. Forsythe, © Lynn M. Forsythe 2009.

DUTY OF CARE

An officer or director must act as a reasonable, prudent person would under the circumstances. This includes making an informed decision based on accurate information. Generally, directors can rely on the information prepared for them by corporate officers and consultants. However, situations can arise when this reliance would not be reasonable. The directors must heed the warning signs of potential problems. In one recent case, shareholders of Abbott Laboratories sued Abbott's board of directors for violating their duty of care. From 1993 to 1999 the Food and Drug Administration (FDA) conducted 13 inspections of Abbott's facilities. The FDA had a number of issues with Abbott, which were eventually settled by Abbott entering into a consent decree with the FDA whereby it would pay a $100 million civil fine, withdraw 125 types of medical diagnostic kits, destroy certain inventory, and make a number of changes in its manufacturing. Information about the inspections and FDA's concerns was available to the directors. Some of the directors received copies of the FDA's letters. In addition, the problems were reported in the Wall Street Journal and Bloomberg News. However, the directors still did not take corrective action. The court concluded that the shareholders should be allowed to proceed with their lawsuit and that it was not necessary for them to make a formal demand on the directors before initiating their suit.[11]

BUSINESS JUDGMENT RULE

The **business judgment rule** (BJR) is used to determine if officers and/or directors have met their duty of care. It protects officers and directors by measuring their performance based on the information available at the time they made the decision, even if eventually the decision is not as profitable as anticipated. All business decisions have some degree of risk. If disinterested and informed officers and/or directors make a decision after a reasonable deliberation, they will be protected under the BJR unless they were grossly negligent or acted in bad faith. There is a presumption that the directors acted appropriately, so the plaintiff must overcome that presumption in court by showing a violation of the duty of care or the duty of loyalty.

When the board of directors is faced with a merger or hostile takeover, the directors can still use the protection of the BJR; however, courts will look at whether the actions taken were really in the interest of the corporation and its shareholders or were an attempt to protect the board members' own interests. Under these unique situations the board should seek legal advice.

Officers and/or directors are not required to personally investigate all the information they use. Such a requirement would place an undue burden on the individuals who hold these positions. They are entitled to rely on information, reports, opinions, and statements prepared by officers, employees, lawyers, accountants, and/or committees. An officer's ability to rely on these documents is more limited than that of a director because an officer is more familiar with the company and its affairs. Courts will not accept reliance by officers or directors if they have other information that indicates reliance is not prudent. In other words, the BJR does not protect officers and directors who ignore red warning flags.

Delaware has enacted a statute that reduces the liability of outside directors, but not inside directors. Under the statute, outside directors are not liable for ordinary negligence, but they remain liable for gross negligence, intentional conduct, or recklessness.[12] Some other states have followed Delaware's lead on the liability of outside directors. The Revised Model Business Corporation Act (RMBCA) includes a similar rule.[13]

DUTY OF LOYALTY

Officers and directors must act in the best interests of the corporation, setting aside any personal financial and professional interests. They should avoid anything that appears to be self-dealing. This duty applies to a range of decisions, from considering a merger to setting executive compensation. They need to actively fulfill their responsibilities and cannot ignore developments that are potentially troubling.

SELF-DEALING

The duty of loyalty indicates that officers and directors should avoid transactions between themselves and the corporation. However, this is not always possible or even advisable. When an officer, such as the CEO, or director wants to enter into a transaction with the corporation, she should assure that all the facts are revealed to the board of directors, including her personal stake in the transaction. She should be meticulous in making sure that nothing is secret from the board. After the full disclosure, she should leave the boardroom and let the rest of the board members discuss the transaction. If the transaction is approved by a vote of the disinterested directors, it is generally acceptable to move forward with the transaction. (It is easier to obtain this approval if the officer who is involved is not a part of the board itself. Board members may feel some degree of loyalty if the proposal involves another board member or his company.) If it is not possible to have a vote of the disinterested board, the board should try to ensure that all the directors are fully informed about the transaction and that it is fair to the company and all the shareholders. These transactions will be suspect if they are not fair to the company.

BUSINESS OPPORTUNITIES

A **business opportunity** in this context is an opportunity that a person tells the officer or director about because of the officer's or director's relationship with the company. In most cases the person is sharing the information because the person wants to know if the corporation would be interested. If an officer or director takes or pursues a business opportunity (also called a corporate opportunity), he is violating his duty of loyalty to the corporation. The officer or director illegally takes a business opportunity if

- the opportunity was presented to the officer or board member in his corporate capacity
- the opportunity was related to the corporation's current business or proposed future business activity
- the corporation has the financial strength to participate in the opportunity
- the officer or director took the opportunity for himself

When an officer or director wrongly usurps a business opportunity, the company can claim the opportunity as its own, and the company can claim any profits that he made. However, it is lawful for the officer or director to pursue the opportunity on his own if the opportunity was fully and accurately presented to the corporation and the corporation turned it down.

CRIMINAL LIABILITY

If an agent, officer, or director violates a criminal statute, he will be personally liable for the violation. For example, he might violate federal or state securities laws. Traditionally, the corporation was not liable for the crime. However, there is a trend toward imposing liability on the corporation, and many district attorneys and attorneys general now actively pursue both the agent and the corporation itself. Corporate liability tends to be based on (1) the fact that the statute itself imposes liability on the corporation, (2) the corporation benefited from the commission of the crime, or (3) the corporation directed the agent to commit the crime or authorized the commission of the crime.

OFFICERS

In most states, if there is only one shareholder, she can act as the only director and the only officer. However, most corporations have four main officers, each of whose powers and authority should be outlined in the bylaws. These officers may have different labels. The board of directors should include detailed descriptions of each officer's authority in the resolutions of the board and, consequently, the minutes of the board meetings. Some state corporation codes mandate the officers a corporation must have. The four main officers are:

- Chief executive officer (also called the president)—acts as the general manager of the corporation, handling its day-to-day business.
- Vice-president—acts in place of the president when she is not available. The vice-president may be given specific duties.
- Chief financial officer—handles the corporation's financial affairs and is responsible for overseeing financial appropriations, directing expenditures, and disseminating financial information. The CFO is responsible for assuring that the financial records provided to shareholders and regulators, such as the U.S. Securities and Exchange Commission (SEC), are correct and accurate.
- Secretary—handles corporate records, such as minutes and resolutions, and transfers of corporate stock.

Some state statutes do not allow the same person to serve as both treasurer and secretary.

In some corporations the board appoints the president and the president appoints the other officers. However, generally, the board appoints the officers, who then serve at the will of the board. The board can terminate an officer even if the officer has a valid employment contract. If the board removes an officer without cause, the corporation may be liable to the officer for breach of contract.

In some corporations the shareholders take a more central role in managing the corporation. Some state statutes and bylaws permit the shareholders to elect some or all of the officers. There is also a trend toward more shareholder involvement in officers' compensation. In some corporations the shareholders make recommendations about the compensation packages for company executives. Recently, there has been negative publicity about the size of compensation packages, especially in companies that are not performing well; so this trend will probably continue.

THE SARBANES-OXLEY ACT

The Sarbanes-Oxley Act (SOX) was introduced in Chapter 4.[14] Many of the SOX provisions apply to U.S. public companies and non-U.S. public companies that are listed in the United States. A number of the SOX provisions apply to officers of the companies. Some of them are described in this paragraph. Under §302, CEOs and CFOs must personally certify to the SEC that the financial statements in the annual and quarterly reports are appropriate and fair. CEOs and CFOs who knowingly certify reports that do not comply with SOX are subject to up to a $1 million fine and a term of up to 10 years in jail or both. The penalties are higher if the behavior is willful. SOX penalties may be imposed in addition to any penalties under other securities laws. The CEOs and CFOs must certify that they reviewed the report and based on their knowledge it does not contain any untrue statement of a material fact or omit a material fact (§302). CEOs and CFOs are responsible for designing, establishing, and maintaining internal controls so that material information can be discovered. During the 90-day period before the report, they must evaluate the efficacy of these controls.

DISCLOSURE COMMITTEE

The SEC recommends the formation of a **disclosure committee** to assist the corporation in complying with Paragraph 4 of §302 of SOX.[15] This section of SOX applies to companies that are issuers. Issuers are companies that are required to file quarterly and annual reports with the SEC. The committee can consist of the general counsel, the principal accounting officer, the chief investor relations officer, and other risk managers.

PROXIES

Officers, directors, and shareholders may ask other shareholders to appoint them as proxies. A proxy is a person authorized to represent another person and act in his or her behalf, such as a proxy appointed to vote for the shareholder at the annual shareholder's meeting.[16] When a shareholder, director, or officer wants to act as a proxy at the shareholders' meeting, he or she will make a proxy solicitation to the shareholders. The solicitation will generally be accompanied by a proxy statement that explains the proposed action(s). The Securities Exchange Act of 1934 imposes special reporting requirements for proxy solicitations in publicly traded companies. Even when reporting to the SEC is not required, the proxy statements should be complete and accurate in order to avoid claims of fraud. Shareholders are more likely to give a proxy (1) if they do not have a large financial stake in the company, (2) if it would be expensive or time consuming to travel to the meeting, and/or (3) if they have a lot of confidence in the person requesting the proxy.

In applying the information in this chapter, the entrepreneur should consider the application questions set out in the box below:

Application Questions

1. Is there one entrepreneur, or are there a group of founders?
2. Who is going to be the promoter(s)?
3. What value, knowledge, and expertise does the entrepreneur bring to the venture?
4. Should the entrepreneur serve as an officer? Which office(s) should she hold?
5. What roles should the other founders have?

6. How many officers does the venture need at this stage of its development? Can some of the positions be combined? The venture may be small and the individuals may have the time and skills to perform multiple roles.

7. How should the roles be described so that officers have a clear understanding of their responsibilities, the important tasks are covered, and duplication of effort is reduced?

8. Who should decide on the compensation and benefit packages for officers? What process should be used?

9. What steps should the venture take to minimize the risks associated with hiring agents?

10. Should the venture agree to reduce the standard of care for officers and directors?

11. Which sections of SOX apply to the venture? Should the venture implement SOX-compliant procedures that are not technically required but are good business practices?

Summary

All types of ventures use a range of agents to act on their behalf, from officers and directors to sales representatives. At different times the entrepreneur will act as the agent, the principal, or the third party when she deals with agents of other businesses. When an agent acts for the venture, the venture will be liable if the agent had authority. There are a number of different types of authority. Generally, the third party would prefer to hold the company liable. However, agents will also be liable if they fail to indicate their capacity, if they intend to be bound, or if they breach their warranties of authority. Agents owe fiduciary duties to their principal. In the past the directors of a corporation only owed their fiduciary duties to the company and its shareholders, but there has been some expansion of who is owed the fiduciary duties. Constituency statutes allow directors to consider other constituents in their decision making.

The duty of care requires officers and directors to act as reasonable and prudent people would act under the same or similar circumstances. This includes making an informed decision based on accurate information. The BJR provides some protection for these decisions. The duty of loyalty dictates that officers and directors act in the best interests of the corporation. When an officer or director does business with the venture, the transaction must be fair to the firm. Also, an officer or director cannot take advantage of a business opportunity unless the corporation rejects the opportunity. Many of the SOX provisions apply to corporate officers, including the entrepreneur, and the officers can be personally liable for their failure to comply with SOX.

Key Terms

business judgment rule	disclosure committee
business opportunity	promoter
constituency statute	warranty of authority

End-of-Chapter Questions

1. In a general partnership, each partner is an agent for the partnership. However, there are limits on each partner's authority. If the entrepreneur is considering entering into a partnership, what restrictions might she want to put on the authority of her partners? Are there any special considerations that the entrepreneur should take in dealing with a strategic partnership?
2. If the entrepreneur has to fire an agent, what should she do to avoid liability for the future contracts of the agent? In other words, what would stop the apparent authority of the agent?
3. Table 5.1 includes this example about Able. "Able is not an agent for Patty's, Inc. However, Able is calling on businesses in town and representing himself as an agent for Patty's. Patty's becomes aware of Able's activities but it does not take any action to protect the public from Able." What steps should Patty's take to protect the public and Patty's reputation?
4. What should the entrepreneur do to avoid personal liability when she is acting as a promoter for the venture?
5. Executive compensation is a touchy issue. What are the arguments in favor of sizeable compensation packages? What are the arguments opposed to them?

Suggested Activities

1. Research whether there is a constituency statute in the state where the venture will be formed. If so, summarize its provisions. If there is no statute, is one proposed?
2. What corporate officers are required in the state where the venture will be formed? Does the state permit the same person to be both the treasurer and secretary?
3. Look up a recent court case involving a business opportunity in the state where the venture will be formed. What does the court say about when an officer or director can accept the opportunity on his own?

Notes

1. Jim Collins, quoted in Jennifer Reingold, "Jim Collins: How Great Companies Turn Crisis Into Opportunity," *Fortune,* 159(2), (February 2, 2009), pp. 48–52, esp. 52.
2. The question of whether a worker is an independent contractor or an employee is relevant for other aspects of their relationship, such as potential liability for the torts of the worker.

3. Under the traditional rule, the third party had to make an election of whether to sue the agent or the principal. The more modern rule is to allow the third party to sue both the agent and principal together. However, either one can force the third party to make an election.

4. *Meinhard v. Salmon*, 249 N.Y. 458, p. 464 (Court of Appeals of New York, 1928).

5. *Smith v. Van Gorkom*, 488 A.2d 858 (Del. 1985).

6. *Dodge v. Ford Motor Co.*, 170 N.W. 668, p. 684 (Mich. 1919).

7. Other scholars have interpreted the case differently. See Ronald J. Colombo, "Ownership, Limited: Reconciling Traditional and Progressive Corporate Law via an Aristotelian Understanding of Ownership," 34 *IOWA J. CORP.* L. 247 (Fall 2008), at footnote 44.

8. Alissa Mickels, "Note: Beyond Corporate Social Responsibility: Reconciling the Ideals of a For-Benefit Corporation with Director Fiduciary Duties in the U.S. and Europe," 32 *HASTINGS INT'L & COMP. L. REV.* 271, (Winter 2009), at footnote 113.

9. A related issue is whether the directors violate their fiduciary duties when they make a charitable donation with company funds.

10. Minnesota Statute §302A.251(5).

11. Demand on the board of directors is a common requirement in shareholder derivative suits. *In re Abbott Laboratories Derivative Shareholders Litigation,* 325 F.3d 795, 2003 U.S. App. LEXIS 5998 (7th Cir. 2003), Rehearing and rehearing en banc denied by *In re Abbott Laboratories Derivative Shareholders Litigation,* 2003 U.S. App. LEXIS 10628 (7th Cir. 2003).

12. Ordinary negligence is the failure to use ordinary care or ordinary diligence. Generally when the term negligence is used by courts and lawyers they mean ordinary negligence. Under gross negligence the standard of conduct is reduced, in other words, the directors are less likely to be held liable. Depending on the state's definition, gross negligence may mean either (1) failure to exercise slight diligence or slight care, or (2) a voluntary act or omission in reckless disregard of a legal duty and the consequences of the act. Most states use the first definition. *Black's Law Dictionary*, 7th edition, Byran A. Garner, ed., West Group, St. Paul, MN., (1999), p. 1057.

13. RMBC §2.02(b)(4).

14. SOX is available on the internet at the SEC Web site at www.sec.gov/about/laws/soa2002.pdf

15. This section of SOX requires CEOs and CFOs to certify the accuracy of the company's financial statements. Jill Gilbert Welytok (2006), *Sarbanes-Oxley for Dummies*, Wiley Publishing, Inc., Hoboken, NJ, p. 128

16. Proxy can also mean the grant of authority or the document that evidences the grant of authority.

CHAPTER

RAISING FUNDS FOR THE VENTURE

Money is the mother's milk of any startup. Access to capital often determines whether a fledgling enterprise succeeds or dies in infancy.[1]

INTRODUCTION

The best idea ever conceived for an entrepreneurial venture will not guarantee success, even if that idea is supported by the best business plan that can possibly be composed. While an entrepreneurial idea is necessary, and while a well-constructed business plan is advisory, without adequate funding the venture is doomed to failure. Putting it as bluntly as possible, the entrepreneur *must* be able to finance the venture in order to have any chance of success. While the task of obtaining funding may seem daunting there are a surprising number of options that may be available for financing the venture, and the financing can even be obtained in stages that correspond with the development of the venture and the growth of the business. Each entrepreneur has to decide which method or methods will be appropriate for his venture; no one method is "best" for every entrepreneur, but some combination of the potential funding sources is likely to provide the necessary capital for every entrepreneur. The secret is for a *particular* entrepreneur to find that combination which will provide *him* with the necessary capital.

Before the entrepreneur begins to seek funding, he needs to determine how much funding he needs. The amount that the entrepreneur *wants* is irrelevant. The relevant amount is the amount that he *needs*, the amount that he absolutely and positively *must* have in order to have a fighting chance of making the venture a success. In order to determine how much he needs, the entrepreneur needs to develop a business plan, and he needs to include his best estimate of his financial needs and opportunities on the basis of substantial market research. Even with his best estimate, the entrepreneur is likely to find that potential investors will want to discount his projected sales figures and income flows, adopting a more pessimistic point of view in evaluating the investment and its likelihood of success. The more funding the entrepreneur requests, the more his business plan, financial statements, and projections will be scrutinized, because a larger investment carries with it the possibility of greater losses if the business venture does not succeed. Thus, in order to get funding, the entrepreneur needs to:

1. Develop a business plan.
2. Prepare financial estimates on the basis of market research and reasonable expectations.
3. Determine how much money is *needed*
   a. at the outset of the venture
   b. during each quarter of the first year
   c. at the end of the first year
4. Calculate how much of the money will be generated by the venture.
5. Determine how much of the funding must come from outside the venture.
6. Seek the necessary outside funding from one or more of the sources discussed below.

Potential sources of outside funding are listed in Table 6.1.

TABLE 6.1 Potential Sources of Funding	
Source of Funds	*Risks*
Bootstrapping	The entrepreneur is likely to be required to put up personal assets as collateral.
	Personal credit is utilized, putting credit rating at risk.
	Likely to be a somewhat limited source of funds.
Family and Friends	Financial harm to family and friends if the venture does not succeed.
	Potential interference from well-meaning (and invested) friends and relatives.
	Keeping the relationship professional despite the personal relationships with the investors.
Commercial Banks and Lenders	Possible need for co-signers and the liability that attaches to them.
	Requirement of adequate collateral puts personal assets at risk.
	Subordination clause in the loan agreement.
	Potential for the lender to call the loan before the expected due date.

(continued)

TABLE 6.1 (continued)	
Source of Funds	*Risks*
Small Business Administration	SBA's emphasis on minority- or female-owned ventures may preclude funding for some applicants.
	SBA's emphasis on inner-city locations may preclude funding for some ventures, e.g., fronting.
Angel Investors	Loss or limit of equity. Angel investors may require stock before investing.
	Increased debt if the angel investors are willing to accept bonds for their investment.
	Need for an antidilution clause may limit other opportunities.
	Angels may require a right of first refusal that hampers the flexibility of the entrepreneur.
Venture Capitalists	Loss of equity. Venture capitalists frequently demand as much as 50% of the equity in the venture in exchange for funding.
	Potential of being pushed out if or when an IPO takes place.
Equity Funding	Dilution of equity for the entrepreneur. Potential of a takeover, whether hostile or not, if equity is traded in the market.

The entrepreneur will also need to be aware of the potential risks faced with each type of funding, especially legal risks that may be incurred. Without some knowledge of these potential risks, the entrepreneur may find that he was able to get the funding to begin the venture, but at a cost that he would not have been willing to pay. This cost may be a loss of many, if not most, of his personal assets if the venture does not meet his initial projections, or it may result in a loss of control—or even ownership—of the venture if his projections prove to be inaccurate. Many of these risks will be discussed below.

BOOTSTRAPPING

There are some circumstances in which an entrepreneur can take his idea for a venture and turn the idea into a successful enterprise by "**bootstrapping**," providing the necessary capital to get the venture from idea to reality through his own creativity and the use of his personal assets. The entrepreneur will use money that he has accumulated in savings and checking accounts, and will also probably obtain loans from banks, using personal assets as collateral for the loans in order to negotiate the best possible terms for repayment. When the entrepreneur uses his own funds, he should make clear whether the funds are a capital contribution or a loan to the enterprise, which can be thought of as a "loan from himself." The characterization of the transaction may affect his ability to withdraw the funds from the enterprise at some time in the future.

Some entrepreneurs will be able to use home equity loans or lines of credit as a source of funding. The advantage to using a home equity loan is that this loan is likely to offer a very favorable interest rate, especially when compared to other types of loans. The disadvantage to using a home equity loan is that the entrepreneur is risking his home to launch his venture. Of course, if the entrepreneur is financing the enterprise by bootstrapping, he is probably risking the family's home, car, and virtually all other assets anyway, and the home equity loan just formalizes that process. Some entrepreneurs have used credit cards as a source of funding for a bootstrapped venture. This is normally a bad idea, since credit cards generally charge a much higher interest rate than other types of loans or credit that might be used. However, an entrepreneur who is careful and who has the time may be able to use the "teaser" rates that many credit card issuers are using today to his advantage. These teaser rates offer the credit card customer a very low rate for an introductory period, often as much as six months. An entrepreneur who is willing to roll over to a new card with a new teaser rate every six months, paying off the older card with the proceeds from the new card, may be able to use the credit cards to procure funds very reasonably. The danger to this approach is that the entrepreneur may forget to roll over in time, or may not be able to find a new card with an attractive teaser rate, locking him into the higher rate that is imposed at the end of the introductory period. There is also the probable negative affect on the entrepreneur's credit rating and credit score from all of these credit card account activities, which is likely to make obtaining credit in the future more difficult and/or more expensive.

Key Point. There is no federal law limiting the maximum interest rate that can be charged on a credit card, and state usury laws do not apply to out-of-state banks. As a result, many credit cards are issued from banks in states with no usury laws or with very high legal rates. For example, Delaware and North Dakota do not have usury limits on credit cards. If the entrepreneur misses a few payments, or is late with a few payments *on any credit account,* he may find that he is categorized as being in universal default,[2] and his credit card rate has increased to 30% or more. Avoid credit cards with a universal default clause.

The entrepreneur who is bootstrapping his enterprise will need to negotiate good, favorable credit terms with his suppliers and customers—seeking longer time periods for making payments to suppliers and shorter time periods for receiving payments from customers. He may want to use barter in lieu of cash on occasion, or share office space and equipment with other entrepreneurs or small businesses to reduce expenses. (Regional small business incubators may be able to provide office space and access to office equipment at a reasonable price.) An entrepreneur can positively affect his cash flow by leasing equipment, at least initially, rather than buying it. The cash outflow from the lease will be less than would occur in a purchase and the entire amount of the lease payment is tax deductible, whereas purchased equipment would have to be depreciated over time. The entrepreneur needs to realize that cutting costs and controlling cash flow are key elements in bootstrapping as a means of financing a venture. (There are numerous Web sites that contain lease contract forms. At least one of these sites, http://www.ilrg.com/forms/equiplease.html, has links to forms commonly used in each state. There is a fee to download such forms at this site.)

The danger in bootstrapping is that the entrepreneur will often be placing everything he owns on the line, risking his financial health on the success of the venture. If the business fails, even for reasons beyond the control of the entrepreneur, the impact on his credit and financial well-being can be devastating. However, the reward if he is able to successfully launch the venture is potentially huge. With no other sources of funds except himself and his assets, the entrepreneur has 100% ownership of the venture and total control of its profits—until such time as he decides to grow the enterprise through external funding.

FAMILY AND FRIENDS

Many entrepreneurs either doubt they have the wherewithal to bootstrap a venture or decide not to risk all of their assets on the idea. Instead, they decide to turn to friends and family members for help in funding the venture, at least initially. In fact, friends and family are likely to be the most common initial source of funding for an entrepreneur who is launching his business. There are several reasons for this, including the fact that friends and family are less likely to want collateral for their loans, as opposed to a bank or commercial lender that would insist on having a security interest. Friends and family are more likely to believe in the entrepreneur than strangers would be, especially strangers who are also business people; so there is less need for the entrepreneur to have a fully developed business plan, although he should still have such a plan. Friends and family are likely to allow the entrepreneur to manage the business, rather than insisting on a voice in management, as some commercial investors may require. Friends and family are less likely to have the business acumen to help the entrepreneur, but they may still give the entrepreneur advice, depending on the family dynamics. The entrepreneur should consider how the family member, for example, his father, will respond if he chooses not to follow the advice. This may be particularly problematic if the venture is experiencing difficulties. Family members may be more adamant about "helping" if they perceive that the venture is in crisis. Friends and family are more likely to be patient if the entrepreneur is not as successful from the start as he optimistically expected—or projected—, thus giving the business some additional time to become established and viable.

Of course, there are also some negative aspects to using friends and family for the funding of the venture. Should the business venture fail, there may be some long-term hurt feelings, dysfunctional impact on the friendship and/or family, and guilt on the part of the entrepreneur, which he might not feel under the same circumstances if a commercial lender or investor was the source of funds. After all, the friends and family members who invested did so, at least to some extent, from a belief in the entrepreneur as much as, or more than, in the business plan supporting the venture. They risked their wealth and financial well-being on a *person* rather than on a *venture*. By contrast, a commercial entity bases its decision to provide funding on the entity's evaluation of the business plan, the likelihood of the venture succeeding, and its expected return on investment. The funding decision was a *business* decision, made without reference to or concern about the individual who was proposing the plan.

If the parties do decide to go forward with a loan, they should be sure that everyone understands the consequences; they should prepare and sign a promissory note before the money changes hands. (There are numerous Web sites that provide templates for promissory notes, so the entrepreneur can select from several options. One such site is provided by ExpertLaw at http://www.expertlaw.com/library/business/promissory_note_form.html) The entrepreneur should have his attorney at least review, if not prepare, the note to be signed by him.

Some things to consider (and discuss with financial and tax advisors) include the repayment schedule; whether the lender will forgive the loan, and if so, under what circumstances; whether the entrepreneur will be required to repay the lender's estate if the lender dies; and what interest rate will be appropriate. The entrepreneur may feel that because the loan is an intra–family transaction he does not have to comply with the established repayment schedule, although the family member may well expect the entrepreneur/borrower to honor the terms of the loan agreement. Loans with below market interest rates may have tax consequences. Many issues will have potential estate planning consequences and may affect the distribution of assets to siblings and other heirs and possibly cause negative feelings within the family. Assume a parent makes a substantial loan to an entrepreneur and the loan does not have to be repaid if the lender dies. If the parent who made the loan does happen to die before the loan has been repaid, the entrepreneur will, in effect, receive a much larger share of the parent's estate than his siblings will receive. This may result is a rift between the entrepreneur and his siblings. This inequity can be adjusted by careful estate planning if the parent remembers and chooses to do so.

The entrepreneur and his friends and family may prefer to treat the funding as an investment rather than a loan, in which case the entrepreneur is giving away a portion of his equity in the venture. While this will relieve the burden of repaying the loans, it dilutes the entrepreneur's ownership interest and, potentially, gives his friends and family a voice in management, and they may decide to proceed in a different direction than the entrepreneur would prefer. It would be best for the entrepreneur to only give non-voting rights to these investors if he desires to retain complete control of the venture. Unfortunately, that will require the creation of a limited partnership (LP), a limited liability partnership (LLP), a limited liability company (LLC), or a corporation, which in turn will require spending more time and money in going through the organizational steps necessary to comply with state statutes in creating one of these structures for the venture.

The benefit to the friends and family when the entrepreneur chooses one of these organizational structures is that they are likely to be shielded from any personal liability in case the venture fails. Limited partners are not liable for the venture's debts, nor are the partners in an LLP or the investors in an LLC or a corporation. The entrepreneur is not shielded from any potential liability in a limited partnership since he will be the general partner. He will also remain liable for any debts of the venture if he is a co-signer or guarantor for the debt, even if he has formed an LP, LLP, LLC, or corporation.

COMMERCIAL BANKS AND LENDERS

For the entrepreneur who is not willing, or not able, to finance the venture through bootstrapping, and who is unable or unwilling to rely on the largesse of family and friends—not to mention the associated guilt if the enterprise should fail—there are several other options. Often, the entrepreneur may decide to seek at least some of his funding from a commercial lender. This is especially likely for the entrepreneur who has decided to form a corporation, an LP, an LLP, or an LLC as his business organization. One reason that the organizational form will influence the decision of how to seek funding is the expectation that the *business* will be the debtor facing liability if the venture fails, but that the *entrepreneur* will have limited liability due to the structure of the venture as a corporation, LP, LLP, or LLC. Thus, only the investment in the business is at risk if anything goes awry and the business fails. Because of this, many entrepreneurs are likely to think that they will be able to shield their personal assets—beyond the amount invested in the enterprise—by choosing one of these organizational forms, investing what they are willing (or able) to risk, and then seeking outside funding for the rest of the monies needed to launch or continue the business.

While investors in a corporation, an LP, an LLP, or an LLC do have limited liability in theory, those in a start-up venture are not likely to be shielded by this limitation. Unless a business has a "track record" on which it can rely in attempting to borrow funds, or has some assets that will comprise adequate collateral, the business is highly unlikely to obtain any loans without some form of external guarantee upon which the lender can rely if the business in unable to repay the loans. The most likely source of this external guarantee is the entrepreneur who is attempting to borrow the money. Thus, even if the entrepreneur forms a corporation, an LP, an LLP, or an LLC, he will probably have to co-sign any loans for the business *personally*, using his personal assets as collateral for the loan to the business. This means that the entrepreneur is still putting his personal assets at risk, if the venture should fail by co-signing. Any other investors who are joining the entrepreneur in launching the venture will also be required to co-sign any loans, or otherwise serve as guarantors. Thus, the initial investors will normally be putting their personal assets at risk, despite the prospect of limited liability; however, the organizational form chosen may provide protection in the form of limited liability for any future investors in the enterprise once it has become a viable enterprise.

Despite these risks, borrowing the funds needed from a commercial lender in order to launch, or continue, the venture may be the most attractive, or at least the most appropriate, funding source for the entrepreneur. A **commercial bank** is less likely to lend money to an entrepreneur for a start-up venture than to an entrepreneur with an on-going business that can show some likelihood of continued success. However, given sufficient collateral available to secure the loan, and with adequate resources available personally, the entrepreneur may be able to obtain a loan from a commercial bank, and such a loan is likely to be less expensive than many of the other potential sources of funding.

The commercial bank will want the same sorts of information from the entrepreneur who is borrowing funds to finance his venture as it would want from any other borrower seeking funds for any other reason. The bank will want a credit report and a credit rating for the entrepreneur; it will want collateral that exceeds the value of the loan being given; it will want a business plan and a forecast of earnings for the venture; and it will probably want a guarantee in the form of one or more co-signers who personally agree to cover any portion of the debt not repaid by the business. The terms of the loan will be affected significantly by the information and commitments the entrepreneur can provide to the bank. The commercial lender is also likely to ask for some concessions and clauses in the contract for a new venture that might not be requested if the enterprise has a "track record" of success.

Because commercial banks are less willing to lend money for start-up ventures, the entrepreneur seeking funding for a start-up venture may prefer applying for financing from a **commercial finance company** rather than from a commercial bank. Commercial finance companies, also known as asset-based lenders, are often willing to make loans when a commercial bank would not be willing to do so. Of course, asset-based lenders are also likely to charge a higher interest rate than would be charged by a commercial bank, increasing the cost of the capital. However, if the entrepreneur can obtain the loan from a commercial finance company, even at a higher rate, he will be able to begin the venture—a reasonable alternative to not being able to launch the business for lack of funds.

Asset-based lenders are more interested in collateral than are commercial banks. Often, the asset-based lender will be willing to extend credit if the borrower is able to provide real estate as collateral, or to secure the loan with accounts receivables, inventory, or equipment. Depending on the need of the entrepreneur, and the type of collateral available, the entrepreneur may be able to obtain a line of credit or a more tradition term loan. Again, the terms of the loan will be affected significantly by the information provided by the entrepreneur, and by the types of collateral he can provide to the lender.

Whether dealing with a commercial bank or a commercial finance company, the lender will often insist on the inclusion of a *subordination clause* in the loan agreement. A subordination clause states that the lender's claim on any debts will take priority over any claims of any future creditors, thus ensuring the lender of a priority position. The inclusion of this clause will give the lender a greater sense of security, thus increasing the likelihood of the entrepreneur getting the loan, but it makes obtaining future credit from other creditors more difficult by making them subordinate to the first lender. The subordination clause will often also state that any loans from the entrepreneur or his other investors are subordinate to the loan by the bank.

The lender may also insist on the inclusion of an *acceleration clause* in the loan, a clause that allows the lender to "call the loan," accelerating payment so that the entire balance becomes due upon the occurrence of some specified event or condition. For example, missing a payment may result in an acceleration, as may the breaking of a loan covenant, such as maintaining a certain level of inventory or carrying a specified amount of insurance. The presence of such a clause puts the entrepreneur at a greater risk since the loan *may* be called for any of the specified reasons and the clause may discourage other potential creditors from extending credit to the venture due to the potential calling of the loan.

Key Point.   The entrepreneur who is seeking financing for a start-up venture is dealing from a position of need, not strength. He will need the credit in order to get the venture "up and running," which means that he will need to accede to most, if not all, of the demands of the lender. Nevertheless, he should make every effort to negotiate terms in the loan that are not unduly harsh. This is especially important in agreeing to an acceleration clause. The entrepreneur should attempt to have some "wiggle room" before the loan can be accelerated. Rather than "any late payment may result in acceleration," perhaps "any payment more than forty-five days late may result in acceleration."

SMALL BUSINESS ADMINISTRATION

"The U.S. Small Business Administration (SBA) was created in 1953 as an independent agency of the federal government to aid, counsel, assist and protect the interests of small business concerns, to preserve free competitive enterprise and to maintain and strengthen the overall economy of our nation."[3] The overriding purpose of the SBA is to help Americans start, build, and grow businesses, and it satisfies this purpose in a number of ways, from offering programs and services to offering loans or loan guarantees for small businesses. While the other services offered by SBA are important components of its overall mission, and while an entrepreneur should be familiar with these other services, it is the lending and guaranteeing of loans that is most relevant here.

The SBA lends money to small businesses in some circumstances and provides loan guarantees to commercial lenders in others. For loan guarantees, the SBA guarantees up to 90% of the amount of the loan and works with commercial lenders to deliver the loans to the small business owner/entrepreneur. In either case, whether making the loan directly to the entrepreneur or working with a commercial lender to obtain a loan for the entrepreneur, the SBA requires the borrower to prepare a loan proposal and complete a loan application. The loan proposal should include a cover letter or an executive summary that clearly spells out the purpose of the loan, the planned time and manner of repayment, and other relevant information.

"Every application needs positive credit merits to be approved,"[4] whether the lender is the SBA or a commercial lender. This means that the entrepreneur must provide information that will be viewed in a positive light in the following areas:[5]

Equity investment	Lenders are not anxious to lend money to an enterprise if the entrepreneur is not willing to risk his own capital in the venture. The lender will look very carefully at the **debt-to-worth ratio**, measuring the amount the lender is being asked to lend (debt) in comparison to the amount the entrepreneur has invested (worth).
Earnings requirements	The business must be able to show that it will generate sufficient cash flow to meet all of its debt obligations as they become due. This will require a showing of when cash will be available (received by the firm) and when debt obligations are due. The SBA will not make any loans unless the borrower can show a reasonable expectation of an ability to repay the loan from the business operation.
Working capital	Unless current assets exceed current liabilities, it is doubtful that the company can meet its short-term debt obligations and, therefore, survive for the immediate future in order to have the opportunity for long-term success.
Collateral	The borrower normally needs to provide adequate collateral to secure the loan. However, the SBA does require a personal guarantee from every person who has a 20% or greater ownership interest in the venture, even if there is adequate collateral to secure the loan.
Resource management	The SBA will evaluate the managerial skills of the entrepreneur, looking at such factors as education, experience, and motivation in determining the overall "quality" of the entrepreneur's resource management abilities, and this factor will weigh heavily in the final granting or denying of the loan.

The SBA also has a new program, "SBA Express," which is intended to streamline the borrowing process by reducing the amount of paperwork normally required for an SBA loan or loan guarantee. With SBA Express, if an entrepreneur can qualify for a loan for up to $150,000 with an SBA-qualified bank, he can obtain the loan—and the SBA guarantee of that loan—without going through the standard SBA application process. The SBA also promises the entrepreneur a decision within 36 hours of the application. However, since loans only carry a 50% guarantee in this program, many SBA-qualified lenders are not participating in it. The SBA, as well as commercial banks and commercial finance companies, is likely to consider the **"five C's of credit"**[6] in deciding whether to lend any money to the entrepreneur seeking funding through a loan.

The SBA also provides other services, including the Small Business Innovation Research (SBIR) and the Small Business Technology Transfer (STTR) programs, through its Office of Technology. Through these two competitive programs, the SBA ensures that the nation's small, high-tech innovative businesses are a significant part of the federal government's research and development efforts. Eleven federal departments participate in the SBIR program, and five departments participate in the STTR program; together they award $2 billion to small high-tech businesses. The U.S National Science Foundation administers the SBIR site on behalf of the federal government. Entrepreneurs who operate small high-tech businesses can seek federal government grants through grants.gov.[7]

The Department of Commerce operates the Minority Business Development Agency (MBDA), the *only* federal agency created specifically to foster the establishment and growth of minority-owned businesses in America. MBDA is an entrepreneurially focused and innovative organization committed to wealth creation in minority communities. The Agency's mission is to actively promote the growth and competitiveness of large, medium, and small minority business enterprises (MBEs). MBDA actively coordinates and leverages public- and private-sector resources that facilitate strategic alliances in support of its mission.[8]

Both the SBA and MBDA strongly encourage businesses that are owned by minority or female entrepreneurs to seek assistance, and both agencies tend to favor such applicants. Unfortunately, this has led to a problem with "fronting," having a person for whom the benefit is intended "front" for a business that is owned and operated by others in order to gain the support of the SBA, including obtaining an SBA loan or loan guarantee. Fronting is a form of fraud, and criminal penalties can attach to anyone convicted of obtaining such benefits through this method.

"ANGELS" AS INVESTORS

"**Angel investors** are individuals who invest in businesses looking for higher returns than they would see from more traditional investments. Many are successful entrepreneurs who want to help other entrepreneurs get their businesses off the ground."[9] In many respects an angel investor is similar to a **venture capitalist** (described below), but usually on a smaller scale.

Angels do not tend to advertise, so finding an angel is not always easy. Often, angels are found through referrals from other entrepreneurs and/or networking within the industry. In addition, the entrepreneur can contact the local chamber of commerce, the executive director of a trade association, or his banker—among others—for the names of investors who might possibly be interested in his venture. Table 6.2 lists a number of ways to locate angel investors. The entrepreneur should not be discouraged by the relative anonymity of angel investors, or the difficulty of finding them, because the SBA estimates that there are at least 250,000 angels actively investing in businesses today, and they are believed to be funding more than $20 billion! By contrast, venture capitalists only fund between $3 and $5 billion per year.[10]

TABLE 6.2   Ten Action Steps for Finding an Angel Investor*
1. Contact the Chamber of Commerce; ask if it hosts a venture capital group.
2. Contact the executive director of the local SBA; ask if he or she knows of angel investment groups in the region.
3. Contact an accountant (perhaps from one of the Big Four accounting firms) who handles entrepreneurial services; ask him or her for names or contacts.
4. Ask legal counsel.
5. Contact a professional venture capitalist; ask if he or she is aware of any angel investors that might be interested in the enterprise.
6. Contact a regional economic development office or agency; ask if anyone there is aware of an angel investment group.
7. Contact the editor of a local business publication; ask if he or she knows of any such groups.
8. Examine the Principle Shareholders section of initial public offering (IPO) prospectuses for companies in the area. These are people who have recently cashed out for significant sums and may be looking for new investment opportunities.
9. Contact the executive director of your trade association; ask if there are any investors who specialize in your industry.
10. Ask your banker. If possible, talk with the bank officer who works with loans of $1 million or less, since this officer is likely to deal with angel investors or investor groups.

*"Venture Capital 101," The Smart Startup, found at http://www.antiventurecapital.com/vc101.html.

Angels are not in the charity business, however, and they will almost certainly scrutinize any potential investments in the same manner as a banker or a venture capitalist would. The angel will review the business plan of the entrepreneur, will examine the financial statements of the enterprise, and will then decide if this venture is likely to provide the type of return he or she expects from the investment. The angel will also want to receive *either* a substantial equity interest in the business *or* bonds, probably convertible bonds, as evidence of the debt/investment. The angel is also likely to require a seat on the board of directors before agreeing to the investment. In addition, the angel may require the entrepreneur to agree *not* to take certain actions or make certain decisions without the prior approval of the angel: decisions such as selling the firm's assets, issuing additional voting stock to the current management, or issuing new shares or classes of preferred stock that would allow the purchasers of this stock to have priority over the angel in the event of a liquidation of the business.

The entrepreneur *must* keep in mind that an angel is going to be more than a source of funds. Angel investors become co-owners or preferred creditors of the venture, and they often insist on the right to pre-approve certain conduct or the ability to veto certain proposals. The investment procured from an angel will be expensive: the angel is likely to demand at least 10% of the firm's equity, and may demand more than 50% of the equity in some circumstances.[11] It is also important for the entrepreneur to perform his "due diligence" when considering the use of an angel investor or an angel investment group. The entrepreneur will be spending a considerable time period dealing with the angel, and will be turning over a significant portion of equity in the firm to him or her. Under these circumstances it only makes sense for the entrepreneur to ensure that he will be comfortable working with the angel or angel group and that they have a common vision and set of goals for the firm.

If the angel investor insists on acquiring stock in exchange for his or her investment, the entrepreneur should make every effort to provide non-voting stock rather than common stock. By using preferred stock the entrepreneur will not be giving the angel voting rights, thus allowing him to retain as much control after the investment as he had prior to the investment. This preferred stock will give the angel investor a priority in liquidation over the common stock holders should the venture fail, but that should be of less concern to the entrepreneur than possibly surrendering control through the issuance of common stock to the angel.

The entrepreneur and the angel should negotiate a "term sheet" that spells out their agreement prior to the investment. One term that is likely to be included in the term sheet is the *antidilution protection* that the investor will normally require. This protection, in the form of an antidilution clause, provides price protection to the investor who invests early in the venture from any reduction in price in subsequent issues of the firm's securities, provides protection in the event of subsequent stock splits or stock options, and generally ensures that the investor's contributions to the venture will not be diluted by later actions of the firm.

Suppose that an angel invests in a firm by purchasing 5000 shares of preferred stock—all the preferred shares issued at that time—at $100 per share. If the firm later sells another 5000 shares of preferred stock to other investors, the angel's percentage of ownership has been diluted from 100% to 50% of this class of stock. Similarly, if the firm later sells another 5000 shares of preferred stock to other investors at $80 per share, the angel's value per share has been diluted by the reduction in the value of each share of preferred stock. Thus, the angel will want to be protected from either or both types of dilution by requiring the inclusion of an antidilution clause. The angel will want a *full ratchet* antidilution clause; the entrepreneur will prefer a *weighted average full ratchet* clause. (Details of how the different types of antidilution clauses affect the parties can be found at numerous Web sites or in a number of finance texts. A few of these Web sites are set out in this endnote.[12])

One possible solution for the entrepreneur is to insert a "pay to play" term into any antidilution clause. Such a term requires the angel to either "pay" (purchase) or suffer dilution. The investor must either purchase his or her pro rata share of any new offerings or suffer the consequences of not playing.[13] Another way to approach this problem is to give the angel investors a provision in the contract granting them a right of first refusal for any new issues of their securities. If the angel exercises this right, his or her percentage of interest is not diluted, but if the angel declines this right, he or she chooses to allow the dilution rather than invest additional funds at that point in time.

Many times the angel will invest in the venture by purchasing convertible bonds, bonds that can be converted into equity (stocks) at certain times or under certain conditions. The venture may prefer to issue bonds rather than stock for two reasons: issuing stock may imply to the investing public that the stock is over-valued, thus causing a drop in stock price; and convertible bonds generally carry a lower interest rate since the bondholder has the right to convert the bonds into stock if the firm does well. The flexibility to be able to convert the bond to stock is the trade-off for the lower interest paid on the bonds.

Key Point. The entrepreneur needs to carefully assess his relative bargaining/ negotiating position with the angel and, to the greatest extent possible, nego-tiate from a position of strength. The angel will "insist" on certain clauses and protections before investing (e.g., subordination clause, antidilution clause, conversion rights), while the entrepreneur will seek to limit his concessions in order to retain more flexibility in dealing with other potential investors. The entrepreneur cannot grant the angel's "demands" too readily. It will benefit the entrepreneur and the venture if the entrepreneur negotiates and seeks trade-offs when and where possible.

VENTURE CAPITALISTS

The initial difficulty for an entrepreneur is establishing his venture as a relatively successful enterprise that has "staying power." Once the entrepreneur clears this hurdle, it is common to seek opportunities for expansion and growth. At this point, many entrepreneurs will turn to *venture capital*, funding provided by an investor or a group of investors who have access to significant capital and are looking for solid growth and return-on-investment opportunities, often requiring a 50% profit margin for a firm before they are willing to invest.[14] It is often diffi-cult to locate an appropriate venture capital group because of the competition for venture capital funds. There are many enterprises seeking venture capital funding at any given time but a limited number of firms or groups providing such funding, so the competition is likely to be fierce for the investors' backing.

"Venture capital" is "capital (as retained corporate earnings or individual savings) invested or available for investment in the ownership element of new or fresh enterprises—called also *risk capital.*"[15] **Venture capitalists** commonly oper-ate in the form of a limited partnership or an LLP, with the managing general partner investing funds on behalf of the group. Many venture capital groups have a "profile," only investing in enterprises operating within specific fields such as biotechnology, while others have a more open approach. In either situation, how-ever, venture capitalists are most commonly looking for investments in a business that has established itself to some extent and is now looking to grow and expand its operations. The investors are also looking for a firm that is poised for fast growth, and one that can return their investment plus a sizeable return on that investment in a relatively short time period. A return and cash-out period of from three to seven years is common. The cash-out often comes from a planned initial public offering (IPO) of stock by the enterprise at the end of the anticipated payback ("cash out") period, which means that part of the agreement with the venture capitalist is an agreement to "go public" with the company, thus diluting the authority of the entrepreneur, or even removing him from the operation.

It must be understood that most venture capitalists are not seeking firms that need small amounts of money; they are looking for firms that need—and can effectively utilize—funds in the millions of dollars. In fact, some venture capital firms will only consider investments of $5 million or more. In exchange for this investment, the venture capitalist is likely to want equity in the firm (the amount of equity will vary with the size of the investment and amount of equity the entrepreneur is willing to surrender), at least one seat on the board of directors, and possibly other areas of influence and/or control of the enterprise.

The loss of equity is perhaps the biggest drawback to using venture capital. The investors are likely to seek as much as 50% of the equity in the enterprise, and whatever equity the venture capitalists acquire is acquired at the expense of the pre-investment equity holders, the entrepreneur in many cases. This means that the original investors will have their holdings diluted, usually significantly, in order to acquire financing from venture capitalists.[16] In exchange for this loss of equity, the entrepreneur gains funding, significant funding in most cases. He also gains access to the contacts, relationships, and expertise that are available to the venture capitalist group and some of its members/investors.

Dealing with a venture capitalist provides a number of advantages to the entrepreneur, especially if he has been able to successfully establish his enterprise. The venture capitalist often has knowledge about the industry and contacts that the entrepreneur can use to his advantage. The potential influx of funds will allow the entrepreneur to expand the business and take his operation "to the next level." There are also a number of disadvantages in dealing with a venture capitalist, not the least of which is the sharing of equity and the likelihood that the venture capitalist intends to "cash out" in the relatively near future. After weighing the pros and cons of dealing with venture capitalists, if the entrepreneur decides to proceed, he should proceed with caution, and he should attempt to:

- Negotiate from a position of strength. If the business *must* have an influx of funds, the entrepreneur will not be able to obtain favorable terms; if the firm can continue to operate successfully, he can obtain much more favorable terms from the investors.
- Establish a relationship that is based on mutual trust.
- Find a venture capitalist with complementary skills, knowledge, and contacts.
- Attempt to include language in the agreement that prevents, or at least discourages, a premature exit by the investors, possibly with the inclusion of certain benchmarks before a withdrawal or cashing out can occur.

The venture capitalist may insist that the firm incorporate if it is not already incorporated.

EQUITY FUNDING

Equity is an ownership interest in a business venture, including a partnership. Each partner in a partnership, an LP, or an LLP has equity in the firm; each investor in an LLC and each stockholder in a corporation has equity in the firm. The entrepreneur may choose equity to fund his venture, rather than relying exclusively on his own assets or borrowing the funds through a commercial lender, an angel, or a venture capitalist. Using equity for funding the venture necessarily involves some loss of control, since there are now other owners involved in the enterprise. In addition, the managers of the enterprise owe fiduciary duties to all the owners, and not just the founders. (Fiduciary duties were discussed in more detail in Chapter 5.) However, there normally is no debt to finance with equity financing, and the investors have a vested interest in the success of the enterprise. These investors also are able to contribute their personal expertise and contacts, thus expanding the scope of expertise available, increasing the number of contacts, and hopefully improving the likelihood for the success of the venture.

Equity funding simply involves surrendering some portion of the ownership of the venture in exchange for the contribution of the investor who is becoming a co-owner of the business. The details will vary with the organizational form of the venture, and may also require compliance with federal and/or state security regulations. For example, in a partnership each partner is a co-owner with certain vested rights and other rights as specified in the partnership agreement. Unless there is a contrary provision in the partnership agreement, each partner is deemed to be an *equal* owner, with a proportionate ownership interest. Thus, an entrepreneur who takes on a partner who invests half of the amount he originally invested will be considered the owner of one half of the venture even though she has only invested one third of the total capital invested, *unless* the partnership agreement specifies a different ownership interest for the new partner. Each partner also has an equal voice in management and is entitled to an equal share of the profits (and is equally liable for losses), unless the agreement specifies otherwise.

If the entrepreneur forms a limited partnership or an LLP, the requirements differ slightly from those of a general partnership. Both a limited partnership and an LLP require a written agreement that must be filed with the state. In a limited partnership there are two classes of partners: general partners, including the entrepreneur, who have the same rights as in a general partnership, and limited partners, who have no voice in management and normally are only entitled to a percentage share of profits as specified in the partnership agreement or a predetermined return on their investments. Limited partners do not face any potential liability beyond their investment. An LLP is similar in many respects; in an LLP all the partners have limited liability unless the liability incurred by the business is due to some wrongdoing by an individual partner or by someone under his or her control and supervision. LLPs are normally more structured than partnerships and limited partnerships. The right of each partner to a percentage of profits is likely to be included in the LLP documentations and filings.

If the entrepreneur decides to form an LLC, he will once again have to file documentation with the state, this time filing articles of organization. There is no presumption of equal ownership with an LLC; the investor's equity share is determined by his or her investment in a manner similar to stock holdings in a corporation. This allows an entrepreneur to retain a greater percentage of ownership and control in an LLC, which can be a very attractive feature of this organizational form. An LLC can be managed by the owners (similar to a general partnership), or it can be managed by a management team hired by the owners (similar to a corporation), at the discretion of the ownership group. In either case, the entrepreneur is likely to retain a significant managerial role within the firm.

If the entrepreneur decides to form a corporation, he must comply with the state incorporation statute, filing articles of incorporation and awaiting receipt of a certificate of incorporation from the state before the corporation legally exists. Equity interests are determined by the percentage of stock owned by each investor, so the entrepreneur controls the amount of potential dilution of his ownership by determining how many shares to retain and how many to make available to the other investors. Other experienced investors, like venture capitalists, may insist on protection from dilution of their interests after their initial investment. They may be concerned about dilution in price, dilution in control (generally called percentage dilution), or both. A corporation is officially run by its board of directors (the entrepreneur is likely to ensure that he has a position on the board), and the board hires the managers of the corporation. The entrepreneur is also likely to take on the position of chief executive officer (CEO), at least initially. The entrepreneur may not be assured of retaining his positions on the board and as CEO as the corporation develops.

SECURITIES LAWS AND THE ENTREPRENEUR

The entrepreneur needs to be aware that selling an interest in a limited partnership, an LLP, an LLC, or a corporation involves the sale of a security, and the sale of securities is likely to entail compliance with federal and state security regulations. Securities regulation is an extremely complex topic, and the entrepreneur will need to consult with his attorney before offering any security for sale to any investors to ensure that he does not run afoul of the regulations, leading to potential fines and expenses that should be avoided through the exercise of adequate care. The attorney may refer the entrepreneur to a specialist in securities regulations. The business plan written by the entrepreneur may be covered by state or federal securities laws. The entrepreneur needs to exercise care even when soliciting family members, consultants, and employees to purchase interests.

Most federal and state securities laws emphasize disclosure to the potential investors. The specifics of what must be disclosed and the format required may differ. With the help of his attorney, the entrepreneur should maintain careful records of the prospectus, business plan, and other solicitation documents, and of who received copies of them and when. Some federal and state securities laws exempt certain types of transactions and/or purchasers: these require careful compliance with the rules and documentation of the compliance. Sales of business interests are also subject to the rules about fraud that govern other contracts.

Since one of the Sarbanes-Oxley (SOX) goals was to improve investor confidence in the stock market, many of its provisions apply to equity funding. These sections of SOX apply to U.S. companies that are publicly traded and non-U.S. companies that are listed on U.S. stock exchanges. (The exchanges exempt certain companies.) As mentioned in Chapter 4, CEOs and chief financial officers (CFOs) must certify that financial statements are appropriate and fair. CEOs and CFOs are subject to penalties if they knowingly certify reports that do not comply with the SOX standards. The penalties are enhanced if they willfully certify reports that do not comply with SOX.

CONCLUSIONS

An entrepreneur must have adequate funds to begin his venture. There are a number of ways to generate these funds, and deciding which method is most appropriate can be a daunting task. Before choosing the method(s) he would like to pursue, the entrepreneur should decide what his needs are, and then determine how best to satisfy those needs. In doing so he should also consider the legal implications involved with each method of funding.

The entrepreneur must also decide what he is willing to risk and how much control of his venture he is willing to surrender in order to get funding. Even if he decides to fund the venture himself, he will be expected to put up collateral for any loans, which means that personal non-venture assets are likely to be "at risk" if the venture does not succeed. Credit cards or home equity loans can provide capital, but the risk is significant if the entrepreneur is late with payments or he defaults. Dealing with friends and family requires either a dilution of equity by issuing securities to the investors or taking on debt in the form of loans. While friends and family may be more patient than other lenders, a failure to repay these debts may lead to lawsuits and liabilities.

If the entrepreneur seeks funding through commercial lenders, angels, or venture capitalists, he needs to decide how much he is willing to surrender prior to any negotiation with the other party. Collateral will be needed for most loans; the entrepreneur may also need to include a subordination clause in any loan agreements or bond issue; he may need to have co-signers for any loans, and these co-signers may demand concessions before they will agree to accept this potential liability. Lenders may insist on a clause allowing them to call their loans under certain circumstances; investors may insist on an antidilution clause in their contracts; buyers may want bonds to be convertible into stock. The entrepreneur needs to determine his relative strength in negotiations with these various parties and then try to negotiate from as strong a position as he can manage. He must be willing to make concessions when necessary, but he should resist "giving away the farm" in order to get funding.

In applying this chapter, the entrepreneur should consider the application questions set out in the box below:

Application Questions

1. Can the entrepreneur bootstrap sufficient funds to start the venture? How will bootstrapping affect his credit rating?

2. Can the entrepreneur obtain loans from commercial banks or commercial finance company for his venture? Will the interest rate be reasonable? Will he be required to co-sign?

3. Where or how does an entrepreneur find angel investors to help finance a venture?

4. What is an angel investor likely to expect in exchange for the investment in the venture?

5. Is the entrepreneur willing to give up equity in the venture to obtain capital?

Summary

"Entrepreneurship is about cashflow creation."[17] New businesses need money in order to go from plan to reality, and there are numerous ways for an entrepreneur to obtain funding for his enterprise. The entrepreneur needs to determine how much money he needs, and then determine the best method or methods for obtaining that money. He may decide to fund the enterprise personally, "bootstrapping" his venture into reality. He may seek funding from family and friends, whether in the form of investments or loans. He may seek loans from commercial banks or commercial finance companies. It is possible that funding can be obtained from an "angel" investor or from a venture capitalist. He may also rely on equity funding.

Each method of obtaining funding has some potential benefits for the entrepreneur, and each carries risks and obligations. Bootstrapping requires the entrepreneur to place his personal wealth and credit at risk, and unless he is already in a position of financial strength, he may not have adequate funds to provide the venture with a realistic chance of success. Financing the enterprise through family and friends is likely to require sharing equity with the people who are supporting the venture, with a corresponding dilution of control and authority, or entering into a debt relationship, either of which can possibly cause irreparable harm to the family or friendship if the venture fails. Debt financing involves the difficulty of getting the loans, involves the cost of interest, and, likely, requires the use of collateral to secure the loans. The entrepreneur may also have to agree to a subordination clause, allowing this loan to have priority over any subsequent loans and also over any of his own claims or those of his fellow investors. He may also have to agree to terms that allow the lender to call the loan, accelerating the due date under certain specified conditions.

Angels and venture capitalists who are willing to provide funding for the venture may be available, but finding such investors can be time consuming, and most such investors would prefer to invest in an established and on-going business rather than in a start-up venture, meaning that neither is likely to provide the initial funding needed to get the business "off the ground." Each is also likely to require a significant percentage of equity in the firm for any investment, and each is likely to demand an antidilution agreement to protect their interest. Both are likely to expect the firm to go public or be sold within a relatively short time period (three to five years).

Equity capital is an excellent source of funding, and provides the opportunity for acquiring significant capital, but in exchange the entrepreneur must be willing to surrender his share of ownership, which will reduce his control over the venture. There are also potential expenses incurred in meeting filing requirements and the possibility of security regulations that impose technical requirements which take time that could be spent operating and growing the business. This "distraction" may operate to the detriment of the fledgling enterprise.

Key Terms

angel investor	debt-to-worth ratio
bootstrapping	equity funding
commercial bank	five C's of credit
commercial finance company	venture capitalist

End-of-Chapter Questions

1. Many credit cards contain a universal default clause. What does the inclusion of such a clause mean? How does this clause possibly affect an entrepreneur who is financing his venture through bootstrapping?
2. Assume that an angel is willing to invest in a venture, but the angel wants an antidilution clause in the agreement before he or she will make the investment. What are the legal implications of including such a clause? What should the entrepreneur do to minimize the impact of such a clause?
3. A commercial lender is willing to make a loan to an entrepreneur, but it wants collateral to secure the loan and insists on a subordination clause in the loan agreement. What are the legal implications of such a clause? How will the inclusion of this clause affect the entrepreneur and his co-investors? Does it make a difference if the entrepreneur and his co-investors purchased equity in the venture or made loans to the venture?

4. When an entrepreneur is considering starting a business, he should consider the type of business organization best for this venture. What factors should he consider in deciding whether to begin as a partnership, an LP, an LLP, an LLC, or a corporation? How important should the concept of limited liability be at this stage of launching the venture?

5. An angel investor or a venture capitalist is likely to require a business to be incorporated before he or she will make a financial commitment to the firm. What legal issues are presented when a firm decides, or is required, to incorporate? How should the entrepreneur address these issues in order to minimize his risk of violating state and/or federal laws or regulations?

Suggested Activities

1. Contact a commercial finance company and a commercial bank and compare their normal requirements and interest rates for lending money to a start-up business.

2. Contact the Chamber of Commerce in your locale and ask about the availability of angels for an entrepreneurial enterprise.

Notes

1. Richard D., Harroch, AllBusiness.com, "The Best Ways to Finance Your Business," SCORE, found at http://www.score.org/best_ways_to_finance.html
2. *Id.*
3. The U.S. Small Business Administration Web site, http://www.sba.gov/aboutsba/index.html
4. *Id.*
5. *Id.*
6. The "Five C's of Credit are: Capacity to repay; Capital; Collateral; Conditions; and Character." See, e.g., InvestorWords.com found at http://www.investorwords.com/1/5_Cs_of_credit.html
7. http://www.sbir.gov/about/index.htm
8. http://www.mbda.gov/?id=2
9. "Angel Investors," Small Business Notes, found at http://www.smallbusiness notes.com/financing/angelinvestors.html
10. *Ibid.*
11. "Angel Investors," Entrepreneur Assist, Enrepreneurs.com, found at http://www.enterpreneur.com/article/printthis/52742.html
12. "The Dilution Dilemma, An Explanation of Ratchet Protection," *Young Venture Capital Society* (October 5, 2005), found at http://www.yvcs.org/uploads/1128485794The%20Dilution%20Dilemma_final.pdf; "Beyond Dante," *The Entrepreneur's Guide—What Goes on in the Dark Spaces Between the Light* (January 15, 2006), found at http://timwolters.blogspot.com/2006/01/term-sheet-terms-anti-dilution-clauses.html

13. "What Is a Pay to Play Provision?" *Startup Company Lawyer* (August 4, 2007), found at http://www.startupcompanylawyer.com/2007/08/04/what-is-a-pay-to-play-provision.
14. "Venture Capital," *BusinessFinance.com*, found at http://www.business finance.com/venture-capital.htm
15. http://www.merriam-webster.com/dictionary/venture%20capital
16. "How Does Venture Capital Work?" *How Stuff Works*, found at http:money. howstuffworks.com/question398.htm
17. "Venture Capital 101," The Smart Startup, found at http://www.antiventure capital.com/vc101.html

CHAPTER 7

AVOIDING TORTS AND MINIMIZING RISKS

Risk comes from not knowing what you're doing.[1]

INTRODUCTION

The United States has a duty-based society. Some duties are imposed by law, while others are voluntarily assumed by the people involved in the relationship. Both tort law and criminal law involve imposed duties, while contract law involves assumed duties. When a person breaches his or her duty, that person faces potential legal liability, whether in the form of civil remedies or in the form of criminal sanctions. See Table 7.1 for a comparison of these types of duties. This chapter will introduce the concepts of tort law. The commission of a tort carries with it the likelihood of civil liability. In order to reduce the likelihood of committing a tort, first the entrepreneur needs to understand what torts are. Then she can explore active steps to reduce the likelihood that torts will occur and thus reduce the risk that she and/or her venture will be liable. (In some situations the entrepreneur may be the injured party, in which case she should contact her attorney about obtaining compensation for the tort.)

An entrepreneurial venture operates through the acts of its workers. Workers who enter into contracts for the venture were discussed in Chapters 4 and 5. In this chapter the discussion will focus on workers who are called employees. Employees are the arms and the legs of the entrepreneur, and as such they engage in physical acts for the venture. In performing these physical acts an employee may, on occasion, commit a tort for which the employer—the entrepreneur—can be held liable. Sometimes it is difficult for the entrepreneur to let go of her "baby" and let someone else do some of the tasks, and the potential liability stemming

TABLE 7.1 A Comparison of Tort Law, Criminal Law, and Contract Law			
Type of Obligation	*Tort Law*	*Criminal Law*	*Contract Law*
How is the obligation created?	Civil law imposes duties on all people	Criminal law prohibits certain conduct or requires certain conduct	Individuals agree on a contract thereby voluntarily assuming duties under the agreement
Who enforces the obligation?	Suit by injured plaintiff	Prosecution by a government entity	Suit by party to the contract
What is the burden of proof in court?	Preponderance of the evidence	Beyond a reasonable doubt	Preponderance of the evidence
What happens if the defendant loses?	Defendant can be required to pay for the injury caused	Defendant can be imprisoned, sentenced to probation, and/or fined	Defendant can be ordered to perform the contract or pay for the injury caused

Source: Courtesy of Lynn M. Forsythe, © Lynn M. Forsythe 2009.

from the actions of employees may invoke fear. Although many entrepreneurs would like to avoid the hassle of hiring employees, that is generally not practical. The entrepreneur cannot do everything herself. So, she hires others because she cannot be everywhere and do everything. She also hires others to obtain the expertise that she lacks. Generally, an entrepreneur does not really want to stay so small that she can operate everything on her own. She wants to grow, and to achieve that growth she must hire employees.

This chapter will discuss common types of risks, how the entrepreneur becomes liable for the risks, and how to minimize the risks. An entrepreneurial enterprise is exposed to different types of risks, but the focus of this chapter is the risks that are encountered while the business performs its normal business functions. Those risks that arise when entering contracts are discussed in other chapters. There are also risks that are enterprise-specific, so the entrepreneur should discuss potential risks with her advisors, mentors, and legal counsel. It is more efficient for the entrepreneur to focus on the risks that are likely in her venture and those that she can control to some extent.

TORTS DEFINED

Torts are commonly defined as civil wrongs. Webster's Dictionary defines a tort as "a wrongful act (not involving a breach of contract) resulting in an injury, loss, or damage, for which the injured party can bring civil action . . . "[2] Many different types of acts may be torts, from **negligence** in operating a company vehicle to defaming a competitor or its goods or services. In the United States, most tort law is state law and consequently it varies by state. In other words, the exact definition, the elements that must be proven to recover, and the defenses that may remove or reduce liability will vary depending on the location where the tort occurred.

An action or series of actions may simultaneously constitute both crimes and torts. Crimes are wrongs against society and are prosecuted by a government entity. A notable example of this is the death of Nicole Brown Simpson. O. J. Simpson was charged with the crimes of murder and voluntary manslaughter, and he was found to be not guilty. Nicole's family subsequently sued him for the tort of wrongful death, and he was found guilty. Murder, voluntary manslaughter, and wrongful death have different legal definitions and elements. Murder and manslaughter are crimes, while wrongful death is a tort. Sometimes when an action is both a crime and a tort, the crime and the tort have the same label; for example, assault, battery, and trespass are the titles for crimes and also the titles for torts. The elements are virtually the same whether the action is being tried in criminal or civil court, but the potential liability or punishment is significantly different. Criminal defendants can be sentenced to a prison term or substantial fine. Civil defendants may be ordered to pay money or take a particular action, such as print a retraction to a defamatory article. Because of the seriousness of crimes, the government has a higher burden of proof than the burden of proof in civil cases. In this context, the term burden of proof means that the litigant carries the risk if she fails to persuade the jury. If the party does not produce sufficient proof, the party will lose the lawsuit. In criminal cases the government has to prove that the defendant committed all the elements of the crime beyond a reasonable doubt. In other words, the jury must start with the presumption that the defendant is innocent. After the evidence is presented, the jury must decide whether there is a real possibility that the defendant is *not* guilty. If there is such a real possibility, the jury must acquit the defendant. In civil cases the burden of proof is generally proof by a preponderance of the evidence; in other words, the plaintiff must prove all the elements of the case by a preponderance of the evidence. In civil cases, the jury is told to find in favor of the party that has the stronger evidence, even though that party's evidence is only slightly stronger than that of the opposition. Business entities, including entrepreneurial ventures, can be charged with crimes, and when they are convicted they are normally fined. The business itself cannot be imprisoned, but its officers and employees can be. If the venture is sued for a tort and loses the suit, the venture will be ordered to pay the other side for its damages. In some instances the entrepreneur (and her co-owners, if any) may have to personally pay for any damages the venture cannot pay.

Many different types of actions are covered under the tort "umbrella"; consequently, it helps to categorize torts as negligent torts, **intentional torts,** and strict liability torts. In order for the court to impose liability in a tort case in any of the three categories, there must be a showing of foreseeability; foreseeability is the knowledge or notice that a particular result is likely to follow from a particular action. For an example using the tort of negligence, if an automobile driver is busy entering her daily appointments in her Blackberry® while driving on a busy street, it is foreseeable that she might have an accident. As a driver she had a duty to observe the rules of the road and to operate her vehicle in a safe and responsible manner. By trying to simultaneously drive her car and make entries in her Blackberry® she breached her duty. If she is involved in an accident, she is likely to be found liable for negligence: she had a duty, she breached that duty, she caused harm, and the results were foreseeable to a reasonable person.

It is probably not possible for an entrepreneur to avoid every single tort that might potentially occur in the operation of her business. If the entrepreneur tried to avoid every tort, she would be likely to never make a decision or take a risk. She and her employees would be reluctant to grab opportunities in the market place for fear of incurring tort liability. This does not mean that she should ignore the possibility that a tort may occur and that she might be held liable for that tort. Rather, she should try to conduct her venture in a manner that recognizes that risks exist, but that opportunities must be taken in the venture if it is to prosper and grow. While torts may happen during the operation of the venture, there are several important reasons to try to reduce the number of torts:

- Torts may cause physical and emotional damage to the enterprise itself.
- Torts and the resulting publicity may injure the enterprise's reputation.
- Potential litigation is expensive, time consuming, and disruptive to the enterprise.
- Torts and any damage awards can be expensive.
- Insurance claims will adversely affect the premiums paid by the enterprise.

NEGLIGENCE

Negligence occurs when a person is careless and that carelessness results in a foreseeable injury to another person or to the property of another person. If the entrepreneur is sued for negligence, her conduct will be compared to that of a reasonable and prudent person; and if her conduct does not measure up to this reasonable and prudent person's behavior, her conduct will be deemed negligent. Courts will examine whether the actor had a duty to the person injured, whether the actor failed to live up to that duty, and whether the failure is what caused the injury. The entrepreneur must have had a reasonable duty to avoid the act or conduct. Often, the duty is a duty of the actor not to create risks to the people around the actor. In litigation the plaintiff must show the fault of the defendant and that the harm suffered by the plaintiff was a foreseeable result of that "fault."

Liability for negligence will not necessarily be limited to the conduct of the entrepreneur. She may also be sued for negligence based on the conduct of one or more of her employees. For example, if the entrepreneur has employees driving around New York City delivering products and samples to customers, the entrepreneur is exposed to the potential risk that one of her employees may negligently cause a vehicular accident. Even though the entrepreneur may have done nothing wrong, and may even have acted with extreme care, if one of her employees is tired or distracted while making deliveries and negligently causes an accident, the entrepreneur/employer will probably face liability for the employee's negligence. As a result, most entrepreneurs and other operators of vehicles will purchase insurance in order to reduce their financial risk, comply with state laws requiring insurance, and protect other assets. Insurance will be discussed in greater detail in Chapter 13.

The entrepreneur should try to reduce the incidents of negligent acts by her employees and herself. A careful analysis of the type of business will often reveal potential problem areas, areas that can be restructured to reduce the risk that a negligent act is likely to occur. For example, a pizza parlor that guarantees delivery of hot pizza in 15 minutes and fines workers who do not make the delivery in time has created a job-related situation that encourages its delivery personnel to take risks in order to meet the 15-minute deadline, and thus avoid the "fine" for being late. This situation creates unsafe driving conditions and is likely to result in an increase in vehicular accidents due to negligence on the part of her employees, and this will result in more potential liability for the employer/entrepreneur. By either eliminating the 15-minute guarantee or removing the fine for "late" deliveries the entrepreneur can reduce this risk to a significant degree.

There are a number of special types of negligence recognized by the legal system. Most entrepreneurs are aware of special types of negligence, such as malpractice by doctors or lawyers. There are also special types of negligence that will apply to entrepreneurs, such as **negligent hiring,** negligent retention, **negligent promotion,** and **negligent supervision**. Exhibit 7.1 illustrates the potential legal liability that may occur when a third party is injured through the negligence of the entrepreneur and/or her employees. Here, the injured party is called the third party because he or she is not a "party" to the employment relationship. The exhibit also illustrates that the entrepreneur can reduce her risk by purchasing insurance.

EXHIBIT 7.1 Liability for Negligence

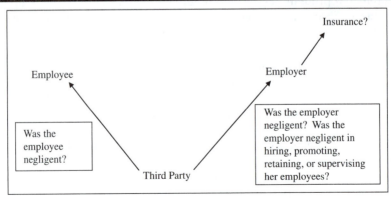

Source: Courtesy of Lynn M. Forsythe, © Lynn M. Forsythe 2009.

NEGLIGENT HIRING

One tort that is being used more frequently against employers is the tort of negligent hiring. Negligent hiring means that the employer chose the wrong person for the specific job duties or did not use due care in the selection process. If an entrepreneur is sued on the basis of an alleged negligent hiring, the question the court will have to decide is whether the entrepreneur exercised the level of care that a prudent employer would exercise in choosing that particular employee for the particular duties he or she was expected to perform. In many states, the tort of negligent hiring applies to the hiring of employees, agents, and independent contractors. For simplicity here, only the term employees will be used.

The tort of negligent hiring is based on the premise that the entrepreneur owes a duty to her customers and the public at large to exercise reasonable care in staffing her venture. In some states, the duty is also owed to the entrepreneur's other employees and agents if they are injured by the negligently hired co-worker. Negligent hiring is based on the assumption that if the entrepreneur had conducted a proper investigation she would have learned of the prior troubling conduct or personality traits and would not have hired this particular employee. She will not be liable for negligent hiring if she conducted a reasonable investigation and did not discover the prior conduct. She would be liable if she did not conduct a reasonable investigation *or* she discovered the prior conduct and hired the employee anyway. For an example, assume the employee is going to have access to large quantities of prescription drugs but the employer does not check his background. The employee has a criminal background of using or dealing in narcotics. This employee would be a poor choice for the position. If the employee harms a customer or third party, the injured party might successfully sue the employer for his loss if she was careless in the selection process and choose the wrong employee. Some states require that the employee's act be in the course and scope of the employment before they impose liability for negligent hiring. This is not a requirement in all states however.

Negligent hiring is a tort, but the problem is greater than potential tort liability. Hiring the "wrong" person can cost the venture in numerous ways. The person could negligently cause accidents at the factory, injure customers negligently or intentionally, embezzle funds, disrupt intra company communication, harass co-workers, refuse to follow instructions or work within company guidelines, and cause emotional distress to the entrepreneur and other employees. The person might even bring a firearm to work and threaten the entrepreneur and other employees. It is understandable why some entrepreneurs try to avoid hiring employees and try to do it "all themselves." Often, this is not practical. Outsourcing may reduce the number of employees but it also has risks and does not guarantee legal protection from torts.

Table 7.2 provides advice on how to limit the possibility that the entrepreneur will be liable for negligent hiring. In making an employment decision, the entrepreneur should consider the nature and type of employment. Traits and conduct

TABLE 7.2   Ten Steps to Avoid Negligent Hiring
1. Have the applicant complete a job application. The entrepreneur should use a job application that is appropriate to the specific job.
2. Obtain a signed release so that the entrepreneur can check criminal records, mental health records, and credit histories. This step is particularly important if the applicant may pose a threat to customers.
3. Conduct a careful and detailed interview with the applicant. Ask about periods of unemployment and other items that seem suspicious or confusing.
4. Ask whether the applicant was convicted of any crimes. In many states, it is illegal to inquire about arrests.
5. Talk to the applicant's prior employers. Ask whether the employee left on good terms. Would the employer rehire the applicant?
6. Check on alcohol use and illegal drug use. This is more critical if the use occurs at work or the use impacts job performance.
7. Ask about driver's licenses, tickets, and driving accidents if the applicant will be driving at work.
8. Check with the department of motor vehicles for appropriate states.
9. Check on potential mental or emotional problems.
10. Maintain a written record of the investigation to show the steps taken to screen applicants and the questions asked of applicants and prior employers. This record will be extremely important if there is a lawsuit.

Source: Courtesy of Lynn M. Forsythe, © Lynn M. Forsythe 2009.

that would be troubling for some types of employment may not be much of a concern for other types. The entrepreneur should consider things such as:

- Is the employee going to have access to business secrets?
- Is the employee going to have access to business bank accounts?
- Is the employee going to have access to alarm codes and/or a master key to the premises?
- Is the employee going to have access to the company computer system?
- Is the employee going to have access to customer files and private information?
- Is the employee going to enter customers' homes or businesses?
- Is the employee going to operate motor vehicles on the premises and/or on public roads?
- Where is the employee going to work and what state or local laws might apply?

Note that some of these questions focus more on protecting the entrepreneur's property and others focus more on protecting customers and the public. Local, state, and federal employment law may limit the types of questions and investigations that are permitted. These limitations will be discussed in Chapter 9. The entrepreneur should consider hiring a professional investigator to investigate applicants in the top tier who may receive job offers. Some entrepreneurs choose to outsource the hiring process and most of the human resources work. The entrepreneur's goal is to avoid putting the wrong person in the position in order to reduce problems within the venture and to reduce potential liability.

Some entrepreneurs may be persuaded to employ family members and friends in the enterprise. The entrepreneur may wish to hire them because of loyalty, or family and friends may pressure the entrepreneur to "share the wealth." It is important to remember that when these people are employees of the entrepreneur, their actions will also potentially expose the entrepreneur to liability. Presumably, the tort of negligent hiring would still be applicable. The entrepreneur is likely to know the family member or friend better than other applicants, including the family member's or friend's strengths and weaknesses.

Negligent Retention

Negligent retention is closely related to negligent hiring. The difference is that the entrepreneur is deemed to be careless because of her decision in retaining or keeping—or lack of a decision in removing—an employee when a reasonable and prudent employer would have dismissed the person. In some cases it is really a lack of a decision by the entrepreneur. For example, a construction company that continues to allow a worker to drive the company truck after a series of vehicular accidents is likely to be guilty of negligent retention. If this same employee is then involved in yet another vehicular accident at work, the person who was injured by the employee will be able to sue the entrepreneur for negligent retention in addition to any other claims the injured party has against the entrepreneur and/or the employee. The entrepreneur can be liable for negligent retention even though she was careful in the initial selection process.

Negligent Promotion

In this tort, the entrepreneur is being sued because of her decision to promote an employee to an inappropriate position or one for which the employee is not qualified. The employee may have been well suited to the prior job, but is not suited to the new position and responsibilities. The entrepreneur can be held liable to the injured party for any losses or liabilities that can be directly connected to the promoted employee's lack of qualifications for the position. For example, an employee with a criminal past is promoted to a position handling customers' funds and credit card information. The employee embezzles funds or uses the credit card information to obtain goods or services for himself at the customer's expense. The employee is liable for this conduct both civilly and criminally, and the entrepreneur is also likely to be held liable for her negligence in making the promotion.

Negligent Supervision

Negligent supervision is found when the entrepreneur is negligent in providing training, instructions, and supervision to employees, resulting in an injury to a third person. For example, assume an employer negligently fails to explain the hazards associated with the equipment or supplies the employees are going to use, and this negligence causes the employee to misuse the equipment in a manner that results in harm to a third person. The employee may be civilly liable for his conduct, and the entrepreneur is also likely to be held liable for her negligent supervision. Suppose that the entrepreneur does not warn her employees of the hazards involved in handling gas canisters at the work site and one of her employees causes an explosion with a gas canister that damages a customer's property. The entrepreneur may be held liable for negligent supervision.

INTENTIONAL TORTS

Intentional torts are based on the concept that the defendant acted in a willful or intentional manner and that the defendant had a duty to avoid the act or conduct in question. Intentional torts also require a showing of fault, and the resulting harm must be foreseeable. The defendant need not have intended to cause any harm.

ASSAULT AND BATTERY

The entrepreneur may be surprised to discover that her employees might commit the torts of assault and battery or that assault and battery could occur in a business setting. In one case, Nabisco was held liable for an assault and battery committed by Ronnell Lynch, its sales person. Lynch committed the assault and battery when he beat the manager of a small grocery store while making deliveries along his route.[3] Assault is the threat of immediate harm or offensive body contact. The contact does not need to occur—it is the threat of the contact that constitutes assault. Battery is the harmful or offensive physical contact. The contact does not have to occur by actually touching the skin of the victim. For example, a rock could be thrown at the victim, or a gun can be discharged and the bullet can hit the victim. Assault and battery frequently occur together, but they can occur independently. Assault and battery are also crimes, but the entrepreneur's main concern will be the tort and the potential litigation and injury to her reputation.

FALSE IMPRISONMENT

False imprisonment occurs when a person is confined or restrained without his or her consent. As with many other torts, there are defenses that the entrepreneur can use during a lawsuit, and a common tort defense is called privilege.[4] Privilege means that the actor was exempt from the normal duty. What particular behavior is privileged depends on the specific tort involved. Most states have passed merchant protection statutes, which give shopkeepers a privilege to detain and investigate suspected shoplifters. For the shopkeeper privilege to apply, most states require that:

- The shopkeeper had reasonable grounds for the suspicion.
- The suspect is only detained for a reasonable period of time.
- The shopkeeper conducted the investigation in a reasonable manner.

Shopkeepers need to use care, or they will be found liable for the tort of false imprisonment.[5]

INTERFERENCE WITH CONTRACTUAL RELATIONS

Interference with contractual relations goes by many labels, including unlawful interference with contractual relations, interference with a contractual relationship, inducement of breach of contract, and procurement of breach of contract. It occurs when the defendant intentionally induces a party to breach his or her contract with the plaintiff, thereby causing damage to the plaintiff.[6] The defendant must be aware that there is a contract. In some jurisdictions the defendant will not be liable if he or she had a good purpose or if he or she acted justifiably. The following example will illustrate the tort.

JamSports, a promoter, entered into a letter of intent with AMA Pro Racing, a company that sanctioned motorcycle racing. Under the letter of intent, the parties agreed to negotiate a supercross promotion agreement with each other exclusively for a 90-day period. Prior to the trial, the court ruled that their letter of intent was a binding contract which (1) required AMA Pro to negotiate with JamSports in good faith for a 90-day period toward a final promotion agreement, (2) prohibited AMA Pro from entering into discussions or negotiations with anyone else, (3) barred the parties from revealing the terms of their letter of intent, and (4) required AMA Pro to promptly notify JamSports if it received another offer. The court concluded that AMA Pro breached its contract with JamSports.[7] In the same suit, JamSports also sued Clear Channel, a competing promoter, for tortious interference with contract. The court found that Clear Channel was aware of the exclusivity provision, that it sent proposals to AMA Pro, and that it induced AMA Pro's representatives to discuss the proposals with Clear Channel in violation of the letter of intent. There was also evidence that Clear Channel contacted supercross stadiums and venue managers and applied pressure on them, so that JamSports would not be able to hold a successful supercross series, and so that AMA Pro would then walk away from the JamSports arrangement and sign a new promotion contract with Clear Channel. Based on this evidence the court concluded that Clear Channel was liable on the tortious interference with contract count.[8]

In some states a defendant may have a privilege to interfere in the contractual relationship. However, the desire to compete with the plaintiff will not be privileged. Some states, like Illinois, use a balancing test, whereby the parties' rights in the contract are balanced against the type of interference, and whether the defendant's conduct preserves another right that the law deems to be of equal or greater value than contract rights. For example, the officers and directors of a company who interfere in a contract entered into by that company have "higher" rights.[9] Many of the cases based on privilege have involved defendants with legal or fiduciary duties.[10]

INTERFERENCE WITH PROSPECTIVE ADVANTAGE

Interference with prospective advantage, also called interference with a business relationship, is based on an intentional, harmful intrusion into another person's or business's *potential* business relationships. Potential business relationships have less protection under the law than actual business relationships. In other words, parties who are still negotiating have fewer rights than parties who have already entered into a contract. Interference with prospective advantage covers both the opportunity to obtain customers and the opportunity to obtain employment. Courts will recognize this tort if the defendant unjustifiably interfered with a relationship the plaintiff was cultivating and this interference caused the plaintiff a loss. *Fair* competition, however, is not tortious. Generally, the elements of this tort are as follows:

- The plaintiff reasonably expected to enter into a business relationship.
- The defendant knew about this potential business relationship.
- The defendant intentionally and unjustifiably interfered with this relationship.
- The defendant's actions caused a termination of the plaintiff's expectation.
- This caused damage to the plaintiff.[11]

In many cases the defendant can use the competition privilege as a defense to litigation based on interference with prospective advantage. This privilege is based on the defendant's intent to advance her own business interests. The privilege entitles an entrepreneur to divert business from her competitors, provided that she is motivated, at least in part, by an intent to further her own business. In other words, she is not solely motivated by spite. Note that competition is *not* a privilege to the tort of interference with contractual relations, discussed in the prior section. If the competition privilege is proven, it can protect the defendant even though some of the defendant's conduct was motivated by spite and ill will. In the JamSports litigation discussed in the previous section, Clear Channel was protected by this privilege even though there was significant evidence of spite by Clear Channel and its personnel.[12]

INVASION OF PRIVACY

Invasion of privacy is a tort that covers many diverse activities that are actionable as unwarranted invasions of privacy. Originally, it covered things like peering into a person's home at night without permission. More current examples would be secretly taking pictures of customers in dressing rooms or restrooms. Over the years, this tort has been expanded to include a number of activities including:

- Publicizing personal information about a person that has not been made public knowledge.
- Intruding on a person's physical solitude without permission.
- Reading a person's mail or email, or wiretapping his phone without permission.
- Using a person's likeness or life story without authorization.
- Presenting a person in false light, such as attributing views and positions to a person that he or she does not hold.
- Appropriating a person's name, face, likeness, or voice without permission for commercial use, such as in an advertisement. This may also be called the tort of misappropriation of the right to publicity or the tort of appropriation, depending on the state.

The tort of invasion of privacy involves an unwarranted intrusion on the victim's "zone of privacy," those areas where the victim has a reasonable expectation of privacy. People talking on their "traditional" (landline) phones in the privacy of their homes have a greater expectation of privacy than people in crowded coffee shops talking—often loudly—on their cell phones. Similarly, celebrities, like Brad Pitt and Angelina Jolie, or public figures, like former president Bush, have less of a reasonable expectation of privacy and thus less protection from invasion of privacy than non-public figures and non-celebrities. People also "lose" some of their protection when they become part of a news story. The entrepreneur should remember to respect the reasonable expectations of privacy of her customers and employees to avoid liability for invasions of that privacy.

PRIVACY ISSUES

Many ventures are susceptible to privacy issues, including Web sites that offer banking services, maintain financial or medical records, or provide dating services. When an entrepreneur commences a venture with privacy issues, she should consider (1) what steps will reduce the likelihood of private information being revealed and (2) what steps might be taken to transfer the legal risks. For Web sites, the former will include up-to-date encryption software, firewalls, and site keys. It may also involve taking a proactive stance against computer viruses and phishing.[13] The latter may include a clear privacy policy on the Web site and a statement of when data sharing will occur and with whom.[14] Once the privacy policy is established and posted, the entrepreneur should use care to comply with her stated policy. The Federal Trade Commission (FTC) or state agencies may bring legal action against the entrepreneur for failure to follow her stated policy. For example, DirectWeb was fined $15,000 by the FTC for selling customer information in violation of its own policy.[15] The privacy policy may also include a statement limiting the entrepreneur's liability.[16] Web sites that may attract children will need to take extra steps to protect the children. Privacy rights are often covered by contracts. Note that the positions the entrepreneur takes on privacy issues may influence potential customers and their willingness to deal with her venture. For example, when a bank has a security breach in its computer system and hackers obtain private information of thousands of customers, the bank often loses customers to its competitors who are perceived as being more secure.

Employees are also entitled to some privacy, and entrepreneurs should take steps to respect that privacy. For example, if an employee has a medical condition, the entrepreneur should avoid disclosing it to others. Sometimes the information may need to be shared with people in the human resources department or the employee's direct supervisor. Care should be used not to share the information with people who do not "need to know."

Other times the sharing may be inadvertent. For example, an entrepreneur encouraged all employees to use Microsoft Outlook for their "appointment books" and to make their calendars available to others as an aid to scheduling meetings. Many employees also put their personal meetings and appointments on their calendars, including the people they were meeting with and why, thus revealing personal medical and financial information that would not otherwise have been available without the employee's knowledge and consent.

Some countries and cultures value privacy to a different degree than the United States. The entrepreneur should be aware of these cultural and legal differences when dealing with people in other countries. For example, in the United States credit card companies must notify consumers that they intend to share data, and consumers can opt out if they so desire. (Some information is required to be shared.) However, in the European Union it is assumed that consumers do not want their data shared. If they are willing to have their data shared, they must opt *into* the sharing of their information.

STRICT LIABILITY

Strict liability is a third category of tort, distinct from negligence and intentional torts. It is based on the duty to make something absolutely safe. When there is strict liability for an activity, an entrepreneur will be responsible for damages whenever there is injury. Strict liability is imposed on a number of different types of activities. Common examples include when the entrepreneur is engaged in ultrahazardous activities, such as the use of explosives, or when the entrepreneur sells a product that is unreasonably dangerous.[17]

Some types of strict liability have been developed through court decisions, and other types have been imposed by legislation. The entrepreneur cannot successfully defend against a strict liability lawsuit by showing that she or her employees were careful. If an injury occurs due to the involvement of the entrepreneur in an inherently dangerous activity, strict liability is likely to be imposed on the entrepreneur.

These are just a few of the torts that may affect the profitability of a venture. Additional torts will be discussed in other chapters; defamation of character is discussed in Chapter 10.

RESPONDEAT SUPERIOR

Respondeat superior is the primary legal doctrine that makes an employee's torts the entrepreneur's problem. The injured third party can sue based on respondeat superior, in addition to any other legal theories such as negligent hiring and negligent supervision. Respondeat superior is a form of vicarious liability, where the entrepreneur who hires the employee is legally liable for the employee's tortious acts *if* the acts are in the course and scope of the job. Respondeat superior does not apply to independent contractors: it only applies to employees. When discussing respondeat superior, generally employees are called servants and employers are called masters. For simplicity, this book will continue to use the terms employees and employers. It is critical to remember that the law is using the terms employees and employers in the legal sense of the words. Exhibit 7.2 shows a diagram of the legal relationships under respondeat superior.

The employer has the right to indemnification if she pays compensation to the third party based on respondeat superior. In many cases the employee will not have adequate financial resources to reimburse her. The entrepreneur may be tempted to retain the employee so that she can recoup the amount owed to her. Retaining the employee is risky owing to the doctrine of negligent retention, previously discussed, and the factors that are used in applying respondeat superior, discussed in the next paragraph.

Courts consider a number of factors in deciding whether respondeat superior should be applied to the particular situation, thereby making the employer liable for the employee's tort. The common factors include:

- Did the act occur during work time and at a work place?
- Was the act the type the employee was hired to perform?

EXHIBIT 7.2   The Legal Relationships under Respondeat Superior

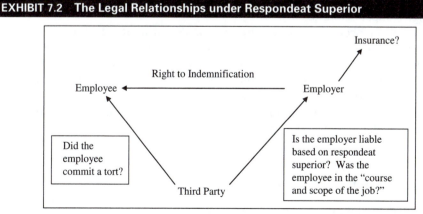

Source: Courtesy of Lynn M. Forsythe, © Lynn M. Forsythe 2009.

- Was the act one commonly done by such employees?
- Was the purpose of the act to serve the employer and/or serve the employee?
- Should the employer expect the use of force if the employee used force?
- Should the employer expect that such an act would be done by the employee?
- Did the employer provide the instrumentality or equipment that was used by the employee in committing the act?
- Was the act a serious crime?[18]

After considering the factors, the jury or judge will make a decision about whether the employee's acts were in the course and scope of the employment. It is difficult to predict accurately when the court will impose respondeat superior and when it will not. In most situations, there will be factors that would lead the jury or judge to believe that there should be respondeat superior and other factors that would lead them to believe that there should not. For example, in the Mary M. case the City of Los Angeles was held liable for the rape committed by Sergeant Schroyer. Schroyer was on duty about 2:30 a.m. when he first observed Mary M.'s erratic driving; however, the officer was not assigned to traffic detail, instead he was a field supervisor responsible for supervising other officers. Obviously, Schroyer was not supposed to rape people, which is a serious crime. It is not an act commonly done by officers. When the courts look at rape cases, they normally view this as a personal activity and not one that serves the interests of the employer. The rape involved the threat of force by Schroyer, and Los Angeles should expect that officers will use force when necessary. Los Angeles had no indication that Schroyer would rape a civilian. In this case, Los Angeles provided the equipment that was used, including the marked police car, the badge, and the gun. Schroyer was in uniform at the time. The court also felt that Los Angeles should have established better procedures that would have reduced the likelihood of this conduct. Los Angeles was held liable based on the doctrine of respondeat superior, but the last point may also be evidence of negligent supervision.[19]

A detour occurs when an employee makes a minor deviation from the employer's business for personal reasons. When the deviation is minor, the court will determine that the employee was in the course and scope of the employment, and the court will "impose" respondeat superior. A frolic, on the other hand, is when the employee makes a significant deviation from the employer's business for personal reasons. If the employee's act is determined to be a frolic, the employer will not be vicariously liable under respondeat superior.

HOW TO REDUCE THE RISKS

One obvious way to reduce risks is to be careful when selecting, promoting, and supervising employees, an issue already addressed in this chapter. Another way is to provide training and instructions to employees.

PROVIDE TRAINING AND INSTRUCTIONS TO EMPLOYEES

Risks may not be obvious to employees, and it is important to train them. It is not sufficient to just warn them to be careful or not hurt anyone. For example, the employees in a fireworks factory regularly smoked cigarettes around the crates of fireworks. In fact, they sat on the crates and smoked during their breaks. One day they caused an explosion. If this occurred in an entrepreneurial venture, and the entrepreneur had not provided adequate training, the entrepreneur could face liability due to negligence and/or negligent supervision. Training materials and programs should be updated, and the programs should be repeated at regular intervals. Care should be used so that the training information is accurate. Otherwise, the entrepreneur may be liable for negligence based on the training. Training should be repeated because employees can use reminders: otherwise, they may get into bad habits. A venture that has many employees driving on the venture's behalf may decide that it is advantageous to offer or require regular defensive driving instruction. Training may also help to reduce the amount paid for insurance premiums. Insurance will be discussed in greater detail in Chapter 13.

ADVANTAGES AND DISADVANTAGES OF OPERATIONS MANUALS

One way for the entrepreneur to reduce risks is to write or adapt an **operations manual** to her venture. The operations manual, if used consistently, can reduce potential legal liability and the likelihood of a loss. An entrepreneur may be able to obtain a sample operations manual from a business mentor, friend, or trade association and adapt it to suit her needs. However, the entrepreneur may have to write her own manual. There are still advantages to an operations manual. Preparing an operations manual is a helpful activity because it focuses attention on the risks inherent in this specific business and techniques for how to best reduce these risks. Much of the risk analysis is common sense. For example, if an entrepreneur is writing the procedures for closing the store in the evening, she will think about things such as checking the lock on the rear exit, removing the excess cash to deposit in the night depository at the bank, locking the front door, and setting the silent burglar alarm. Analyzing the risk, thinking about how to reduce the risk, and then taking the necessary steps will reduce the entrepreneur's exposure to the risks. Not all of the risks will be legal risks. The entrepreneur may be exposed to losses from theft or damage to her reputation.

Training of the employees will be more consistent if the entrepreneur shares the operations manual with each of them. In addition, employees can provide helpful feedback and suggestions to improve the operations manual and the business procedures. Employee suggestions may result in revisions to the operations manual. Writing and using an operations manual has the potential to reduce problems for the entrepreneur.

Obviously, the operations manual will be more effective if it is used. What if it is not used? If the entrepreneur or her employees do not follow the listed procedures, this could be damaging evidence in a tort law suit because it would provide further evidence of negligence. An exception would be if under the particular circumstances the actions actually taken were more careful than the actions specified in the manual.

FORM A SAFETY COMMITTEE

The entrepreneur should consider establishing a safety committee of employees and managers. The committee should meet regularly to discuss safety issues and how to address them. The employees have a unique vantage point to observe safety hazards and recommend practical solutions. (In some environments including employees on the safety committee may pose other issues, so the entrepreneur should check with her attorney first.)

MONITOR EMPLOYEES

The entrepreneur needs to use care when selecting employees, but that will not be sufficient. She also needs to monitor the employees. The amount of monitoring depends on the type of employees and the situation. For example, if her employees spend much of their workday on the Internet, she may be concerned about how much time they spend sending jokes and watching videos on YouTube instead of working. A failure to monitor the employees may result in many wasted hours that should have been put to a more productive use. Technology is available to watch what sites employees visit while on the Internet. In most states, the entrepreneur will be allowed to implement this technology if she is providing computers and Internet access for work purposes. It will strengthen her legal position if she warns employees that she or her managers will be monitoring their activities. This "warning" can be included in the employee handbook. Once the employees are informed about the monitoring, they will have a more difficult time arguing that they had a reasonable expectation of privacy.

When monitoring employees, the entrepreneur should exercise care not to violate employee rights. For example, generally she cannot restrict the use of alcohol by adult employees during non-work hours if it does not interfere with the employees' work performance. Some employers require job applicants and employees to take drug tests. Courts generally allow the drug testing of applicants, but the entrepreneur should consult with attorneys in the state where the facility is located. Testing of current employees is generally permitted if it is required after an accident or if the entrepreneur has a reasonable suspicion that an employee is impaired due to drugs. One of the concerns about drug testing is that, in addition to information about the possible use of illegal drugs, the results also reveal information about some legitimate prescription drugs and, consequently, some medical conditions. Drug testing will be discussed in more detail in Chapter 9.

BEWARE OF BORED EMPLOYEES

Employees who are bored tend to get into mischief, sometimes in ways the entrepreneur could never imagine. She should try to create positions that are interesting and that allow employees some degree of job satisfaction and fulfillment. When employees are required to remain on the work premises, she should arrange for them to work. The most problematic are employees who are required to remain on the work premises because of the nature of the job but do not have tasks to do. For example, the dock workers at one port were required to stay at the dock their entire shift whether or not they had work to perform. In order to amuse themselves, the dock workers would play with the booms used to load the vessels. They would swing the booms and use them in a playful but non-productive manner. One day they hit a man who was walking on the dock with the swinging boom. The man required an extended hospital stay. The employer in such a situation is likely to be held liable for the conduct of the employees even though their conduct was neither authorized nor condoned.

SET A GOOD EXAMPLE

Albert Schweitzer said, "Example is not the main thing in influencing others. It is the only thing."[20] The entrepreneur should follow her own rules. If she does not, her employees will not follow the rules either. They *may* comply with the rules while she is present, but they will violate them when she is not present. For example, if the entrepreneur is operating a bar and she does not want her employees to drink alcohol during work hours, she should not drink at work.

MANAGING THE RISKS

The entrepreneur should consider the risks that are likely in her enterprise and address them. Risks can and should be managed. The entrepreneur should consider the checklist in Table 7.3 for helpful suggestions on managing the risks.

The entrepreneur should consider the application questions set out in the box below as a first step in avoiding liability for torts.

TABLE 7.3   Managing the Risks

- Designate a person to be responsible for risk management. He should receive copies of all claims and should determine the problem areas. He should report incidents and problem areas to the entrepreneur, chief executive officer, and/or the board of directors.
- Establish a safety committee consisting of managers and non-managerial employees.
- Consider an applicant's safety record before making a hiring decision. Consider an employee's safety record before making decisions about promotions.
- Create education programs to cover all sources of tort liability. Education programs should be ongoing. It is helpful to periodically remind employees about reducing risks.
- Establish policies that protect the environment, workers, and customers from exposure to toxic substances. Keep current on potential toxins. Additional substances are added to the list as scientists learn the effects of exposure. The venture should test and monitor the amount of exposure in the work environment.
- Consider removing toxic substances or substituting less toxic alternatives.
- Test products that the venture does not manufacture to assure that the products comply with the venture's specifications.

Application Questions

1. What types of torts are likely to occur with this venture?

2. What skills and traits are important in employees? How should the entrepreneur assure that her employees have those skills and traits?

3. What steps should the entrepreneur take to avoid negligent hiring?

4. Are employees operating motor vehicles or heavy equipment on behalf of the enterprise?

5. What should the entrepreneur do to remind employees about safety?

6. How should the entrepreneur instruct and supervise her employees?

7. How should the entrepreneur "reward" individual employees and divisions for safe operations?

8. Should the entrepreneur write an operations manual for the venture? If so, what types of information should it contain?

Summary

Different ventures have different risks and it is not possible to avoid them all. The entrepreneur should focus on the risks that are most likely with her particular type of venture and those that could be the most devastating. The entrepreneur wants to surround herself with talented individuals who can perform well. She wants to use reasonable selection criteria and procedures to screen out employees who will cause problems for her, her other employees, and her customers.

There is a risk that the entrepreneur or one of her employees will commit a tort, which is a civil wrong. Torts can be divided into negligence, intentional torts, and strict liability. There are a number of traditional torts, such as assault, battery, defamation, and invasion of privacy. There are other torts that may occur in business settings, such as interference with prospective advantage and interference with contract. Courts will use the doctrine of respondeat superior to hold the entrepreneur liable if a tort was committed by an employee in the course and scope of the employment. The judge or jury considers a number of factors before reaching a conclusion about respondeat superior.

One way to focus on the risks is to write an operations manual, addressing the various risks that are prevalent in this type of venture and how to reduce them. The manual should be shared with employees, and they should follow the procedures. The entrepreneur is not the only source of knowledge. She should also ask her employees about potential risks and how to reduce them. She may create a safety committee to address some concerns.

Key Terms

interference with contractual relations
interference with prospective advantage
intentional torts
invasion of privacy
operations manual
negligence

negligent hiring
negligent promotion
negligent supervision
respondeat superior
strict liability

End-of-Chapter Questions

1. California enacted a law making it a crime to talk on cell phones while operating a motor vehicle unless the driver is using a hands free device.[21] This
statute caused great concern to entrepreneurs because many of them have
employees operating motor vehicles on the streets. Some of these employees
may be using cell phones provided by the venture or their own personal cell
phones. Even in states that have not enacted similar statutes, an entrepreneur
may be liable if an employee is distracted by a business call. What should an
entrepreneur tell her employees to reduce the likelihood of an accident
and/or litigation? Some states or communities have adopted similar statutes
or ordinances prohibiting "dashboard dining," eating while operating a motor
vehicle. Should the entrepreneur consider including a section of the employee
handbook addressing such topics as cell phone use or dashboard dining while
operating a vehicle while working, and the sanctions for violations?
2. Considering the entrepreneur's business concept, what questions should she
ask the applicants' prior employers during the hiring process? What types of
questions should not be asked?
3. Explain the different types of invasion of privacy. A business venture is likely
to violate which ones? Why?
4. What are the advantages and disadvantages of writing an operations manual?
With a particular venture in mind, do the advantages outweigh the disadvantages? Why or why not?

Suggested Activities

1. Find a potential example of negligent hiring in a local or national newspaper.
What questions should the employer have asked the applicant to avoid or
reduce liability?
2. Write a privacy statement for a Web-based business.
3. Search the Internet for a good example of an operations manual that could
be modified to suit the entrepreneur's venture.
4. Choose an idea for a new venture. Write an operations manual for this venture.
What are the particular risks for this venture, and how can these risks be
reduced? What procedures should employees follow?

Notes

1. Warren Buffett, found at http://www.brainyquote.com/quotes/quotes/w/ warrenbuff138173.html
2. Webster's Dictionary of the English Language, Unabridged, *Encyclopedic Edition*, © 1977 J. G. Ferguson Publishing Company, Webster's Press, New York, p. 1926.
3. *Lange v. National Biscuit Company*, 211 N.W.2d 783 (Minn. 1973).
4. Bryan A. Garner, Editor in Chief, "Privilege—a special legal right, exemption, or immunity granted to a person or class of persons; an exception to a duty." *Black's Law Dictionary*, (1999), 7th edition, West Group, St. Paul, p. 1215.
5. In the process of detaining and charging the customer, depending on state law the shopkeeper may also commit other torts such as assault, battery, intentional infliction of emotional distress, libel, malicious prosecution, and outrageous conduct.
6. In one famous case, Pennzoil had a contract to purchase the Getty Oil company. Texaco encouraged Getty Oil to breach the agreement by offering Getty Oil a better price. Pennzoil sued Texaco and was awarded damages. *Texaco, Inc. v. Pennzoil Co.*, 729 S.W.2d 768, 1987 Tex. App. LEXIS 6484 (Tex. App. 1987). There were numerous appeals in this dispute until the parties eventually settled the dispute.
7. *Jamsports & Entm't, LLC v. Paradama Prods.*, 382 F. Supp. 2d 1056, 2005 U.S. Dist. LEXIS 17452 (N. Dist. Ill., E. Div. 2005), pp. 1058 and 1059. The judge in this case is deciding the post trial motions.
8. The court granted a new trial on the issue of damages because of ambiguities in interpreting the jury award.
9. *Jamsports & Entm't, LLC v. Paradama Prods.*, p. 1063.
10. *Id.*
11. *Id.*, p. 1060.
12. *Id.*, p. 1063. The evidence of Clear Channel's spiteful behavior probably contributed to the $73,000,000 punitive damages award by the initial jury.
13. Phishing is a fraudulent technique used to obtain sensitive or personal information by pretending to be another company. For example, a person sends out emails pretending to be Bank of America. The email informs the reader that Bank of America needs to confirm his or her user name and password and directs the reader to a Web site for the "verification" process. The original email and the Web site look similar to the real company to aid in the deception. The email address and the URL may also look legitimate.
14. The European Union requires that a business post a privacy policy if it deals with European Union residents. Fred Steingold, (2001) *How to Get Your Business on the Web: A Legal Guide to E-Commerce*, Nolo, Berkeley, CA, p. 12/8.
15. *Id.*, p. 12/9.
16. These statements are not always effective, but they may provide another layer of protection.

17. Strict liability for products is based on the fact that the goods were unreasonably dangerous. A plaintiff suing under this tort must prove that the (1) seller was in the business of selling goods, (2) the goods were defective when they were in the seller's possession, (3) the defect caused the plaintiff's injury, and (4) the product was expected to and did reach the consumer without substantial change in its condition.

18. *Restatement (Second) of Agency* (Philadelphia: American Law Institute, 1958), §§228 (1) and 229 (2).

19. *Mary M. v. City of Los Angeles*, 814 P.2d 1341 (Cal. 1991).

20. Albert Schweitzer, found at http://www.quotationspage.com/quote/ 34600. html

21. California Vehicle Code §§12810.3, 23123, 2006 Stat. Ch. 290. A number of other states have similar laws for adult drivers, including New York, New Jersey, and Washington, DC. Erin Barmby, "Review of Selected 2007 California Legislation: Vehicle: Chapter 290: California's Message to Hang Up and Pay Attention," *McGeorge Law Review*, Vol. 38, pp. 342, 344.

CHAPTER 8

SUPERVISING WORKERS TO REDUCE THE RISKS

*You get what you reward. Be clear about what you want
to get and systematically reward it.[1]*

INTRODUCTION

The process of hiring and supervising workers necessarily takes attention away from the core business activities. However, most entrepreneurs want to grow their enterprises. During that growth they will reach a point where they cannot do it all themselves. In addition, the entrepreneur can hire workers with the knowledge, skills, and traits that he lacks. Hiring a talented workforce and properly motivating them are essential to most ventures. This chapter will discuss many aspects of hiring and supervising workers. As mentioned in Chapter 7, what an **employee** does in the course and scope of employment will generally be attributed to the entrepreneur under the doctrine of respondeat superior. In Chapter 5 this Companion discussed hiring **agents** who enter into contracts on behalf of the entrepreneur, and this chapter will focus more on workers who provide physical effort for the entrepreneur. A worker can do both. See Figure 8.1 for an illustration of this idea. When a dispute arises with a member of the public, called a third party, one of the first questions that the court will usually ask is whether the problem arose because of a contract or a tort. In other words, is the third party complaining about a contract she entered into with an agent, or is she complaining about a tort committed by a worker? This chapter will also explore in more detail the distinctions between two types of workers—employees and **independent contractors**.

FIGURE 8.1   **Individuals Can Serve Dual Roles**

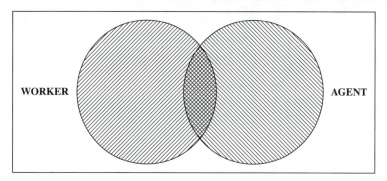

WORKER   AGENT

Source: Courtesy of Lynn M. Forsythe, © Lynn M. Forsythe 2009.

The focus of this chapter will be the workers that the entrepreneur hires. However, clients may hire the entrepreneur, so he also may be a worker for his clients. The entrepreneur should consider the relationships from that direction as well. A worker will be legally liable for the torts he commits, whether or not the torts are in the course and scope of the employment. Consequently, the entrepreneur should use care to avoid conduct that may result in liability.

After considering his needs for employees, the entrepreneur may decide that he does not need full-time employees and that some other type of work relationship would be preferable. Some possibilities include independent contactors, leased employees, temporary help, and outsourcing. See Table 8.1 for definitions of these work relationships. The entrepreneur may also find that a paid or unpaid intern from a local university can help with some of the tasks. The entrepreneur should begin the analysis by considering his needs. Much of the needs assessment discussed in the next section will apply to multiple types of work arrangements.

HIRING AND SUPERVISING EMPLOYEES

The entrepreneur may solicit referrals for prospective employees from friends, family, former co-workers, and business associates. In fact, the individuals providing these leads may also want to work for the enterprise, but that may complicate the work environment *and* personal relationships.

The entrepreneur should use care in hiring employees to avoid potential liability for negligent hiring and respondeat superior, both of which were discussed in Chapter 7. When the entrepreneur is careful in the hiring process, it will reduce later problems and the entrepreneur's potential liability for the actions of his employees. The entrepreneur should consider what his needs are before hiring employees. For example, generally regular employees do not want to work for a few hectic months with many overtime hours and then be unemployed for the rest

TABLE 8.1 Types of Work Relationships

Type	Description
Employee	These workers perform tasks for the entrepreneur. Generally, they work at the entrepreneur's work site and use his equipment and tools. They are subject to the control of the entrepreneur, who may be liable for their actions under respondeat superior.
Independent Contractor	These workers are generally hired for a project or series of projects. They generally work at their own work location, using their own equipment and tools. The entrepreneur can provide specifications for the completed project. The entrepreneur does not control how the work is actually performed. He will not be liable for the independent contractor's acts under respondeat superior.
Leased Employees	These workers are employed by another company, which is responsible for their pay, benefits, and taxes. They generally work at the entrepreneur's premises. The entrepreneur pays the leasing company the agreed amount. Note that the entrepreneur may be liable for these leased employee's actions under respondeat superior.*
Temporary Help	An arrangement where the entrepreneur contracts with a temporary help agency to hire workers on a temporary basis. This is particularly effective in the short term, such as when the entrepreneur's administrative assistant takes a three-week vacation or there is a temporary increase in the work load. Temporary workers can also be helpful if the entrepreneur needs workers in another country for a short time. Employment laws in other countries or in foreign countries can be complex and confusing. Whether the entrepreneur is using the temporary workers in the United States or in foreign countries, he should ask the temporary personnel agency to agree, in writing, to indemnify him for all liabilities due to violations of employment laws. Note that the entrepreneur may be liable for the temporary employee's actions under respondeat superior.†
Outsourcing	An arrangement where the entrepreneur hires a company or individual to take care of most or all of his needs in a particular area, for example, the production and maintenance of his Web site or advertising for the venture.‡

* For examples of employee leasing companies, visit Agility Solutions Group at http://www.agilitysolutionsgroup.com/ and First Financial Employee Leasing, Inc. at http://www.ffel.net/

† If the entrepreneur needs employees for the long term, he may find that temporary help does not suit his needs. He may have to deal with turnover as these employees may leave their employer. Many employees who work for temp agencies are really seeking permanent employment. If the employee is working well and the entrepreneur determines that he needs a permanent employee, he may try to hire her. The entrepreneur's contract and/or the temporary employee's contract with the agency may prohibit her from accepting a permanent position with the entrepreneur. For examples of companies that provide temporary help, visit Advantage Human Resourcing at http://www.advhr.com/; Kelly Services at http://www.kellyservices.ca/web/ca/services/en/pages/; Manpower, Inc. at http://www.manpower.com/; and Stivers Staffing Services at http://www.stivers.com/history.html Some of these companies also assist an employer in locating permanent staffing.

‡ For an example of a human resources outsourcing company, visit the Emplicity Web site at http://www.emplicity.com/lp/PEO/PEO-10-things-you-need-to-know-about.php

Source: Courtesy of Lynn M. Forsythe, © Lynn M. Forsythe 2009.

of the year. In these situations, hiring temporary workers through an agency may make more sense. The entrepreneur should consider:

- What skills does he need now? He should also consider skills that he may lack, such as accounting or computer programming skills.
- What does he need the other person (or persons) to do?
- How much work is there? Is there enough work to justify a full-time employee or only a part-time employee? Even if there is enough work for a full-time employee, the entrepreneur may be better served by a couple of part-time employees, or by job sharing.
- What will he need in the future—both the next couple months and the next year? Is the work seasonal? For example, does he need extra sales people during the holiday season?
- What is the job market for these types of employees?[2] Are they difficult or easy to find and train?
- What will the employee cost, including any salary or hourly wage, benefits, insurance, worker's compensation, taxes, and the cost of a work station and other equipment?
- Where will the employee fit in the organization chart? Who will supervise the employee and be responsible for her performance review?
- Can the entrepreneur make other arrangements to have the work performed effectively and at a reasonable price? For example, many businesses now out-source their payroll processing and human relations management. Some even outsource the hiring process.

After completing a needs assessment, the entrepreneur should write a job description, listing the skills and qualifications necessary. To the degree possible, the position should be challenging and interesting. It is easier to motivate workers who are experiencing job satisfaction. The entrepreneur should try to minimize the amount of employee boredom because bored employees can get into mischief and cause damage to third parties and potential liability for the entrepreneur. They can also act in ways that will discredit the entrepreneur's reputation.[3]

The entrepreneur should list each essential job function of the position and rank them in the order of their importance. He should also include the skills and abilities needed for each function.[4] A good job description will help the entrepreneur focus his search. It can also be helpful if there is litigation over his hiring practices. Many of the sources of potential litigation will be discussed in Chapter 9. The entrepreneur should also write a job application form or select an application form and modify it so that it will be appropriate for this position. The entrepreneur should also write a standard list of questions for the interviews. Using the same application form and the same questions for each applicant make it easier to compare the applicants to each other and to disprove any claim of illegal discrimination. In Chapter 9 this Legal Companion will discuss some of the questions that are not permitted. During the interview process, the entrepreneur should take notes on all the interviewees and keep them in his personnel files. He should retain the notes even for those who are not subsequently hired. These notes can be very helpful if litigation ensues. The entrepreneur should also note nonverbal cues of job candidates, such as dress, manners, posture, facial expressions, tone of voice, and how interested the interviewee seems in the position. Depending on the job market, the entrepreneur may not find a qualified employee, and he may decide to hire someone less qualified and provide training to the new hire. If the entrepreneur is not able to compete with other employers on salary, he may be able to offer no-cost or low-cost benefits. For example, providing a flexible schedule or split shift to work around a student's class schedule may not increase the entrepreneur's costs.[5] Another example would be to permit job sharing, where two employees share one job.

The entrepreneur can and should monitor his employees. It will let him know how productive his employees are, whether they are completing personal tasks on company time, whether they are stealing company supplies or secrets, and whether they are harassing other workers. He needs to be aware that there are limitations on his monitoring of employees. The law is continuing to change and evolve concerning an entrepreneur's rights to monitor his employees' use of the company's computers, the Internet, phone, email, and voicemail.[6]

SHOULD EMPLOYEES BE HIRED AT WILL, OR SHOULD THERE BE A CONTRACT FOR A PERIOD OF TIME?

The entrepreneur can hire his employees "at will" or for a set contract period. When the employment is at will, there is no set length for the employment period, and *either* party is free to terminate the relationship at any time, with or without cause.[7] Conversely, when there is a contract period, the contract may not be terminated during the established time without legal consequences. However, most carefully written employment contracts will specify certain circumstances that justify termination during the contract period. Most employees in the United States are at will employees.

Most entrepreneurs choose to hire employees at will.[8] The advantages include the flexibility and ability to make changes as needed. This is particularly important because of changes in (1) the economy, (2) the market, and (3) the expertise and skills that the venture needs. In addition, if the entrepreneur's exit strategy is to sell the enterprise, the buyer would generally prefer not to be required to retain employees. The following paragraph is a sample of language indicating that the employment is at will.

> Employee and Employer understand and expressly agree that Employee's employment may be terminated by Employer or by Employee at any time, with or without notice and with or without cause. Employee and Employer expressly agree that this provision is intended by Employee and by Employer to be the complete and final expression of their understanding regarding the terms and conditions under which Employee's employment may be terminated. Employee and Employer further understand and

agree that no representation contrary to this provision is valid, and that this provision may not be augmented, contradicted or modified in any way, except by a writing signed by Employee and by the [Company] President.[9]

The entrepreneur would probably choose **employment at will** for low-level employees who are easy to replace. However, there are situations where he might prefer a contract period: these include (1) a tight labor market where it is hard to locate qualified employees, (2) the entrepreneur has provided costly training to the employees, (3) the employees have access to important company secrets, and/or (4) the employees have unusual or complicated compensation agreements. An employee may want a set period when she is leaving a stable position to accept a position at a start-up, and/or she is making an expensive move to a new location. When a potential employee requests a contract, the entrepreneur and the potential employee will negotiate on this point. Whether the entrepreneur agrees will depend on the employee's bargaining power and the value the employee will bring to the venture.

Contracts will be discussed in more detail in Chapter 12. However, if the entrepreneur does agree to hire the employee for a set period, there are a number of items that they can and should cover in the contract, including the length of the employment period, the length of any probationary period, contract renewals, employee benefits, health insurance, normal work place and work hours, sick leave, vacations and holidays, reimbursement of moving expenses, dress code, policy on drug and alcohol use, ownership of inventions, non-disclosure agreements, agreements not to compete,[10] anti-raid agreements, and actions or occurrences that justify the early termination of the agreement.[11] As with most contracts, there are very few legal restrictions on the contract provisions, providing a great deal of flexibility in the entrepreneur's choices of provisions. However, once the parties have entered into a contract, much of the flexibility disappears, because their agreement is now governed by the words of the contract. The employment relationship does not need to terminate at the end of the contract period. The entrepreneur and his employee can decide to renew the contract. Depending on the employee's skills, and the job market for those skills, the negotiation period may be quite intense.[12] There are no limits on the number of contract renewals to which the parties can agree. Unless otherwise indicated, throughout the rest of this Legal Companion the use of the term employee includes both at will employees and employees who are under contract for a term.

In either type of employment the entrepreneur may establish a probationary period for newly hired employees. It is common for the probationary period to be either 60 or 90 days. The probationary period policy, including the length of the probationary period, should be in writing and provided to the employee. This is commonly done on the application form that the applicant signed, but it can be reinforced in the employee handbook and at other places, as well. This probationary period should be the same for all new hires and provides the entrepreneur an opportunity to observe the employee and how she interacts with others inside and outside the venture. If she is having problems completing tasks competently and fitting into the work environment, she can be terminated without providing an explanation or justification. The entrepreneur may have performance reviews during the probationary period, depending on the situation. He should have a performance review at the end of the probationary period, and he should continue to have performance reviews at least once a year thereafter.

The entrepreneur should exercise care when hiring employees in other countries: their employment laws may vary significantly from the approaches in the United States. For example, European Union (EU) countries may have different views about the length or term of employment. In some of them the general rule is employment for the life of the employee.

HOW TO REDUCE RISKS ASSOCIATED WITH HIRING AND SUPERVISING EMPLOYEES

There are a number of varied risks associated with hiring employees. The employees may commit crimes, commit torts, disrupt channels of communication within the enterprise, steal the entrepreneur's trade secrets, and embezzle the entrepreneur's funds. Their actions may create legal liabilities for the entrepreneur as well. The entrepreneur can "manage" this important resource of the venture, however. For example, the concept of operations manuals was discussed in Chapter 7.

PERFORMANCE REVIEWS

The entrepreneur can obtain valuable information from the performance review process. He should avoid summarily expressing that performance is good or excellent. This is an opportunity to improve the working relationship. During the process he may also discover problems the employee is facing on the job, such as sexual harassment. Also, it becomes difficult to fire an employee later for substandard work if the employment files do not support and document this. (For example, assume the entrepreneur wants to fire an employee, however in prior years he simply noted that performance was good because he did not give much attention to performance reviews.) If an employee has been informed that her job performance does not meet the required standards and that she may lose her job if she does not improve, she will not be shocked if she is subsequently fired. If she knows that she *may* be fired, she is less likely to react with violence and/or an employee lawsuit. Also, if there is a paper trail that documents the personnel issues, the firing is less likely to appear to be retaliation for whistle-blowing, filing a claim for illegal discrimination, complaining about sexual harassment, or raising other employment-related issues. These issues are discussed in Chapter 9. The entrepreneur should also try to notice changes between performance reviews and deal with them in a timely manner.

INVENTIONS

The entrepreneur should consider a pre-invention agreement with his employees, especially his creative and inventive employees. This agreement or contract generally specifies that any discovery or invention that the employee makes along the lines of the venture belongs to the venture. Normally, the language of the agreement extends beyond inventions that are patentable, but the authors will call them inventions for the remainder of the discussion. The entrepreneur and his employee can agree to share these rights so that the discovery or invention belongs to them jointly or the employee receives some sort of bonus or recognition for the idea. The justification for pre-invention agreements is that the ideas or inventions that the employee conceives are likely to be related to the entrepreneur's enterprise and "spawned" by the work performed for the entrepreneur. The agreement can include inventions created prior to, during, and/or for a set period of time after the employment ends. The reason for extending the agreement beyond the employment term is to prevent an employee with a marketable idea from terminating his or her employment so that he or she will "own" the idea.

If the entrepreneur does not have an effective pre-invention agreement with his employee, he may seek recognition by the court that he has a shop right.[13] Courts consider the circumstances surrounding the development of an invention and the employee's activities once the invention or idea is created. The court tends to grant a shop right if the employee used the entrepreneur's computers, equipment, offices, phones, or laboratories in the development of the employee's invention. However, courts have also held that the use of a small amount of materials and equipment did not justify a shop right by itself.[14] A shop right gives the entrepreneur the right to use the employee's discovery or invention. However, the entrepreneur cannot stop others from using the right, and he cannot transfer the right. In other words, the right is nonexclusive and nontransferable.

The entrepreneur who is just starting out may need to check the agreements he signed with his current employer: he may discover that he too has entered into a pre-invention agreement.

TRADE SECRETS AND NON-DISCLOSURE AGREEMENTS

Trade secrets will be discussed in more detail in Chapter 11. An employee will have a legal obligation not to disclose trade secrets. However, a non-disclosure agreement (NDA) with employees serves a number of important functions. It puts employees on notice that they are going to be exposed to trade secrets, and it informs them that they have obligations to keep such information secret even after the termination of their employment. NDAs are discussed in further detail in Chapter 12.

The entrepreneur can request that the court apply the inevitable disclosure doctrine to prevent a former employee from working for a competitor for a limited period of time. The court will grant the request *if* the entrepreneur is able to convince the court that the new employment will inevitably lead the former employee to rely on the entrepreneur's trade secrets. For example, a court enjoined William Redmond, a former general manager from PepsiCo, from divulging any trade secrets to the Quaker Oats Company, his new employer, and from assuming any duties relating to "beverage pricing, marketing, and distribution" for Quaker Oats for about half a year. While working for PepsiCo, Redmond had participated in confidential and strategic plans for sports drinks, tea products, and fruit drinks. The court felt that Redmond possessed extensive confidential information and inevitably would rely on this information when making decisions at Quaker Oats about the beverages Gatorade and Snapple.[15]

How to Reduce the Risks Associated with Firing Employees

It may be difficult or unpleasant to fire an employee who is not working up to expectations or who is disruptive to the business environment. It can be even more difficult if that employee is a family member or close friend. It is not fair to the entrepreneur or his other employees to keep an employee who is not working out. Firing employees is sometimes unavoidable. The entrepreneur should consider carefully why he wants to fire a particular employee. He needs to make sure that he is not behaving in a manner that is unlawful, such as retaliating against a whistle–blower or discriminating on the basis of race, religion, national origin, or some other unlawful grounds. The problem may not necessarily be the employee's fault. For example, in one enterprise the entrepreneur suspected that a particular employee was disruptive to the business setting. In reality, the problem was the entrepreneur's son who also worked for the venture. The son's behavior was counterproductive to a number of segments of the enterprise, and the entrepreneur needed to take corrective action. Before the entrepreneur decides to fire an employee, he should counsel the employee in private: he should tell the employee clearly what behavior needs to be changed and give the employee the opportunity to make changes. The entrepreneur should write notes for the employee's personnel file, documenting the discussions and warnings as they occur. It is best if there are both verbal and written warnings to the employee. This documentation will be essential if there is litigation about the firing. It is best to handle each meeting in a calm, firm, honest, and humane manner.

The entrepreneur should consider some other options which *may* reduce the likelihood of litigation. One possibility is to assign the employee to another position, or to redesign the employee's job. Another possibility is offering the employee a chance to resign from the position, and thus save face. However, if it is presented to the employee as a firm choice to either resign or be fired, the employee will still probably be eligible for unemployment compensation and can still probably sue for wrongful termination, assuming that she has legal grounds for the suit. Another possibility is offering the employee a positive reference. This option may work for an employee with positive traits but who was not a good fit for the entrepreneur's venture. Before making this commitment though, the entrepreneur should be sure that he is comfortable making a positive recommendation and that he believes it would be accurate. The entrepreneur can be legally liable if he makes false statements orally or in writing: persons injured by the employee at her new job can successfully sue the entrepreneur. The entrepreneur who makes a commitment to give a positive recommendation should follow through with the commitment. Another option is to offer to help the employee find a new job that is better suited to her. For example, the entrepreneur could pay the fees at a placement agency.

The entrepreneur should consider all the potential ramifications of the termination, including the risk of protracted litigation, before going forward with firing the employee. If the entrepreneur has any concerns about where he would stand legally, he should consult his lawyers. If he is currently in a weak legal position, he may be able to collect additional evidence to support the firing. The entrepreneur and his attorney will want to have a strong paper trail.[16] The firing will have an affect on the entrepreneur's other employees. Even those employees who understand why the employee was fired may be somewhat traumatized by the firing.

If the entrepreneur decides to go ahead and fire the employee, he should prepare a termination letter and prepare to have a termination meeting. The termination letter should describe any severance package that is being offered to the employee and the terms and conditions of the severance package.[17] The entrepreneur should give careful consideration to whether he wants to ask the employee to sign a release of any claims she has against the business: she may not have thought about suing the venture until the entrepreneur mentions it. If the entrepreneur wants the employee to sign a release, he needs to offer her consideration. (As discussed in Chapter 12, consideration is something of value that the employee is not already entitled to receive by contract or state law.) The entrepreneur should consider reviewing with the employee any non-disclosure agreements or agreements not to compete that she had previously signed. The entrepreneur will also want to collect any property that the venture has entrusted to the employee, including access codes, keys, identification cards, and laptop computers. The timing of the collection will depend on the situation and the threat posed by the employee.

The entrepreneur should plan carefully what he is going to say, and should avoid any language that hints the person had good job performance or that could be interpreted as discriminatory. The entrepreneur should limit the discussion to the specific behavior the employee was already warned about. He should also remind the employee that she was given adequate warning and an opportunity to change her behavior. The entrepreneur should tell the fired employee that her personnel issues will not be discussed with her co-workers. Troubled and potentially violent employees often exhibit clues that should serve as warning signs and should not be ignored. These clues include "high absenteeism, known substance abuse, chronic tardiness, fascination with weapons, and harassing and threatening"[18] behavior. If the entrepreneur is about to fire such an employee, he may wish to consult with a psychologist who has expertise in workplace issues.

Most states have rules about the time frame in which the owner must issue the final paycheck to the terminated employee. For example, in California the final paycheck is due immediately when an employee is fired.[19] The entrepreneur should use care not to disclose private personnel matters to others. The fired employee may be looking for good grounds for a lawsuit against the entrepreneur. Often, fired employees sue for defamation of character or invasion of privacy on the basis of the entrepreneur's statements about them.[20]

USING INDEPENDENT CONTRACTORS TO REDUCE COSTS AND RISKS

WHAT IS THE DIFFERENCE BETWEEN AN INDEPENDENT CONTRACTOR AND AN EMPLOYEE?

Entrepreneurs can sometimes use independent contractors to reduce expenses and liability. What is an independent contractor and how does an independent contractor differ from an employee? Employees include both at will employees and those who are under contract with the entrepreneur. With an independent contractor, the entrepreneur will specify the project he wants to have completed, the standards for successful completion, and the deadline for the work. However, the entrepreneur will lack control over the details of how the job is completed. One of the key differences between independent contractors and employees is that the entrepreneur has less control (or right to control) over the independent contractor. See Exhibit 8.1 for an illustration of the control continuum. It shows the independent contractor on the far left where there is less control: Control is limited to the specifications for the completed project. The entrepreneur would not be able to specify when the independent contractor starts work, stops for the day, how long she takes for lunch, whether she hires assistants, or when she takes a day off. An independent contractor will not *generally* be at the entrepreneur's work site. Many independent contractors work from their own homes or offices. The employee is on the far right of the control continuum, where the entrepreneur can control the particulars of the job. Generally, the entrepreneur will be able to control the hours the employee works, including when the worker takes breaks, the location where the employee works, the tools the employee uses, and the method or techniques the employee uses.

The "line" between independent contractors and employees is not always clear, even to the courts. It is not sufficient to label workers as independent contractors. Courts will not be controlled by that label. Courts will look beyond the label to the actual relationship. Although the label used is not controlling, if there is any litigation it is certainly helpful if the entrepreneur was consistent in

EXHIBIT 8.1   Control Continuum
How much control does the entrepreneur have?
Least Control   Most Control
├──┤
Independent Contractor   Employee

Source: Courtesy of Lynn M. Forsythe, © Lynn M. Forsythe 2009.

the label he used. For example, the entrepreneur should not require the worker to sign an independent contractor agreement on one hand and then ask her to conform to rules in the employee handbook. In a recent California case, the courts held that for the purposes of the state labor code, FedEx's drivers were employees and not independent contractors, despite the operating agreements signed by the drivers stating that they were independent contractors.[21] In this case, the drivers provided their own trucks and were responsible for the trucks' condition. Although the operating agreement indicated that the drivers could determine "the manner and means"[22] used to perform the deliveries, the evidence showed that FedEx exerted significant control over the deliveries. FedEx controlled numerous aspects of the drivers' work, including the drivers' color of socks, hair style, earrings, hours and days of work, color of truck, and logo on truck. FedEx paid the drivers weekly. Drivers were not free to reject a job, and they were not permitted to work for other delivery services.[23]

Numerous individuals and government entities can raise the issue of whether a worker is really an independent contractor. In the California case the drivers sued FedEx for reimbursement of expenses. Some others who may raise the issue include the entrepreneur's other employees who envy the "independent contractors," the Department of Labor, the Internal Revenue Service (IRS), the state tax department, and the state department handling worker's compensation and/or unemployment. The various state and federal agencies use slightly different tests or factors in making their decision. Generally, when courts have to decide whether a worker is an independent contractor, they look at the following:

- Does the hiring party have control or the right to control the worker, including the details of the work?
- Does the worker hire assistants to help her?
- Is the worker paid a salary, an hourly wage, or by the job?
- Are the worker's expenses reimbursed by the hiring party?
- Does the hiring party provide employee-type benefits, such as health insurance, pension plans, and paid vacation?
- How long are services going to be performed by this worker? How long will this relationship continue?
- Who is going to provide the tools, supplies, and equipment needed?
- Where is the work going to be performed?
- Does the worker have a separate business or distinct occupation?
- Is the work a regular part of the hiring party's business, or is it something that is done occasionally?

After providing its own list of factors, the IRS summarizes the decision making like this: "Businesses must weigh all these factors when determining whether a worker is an employee or independent contractor. Some factors may indicate that the worker is an employee, while other factors indicate that the worker is an independent contractor. There is no 'magic' or set number of factors that 'makes' the worker an employee or an independent contractor, and no one factor stands alone in making this determination. . . . The keys are to look at the entire relationship, considering the degree or extent of the right to direct and control, and finally, to document each of the factors used in coming up with the determination."[24] If the entrepreneur decides that he wants to hire an independent contractor, he should carefully structure the relationship and draft the appropriate documents to support his decision that the worker is an independent contractor.[25]

WHY DOES IT MATTER IF THE WORKER IS AN INDEPENDENT CONTRACTOR OR AN EMPLOYEE?

Why does it matter whether the worker is one or the other? Table 8.2 illustrates a number of the differences between them. An entrepreneur may be an independent contractor for others. Consequently, he should be aware that independent contractors will be liable for their own torts. As mentioned in Chapter 7, employees are also liable for their own torts.

ADVANTAGES AND DISADVANTAGES OF INDEPENDENT CONTRACTORS

There are a number of advantages to hiring independent contractors to complete projects. These include:

- Independent contractors provide expertise and flexibility, especially when the entrepreneur does not need a full-time person for these duties.[26]
- Independent contractors are not protected by employment laws that are designed to protect employees, including laws prohibiting discrimination and wrongful termination, and laws providing the right to unionize. Many of these laws are discussed in Chapter 9.
- Independent contractors do not require as much cash at the outset because they provide their own work space and equipment, unless the contract provides otherwise.
- The entrepreneur will generally not have to provide training for the independent contractor.
- The entrepreneur will not have to pay a number of federal taxes, including Social Security and Medicare taxes.
- The entrepreneur will not have to withhold state or federal income taxes for the worker.
- The entrepreneur will not have to pay unemployment tax or unemployment insurance for the worker.
- The entrepreneur will not have to pay for worker's compensation coverage through taxes or insurance.
- The entrepreneur will not have to pay for employee benefits.

TABLE 8.2 What Are the Differences Between Employees and Independent Contractors?		
	*Employee**	*Independent Contractor*
Entrepreneur has potential liability under respondeat superior	Yes	No
Entrepreneur generally provides the tools and machines necessary to do the work	Yes	No
Entrepreneur generally provides the work place	Yes	No
Entrepreneur must withhold income taxes from pay	Yes	No†
Entrepreneur must withhold and pay Social Security and Medicare taxes	Yes	No
Entrepreneur will provide fringe benefits, such as paid holidays, sick leave, health insurance, retirement plans	Yes	No
Worker is entitled to unemployment compensation‡	Yes	No
Worker is entitled to worker's compensation§	Yes	Not in most states/not in most situations**
Worker is entitled to minimum wage and overtime under federal or state statutes	Yes	No

* The IRS calls this a common-law employee. Common law in this context means law that was developed by court decisions as opposed to statutory law.

† The entrepreneur will pay the independent contractor the gross amount. The independent contractor will pay her tax liability directly to the state and federal governments. Depending on the situation, the entrepreneur may still need to file an informational return with the tax agencies. Some workers may be deemed statutory employees under the Internal Revenue Service (IRS) guidelines. The entrepreneur will have to withhold income taxes for statutory employees. If the entrepreneur characterizes a worker as an independent contractor, and the IRS or a court determines that she should have been treated as an employee, the entrepreneur can face a significant bill for past taxes.

‡ The entrepreneur must pay unemployment tax on the wages paid to the worker during the employment period if the worker is entitled to unemployment compensation.

§ The entrepreneur will have to pay for worker's compensation coverage if the worker is covered by the state worker's compensation program.

** The independent contractor may be able to sue if she is injured while working at the entrepreneur's work site or with the entrepreneur's equipment.

Source: Courtesy of Lynn M. Forsythe, © Lynn M. Forsythe 2009.

However, there are also some significant disadvantages to hiring independent contractors instead of employees. It is unlikely that the growing venture would want to hire only independent contractors. One disadvantage is the lack of control over how the independent contractor does the job. The entrepreneur can and should specify the qualities of the final project; however, the entrepreneur lacks control over the details of the job. If the entrepreneur tries to dictate the specifics, many independent contractors will balk. This is not as much of an issue when the entrepreneur is relying on the independent contractor's expertise. The disadvantages to using independent contractors include:

- The risk that a federal or state government entity will audit the venture and reclassify the workers.

- The risk that an independent contractor will file for employment-related benefits, such as unemployment compensation or worker's compensation, prompting a government agency to investigate the entrepreneur's classification of the worker, and perhaps other workers.

- An independent contractor may sue for work-related injuries, claiming that the entrepreneur or his employees are responsible for the injuries.

- The entrepreneur will not have the same degree of control over the independent contractor as he would have over an employee. The entrepreneur should allow the independent contractor to do the job the way she chooses, or he risks having the worker reclassified.

- The independent contractor will not have the same degree of loyalty as an employee.

- The entrepreneur will lose continuity as independent contractors change. Each new independent contractor will result in a learning curve as she becomes familiar with the entrepreneur and his venture and he establishes a new working relationship.

- Independent contractors work for themselves and, consequently, they generally work for a number of other businesses. They may work for the entrepreneur's competitors unless there is an agreement to the contrary. Any such agreement would need to clearly define who is a competitor to the entrepreneur. The entrepreneur should not indicate that the independent contractor can only work for his venture. FedEx had such a provision in the case previously mentioned.

- The independent contractor may not be able to complete assigned tasks as quickly as possible owing to the priorities of her other clients. The independent contractor may not be able or willing to drop everything to assist the entrepreneur because of her other work commitments. For example, a truck driver who is an independent contractor will arrange as many trips as she can. When the entrepreneur wants the driver for an emergency trip, the trucker may already be committed to other jobs.

- The independent contractor's relationship is governed by contract and is not generally an at will relationship.

The entrepreneur who hires an independent contractor generally does so to complete a project for him. If the independent contractor enters into a contract to complete a project, she is legally liable to complete the project. However, if the entrepreneur sues the independent contractor for breach of contract and wins, the court will generally not force the independent contractor to do the work.

Instead, the court will require her to pay for damages. Unfortunately, this may cause a substantial delay in project completion; so the entrepreneur should choose his independent contractors with care.[27] On the other hand, the court would not require an employee (or former employee) to complete a task either.

If an independent contractor is hired to create intellectual property, such as a play manuscript or an invention, the entrepreneur should make sure that the contract clearly states who will own the rights to the intellectual property. This will deter future litigation over ownership.

STATUTORY EMPLOYEES AND STATUTORY NONEMPLOYEES

As if the distinctions between employees and independent contractors were not confusing enough, some workers who are independent contractors under the common law, using the traditional tests, are treated as employees by statute. They are called **statutory employees**, because they are deemed to be employees by statute. There are also workers who would be employees under common law, but the statute treats them as independent contractors, that is, statutory nonemployees. Statutory employees are much more common than statutory nonemployees because governments generally feel that it is to their benefit, and society's benefit, to classify workers as employees, because employment taxes are based on employee payroll and taxes are withheld from employees' pay. The question as to who is a statutory employee or statutory nonemployee will depend on the applicable state or federal statute, and there are a myriad of statutes. In other words, the statutes are not consistent, and a worker may be a statutory employee for one purpose but not for another. For example, under the federal tax law statutory employees are not liable for self-employment tax, because their employers must treat them as employees for Social Security and Medicare taxes.[28] One example of a statutory employee for Social Security and Medicare taxes is an individual who works at home on materials or goods supplied by the entrepreneur that must be returned to the entrepreneur or his representative *if* the following requirements are met (1) the entrepreneur establishes the specifications for the work to be done, (2) the contract states or implies that substantially all the work is to be performed personally by the worker, (3) the worker does not have a substantial investment in the equipment and property to be used, and (4) the work is performed on a continuing basis for the entrepreneur. The entrepreneur would have to withhold Social Security and Medicare taxes for this worker, and he would have to pay the matching employer's contribution for these taxes.[29] The entrepreneur would not have to withhold income taxes from the worker's pay, however, because the worker is not a statutory worker for income tax purposes.[30]

MISCLASSIFIED WORKERS

"An estimated thirty-eight percent of small businesses misclassify employees as independent contractors."[31]

Misclassification is a serious problem for all businesses and government entities. Federal and state governments may decide to be more aggressive in their attempts to collect employment-related taxes. There is evidence that at least the federal Congress is going to move in this direction.[32] Generally, an entrepreneur who hires employees must withhold income taxes for the employee, must withhold and pay Social Security and Medicare taxes, and must pay unemployment taxes on wages paid to the employee. What is an entrepreneur to do? An entrepreneur can minimize or avoid the problem by (1) hiring his workers as employees, (2) leasing employees from a leasing company, (3) hiring workers from a temporary help agency, (4) contacting the various federal and state agencies and researching the tests they use, and (5) consulting with his attorney about this legal and practical quagmire.[33]

To an entrepreneur, one of the biggest financial risks of misclassifying a worker as an independent contractor is the resulting bill: the entrepreneur may owe back taxes for a number of years plus interest and penalties.[34] If the entrepreneur and his attorney review the factors, and still cannot confidently categorize the worker for federal tax purposes, he can ask the IRS for its determination. (The worker can also ask the IRS for a determination.) The entrepreneur can file Form SS-8, Determination of Worker Status for Purposes of Federal Employment Taxes and Income Tax Withholding, which is available online. The IRS may take up to six months to make an official determination about the worker's status. As the form suggests, this determination of status will be binding for only federal tax purposes.[35] The disadvantage to this approach is that the entrepreneur will be "bound" by the decision.

LIABILITY FOR THE ACTS OF INDEPENDENT CONTRACTORS

Assuming that the worker is properly classified as an independent contractor, the entrepreneur may still be liable for the independent contractor's acts, even though there is no respondeat superior. The trend is to increase the number of situations in which liability is imposed on the entrepreneur. In many states, the entrepreneur will be liable if:

- The independent contractor is hired for ultrahazardous activities. The standard is hazardous activities in some states.
- The independent contractor is hired to commit a crime.
- The hiring party reserves the right to supervise or control the independent contractor.
- The hiring party directs the independent contractor to do something careless or wrong.
- The hiring party observes the independent contractor doing something wrong and does not stop the activity.
- The hiring party does not adequately supervise the independent contractor.
- The hiring party is negligent in choosing the independent contractor.

So, even though there is no respondeat superior for acts of the independent contractor, the entrepreneur can still be liable for the independent contractor's physical acts.

GRATUITOUS EMPLOYEES AND AGENTS

One of the common duties that an entrepreneur will owe to his employees and agents is to compensate them according to their agreement. The agency relationship was discussed in Chapter 5. Employees or agents, generally, are paid or receive other compensation; however, that is not a legal requirement for the establishment of either an employment or agency relationship. Consequently, family members, friends, and unpaid interns may be considered employees or agents of the venture. The entrepreneur may ask a family member or friend to deliver documents to the attorney's office, take the packages to the post office, or clean the office after hours. (These requests are even more prevalent in beginning enterprises or when the entrepreneur is particularly busy.) When the family member "accepts" the task, she may be acting as an employee or agent, depending on the task. So, for example, the entrepreneur may find that he is liable under respondeat superior when his wife has an auto accident while on an errand for the venture even though she does not have an official position with the venture. He may also be contractually liable when his wife signs a legal document for the venture at his request.

The third party may try to hold the entrepreneur liable for acts of other people who are not paid. In one case, Brendon Bosse was dining at Chili's Grill and Bar with three other teenagers. The four teenagers decided to leave the restaurant without paying. Another customer of Chili's went after them, and a high-speed pursuit occurred. The teenagers' car hit a brick or cement wall, and Bosse was seriously injured. Bosse tried to sue Chili's under respondeat superior for the acts of the other patron. (Bosse could not sue the patron because the patron was not identified: he left the scene after the car hit the wall.) The court sided with Chili's because it felt that there was no evidence that Chili's asked the patron to pursue the teenagers in its behalf or consented to having the patron act in its behalf. In addition, Chili's lacked the control or right of control necessary to establish an "employment" relationship necessary for respondeat superior.[36]

Another common problem may occur when an entrepreneur shares office space with others. For example, the entrepreneur has his first office at the local business incubator, which he shares with four other businesses. The entrepreneur needs to be aware that the incubator staff, and even the other business owners, may be perceived by third parties to be his agents and/or employees. Depending on the situation, the court may confirm that the third party was reasonable in her belief that the incubator staff member was acting as an agent for the entrepreneur, for example when the staff member signed for a delivery. The same situation can occur when he shares a commercial office space with other businesses. This legal result is even more likely when the businesses share not only the office space, but also share the office equipment and receptionist.

EMPLOYEE HANDBOOKS

An entrepreneur can use an employee handbook to his advantage to carefully communicate company policies to employees. The handbook also provides an opportunity to provide required legal notices to employees, and to set out policies for the probationary period, the termination of employees, the temporary lay off of employees, etc. If the entrepreneur establishes clear policies, communicates them to his employees, and follows them, he can reduce his exposure to lawsuits, and he is less likely to seem arbitrary and capricious to his employees. The statements in the employee handbook help define the legal relationship between the entrepreneur and his employees. If the employees are at will employees, the handbook is a good place to repeat that information. Care should be used not to make promises in the employee handbook that the entrepreneur may be unable or unwilling to keep. Courts may interpret these promises as legally binding commitments to employees. There are a number of examples of employee handbooks on the Internet, including the handbooks of other companies and universities. Whether the entrepreneur or his staff create the handbook or purchase it from a company, he should have his attorney carefully review the handbook, and the entrepreneur should make sure that he understands the legal significance of the document.

The advantages of an employee handbook include:

- The handbook can include legal notices that the entrepreneur must provide his employees.
- The handbook can help establish clear standards for employee conduct (e.g., consequences of not reporting for work or calling into work, required uniforms, use of safety equipment).
- The handbook can provide clear statements of company policies to employees. If all employees receive a copy, it can be used to rebut an employee's claim that she was not aware of a rule.
- The handbook can encourage and promote consistent management practices.
- The handbook can demonstrate that the entrepreneur is committed to treating his employees equally.
- The handbook can reduce the likelihood of accidental illegal behavior.
- The handbook can help reduce disputes and litigation.

The disadvantages of an employee handbook include:

- Courts will often interpret statements in the handbook to be contracts or contractual types of promises to employees.
- If the language in the handbook is ambiguous, it will probably be interpreted against the entrepreneur who drafted it.
- The language in the handbook may limit the enterprise's ability to handle situations on a case-by-case basis.

Some of these disadvantages can be minimized by the careful selection of language in the handbook. The entrepreneur should use care to make sure that he *and* his other managers use the policies once they are established. It is probably preferable not to establish any policy than to have a policy and not follow it. Table 8.3 provides advice on drafting an employee handbook.

TABLE 8.3 What Topics Should the Entrepreneur Include in His Employee Handbooks?

- If the entrepreneur decides the venture should have an employee handbook, he should decide the purpose(s) of the handbook. One common goal is to reduce litigation and help defend against litigation. If that is the objective, the entrepreneur should consider areas where litigation is common.* Other common goals are to improve employee morale[†] and organizational needs.[‡]

- The entrepreneur should include an acknowledgement sheet verifying that employees received a copy and understand their obligation to read, understand, and comply with the handbook. (Some entrepreneurs may want to use a form that indicates employees actually read and understood the provisions in the handbook. This latter form will probably only be effective if employees are given an opportunity to read and study the handbooks before being asked to sign and return the acknowledgement sheets.) The acknowledgement sheets should be signed and dated by the employees and put in their employee personnel files.

- The entrepreneur should include a carefully worded disclaimer. However, the disclaimer should use simple, easy to understand language. The disclaimer should state that (1) the handbook is not intended to create an express or implied employment contract; (2) all employment with the company is employment at will (assuming that this in the entrepreneur's intent); (3) the handbook is not a complete description of the company's policies and practices; and (4) the company reserves the right to change, revise, add to, suspend, or discontinue the policies at any time. The disclaimer will not protect the entrepreneur from litigation by his employees, but it will help deter litigation, and will also be helpful in the event there is litigation.

- The disclaimer should be well publicized and placed in a prominent place to best protect the company. It may be advantageous to place the disclaimer in multiple locations.

- The handbook should avoid using the term "rights of employees" or other language with a similar connotation.

- The handbook will probably include statements about the venture's disciplinary policies. If the entrepreneur makes a clear statement of the policies, and carefully follows them, it can be very helpful in employment-related litigation. If the policy indicates the normal progressive disciplinary steps to be followed, it should also indicate that the venture can skip any or all of these steps when it deems appropriate.

- The handbook should also address other policies, such as the policy on sexual harassment and absenteeism.

- Before including any policy in the handbook, the entrepreneur should make sure that the venture can implement the policy. Managers and employees should be able to understand the policy. The policies need to be consistent with the venture's structure and capabilities.

(continued)

TABLE 8.3 *(continued)*

- The entrepreneur should also consider whether there are any unique situations in the firm that should be addressed.
- If the handbook discusses benefit plans, the discussion should be general and refer to the plans. It should *not* try to restate aspects of the plan. If there are any inaccurate restatements, the venture may be liable for what is represented in the handbook but not actually covered by the plan.
- If the workforce is unionized, the entrepreneur should not include provisions that are subject to union bargaining. It is likely to cause unnecessary confusion.
- The handbook should not be so long that employees do not read and remember it.

* Common areas of litigation may include: (1) alcohol and drug use, (2) attendance, (3) being tardy, (4) confidentiality and ownership of the entrepreneur's information and trade secrets, (5) conflicts of interest, (6) discipline, (7) safety at work, (8) sexual harassment, (9) termination, and (10) proper use of email, Internet, and computer equipment. The entrepreneur may want to consider an arbitration clause.

† When morale is the issue, the handbook may focus on (1) benefits, (2) compensation, (3) holidays, (4) leaves with pay, and (5) vacation.

‡ In these cases, the handbook may address (1) advancement, (2) employer reimbursement for college tuition, (3) job training and development, (4) mentoring, (5) recruiting new employees, including referral bonuses, and (6) retention of employees.

EMPLOYMENT POLICIES

Whether or not the entrepreneur drafts an employee handbook, there are some additional policies he may want to consider. He needs to be careful to apply company policies in an even way. In other words, he cannot choose to ignore the behavior from some employees and be very strict with others. Uneven application of policies is likely to cause discontent among employees, and litigation.

NONSOLICITATION AND ANTIPIRACY AGREEMENTS

The entrepreneur may want his employees and/or independent contractors to sign **nonsolicitation agreements**. In these agreements the entrepreneur can state that independent contractors or employees who leave will not solicit fellow employees and/or the entrepreneur's clients or customers. Nonsolicitation agreements *may* even be enforced in states like California that do not generally enforce covenants not to compete against employees.[37] As with many contract provisions the law may vary significantly from state to state, so the entrepreneur should consult with his attorney to make sure that the proposed agreement will be upheld in the state where the workers are employed. In most states the entrepreneur will need a legitimate business reason and the scope of the agreement will have to be reasonable. It will not necessarily have a geographic limitation, though. Nonsolicitation agreements may also be advantageous in some contracts with the entrepreneur's clients. In this form the agreement generally states that the client will not solicit the entrepreneur's employees. Otherwise, when the entrepreneur provides services to his clients, he runs the risk that the client will decide to hire away a good employee and start performing the service in-house.[38]

On the other hand, antipiracy or no-raid agreements expressly forbid employees when they leave from soliciting other employees to join them at their new companies, inducing other employees to leave the entrepreneur, or hiring other employees for a stated period of time. Often, the courts say that a departing employee can tell co-workers about her plans, although she cannot solicit them. Depending on the situation, the co-workers may be allowed to pursue employment with the departing employee on their own. Prudent use of nonsolicitation or antipiracy agreements can help the entrepreneur avoid the situation where he loses three or four key employees in a short period of time.

NEPOTISM POLICY

The legal system does not forbid **nepotism**, or the hiring of relatives, in private businesses. However, many larger enterprises have policies against nepotism because of the concerns that an employer or manager will favor family members over other employees.[39] The other employees may perceive that there is favoritism even when there is not. Some of the antinepotism policies indicate that one person should not supervise members of his or her family, in other words, he should not be responsible for their hiring, promotions, bonuses, and scheduling. In addition, it may be somewhat challenging to work with relatives or the relatives of other employees. For example, in one enterprise the CEO and his wife worked for the same company, and they often "paired up" against other officers of the venture. Despite the possible problems, the entrepreneur should not automatically adopt a policy against nepotism. He should think:

- Who does he plan to hire immediately, *and* in the future?
- What about spouses, children, and grandchildren?
- Who will be the future leaders of the enterprise?
- What is his exit strategy? Does he intend to make it a family business? Does he want it to continue for future generations? If so, he will need to train the future generations to take over.

Employment discrimination will be addressed in Chapter 9. However, if the entrepreneur hires primarily family members and close friends, he may inadvertently discriminate against people of other races, religions, and national origins.

NO-MOONLIGHTING CLAUSE

Some entrepreneurs have a policy preventing their employees from working for other businesses during the employment. This policy often includes all other businesses, and is not restricted to competing businesses. A less restrictive approach is for the entrepreneur to require approval in advance before the employee takes a second job or starts her own enterprise.

In hiring and managing his workers, the entrepreneur should consider the application questions set out in the box below:

Application Questions

1. Should the entrepreneur hire independent contractors, leased employees, temporary help, employees, or a combination of them?

2. If the entrepreneur hires independent contractors, what can he do to avoid having them reclassified as employees?

3. If the entrepreneur hires employees, should the employees be at will, or should they have a contract term?

4. When should the entrepreneur "accept" the labor and assistance of family members, either with pay or without pay?

5. Should the entrepreneur require employees (and family members) to sign non-disclosure agreements, nonsolicitation agreements, and/or non-compete agreements?

6. Should the entrepreneur arrange to have an employee handbook written? If so, what would be the purpose of the handbook, and what provisions should it include?

7. What steps should the entrepreneur take to avoid industrial espionage and theft of trade secrets by employees?

8. What policies should the entrepreneur implement for termination of employees? Does it matter whether the employee is a manager or not?

Summary

The entrepreneur starts with a vision, and once he starts to grow his enterprise, he will find that he needs help. He does not really want to be so small that he can do everything himself. He needs to decide what type of help he needs and whether he can obtain it efficiently by leasing employees, hiring temporary employees, or outsourcing the work. If these techniques will not work, the entrepreneur should decide whether this is a job for an employee or an independent contractor. There are a number of advantages to hiring independent contractors; however, the entrepreneur will have more control and right to control over employees. For example, the entrepreneur is more likely to be able to control the work days and work hours, how the job is performed, how the worker dresses, and whether the worker hires assistants if the worker is an employee. The control continuum shows independent contractors and employees at the ends of the continuum, but sometimes it is difficult to tell whether a worker is one or the other. In these cases the courts look at a number of factors before reaching a decision. The label the entrepreneur uses is important, but it will not control the court's decision. One of the advantages to hiring independent contractors is that there is no respondeat superior for their actions. However, courts seem to be increasing the number of situations in which the hiring party will be liable for the acts of the independent contractor. Employees and independent contractors will also be liable for their own torts.

The entrepreneur should use care in the hiring process and try to select the worker who will be the best fit for the venture. He still needs to monitor the worker and her progress. Occasionally, he will need to fire workers. He also needs to communicate with his workers, and a common tool used for communicating with workers is an employee handbook. The entrepreneur should use care not to make statements that can be perceived as promises to his employees. Otherwise, the court may decide that the employees are entitled to benefits that the entrepreneur did not intend to grant. For example, depending on the language used, the court might decide that there are limits on the entrepreneur's right to discharge employees.

Key Terms

agent
employee
employment at will
independent contractor

nepotism
no-moonlighting clause
nonsolicitation agreement
statutory employee

End-of-Chapter Questions

1. When might an entrepreneur want to hire leased employees, or temporary help? In what types of situations would these arrangements be advantageous?
2. What are the disadvantages to hiring employees at will? Explain why these are disadvantages.
3. How might an entrepreneur be frustrated by his lack of control over independent contractors?
4. What are the advantages to the entrepreneur of a no-moonlighting clause?
5. What is a statutory employee? What is the effect of having statutory employees working in the enterprise?
6. What are the advantages and disadvantages of a nepotism policy? Why might such a policy be problematic for an entrepreneur? What potential difficulties might the entrepreneur face when he hires family members and/or friends?

Suggested Activities

1. Find a contract between a sports team and a professional athlete. What provisions could an entrepreneur adapt to use in a contract with an employee? Why would these provisions be suitable?
2. Use the U.S. Department of Labor's *Occupational Outlook Handbook* available at www.bls.gov/oco/home.htm to find information about the position of administrative assistant (secretary). Write a job description based on this information. What salary range should the entrepreneur expect to pay?
3. Search the Internet for a sample job application form that the entrepreneur can adapt for his needs. What modifications should the entrepreneur make? Why?

4. Write a list of interview questions to ask applicants for a position in the information technology (I.T.) department.

5. Use the Internet to locate a "model" employee handbook that the entrepreneur can modify to fit his enterprise. What are the strengths and weaknesses of the model?

Notes

1. Bob Nelson, quote from Brainy Quote found at http://www.brainyquote. com/quotes/quotes/b/bobnelson194824.html

2. For information on job titles, duties, and wages, the entrepreneur can check the U.S. Department of Labor's *Occupational Outlook Handbook,* found at www.bls.gov/oco/home.htm

3. In 2009 two employees at a Domino's Pizza franchise in Conover, North Carolina, created a video showing one of them engaging in unsanitary acts such as putting cheese in his nostril. The pair then posted the video on YouTube. Associated Press, "Domino's Workers Fired for Antics in YouTube Video," *The Detroit News*, detnews.com, (April 15, 2009), found at www.detnews.com/article/20090415/METRO/904150428 and Brand Republic, "Domino's Pizza to Take Snot Pair to Court," (April 15, 2009), found at http://www.brandrepublic.com/News/898704/Dominos-Pizza-snot-video-pair-court/

4. This will help the entrepreneur comply with employment laws such as the Americans with Disabilities Act which is discussed in Chapter 9.

5. In fact, some restaurants prefer the split shift where employees work during peak meal times but are off during the mid-morning or mid-afternoon.

6. For a more thorough discussion see Chapter 11, Employee Privacy, of Fred S. Steingold (2007), *The Employer's Legal Handbook*, 8th edition, Nolo, Berkeley, CA.

7. When an entrepreneur plans to terminate an "at will" employee, he should consult with his attorney. Courts and some statutes limit this right to fire "at will" employees: for example, courts will hold an entrepreneur liable if the discharge violates public policy.

8. Some states have laws that modify the traditional concept of "at will" employment and limit an entrepreneur's ability to fire employees. For example, Montana enacted its Wrongful Discharge from Employment Act. Fred S. Steingold (2008), *Hiring Your First Employee, A Step-by-Step Guide*, 1st edition, Nolo, Berkeley, CA, p. 21.

9. *Colvin v. Comm'r*, T.C. Memo 2007-157, pp. 5 and 6.

10. Nondisclosure agreements and agreements not to compete are discussed in more detail in Chapter 12.

11. Some actions that can be included are the bankruptcy of the venture, the sale of the division where the employee works, and specific employee behavior that justifies termination. Some common examples of clauses indicating the employee will be terminated include a morals clause specifying immoral

behavior will justify termination, a quota clause specifying a required minimum sales quota for the employee, and a clause specifying that behavior that reflects poorly on the company will justify termination. For example, the employee is arrested for driving under the influence after work hours and when the situation is reported in the media the newscasters frequently mention that the driver is an employee of the entrepreneur's venture.

12. The entrepreneur may note the discussion in the media about contract negotiations for professional athletes or coaches.

13. A shop right is an implied license to use the invention or process.

14. "Circumstances in Which Shop Right Does Not Arise," 27 Am Jur 2d Employment Relationship §191, © 2008 West Group.

15. *PepsiCo, Inc. v. Redmond*, 54 F.3d 1262 (7th Cir. 1995). The quote is from p. 1263. The court noted that there was fierce competition in the beverage industry.

16. If there is pending litigation or even the hint of litigation, the entrepreneur should not destroy any records without consulting with his attorney.

17. Some states require in certain circumstances that the employer give the employee a "letter of dismissal" with an accurate statement of why the employee is being dismissed. Thomas M. Hanna (2007), *The Employer's Legal Advisor: Handling Problem Employees Effectively, Knowing When and How to Work with an Attorney, Staying Out of Court—or Winning Your Case if You Get There*, AMACOM, New York, p. 109. One item that the entrepreneur might offer is to continue to pay for benefits for a period of time.

18. Fred S. Steingold (2005), *The Employer's Legal Handbook*, 7th edition, Nolo, Berkeley, CA, p. 10/19.

19. See the Appendix entitled "State Laws That Control Final Paychecks" in Steingold (2007), pp. 349–354.

20. Additional information on firing employees is found at Web sites, such as Business Town, "Managing People – Firing Employees" at www.businesstown.com/people/firing.asp and its "Streetwise Tips on Firing Employees" at http://www.businesstown.com/people/firing-advice.asp

21. The trial court decision that the drivers were employees was affirmed by the court of appeals. *Estrada v. FedEx Ground Package System, Inc.*, 154 Cal. App. 4th 1, 2007 Cal. App. LEXIS 1302 (2nd Dist. Div. 1 2007). This class action case was limited to full time drivers who had a single work area or route (SWAs). In the words of the court, " In practice . . . the work performed by the drivers is wholly integrated into FedEx's operation. The drivers look like FedEx employees, act like FedEx employees, are paid like FedEx employees, and receive many employee benefits." *Estrada v. FedEx Ground Package System, Inc.*, p. 9.

22. *Estrada v. FedEx Ground Package System, Inc.*, p. 11.

23. Another federal court case against FedEx is still pending in South Bend, IN. Associated Press, "FedEx Drivers Awarded $14.4 Million," MSNBC, found at http://www.msnbc.msn.com/id/27284792/ (October 20, 2008). See also "FedEx Drivers in California Awarded $14.4 million in Landmark Employee Misclassification," Reuters, found at http://www.reuters.com/article/pressRelease/idUS189653+20-Oct-2008+PRN20081020 (October 20, 2008).

24. IRS web page entitled "Independent Contractor (Self-Employed) or Employee?" found at http://www.irs.gov/businesses/small/article/0,id=99921,00.html

25. See Amy DelPo and Lisa Guerin (2005), *The Manager's Legal Handbook*, 3rd edition, Nolo, Berkeley, CA, pp. 9/12–9/20, for a discussion of the documents the entrepreneur should use when hiring an independent contractor.

26. This flexibility can help an entrepreneur run a lean and responsive venture.

27. As mentioned in Chapter 7, in many states the entrepreneur can be held liable for the negligent hiring of an independent contractor.

28. IRS web pages entitled "Who is a Statutory Employee?" found at http://www.irs.gov/charities/article/0,id=131138,00.html and "Statutory Employees" found at http://www.irs.gov/businesses/small/article/0,id=179118,00.html. The latter page describes the rules for who is a statutory employee.

29. "Statutory Employees" and Steingold (2007), p. 114.

30. Steingold (2007), p. 114.

31. Judson D. Stelter "Note: The IRS' Classification Settlement Program: Is it an Adequate Tool to Relieve Taxpayer Burden for Small Businesses That Have Misclassified Workers as Independent Contractors?," 56 *CLEV. ST. L. REV. 451*, 452 (2008), citing Walter H. Nunnallee, "Why Congress Needs to Fix the Employee/Independent Contractor Tax Rules: Principles, Perceptions, Problems, and Proposals," 20 *N.C.L. REV.* 93, 94 (1992). The Stelter article reviews possible systemic solutions to the classification problem and discusses the Classification Settlement Program (CSP), under which the IRS can offer to settle a classification dispute that it has with an employer.

32. Stelter (2008), p. 452, citing Edmund Andrews (2007), "Democrats Seek Unpaid Taxes, Inviting Clash," *New York Times* (February 5, 2007), p. A1.

33. The IRS will provide information to taxpayers a number of ways including its Web site and booklets, the toll free information number, Private Letter Rulings, and Revenue Rulings and Revenue Procedures. The discussion in this chapter is limited to obtaining IRS assistance with worker classification questions.

34. The governing law will determine how many years back the agency can go in its assessment.

35. "Independent Contractor (Self-Employed) or Employee?" If an entrepreneur has misclassified a worker as an independent contractor and he has a reasonable basis for this classification, he may be relieved from having to pay back employment taxes for that worker. To see if the entrepreneur is eligible for the relief provisions, he should review *IRS Publication 1976, Section 530 Employment Tax Relief Requirements.*

36. Chili's may also have benefited from the fact that it had an expressed, but unwritten policy not to pursue outside of the building customers who leave without paying their bill. *Bosse v. Brinker Restaurant Corporation, d.b.a. Chili's Grill and Bar*, 2005 Mass. Super. LEXIS 372 (Superior Ct., 2005).

37. Covenants not to compete will be discussed in more detail in Chapter 12.

38. Charles H. Fleischer (2004), *Employer's Rights, Your Legal Handbook from Hiring to Termination and Everything in Between*, Sphinx Publishing, Naperville, IL, pp. 280–281.
39. In some family businesses, family members are given preferential treatment and salaries to the detriment of qualified nonfamily employees. These businesses are often labeled "family first" businesses because of their focus on family. Qualified employees and potential managers may be reluctant to join any family business due to their concerns that there will be limited opportunities for advancement for nonfamily members.

CHAPTER 9

COMPLYING WITH EMPLOYMENT LAWS

*Right is right, even if everyone is against it; and wrong
is wrong even if everyone is for it.*[1]

INTRODUCTION

When the entrepreneur hires workers she must comply with federal, state, and
local employment laws. In some areas, she may discover that the federal rule is
most strict and in other areas the state rule is most strict. As a general rule the
entrepreneur must follow the law that is the most strict. While there are a myriad
of employment statutes, this Legal Companion will only focus on some of the
more important federal laws. Many employment statutes provide their own definitions of an employee and the types of employment and workplaces that are
covered by the act. For example, if the entrepreneur has 50 or more employees,
her absenteeism policy must comply with the Family and Medical Leave Act.
Some of the statutes provide for fines that can be imposed on ventures that violate the rules; however, the entrepreneur also needs to consider the disruption to
her venture and the time and effort that she will have to expend on any claims
and lawsuits that are filed. It is to her advantage to minimize these disruptions by
being aware of the law and complying with it as fully as possible.

Employment laws often specify that notices must be posted in the workplace
and/or the information must be provided to employees in written form. Even
very small businesses may be subject to the signage requirements. Numerous
businesses and government agencies provide posters and pamphlets that comply
with the law.[2] The entrepreneur should look for a reliable vendor, such as her
local or state chamber of commerce.[3] The entrepreneur should avoid purchasing

overpriced posters and posters that are out of date. Obviously, in addition to posting the required signs she needs to comply with the law.

The entrepreneur should be aware that, consistently, the top reasons for insurance claims and litigation within companies are:

- workplace safety and **worker's compensation**
- wrongful termination
- **sexual harassment**[4]

This chapter will focus on the federal laws prohibiting discrimination and sexual harassment. It will also address the entrepreneur's obligation to provide a safe place to work and worker's compensation.

DISCRIMINATION

LEGAL AND ILLEGAL DISCRIMINATION

Discrimination has a negative connotation; however, the entrepreneur should be aware that there are two types of discrimination—legal and illegal discrimination. It is permissible to discriminate among job applicants based on the education, job skills, and knowledge that are necessary for the job. For example, a law firm can require that the lawyers it hires graduate from law school and pass the state bar exam. There are a number of bases on which the entrepreneur cannot discriminate in her employment processes. The prohibition applies to all parts of the employment process, including "preparing job descriptions, writing ads, conducting interviews, deciding whom [sic] to hire, setting salaries and job benefits, promoting employees, and disciplining and firing them."[5] Although the prohibition applies throughout the hiring process, for simplicity this Legal Companion will use the term "employees" instead of the more cumbersome phrase "potential applicants, applicants, and employees." The entrepreneur may want to include the statement, "An Equal Opportunity Employer," or "EOE" in her job advertisements as a signal that she does not illegally discriminate in her employment practices.[6] The discussion that follows will focus on the federal laws; however, the entrepreneur should be aware that cities and states also have laws prohibiting certain types of discrimination that may apply to the entrepreneur even though the federal laws do not.[7] For example, some federal laws only apply to larger enterprises, and the more local laws may apply even when the entrepreneur has only one employee.

The entrepreneur is entitled to make hiring decisions that work for her business. However, she will run into difficulty when she treats an employee (or group of employees) differently because the employee belongs to a protected class. Under **Title VII** of the federal Civil Rights Act of 1964, the primary protected classes are race, color, religion, gender, and national origin.[8] Title VII authorized the creation of the **Equal Employment Opportunity Commission** (EEOC), and prohibits discrimination by employers, employment agencies, and unions. The

TABLE 9.1 Federal Laws Forbidding Employment Discrimination		
Law	*Protected Attributes*	*Employers Covered by Law*
Americans with Disabilities Act (ADA), Title I	Physical or mental impairment that substantially limits one or more major life activities*	Employers with 15 or more employees
Immigration Reform and Control Act (IRCA)	Citizenship status, national origin	Employers with 4 or more employees
Title VII	Color, gender, national origin, race, religion	Employers with 15 or more employees

* The ADA also covers employees who have a record of substantial impairment or are perceived as having a substantial impairment.

Source: Courtesy of Lynn M. Forsythe, © Lynn M. Forsythe 2009.

employers covered by Title VII include private employers with 15 or more employees, state governments and their agencies, and the federal government. See Table 9.1 for a summary of some of the federal antidiscrimination statutes.

When the entrepreneur is perceived as discriminating illegally, she can be sued by an applicant, an employee, a federal agency, and/or a state agency. The allegations may result in negative publicity that can deter other qualified applicants from applying for her positions, while current and potential customers may also decide not to support her business. For example, in 2004 the EEOC filed suit against the national retail store Abercrombie & Fitch, alleging that the store was violating Title VII by not hiring female and nonwhite applicants because the applicants did not meet the image the company was trying to project. The lawsuit was settled by consent decree, with Abercrombie & Fitch agreeing to pay $50 million, and also to develop and implement training programs and hiring practices to end the alleged discriminatory practices.[9] Many of the people who claimed to be victims of this alleged discrimination were Asian Americans. After hearing the news stories, it is possible that a number of Asian American customers may have decided to shop elsewhere, due at least in part to the perceived discrimination against people of Asian descent.[10] *If* this occurred, this would cause additional losses on top of the $50 million Abercrombie & Fitch already owed for its 2004 settlement with the EEOC.[11]

The discussion in this section will focus on Title VII. However, Title VII is not the only federal statute dealing with discrimination. The Immigration Reform and Control Act of 1986 (IRCA),[12] which applies to employers with four or more employees, prohibits discrimination against employees based on their citizenship or national origin. However, it also makes it illegal for employers to knowingly hire employees who are not legally authorized to work in the United States. It also requires that employers maintain records verifying their employees' right to work in the United States.

A venture can be held liable for discrimination even when it does not have an express policy of discrimination. For example, if the venture has 75 employees but has never hired someone who is Jewish, there is a strong likelihood that the venture is discriminating.[13] If the entrepreneur is sued, she should be prepared to show her efforts to have a diverse pool of applicants and to support how she used objective criteria to choose the best applicant in each case.

DISPARATE TREATMENT AND DISPARATE IMPACT

Disparate treatment occurs when the entrepreneur openly discriminates against a protected group. For example, the entrepreneur hires only women to be washroom attendants in the ladies restroom. Disparate treatment based on sex *can* be legal, and it probably would be legal in the washroom example. See the discussion of **bona fide occupational qualifications** that follows. In many cases disparate treatment is not legal. In the Johnson Controls case, the employer decided to hire only men to work with hazardous materials because exposure to the materials were dangerous to a woman's reproductive health and the health of her unborn child if she was pregnant. Women sued because they wanted these higher paying positions. In this case the court decided that the disparate treatment was not legal.[14] **Disparate impact** occurs when the entrepreneur has a rule that seems neutral on its face but has a disproportionate impact on a protected class of people. Some of the discrimination may not be immediately obvious to the entrepreneur. The entrepreneur should review her hiring practices annually to make sure that she has not inadvertently created a system with disparate impact. She should also consider employee complaints, because policies that seem neutral to her may have discriminatory consequences that she may not realize. For example, a height requirement for a position would have a disparate impact on women and people of Asian descent. For some positions, the height requirement may be a necessary job requirement, but for many positions it would not be.

BONA FIDE OCCUPATIONAL QUALIFICATIONS

Under the antidiscrimination laws, an entrepreneur can discriminate based on gender, religion, or national origin if the position has such a special requirement that makes the discrimination necessary. For example, if the producer of a movie wanted a woman to play the role of the mother in a film the producer was making, being a woman could be a special requirement. These special requirements are called bona fide occupational qualifications or BFOQs. However, race cannot be a BFOQ. If there is litigation, the entrepreneur would have the burden of convincing the court that the job requirement is necessary. It seems particularly difficult to prove that national origin is a BFOQ.[15] Prior to the passage of the Civil Rights Act, most commercial aircraft had women flight attendants called stewardesses. Some airlines continued to refuse to hire male flight attendants after the passage of the act, and men filed suits. The airlines tried to convince the courts that being a woman was a BFOQ for flight attendants. The courts rejected their arguments on the basis that men could also be responsible for passenger safety and serving passengers.

One area of particular concern for entrepreneurs is educational requirements. In one case, Duke Power Company hired both black and white employees, but only white employees held white-collar managerial positions. The company decided to change the requirements for managerial positions and to require high school graduation. It "grandfathered" the current holders of managerial positions, so the requirement only affected new promotions. When Duke Power was sued for job discrimination, it argued that high school graduation was a BFOQ. The court noted the discriminatory effect of the requirement since very few blacks in the area had graduated from high school. It also noted that there was no convincing evidence that high school graduates were better managers than those who did not graduate. In fact, some of the better managers did not graduate high school. Consequently, the court concluded that high school graduation was not a BFOQ.[16] One way the entrepreneur can avoid discrimination or the appearance of discrimination is to require that job applicants have a degree or "equivalent experience."

DISCRIMINATION BASED ON RELIGION

As already mentioned, the entrepreneur cannot discriminate against employees or applicants on the basis of their religion. The law also requires that the entrepreneur *reasonably accommodate* an employee's or job applicant's religious observances or practices unless doing so would constitute an undue hardship on the business. The decision is made on a case-by-case basis. Reasonable accommodation does not mean that all the employee's desires be accommodated, and the accommodation does not need to be perfect. The entrepreneur can consider the following factors in making a decision about a reasonable accommodation: business necessity, financial costs and expenses, and resulting personnel problems. The entrepreneur may be asked to make accommodations to allow her employees to:

- observe their Sabbath or religious holidays
- have a prayer break during the workday
- follow their religious dietary requirements
- take time off during the mourning period for a deceased relative
- decline medical examinations that violate religious beliefs
- decline membership in labor organizations that violate religious beliefs
- dress and groom themselves in compliance with religious practices

Whether or not an entrepreneur can reasonably accommodate these religious practices will depend on the situation.

When an employee requests a reasonable accommodation, the entrepreneur will need to negotiate with the employee in an effort to find a reasonable accommodation. During the negotiation process, both the employee and the entrepreneur will offer suggestions. When there are multiple options to reasonably accommodate the employee, the entrepreneur can select the option that poses the least hardship on her business. However, she should avoid the options that disadvantage the employee in his employment opportunities. If the entrepreneur can show that all suggested accommodations would create undue hardship, she may order the employee to perform the work and discharge him if he refuses. However, the entrepreneur should consult with a specialist in labor law before she takes this position.

Religious discrimination cases can be quite subtle and require the entrepreneur to be sensitive to how her practices and activities might be viewed by other religions. Many of the cases involve the entrepreneur's or manager's practices that interfere with the employee's religious practices. Some of the behaviors that can cause difficulty for the entrepreneur include:

- requiring employees to work on their Sabbath or religious holidays[17]
- pressuring employees to attend prayer or Bible study sessions at work
- not stopping co-workers from recruiting members for their religion or place of worship
- not allowing members of other religions to schedule the conference room to discuss their religion
- not accommodating religious requirements in food choices, such as offering vegetarian options
- establishing a dress code that requires or forbids clothing that is mandated by religious beliefs (For example, prohibiting headwear worn for religious reasons.)
- requiring men to shave their beards contrary to their religious practices

Religious discrimination issues also require the entrepreneur to be sensitive to how other religious groups might feel about company activities, such as an undue emphasis on Easter or Christmas.[18] This sensitivity is particularly essential in a venture predominated by family members who practice the same religion as the entrepreneur. If the entrepreneur is sensitive to how employment practices will affect members of different religions, she can minimize the disruption and help her employees be more content and productive.

SEXUAL HARASSMENT

Title VII does not specifically mention harassment, but the EEOC decided that it was illegal to harass a person because of color, race, religion, gender, or national origin, and the courts have upheld this determination. The harassment that causes the most difficulty is sexual harassment. In many cases it should be obvious that the behavior is inappropriate, but in other cases it is more difficult to decide.

Offenders often claim that they were only joking around and did not mean anything by their conduct. There are situations when that argument might be persuasive. People do sometimes have trouble recognizing whether a behavior is sexual harassment. A practical test that is often recommended is, if the behavior is directed at a woman, ask the question—how would you feel if someone acted that way towards your mother, your wife, your sister, or your daughter? Obviously, the genders can be reversed if the conduct is directed at a man. Sexual harassment can be committed by men or women, and men or women can be the targets. Courts have interpreted sexual harassment as including:

- offering unwelcome sexual advances in exchange for job benefits and/or advancement
- demanding sexual favors in exchange for job benefits and/or advancement
- posting sexually explicit pictures
- telling sex-related jokes
- repeatedly asking for dates when the other person is not interested
- making inappropriate comments about an employee's appearance
- hiring strippers for business functions
- stating that one gender is unable to perform the work

Any sexually charged offensive behavior can constitute illegal sexual harassment. The entrepreneur has a duty to protect her employees from sexual harassment by managers, other workers, and people who enter the business, such as customers.

In addition to the potential legal liability, sexual harassment is very costly in terms of work productivity. In one case the worker who was being harassed did just about anything she could to avoid being with the harasser. She spent most of her workday hiding from him. If the entrepreneur learns of conditions or activities that might make some workers uncomfortable, she should take prompt action. Sexual harassment contributes to poor employee morale and high absenteeism, not just in the employee being harassed but in other employees as well. (However, chances are that if a person is harassing one employee, he or she is harassing others, too.)

In one case, Teresa Harris worked as a manager at Forklift Systems, Inc., an equipment rental company. The company president, Charles Hardy, frequently insulted her in front of others because she was a woman, and made sexual innuendos. He said things such as, "You're a woman, what do you know" and "We need a man as the rental manager." He suggested that they "go to the Holiday Inn" to negotiate Harris' raise. He also asked her if she had promised a customer sex. Hardy asked female employees, including Harris, to retrieve coins from his front pants pockets. Harris quit and sued Forklift on the theory that Hardy's behavior created an abusive work environment. Harris is the only employee who sued, but Hardy harassed other women employees as well. The U.S. Supreme Court agreed with Harris that the behavior constituted sexual harassment.[19]

It is in the interest of the entrepreneur to take steps to eliminate sexual harassment at her business. She should:

- take a proactive stand when she observes behavior that may make employces uncomfortable, such as pornographic pictures, magazines, or jokes with a sexual connotation. She should not wait until an employee complains.

- make it clear that sexual harassment will not be tolerated.

- create a formal written policy against sexual harassment.

- distribute the written policy to employees by including it in the employee handbook or making it a separate statement or both.

- inform employees who they should talk to if they have a complaint. The entrepreneur should have more than one person to receive complaints in case the person designated to receive the complaint is the alleged harasser or is someone the employee has trouble talking to.[20]

- conduct regular training on employees' rights to be free from sexual harassment. This helps remind employees that it is a priority, who they should complain to, and the types of behavior that might constitute sexual harassment. Often, the training is held annually.

- handle complaints as confidentially as possible.

- remind employees that they will not be retaliated against for filing a sexual harassment complaint or assisting in the investigation of the complaint.

- make sure that complaints are quickly and properly investigated and that appropriate disciplinary action is taken regardless of who the harasser is.[21] Failure to do so will "signal" to employees that the entrepreneur is not really serious about the policy, and it will also be damaging evidence if there is litigation.

The entrepreneur should also be aware that there are situations where employee conduct is more problematic, such as company travel and company parties involving alcohol.

ONCE A DISCRIMINATION COMPLAINT IS FILED

Employment discrimination laws are complex. If the entrepreneur is sued for employment discrimination, she should consult with a lawyer who has expertise in this area of the law. It is illegal for the entrepreneur to retaliate against (1) an employee who objects to illegal discrimination, (2) an employee who files a complaint under Title VII, or (3) an employee who cooperates in the investigation of a Title VII complaint. In other words, the entrepreneur cannot take a negative action against the employee because of his participation in the discrimination complaint. The entrepreneur can take a negative action against the employee for other reasons, such as excessive absenteeism, poor job performance, or tardiness. However, generally the employee will contend that the negative action was retaliatory. Consequently, if the entrepreneur needs to take negative action against such an employee, she should be prepared to defend her action and show that it was unrelated to the complaint and consistent with her treatment of other employees. If the entrepreneur employs family members and close friends, it is particularly important that she be consistent with all her employees. It would be extremely helpful to have prior written warnings and other written documentation of employee misconduct. The entrepreneur should also discuss the best way to proceed with her attorney.

WORKPLACE ROMANCES

Entrepreneurs should be concerned about workplace romances because they may be disruptive to the work environment, both during the dating period and during any subsequent break up. Workplace romances can affect the productivity of the workers involved and other workers in the business. The workers who are involved with each other may flirt at work, making other workers feel uncomfortable. Other employees may claim that there was sexual harassment because of a hostile work environment. If the couple is having a difficult time in their relationship, it may spill over to the work environment and make everyone feel uncomfortable. Of particular concern are relationships between supervisors and workers who are subordinate to them. If these relationships break up, there is the possibility that the subordinate will sue for sexual harassment.

Larger businesses often establish policies about employees dating each other. Sometimes these policies extend to employees dating customers and suppliers. Such a policy is generally not practical in a small business, especially one that employs family members. If the entrepreneur is employing her spouse, it is difficult for her to say that other employees cannot start dating. Still, situations can be strained. One entrepreneur started a business with his wife, where she was the office manager. When they had marital problems and a trial separation, they still had to work together on a daily basis.

If the entrepreneur does establish a policy about dating, she needs to make sure that all employees are aware of the policy. She also needs to be consistent in the application of the policy. California, Colorado, New York, and North Dakota have broad statutes that state that an employer cannot prohibit employees from engaging in lawful activity once they leave the work premises unless the activity conflicts with the employer's business interests.[22] If the venture has workers in one of these states, the entrepreneur should be prepared to explain how the dating conflicts with her business interests.

AMERICANS WITH DISABILITIES ACT

According to the U.S. Census Bureau, approximately 15% of U.S. residents over the age of five have a disability.[23] The **Americans with Disabilities Act** (ADA)[24] is a federal statute that applies to entrepreneurs in two areas—in the employment area and in the public accommodation area (property that is open to the public). Title III of the ADA regulates public accommodations, for example, casinos, bars, restaurants, hotels, motels, movie theaters, and stores. Newly constructed public accommodations should be designed and constructed to accommodate handicapped individuals. This is sometimes called universal design. If the entrepreneur renovates her space or part of it, the part that is renovated also needs to accommodate handicapped individuals. The Department of Justice establishes regulations for the design of new construction and renovation. Either disabled individuals or the Department of Justice can bring litigation against the business operating the public accommodation. Some handicapped individuals have targeted businesses and filed numerous suits to the detriment of many small businesses.[25] Critics of Title III complain that it is unclear what handicaps must be accommodated and how they must be accommodated: however, government agencies are working to clarify the standards.

EMPLOYMENT PROVISIONS OF THE ADA

The ADA also makes it illegal for the entrepreneur to discriminate in employment against individuals who are disabled. Title I of the ADA applies to job applicants and employees if the entrepreneur has 15 or more employees working for her for 20 or more weeks during the current calendar year or the prior calendar year. When counting employees, the ADA counts both full-time and part-time employees. Many states have similar statutes, and these state statutes may apply to ventures with fewer employees. The entrepreneur should avoid discrimination against workers with disabilities, and she needs to prevent harassment of workers with disabilities. As with other employment laws, the ADA prohibits discrimination in many aspects of the employment process from job applications to job benefits. Consequently, in the hiring process, the entrepreneur should:

1. focus on core tasks in job descriptions to avoid discriminating against applicants because of less important or marginal job tasks

2. avoid asking about possible disabilities on job applications and during interviews

3. not ask about medical conditions and not schedule medical exams until after the entrepreneur has made a conditional offer of employment

In addition to not discriminating against an applicant or employee because of his own disability, the entrepreneur cannot discriminate against an applicant or employee if he is related to or associated with someone who has a disability, including his child, spouse, or dependent.[26]

The ADA's definition of a disability probably differs from that used by the Census Bureau. As with many statutes, it has a technical definition. Under the ADA, a person has a disability if:

1. The person has a physical or mental impairment that substantially limits one or more major life activities.

2. The person has a record of being substantially limited. For example, this provision protects people with a history of cancer, heart problems, or mental illness.

3. The person is regarded as being substantially limited. For example, the entrepreneur or other people may believe the person is limited.

To elaborate under number 1 above, the entrepreneur should ask herself these questions:

- Does the person have a physical or mental impairment as that is defined under the statute? Physical impairments include any anatomical loss, condition, cosmetic disfigurement, or disorder. Mental impairments include any mental or psychological disorder.

- Does the impairment substantially limit one or more major life activities? Under the ADA, some major life activities include breathing, learning, reading, seeing, sitting, and walking. This list provides some examples for illustration purposes: it is not an exhaustive list. The impairment must substantially limit the activity. For example, an applicant may have difficulty seeing, but that may be fixed by corrective lenses. The vision problem would not substantially limit the applicant's activities. In making a decision, the entrepreneur should look at how the disability affects this person's activities.

The entrepreneur should avoid making decisions based on her assumptions. She should obtain accurate information about the employee's abilities and then make informed decisions on legitimate, nondiscriminatory reasons.

The ADA states that it is illegal to discriminate against an applicant or employee if the person is qualified to perform the work or could perform the work if a reasonable accommodation is made. The key is whether the person is qualified to do the job. The ADA requires reasonable accommodations, unless the accommodations would cause undue hardship. The following resources can assist the entrepreneur in obtaining information and advice about making reasonable accommodations:

- Job Accommodation Network (JAN), a federally funded service, available at 800-526-7234 or www.jan.wvu.edu
- U.S. Equal Opportunity Commission
- State or local vocational rehabilitation agencies
- State or local organizations that help individuals with disabilities

PROVIDING A SAFE PLACE TO WORK AND WORKER'S COMPENSATION

One of the obligations that an entrepreneur owes her workers, especially employees, is a safe place to work. Providing a safe place to work also has a positive impact on the employer–employee relationship and employee morale. Failure to provide a safe place to work signals a disregard for employees, which is likely to negatively affect morale, employee loyalty, and even employee retention. Most state and federal laws grant employees the right to complain about unsafe work conditions and to refuse to work in conditions that may endanger themselves or others. Employees who exercise these rights are protected, so the entrepreneur cannot discipline them or take other negative action against them due to their complaints or refusals. When the work or work site is inherently dangerous, the entrepreneur should take reasonable steps to reduce the risks. Some of these steps may be relatively inexpensive. She should also reinforce the importance of safety to her employees. The safety issues will vary depending on the type of venture. Potential safety concerns may include:

- exposing employees to dangerous chemicals
- exposing employees to excessive levels of noise
- failing to provide adequate first aid and medical treatment
- failing to supply protective gear, and failing to make sure that employees use the gear
- failing to provide fire protection
- failing to provide adequate ventilation and suitable workplace temperatures
- failing to train and provide proper instructions to employees

The entrepreneur may also have a legal obligation to inform her employees about hazardous chemicals at the work site.[27] The list of hazardous chemicals tends to increase as medicine and science discover the side effects of human exposure to chemicals.

The federal Occupational Safety and Health Administration (OSHA) and state agencies regulate workplace safety and provide helpful information to employers about workplace safety.[28] In many states the entrepreneur can obtain a free and confidential consultation at her work site through an OSHA-sponsored agency.[29] OSHA has the ability to fine employers for unsafe work conditions. If OSHA identifies a hazard and the entrepreneur fails to eliminate it, OSHA can impose a fine of up to $7,000 per day until the hazard is corrected.[30] In one recent example, OSHA announced that it is going to fine Wal-Mart Stores, Inc., $7,000 for inadequate crowd management in the death of a temporary employee on November 28, 2008. The employee was crushed in a stampede at the after Thanksgiving sale.[31] Even though there is a potential for high fines, entrepreneurs are more likely to be fined if the workplace is highly dangerous and the entrepreneur has ignored prior complaints about the work conditions.

One area that should concern the entrepreneur is the increase in the number of ordinances and statutes that prohibit smoking. The entrepreneur will need to comply with state and local laws, commonly called "clean indoor air laws," that prohibit or restrict smoking in the workplace.[32] In addition she may need to make reasonable accommodations to reduce or eliminate smoking at work under the ADA if she has a disabled employee whose disability is negatively impacted by the smoke. The entrepreneur might also want to write a policy about smoking at work, but she must make sure that it complies with the applicable laws. In addition, many states prohibit policies restricting the legal use of tobacco products when the employee is not at work.

Rights of the Injured Worker

Under the common law, when an employee was injured at work he or she could try to sue the entrepreneur. However, there were a number of legal defenses that the entrepreneur could use. These defenses are summarized in Table 9.2. Contributory negligence, comparative negligence, and assumption of the risk are basic concepts of tort law that are being applied to the injured worker. Most states have replaced contributory negligence with comparative negligence, but some states have retained the more traditional doctrine of contributory negligence. Some states are reluctant to apply assumption of the risk to employment situations. The fellow-employee doctrine prevents an employee from recovering if he or she was injured by the acts of another employee who works for the same employer. As indicated in Table 9.2, it bars recovery. An example would be if the entrepreneur's truck driver has a vehicular accident because the company mechanic was negligent in repairing the truck. The truck driver could not recover because of the fellow employee doctrine. The result of these defenses is that most injured workers did not receive compensation for work-related injuries. Worker's compensation statutes were enacted as a response to the way these theories "combined" to prevent recovery.[33] Worker's compensation provided employees a possible avenue for recovery. Generally, the entrepreneur will be required to pay for worker's compensation as discussed below. In most states, employees have to choose to seek recovery either under the common law principles or under the worker's compensation statute. Some states do not allow an election and require employees to use worker's compensation. Intentional injuries caused by the employer are an exception to these rules in most states.

Worker's Compensation

Worker's compensation coverage will pay employees who are injured at work.[34] The state coverage may pay for medical expenses, temporary disability benefits, permanent disability benefits, supplemental job displacement benefits, vocational rehabilitation, and death benefits.[35] Workers are covered whether or not the

TABLE 9.2 Common Law Defenses Available to the Entrepreneur When Sued for Work-Related Injuries	
Legal Defense	*Consequence*
Contributory negligence of the injured employee*	Bars recovery
Comparative negligence of the injured employee*	Reduces recovery
Assumption of the risk by the injured employee	Bars recovery
Fellow employee doctrine (Fellow servant doctrine)	Bars recovery

* The state will use either the contributory negligence or comparative negligence approach.
Source: Courtesy of Lynn M. Forsythe, © Lynn M. Forsythe 2009.

entrepreneur is at fault in causing the injury. Generally, the entrepreneur pays for the worker's compensation coverage by paying into a state fund or buying private insurance. Some states have only a state fund or only private insurance, but others have both. The entrepreneur will need to compare prices among her options. When the state uses an insurance approach to worker's compensation, the amount the entrepreneur is charged will be based on the perceived risk attributed to the enterprise,[36] the number of employees, and the job classification of the employees.[37] Many states permit employers to self-insure by posting a security deposit and submitting to audits.[38] Entrepreneurs generally do not have sufficient liquid assets to self-insure, nor would self-insurance be a prudent use of the entrepreneur's capital.

There is significant variation among the states as to who is covered by worker's compensation and what situations will be covered. Depending on the state, insurance may be optional for all employers or some small employers, for example, employers who do not have more than two or three employees. However, some states may require entrepreneurs with no employees to carry worker's compensation coverage. For example, California requires roofers without any employees to carry worker's compensation insurance.[39] States also exempt certain types of workers, such as business owners, independent contractors, farm workers, and unpaid volunteers. Many states do not provide worker's compensation coverage when an employee's injury is due to:

- an accident caused by the worker's use of alcohol or illegal drugs
- self-inflicted injuries
- a fight initiated by the employee
- the commission of a serious crime
- activities that violate company policy
- activities that are not job related[40]

Even when worker's compensation insurance is not required, it may be a wise purchase for the entrepreneur. Many workers who are employees at will decide to sue their employers for worker's compensation when they are fired or laid off. In fact, unscrupulous lawyers and doctors offices have been known to "troll" the unemployment offices looking for clients who can sue their former employers.

WORKPLACE VIOLENCE

An entrepreneur should take proactive steps to provide a safe workplace, free of violence. This will benefit the entrepreneur, her employees, and her customers. Workplace violence, and the threat of possible workplace violence, disrupts work productivity. In addition, the litigation and all the resulting distraction takes away from the core business. "Assigning a convicted rapist to work with a female employee has resulted in more than one successful lawsuit following an assault."[41]

What can an entrepreneur do to reduce workplace violence? She can:

- take the potential threat seriously. Do not think it cannot occur in her company.
- make safety at work a priority.
- plan a company-wide safety program based on expert advice from security and mental health experts.
- try to spot dangerous employees, paying particular attention to employees who have uncontrolled tempers, are obsessed with firearms, lack self-control, make threats, or seem to have a dark secretive side.
- evaluate the work site and improve security features. Consider installing adequate lighting in parking lots and hallways, hiring security guards, using security cameras, and using identification cards that are difficult to counterfeit.
- use appropriate screening of job applicants to avoid negligent hiring, negligent promotion, and negligent supervision (discussed in Chapter 7).
- respond quickly to dangerous or bizarre behavior. In many instances, the offender behaved strangely but his or her supervisors did not believe the situation was serious.
- provide employee assistance programs and counseling to diffuse potential problems.
- fire employees when necessary. Problem employees may be more dangerous than the entrepreneur wants to believe.

DRUG TESTING

The entrepreneur can have a drug-free workplace if she chooses. In fact, if she is a federal contractor or grantee, she may be required to have a drug-free workplace. However, programs of drug testing may conflict with her employees' rights to privacy. Her employees may feel that what they do on their own time is their own business. In addition, many drug tests will reveal information about legal prescription drugs, thereby revealing information about the employees' health. State laws are in a state of flux as legislators and judges try to balance these competing interests.[42] Generally, the law is more lenient in permitting the testing of job applicants than the testing of employees. If the entrepreneur is going to use testing, she should tell the applicants or employees in writing. For example, she can include that information on the job application that applicants sign. If the applicants or employees know in advance, it is more difficult for them to make a convincing case that they expected privacy. Drug testing is usually permitted if the employee has been involved in a work-related accident. If the entrepreneur decides to use drug testing, she should:

- consult with her lawyer
- utilize the expertise of the Center for Substance Abuse Prevention Workplace Hotline at 800-967-5752 or http://prevention.samhsa.gov

- treat all workers/applicants consistently
- consult with knowledgeable drug testing experts to assure that her test procedures are as accurate as possible (Of particular concern are false positive results, i.e., incorrect results that indicate that a person has used illegal drugs.)

The entrepreneur should also be aware that recovering drug addicts and alcoholics are protected from discrimination under the ADA.

MINIMUM WAGE LAWS

Depending on the size and type of venture, the entrepreneur may need to comply with federal,[43] state, and/or city minimum wage laws. Many states raise their minimum wage each year. The current minimum wage is often posted on the state government Web site.[44] Some employees receive tips as part of their compensation. Under federal law, employees who regularly earn at least $30 per month in tips can be paid less per hour.[45] However, the amount of pay plus the amount of tips must meet the federal minimum wage. If it is less, the entrepreneur must pay the difference. Some states, such as California, do not allow a reduced wage for employees who receive tips; these employees must be paid the state minimum wage.[46] Under federal law, the entrepreneur can count commissions she pays to sales employees toward the minimum wage: the total of the wages and commissions must equal or exceed the minimum wage, or she will have to make up the difference. The federal Fair Labor Standards Act (FLSA) requires that employees be paid at least once a month; however, state laws may require that pay checks be issued more frequently.[47]

Entrepreneurs frequently wrestle with the issue of overtime pay for employees. The federal government provides three resources that are helpful. They are:

- overtime Security Advisor at http://www.dol.gov/elaws/overtime.htm, which helps determine which employees are exempt from the FLSA minimum wage and overtime regulations.
- hours Worked Advisor at http://www.dol.gov/elaws/esa/flsa/hoursworked/default. asp, which helps determine which hours are hours worked under the FLSA.
- overtime Calculator Advisor at http://www.dol.gov/elaws/otcalculator.htm, which helps compute the amount of overtime pay due for a pay period based on data provided by the entrepreneur.

State law may have different rules about who is exempt and how the calculation is to be made.

REQUIRED BREAKS

In addition to minimum wage laws, many states also have laws requiring lunch periods and breaks. Before hiring workers, the entrepreneur should check to see what breaks are required and whether or not the employer and employee can agree to waive them. Certain occupations and industries may be entitled to special breaks or may not be entitled to breaks.[48] Some states, such as California, impose significant fines on entrepreneurs who violate the break requirements.

WHISTLE-BLOWER PROTECTION

Employees may be protected by state and federal laws if they blow the whistle.[49] **Whistle-blowers** alert people within the company and/or outsiders to potential breaches in internal company policy or government regulation.[50] The entrepreneur would prefer that they inform insiders first. It is best not to treat whistle-blowers as annoying whiners or tattle tails: they can alert the entrepreneur to potential problems that may need to be resolved in order to protect her venture. Although she may prefer internal whistle-blowing, she cannot stop whistle-blowing to outsiders, nor should she try. Most of the statutes protect whistle-blowing to outsiders, including government agencies, and some even create a duty to whistle-blow. One example of a whistle-blowing statute is §806 of the Sarbanes-Oxley Act (SOX), under which employees of U.S. public companies who lawfully provide information to their supervisors, the U.S. government, or Congress about behavior they reasonably believe violates securities laws or antifraud laws are protected from retaliatory discharge or other adverse employment action. Under SOX this protection extends beyond employees to contractors, subcontractors, and agents of U.S. companies.

Whistle-blower protection can be a serious issue for the entrepreneur even if her employees are employees at will. If an employee has reported alleged wrongdoing, the entrepreneur should consult with her legal counsel before firing, demoting, or transferring the employee to another work unit without the employee's consent. These actions may be interpreted to be adverse employment actions. Legal counsel and good human resource practices can help the entrepreneur avoid the cost and distraction of litigation. The entrepreneur may wish to establish a policy to protect whistle-blowers and encourage whistle-blowing at least within the organization. Table 9.3 has some suggestions on implementing a whistle-blower protection policy.

TABLE 9.3 Whistle-blower Protection

- Establish a whistle-blower protection policy.
- Establish multiple approaches for internal reporting, such as contact the company ombudsman or other company manager, call a company hotline, or email a particular address.
- Establish a method for reporting waste, fraud, or abuse.
- Value the feedback and the employees who provide it.
- Make a clear statement that there will be no retaliation, including firing, demotion, or suspension, against an employee for making a report.
- Include procedures for conducting investigations.
- Include information about how the findings will be disseminated after review by legal counsel. Information should be provided to the person who filed the report.
- Deal with the issues raised and make any operational and/or personnel changes necessary.
- Report any criminal activities, if warranted.

Many of these suggestions would also work in establishing a policy to report sexual harassment. In both cases, it is important to make it clear that the entrepreneur values the feedback.

UNIONS

An entrepreneur should not threaten or fire employees who want to unionize the workplace. However, the entrepreneur can take some actions so that employees are less likely to want to unionize. Satisfied workers often do not seek to unionize. An entrepreneur can work to avoid unions by:

- being sensitive to what is happening in the workplace and making reasonable changes if required. When changes are not possible, she should explain the situation to the workers.

- encouraging employees to come to the entrepreneur's office with workplace concerns and listening carefully to what they say. They may even have ideas for possible solutions.

- fixing health or safety problems.

- keeping workers steadily employed. Workers are insecure and have high levels of anxiety when they are hired, then laid off, and then rehired. If the entrepreneur has a lot of seasonal work, she should consider hiring temporary workers.

- changing workplace procedures if they are annoying or seem unfair to workers.

- being consistent in enforcing work rules and disciplining workers. This may be particularly tricky for an entrepreneur who has hired family members, such as parents and children, and close friends.

- allowing workers autonomy on how to do their jobs if it is possible.

- surveying the salary and benefits offered by similar businesses. The entrepreneur should compensate her workers at a competitive level.

- providing incentives for excellent work.

These actions may also reduce the likelihood of litigation by employees and former employees. Not all employment issues need a significant influx of funds. Some can be solved for little or no cash. For example, some entrepreneurs find they can improve the workplace atmosphere by treating their employees to coffee and doughnuts once a week and sitting and talking with them during the "coffee break."

If the entrepreneur's workers are considering unionizing, she should seek the help of an experienced labor law attorney. The entrepreneur cannot threaten or dismiss the workers who are in favor of unionizing, nor can she promise benefits to those who vote against the union. Discrimination among employees based on whether or not the employees are union members is prohibited under the National Labor Relations Act (NLRA).[51] Currently, workers are entitled to secret elections supervised by the National Labor Relations Board (NLRB).[52] Whether the entrepreneur can restrict discussions about the union and the distribution of union literature is a very sophisticated area of law, and she should discuss any proposed

restrictions with her labor lawyer. She should be especially careful not to selec-
tively enforce any policies against the union and union organizers.[53] It is currently
uncertain whether the entrepreneur can prevent union organizers from using the
company email accounts for union-related information.[54]

If the entrepreneur has a union at her workplace, and she is experiencing
discord with the union, she will need to be careful with actions such as plant
closures and large scale reorganizations. It would be wise to consult with her
labor law attorney, because the union is likely to claim that she is trying to "break
the union." An entrepreneur may also want to discuss her plans for employee
committees with a labor law expert because these committees may be deemed to
be illegal employer-dominated labor organizations.[55]

If the entrepreneur has a union, the union may want the entrepreneur to
enter into a "union security agreement." These agreements cannot require a
worker to join the union, which would be a violation of the NLRA. However,
under such an agreement, a worker who does not join the union can be required
to pay an "agency fee" to the union as a condition of getting or keeping his job.
One intent of this fee is to compensate the union for services that it provides to
nonmembers. Some states have laws that prohibit "union security agreements":
these states laws are called right to work laws.[56]

In applying the information in this chapter, the entrepreneur should consider
the application questions set out in the box below:

Application Questions

1. Where should the entrepreneur advertise positions to secure the broadest
   pool of eligible applicants?
2. What is the underlying culture of the venture? Are there any aspects of
   the culture that are troubling?
3. Should the entrepreneur establish a policy about employee dating?
4. What can the entrepreneur do to prevent or discourage sexual harassment?
5. What should the entrepreneur include in her sexual harassment policy?
6. Is the venture open to the public, such as a bar, restaurant, or store, and
   subject to the ADA provisions on public accommodations?
7. Is the ADA applicable to the venture, requiring accommodations for
   employees? If so, what reasonable accommodation may be required?
   What are the core tasks of the job, and what tasks are marginal?
8. Is the venture subject to the state minimum wage laws?
9. What can the entrepreneur do to make the unionization of her labor
   force less likely?
10. Does the entrepreneur's state allow "union security agreements"?

Summary

Once the entrepreneur's venture has grown to the size where she needs employees, she will be required to deal with local, state, and federal employment laws. Some of the laws will only apply to larger ventures, but many will apply to the entrepreneur when she has one or more employees. She will find that sometimes the local or state laws may be more strict and sometimes the federal laws will be more strict.

Under Title VII, she may not discriminate against applicants and employees based on color, gender, race, religion, or national origin. This applies throughout the application process and the actual employment, including promotions. There are two types of illegal discrimination—disparate treatment and disparate impact. In the first, the entrepreneur openly discriminates, for example, only hiring men for certain positions. In the second, she has job requirements that in effect prevent some people from being eligible for the job, for example, requiring applicants to be able to bench press 200 pounds. If there is litigation over the entrepreneur's job requirements, she will try to persuade the court that the job requirement is a BFOQ. The entrepreneur must not harass employees based on their gender or race, and she also needs to take active steps to make sure that other employees, supervisors, and others who enter the workplace do not harass employees on these bases.

The ADA has two provisions that may affect the entrepreneur: one says that public accommodations must be accessible to handicapped individuals and the other says that employers cannot discriminate against handicapped applicants and workers. The statute takes a very technical approach as to who is handicapped under the ADA. If the applicant or employee is handicapped but is otherwise qualified and can do the job, the entrepreneur must make reasonable accommodations to allow them to do the job.

The entrepreneur owes her employees a safe place to work. If her employees are injured at work, they will probably file claims under the state worker's compensation statute. Many statutes prohibit retaliation against whistle-blowers. Many of the entrepreneur's responsibilities make "good sense" in addition to complying with her legal obligations.

Key Terms

Americans with Disabilities
   Act (ADA)
bona fide occupational qualification
   (BFOQ)
disparate impact
disparate treatment

Equal Employment Opportunity
   Commission (EEOC)
sexual harassment
Title VII
whistle-blower
worker's compensation

End-of-Chapter Questions

1. Under what conditions might obesity be a disability or a perceived disability under the ADA? Why?[57]
2. Assume that an entrepreneur wants to establish a policy against employees dating other employees (and supervisors). Write the justification as to why this policy protects the entrepreneur's business interests.
3. What can an entrepreneur do to minimize the risks of worker's compensation claims against her venture?
4. Why should the entrepreneur welcome and encourage whistle-blowers who come forward within the organization?
5. What factors will make it more likely that the entrepreneur's employees will form or join a union?

Suggested Activities

1. Find the state labor department for the state where the employees will work. What is the state department's phone number, street address, and Web address?
2. Using the Internet, locate the worker's compensation laws of the state where the venture will be located. Summarize the approach to worker's compensation used by this state.
3. Return to your answer to Suggested Activity Number 4 from Chapter 8. Based on the information in this chapter, which of these questions would be legal pre-employment inquiries, and which ones would not be legal in the state where the venture will operate? Explain.

Notes

1. William Penn, as quoted in Ashton Applewhite, William R. Evans, III, and Andrew Frothingham (1992), *And I Quote, The Definitive Collection of Quotes, Sayings, and Jokes for the Contemporary Speechmaker*, A Thomas-Dunne Book, St. Martin's Press, New York, p. 95.
2. The entrepreneur can obtain information about what federal posters are required from the "Poster Advisor" of the U.S. Department of Labor found at www.dol.gov/elaws/asp/posters/industry.asp
3. For example, CalBizCentral from the California Chamber of Commerce sells notices that comply with California and federal laws. CalBizCentral c/o California Chamber of Commerce, 1332 North Market Blvd., Sacramento, CA 95834-9928, 1-800-331-8877.
4. Peggy M. Jackson (2006), *Sarbanes-Oxley for Small Businesses, Leveraging Compliance for Maximum Advantage*, John Wiley & Sons, Inc., Hoboken, NJ, p. 141.
5. Fred S. Steingold (2005), *The Employer's Legal Handbook*, 7th edition, Nolo, Berkeley, CA, p. 1/4.
6. This language is required if the entrepreneur is a federal contractor.

7. See the appendices entitled State Laws Prohibiting Discrimination in Employment, pp. A/58–A/67, and Agencies That Enforce Laws Prohibiting Discrimination in Employment, pp. A/68–A/71 in Steingold (2005).

8. Title VII applies to the entrepreneur's business if she has 15 or more full-time and part-time employees. Other federal laws also prohibit discrimination against workers who are 40 or older in employment *and* employee benefit programs. State laws may prohibit age discrimination against workers of other ages as well. Racial harassment and sexual harassment are prohibited as varieties of illegal discrimination.

9. "EEOC Agrees to Landmark Resolution of Discrimination Case Against Abercrombie and Fitch," EEOC Press Release (November18, 2004), found at http://www.eeoc.gov/press/11-18-04.html

10. This potential loss has not been verified by research.

11. Amy DelPo and Lisa Guerin (2005), *The Manager's Legal Handbook*, 3rd edition, Nolo, Berkeley, CA, p. 3/12.

12. 8 U.S.C. §1324.

13. In fact, a company's culture may be very discriminatory.

14. *Johnson Controls v. United Association of Journeymen*, 39 F. 3d 821 (7th Cir. 1994). Some women employees voluntarily were sterilized to be eligible for jobs in the division.

15. This may be due, in part, to the close relationship between national origin and race.

16. *Griggs v. Duke Power Co.*, 401 U.S. 424 (1971).

17. Problems can often be avoided by providing employees with personal holidays that they can use for religious holidays and observances.

18. For example, some employers have asked employees not to wear Christmas themed clothing at work.

19. *Harris v. Forklift Systems*, 510 U.S. 17 (1993). The lower courts were not convinced that Hardy's behavior met the standard of abusive work environment, because Harris had not suffered physical or psychological injury.

20. It is generally very difficult for employees to talk about sexual harassment even when they are not the person being harassed.

21. For example, in one case the harasser was the owner's brother.

22. Fred S. Steingold (2007), *The Employer's Legal Handbook*, 8th edition, Berkely, CA: Nolo, p. 231.

23. This is based on the 2005–2007 data set. The U.S. Census Bureau American FactFinder, found at http://factfinder.census.gov/servlet/NPTable?_bm=y&-geo_id=01000US&-qr_name=ACS_2007_3YR_G00_NP01&-ds_name=&-redoLog=false

24. 29 U.S.C. §706 et seq.

25. For example, Jarek Molski is confined to a wheelchair due to a motorcycle accident. He has filed over 400 lawsuits under the ADA, requesting that business owners be fined $4,000 per day for every day their facilities were not in compliance. However, a federal judge has barred Molski from future

litigation, calling him a "hit-and-run plaintiff." The judge also barred his legal counsel from filing additional cases without the judge's permission. Carol J. Williams, "Litigious Man Barred from More Lawsuits," *The Fresno Bee* (November 18, 2008), p. B3.

26. It is illegal to discriminate because the employee's relative has a disability not covered by the entrepreneur's health plan or a disability that can increase the costs of the health plan. It is also illegal to discriminate because the employee has a roommate or close friend with AIDS.

27. The legal notification laws are commonly called "Right-to-Know Laws." The applicable state code sections are listed on p. A/57 in Steingold (2005).

28. Three OSHA publications that are particularly helpful are: *OSHA Publication 2209, Handbook for Small Business; OSHA Publication 3151, Assessing the Need for Personal Protective Equipment; and OSHA Publication 3084, Chemical Hazard Communication*. All three are available through the OSHA Web site at www.osha.gov.

29. The entrepreneur can obtain information about the free, confidential inspections found at www.osha.gov/dcsp/smallbusiness/consult_directory.html

30. DelPo and Guerin (2005), p. 7/4.

31. Business Briefs, "Wal-Mart Cited for Death on Black Friday," *The Fresno Bee* (May 27, 2009), p. B3.

32. For a summary of some state laws about smoking at work, see Steingold (2005), p. 7/18.

33. The three common law theories that originally prevented recovery—contributory negligence, assumption of the risk, and the fellow servant doctrine—were referred to as the "three wicked sisters." Bryan A. Garner (1999), Editor in Chief, *Black's Law Dictionary*, 7th edition, West Group, St. Paul, MN, p. 1490.

34. When the entrepreneur has employees who telecommute, it will be difficult for the entrepreneur to find out exactly how the injury occurred.

35. For information about worker's compensation laws in a particular state, the entrepreneur can refer to www.workercompensation.com

36. Most programs rely on an experience modification factor, which is a number that represents the venture's accident and injury record compared to the average for the industry. The entrepreneur will want to keep this number as low as possible. When the experience modification number is high, the cost of the insurance will also be high. Insurance companies and states will make assumptions about the risk when a venture is new and does not have a record yet.

37. Each employee or job classification is assigned a rating based on the estimated level of risk involved in that particular job. Additional information can be obtained from the state Department of Insurance.

38. For example, see the California Department of Industrial Relations Web page on Self Insurance Plans (SIP), found at http://www.dir.ca.gov/sip/sip.html

39. California Department of Industrial Relations Web page on Division of Workers' Compensation—Employer Information, found at http://www.dir.ca.gov/dwc/Employer.htm Although independent contractors are not generally covered by worker's compensation, California requires real estate brokers to

obtain worker's compensation insurance for their agents even if the agents are independent contractors. *Id.*

40. DelPo and Guerin (2005), p. 7/6.

41. Thomas M. Hanna (2007), *The Employer's Legal Advisor: Handling Problem Employees Effectively, Knowing When and How to Work with an Attorney, Staying Out of Court—or Winning Your Case If You Get There*, AMACOM, New York, p. 130.

42. For a summary of state laws about drug and alcohol testing, see Steingold (2005), pp. A/3–A/12.

43. The federal minimum wage laws are administered by the regional offices of the Wage and Hour Division of the Department of Labor. Contact information for the regional offices is found at www.dol.gov/esa/contacts/whd/america2.htm

44. See the U.S. Department of Labor Web site for a list of state labor departments and other state labor resources. Its address is www.dol.gov/dol/location.htm It has information about the minimum wages in the states found at www.dol.gov/esa/minwage/america.htm

45. This amount is currently $2.13 an hour. DelPo and Guerin (2005), pp. 2/3–2/4.

46. *Id.* See the State Minimum Wage Laws for Tipped and Regular Employees chart on pp. 2/36–2/42.

47. Fred S. Steingold (2004), *The Employer's Legal Handbook*, 6th edition, Nolo, Berkeley, CA, p. 3/21.

48. See the State Meal and Rest Breaks Laws Appendix in Steingold (2007), pp. 306–310.

49. For example, employees who bring claims under the False Claims Act for their employer's fraud against the U.S. government are protected under 31 U.S.C. §3730 of the False Claims Act and employees of publicly traded companies who provide information or who testify as part of an investigation of securities fraud are protected under P.L. 107–204 of the Sarbanes-Oxley Act.

50. Some whistle-blowers alert entities outside the company, such as government agencies. As a practical matter, many of these whistle-blowers tried reporting the problems within the company and only went outside when they were ignored by those within the company.

51. 29 U.S.C. §151 et seq.

52. There are proposals before Congress to remove the secret elections and substitute "card check."

53. DelPo and Guerin (2005), pp. 8/8–8/11 and p. 8/19.

54. *Id.*, pp. 8/10–8/11.

55. *Id.*, p. 8/16.

56. *Id.*, p. 8/11 and a Chart of the State Right to Work Laws, p. 8/22.

57. Note that there is currently litigation in this area. The decisions do not yet provide a clear picture of when obesity will or will not be a disability.

CHAPTER 10

PROTECTING THE VENTURE'S NAME AND REPUTATION

A good name, like good will, is got by many actions and lost by one.[1]

INTRODUCTION

A person's good name and reputation can be invaluable. No one wants to do business with an individual if that individual is not deemed trustworthy, nor with one who has a reputation for acting in an inappropriate manner in his commercial or contractual dealings. Similarly, a business has a name and a reputation, and both the name and the reputation can directly impact the success, or lack thereof, that the business might enjoy. In 1982 someone in the Chicago area tampered with Tylenol, putting cyanide into Tylenol capsules. Seven people died from use of the adulterated product, and Johnson & Johnson, the maker of Tylenol, promptly pulled Tylenol from the market. Many experts believed that Tylenol would never again be a significant product in the pain relief market because of the harm done to its name by the deaths attributed to the product, the fear of using the product generated by these deaths, and the surrounding publicity. However, Johnson & Johnson believed in the product and in the reputation of both the product and the company. Johnson & Johnson developed a tamper-resistant package for the product, and reintroduced it to the market in its new package. Despite the misgivings of many experts, Tylenol quickly regained 70% of its previous market share within five months of reintroducing the product: Its market share had dropped from 37% of the market prior to the scare to a low of 7%.[2] Tylenol continues to maintain a significant share of the pain relief market to this day. One reason for this rebound was the public perception of the product and the parent company, both of which had strong reputations and were highly regarded by the public. The "good name" of Tylenol and of Johnson & Johnson had a significant positive impact in this situation. Its handling of the situation contributed to the positive perception of the brand and the company.

For an entrepreneur there is often an "overlap" between his name and reputation and the name and reputation of the venture he is creating and/or operating. Recall from the discussion in Chapter 6 concerning the "five C's of credit" that the fifth C is character. Lenders want to know about the character of the entrepreneur before extending him credit, and will consider the personal impression made by the entrepreneur, based in part on the education and experience of the entrepreneur, and also on the references provided. While lenders and investors will take the time to make these sorts of inquiries, most customers or clients will not have the time or the means to do so. Instead, customers and clients must rely on appearances, and upon the general public perception of the entrepreneur, the enterprise he operates, and the goods or services he provides. Lenders and investors will look closely at some, if not all, of the five C's in deciding whether to lend or invest money in the venture, but customers and clients do not have this luxury. This, in turn, means that it is extremely important for the entrepreneur to protect his name and reputation and the name and reputation of the venture and its goods and/or services.

Many entrepreneurs are involved in a franchising arrangement, either as the franchisor or the franchisee. A standard clause in a franchise agreement involves restrictions on the activities of the franchisee, with a possible loss of the franchise if the franchisee engages in certain prohibited types of behavior. One reason for this emphasis on the conduct of the franchisee is that a few "bad actors" can spoil the value of the brand and franchise for the franchisor and for other franchisees. One or two poorly run stores can have a significant negative impact on others, and the franchisor has a duty to protect its good name for the benefit of all concerned. Reputation matters in a franchising arrangement, and every franchised location potentially impacts on every other location.

The reputation of a business has value that generates profits.[3] Very often the reputation of an entrepreneurial business is closely tied and identified with the reputation of the entrepreneur who launches the venture. This means that the entrepreneur needs to develop, and if necessary defend, a strong reputation for himself and for the venture. The entrepreneur will need to be aware of attacks on his reputation, most likely in the form of **defamation**; attacks on the reputation of the venture, probably in the form of product **disparagement**; and attempts by competitors to "steal" the value of that reputation by **palming off** goods produced by those competitors as being goods produced by the entrepreneur's venture. He will also need to be aware how product liability claims affect that reputation and the financial well-being of the venture.

DEFAMATION

An entrepreneur's reputation can be harmed by comments or communications made by others who hold the entrepreneur up to ridicule or allege improper or inappropriate conduct. The person making these comments and allegations may be a jealous competitor, a disgruntled employee, an unhappy customer, or anyone else who has a grudge—real or imagined—against the entrepreneur. However, once made these comments or allegations may take on lives of their own, being repeated or passed on by means of the "grapevine" or the "rumor mill." In any event, these communications may constitute defamations, and if so, the entrepreneur may have legal recourse, suing the party or parties who have communicated the information.

Defamation, often referred to as defamation of character, is an intentional tort (civil wrong) for which the victim, the defamed party, can sue the defaming party for damages. Defamation is "the offense of injuring a person's character, fame, or reputation by false and malicious statements."[4] There must be three parties involved to have a defamation: the defaming party, the defamed party, and a third person to whom the defamatory information is communicated. There must be a communication between the defaming party and the third person, the information communicated must be false (truth is an absolute defense to a charge of defamation), and the information must injure the character, fame, or reputation of the victim. For example, if a disgruntled employee confronts the entrepreneur in his office, with no one else within earshot, and accuses the entrepreneur of lying about the job or cheating the employee out of a bonus, no defamation has occurred, even if the accusations are untrue. There was no communication to a third party, an essential element for defamation. Similarly, if the employee communicated these accusations to a third party and the accusations were true, there would be no defamation since truth is an absolute defense. However, if the employee communicated these accusations to a third person and the accusations were untrue, the employee would have defamed the entrepreneur and could be sued for the harm caused to the reputation of the entrepreneur.

There are two types of defamation, **libel** and **slander**. Libel is defamation in print, writing, pictures, signs, or other enduring forms. Libel is often considered the more serious type of defamation because of its enduring nature. The statement is made in a manner that allows others to see it, read it, or hear it multiple times, and it remains "out there" for all the world to see, often long after the initial communication was made. When a libel occurs, the victim will usually seek damages for the defamation, and will seek to have an apology for and/or a retraction of the publication of the information. The Internet has significantly increased the severity of libel. A libelous statement posted on the Internet may be picked up by others and posted to a multitude of sites, making any effective retraction or deletion of the communication virtually impossible. A libelous communication posted on one or more popular sites such as YouTube may be seen by literally millions of people, especially if the initial posting is copied or downloaded and reposted or forwarded by browsers who found it interesting or amusing. Many of these people will have no malice toward the entrepreneur and may not even know who he is, but many of the people who see the posting will assume that it is true because it was on the Internet. The ensuing harm to the entrepreneur's reputation may well be immeasurable and irreversible.

Slander, by contrast, is spoken defamation. When a defaming party makes an oral accusation to or in front of a third person that falsely harms the reputation of the entrepreneur, the defaming party has committed slander. However, once the statement is made it is finished. There is but one fleeting comment, not something in an enduring form that can be viewed and reviewed into the future. As a result, slander is often viewed as less severe than libel. However, the slanderous comment may contain a devastatingly negative allegation that does a great deal of harm to the entrepreneur, so the impact can be as great as — or in some instances even greater than — a libelous statement. Slander is more difficult to prove in court than libel. In order to prove that a slander occurred, the entrepreneur will need to have one or more witnesses testify as to what the defaming party said. There is no tangible evidence of the communication as would be present in a libel case, and the credibility of the witnesses becomes an essential part of establishing the tort of defamation when slander is involved.

Given these potential problems, how is an entrepreneur to protect his reputation from the harm that defamation can cause? Obviously, there is no guarantee that others will not make comments that are harmful to his reputation, or that false allegations which portray him in a negative light or cause embarrassment to his good name will be prevented. Perhaps there are only two things that the entrepreneur can do to protect himself to any appreciable degree from the negative impact of any defamatory comments. First, he needs to conduct his life, both personal and professional, in an appropriate manner. The entrepreneur needs to act in a positive manner in his personal life. He needs to act in an appropriate manner when out in public, and he needs to be scrupulously professional in his business affairs. He should, to the extent feasible, be active in civic organizations, and he should treat his employees and his customers as he would like to be treated by an employer or another business person. He should also be aware of public communications that refer to him or to his business, and if there are any negative connotations in these communications he needs to determine whether these negative connotations are justified. If so, he needs to address his conduct, or the conduct of his venture, to remove the negative implications and provide a more positive image. Second, he needs to be willing to take legal action against any defamatory comments that he deems unmerited, preferably seeking an apology or a retraction, as well. He should discuss possible litigation with his attorney. Any litigation may result in additional publicity and the repeating of the defamatory remarks to his detriment. Third, he can launch a public relations campaign to improve his image. However, most people will see through the public relations campaign if it is merely "window dressing" and not based on reality.

Another thing the entrepreneur may want to consider is exercising extreme caution in posting anything on the Internet that might cause harm to his reputation.

There are numerous examples of people who have posted things on Internet sites such as MySpace and FaceBook that, in hindsight, probably should not have been posted. What was meant to be humorous can sometimes turn out to be misconstrued by others. The entrepreneur needs to be aware that a reputation he spent years developing can be lost in an instant with one inappropriate act, and that to the public perception becomes reality. If the public perceives the entrepreneur as untrustworthy, he *becomes* untrustworthy despite any and all prior actions that indicated he is of high character and deserving of trust!

DISPARAGEMENT

The reputation of an entrepreneur's product or service is likely to be more important than the reputation of the entrepreneur, especially if the enterprise has been in existence for a while. Once the entrepreneur has the venture "up and running," the public perception of the *venture* becomes paramount, which makes protection of the venture's reputation extremely important for the entrepreneur. Research shows that customers "are most likely to do business with people or organizations [they] trust. And . . . trust is built on reputation in the marketplace."[5] The reputation of a business directly affects the profitability of the business, and a loss of reputation will normally lead to a loss in profits.

An entrepreneur can do a great deal to build a positive reputation for his business, but the process is not completely under his control. He can implement quality control standards, ensuring to the greatest extent possible that the enterprise produces only well-made and well-designed products, or provides only quality services. He can emphasize customer service, taking positive steps to ensure that customers are treated with respect and made to feel as if the business cares about them. He can use public relations releases that highlight the positive things the venture is doing and present the enterprise in the most flattering light possible. All of these things should enhance the positive reputation of the firm, and the entrepreneur should make an effort to incorporate each of these into the venture's operations. However, even if the entrepreneur does all of these things, he is not protected from disparagement, and this disparagement might be sufficient to negate all of the positive steps designed to improve the firm's reputation.

Disparagement is "a false and injurious statement that discredits or detracts from the reputation of another's property, product, or business. To recover in tort for disparagement, the plaintiff must prove that the statement caused a third party to take some action resulting in specific pecuniary loss to the plaintiff."[6] When a person —whether customer, competitor, or other—makes a false statement that harms the reputation of the entrepreneur's products or services, that person has *disparaged* the products or services. If this false statement causes financial harm or losses for the enterprise, the enterprise can file suit seeking damages just as the entrepreneur could do personally if his name or reputation was defamed. There is a problem with recovering damages due to disparagement, however. Most courts deciding disparagement cases have concluded that the plaintiff must show actual malice in order to prevail. The courts apparently view a business as a "public figure" rather than a "private person" (a business entity is usually treated as a legal person), and the courts have applied the same requirements in proving disparagement as they require when a public figure sues for defamation.[7] Thus, in order to prevail in a claim of disparagement, the entrepreneur must show that:

1. A false and injurious statement was made.
2. The statement discredited or detracted from the reputation of his business.
3. The enterprise suffered financial losses due to the publication of the statement.
4. The person making the statement did so with malice toward the entrepreneur and/or the venture.

This is a significant burden of proof that makes establishing disparagement difficult; it may discourage the entrepreneur from seeking redress when he believes that his venture has been the victim of disparaging comments that have negatively affected its reputation.

Given the importance of the reputation of the venture, and considering the difficulty of establishing that a disparagement has occurred, what should the entrepreneur do to develop a positive reputation for the enterprise while minimizing the potential impact of any false and injurious statements that may be made by others? The **Reputation Institute**,[8] a private advisory and research firm that specializes in corporate reputation management, recognizes four key principles in developing a firm's **reputation quotient** (RQ). These four principles are set out in Table 10.1. The Reputation Institute states that "it's common knowledge that a good 50 percent of most companies' market value is made up of what accountants call intangible assets that are not on the balance sheet . . . reputation is one of those assets."[9] The Institute views reputation as a magnet that can

TABLE 10.1 Four Principles of a Reputation Quotient	
Characteristic	*Elements*
Distinctiveness	Brand positioning; marketing efforts; creation of an image in the minds of consumers and stakeholders.
Authenticity	The firm must be able to "walk the talk," being genuine by acting in accordance with the image created; media relations, governance, and performance must all genuinely be in accord with the image.
Transparency	The venture must be transparent in its business affairs. Communication is essential and the firm must strive to develop a visible presence with the media and its stakeholders.
Consistency	The enterprise needs to develop a core theme and then focus its actions and communications around that theme. This will, over time, create a belief in the customers and stakeholders that they know what to expect of the venture.

attract resources, and believes that a strong reputation directly affects the ability of a firm to do well financially. An entrepreneur who desires an enhanced reputation for his venture should therefore consider building a strong reputation by developing a positive RQ, and this can be done by applying the four principles set out by the Institute as a means of improving—and protecting—the reputation of the enterprise.

The four principles of an RQ show that "it's all about the message."[10] By extension, the venture's customer and stakeholder perceptions become the venture's reputation, and once this reputation is established, it becomes very difficult to destroy it, so long as the entrepreneur adheres to the four principles and remains vigilant. In order to establish the message, the foundation for the RQ, and the basis of the reputation, the entrepreneur needs to determine *what* the message should be. He must then *construct* the message through a communication plan that gets the message out to the public. Finally, he must *orchestrate* the message so that the name of the firm becomes synonymous with the message.[11] He also should use care so that his advertising message does not conflict with the image that he is attempting to establish. A message that is considered too sexy or too chauvinistic, for example, may create a negative image of the venture in the minds of the targeted customers, thus defeating the ultimate goal of the advertising.

PALMING OFF

It can be a daunting task to start an enterprise and nurture and develop the business when an entrepreneur is facing fair competition. It becomes much more difficult when the entrepreneur is forced to deal with *unfair* competition. For example, a competitor may unfairly compete with the entrepreneur by "palming off" its goods, simultaneously taking part of the entrepreneur's market and, normally, harming the reputation of the entrepreneur and/or his venture. A business is guilty of palming off under either of two distinct circumstances:

1. The business represents that the goods offered to the public are goods produced by another—likely more reputable—firm.
2. The business sells goods produced by another firm—again, likely more reputable or better known—and claims that it produced the goods.

In the first circumstance, the business is palming off its goods by claiming that the goods, presumably inferior or less well-known, are produced by a competing firm, presumably one with a better reputation for quality or a more recognized name. Suppose that a competing firm begins to sell goods, claiming that the entrepreneur's enterprise is the manufacturer. If the competing firm is producing merchandise of lesser quality, and consumers believe that they are purchasing goods produced by entrepreneur's firm, the reputation of the alleged manufacturer, the entrepreneur's firm, will be harmed by the public's dissatisfaction with the goods and the perception of a lowering of quality. For example, if a retailer claims to be selling a particular brand of computer but in reality is selling a lower quality computer, which is housed in a case very similar to the case of the particular brand, the retailer is palming off the computers it sells. However, if this same retailer is only selling the lower quality computers without claiming that they are selling the higher quality brand, and some consumers are confused about the manufacturer owing to the similarity in the cases, palming off probably cannot be proven, and the retailer has not committed an unfair trade practice.[12]

In the second circumstance, the competitor's business is guilty of palming off because it is claiming that it produced or manufactured the goods although, in reality, the goods were produced by the entrepreneur's firm. The competing business is using the quality of the entrepreneur's firm to enhance its own reputation by claiming that it produced the goods, when it fact it has only resold the goods, probably after repackaging them to hide the identity of the entrepreneur's firm, the true manufacturer. For example, suppose that a firm purchased several barrels of a well-known wine, bottled the wine, and then labeled the bottles with the name of the purchaser rather than the vintner. Selling this wine under the name of the purchaser would constitute palming off—to the detriment of the vintner and, potentially, benefit of the purchaser.

When an entrepreneur believes that his enterprise is the victim of a competitor palming off its goods to the entrepreneur's detriment, he needs to seek legal relief as quickly as is practical. The entrepreneur needs to seek a preliminary injunction against the competitor, alleging that the competitor is palming off its goods to the detriment of the entrepreneur. If the entrepreneur seeks the preliminary injunction quickly enough, and the court issues the injunction, the matter may well be resolved. The party accused of palming off will have to either change its packaging or quit selling the product, either of which will end the confusion among consumers and, thus, protect the reputation of the entrepreneur.[13]

Palming off is not just a tort based on unfair competition; it is also closely related to intellectual property laws and protections, topics to be discussed in Chapter 11. The discussion of these topics will provide additional methods the entrepreneur can use to protect his venture's name and reputation.

PRODUCT LIABILITY

An entrepreneur will want his venture to establish a reputation for quality in its goods or services. If the customers believe that the enterprise produces goods of high quality or provides excellent services, the value and reputation of the firm will be enhanced, allowing it to develop brand loyalty. However, if the goods produced by the enterprise are perceived to be of low quality, or if the services provided are viewed as below average, the venture will have a reduced reputation with a corresponding loss of value. This means that the entrepreneur needs to emphasize quality in the production of the goods or provision of the services. But even when there is an emphasis on quality, some products will be produced that are not "up to par," and some of the services provided will not meet the expectations of the customer. So long as these situations are the exception rather than the rule, the reputation of the enterprise will not be unduly harmed. But if poor quality of the goods or services is seen as the norm, the firm will suffer a serious setback in both reputation and value. The one thing most likely to cause this sort of perception is a lawsuit alleging product liability and the publicity of the lawsuit itself. For example, the European food producer Nestle has recently encountered a serious legal problem due to tainted products produced at one of its facilities in China. "Tests in Taiwan have found minor doses of the industrial chemical melamine in milk powders produced in China . . . and those products are being withdrawn."[14] At least four children have died and more than 50,000 have been sickened by the contaminated milk powder, and civil suits have been filed in the case. While Nestle is not an entrepreneurial venture, similar cases could involve an entrepreneurship, which is not likely to have the resources that Nestle has to settle the cases or effectively defend itself in such a case. Suppose that an entrepreneur opens a toy store. He is able to purchase a number of very popular toys from various manufacturers, including Mattel[15] and Fisher-Price,[16] and he enjoys a great deal of success in his store from its initial opening. Then he gets sued because the toys he sold contained lead paint that resulted in harm to the children of several of his customers. The fact that he may be able to subsequently recover from the manufacturer of the toys who sold them to him will be little solace, especially if the lawsuits he is facing force him out of business before he is able to recoup his losses caused by this initial imposition of product liability.

WARRANTIES

Product liability can be based on a breach of warranty or on negligence, or, in some circumstances, strict liability can be imposed without any showing of fault. Warranties are a part of the sales contract when goods are sold. Some warranties, called express warranties, are created by the seller through the circumstances surrounding the sale of the goods. Express warranties arise when a seller creates a belief in the mind of the buyer as to the character, quality, or nature of the goods. The seller does not have to intend to create a warranty, nor does he have to use words such as warranty or guarantee in order to create these warranties. Pre- or post-contract discussions or comments can be viewed as creating such a belief in the mind of the buyer and, thus, as giving express warranties to the buyer. This means that entrepreneurs need to be careful in their conversations with customers, especially when making statements that are likely to be viewed as factual. While statements of opinion ("This is a good car.") are not likely to be seen as creating a warranty, statements of fact ("This car will get 30 miles per gallon in city driving.") will normally be viewed as part of the contract and, thus, as express warranties. Since the seller creates these warranties, he can also limit or restrict them in the same discussions. Suppose that the entrepreneur decides that he wants to give a warranty on his product but does not want to have the warranty extend too far into the future. He may decide to give the buyer an **express warranty** covering parts and labor needed to repair the product for six months. If he does so, he has warranted (guaranteed) the product for six months. After six months and one day the warranty expires, and any potential liability on the product under the express warranty ends.

Because express warranties only exist when they are given by the seller, the seller can limit or even prevent the existence of express warranties in the sale of goods through careful use of language. And since warranties carry the potential for liability, many sellers attempt to exclude *any* and *all* warranties when they enter into contracts for the sale of goods, through the use of language such as "there are no warranties, express or implied, in this contract." Before taking this approach, the entrepreneur should consider the impact on sales if he does not provide the warranties that are common in the industry and are being offered by the competition. The Uniform Commercial Code (UCC) provides for some **implied warranties** in the sale of goods (Article 2) as a matter of law. Depending on the circumstances of the sale and status of the parties, these implied warranties exist in the contract unless the buyer surrenders them: "surrender" often occurs through exclusionary language included in the contract by the seller. There are four possible implied warranties:

1. the warranty of title
2. the warranty against infringements
3. the warranty of merchantability
4. the warranty of fitness for a particular purpose

The breach of any of these warranties opens the entrepreneur to potential liability in a suit for breach of warranty for any harm suffered by the buyer. Warranty coverage also extends to some third parties who may be harmed by the product. Generally speaking, warranty protection runs to the buyer and to third persons who could reasonably be expected to use, consume, or be affected by the goods. At a minimum the protection will run to the buyer, and his or her family, household, and guests.[17] The scope and applicability of these implied warranties are set out in Table 10.2.

Excluding implied warranties is possible, but it requires the seller to be relatively specific; the exclusions should be in writing in order to provide the greatest protection in the event a buyer files suit alleging that one of these warranties was breached. Care must be exercised in attempting to exclude a warranty, even if the exclusion is in writing. The courts will, on occasion, examine such exclusions very carefully, and if the exclusions are found to be unconscionable, the courts will refuse to enforce the exclusion. In *Walker v. American Cyanamid Co.*,[18] the court refused to enforce a warranty exclusion contained on the label of an herbicide sold by American Cyanamid, ruling that it was both procedurally and substantively unconscionable.[19]

The Magnuson-Moss Warranty Act[20] may also affect the entrepreneur. Magnuson-Moss requires a merchant selling goods to consumers to make warranty information available to the consumer *prior* to entering into the contract. The merchant can choose to offer the buyer a **full warranty**, a **limited warranty**, or *no* warranty. If the merchant provides a written warranty, he may not exclude or

TABLE 10.2 Implied Warranties in the Sale of Goods		
Warranty	*Warrants (Assures) (Scope)*	*Given by (Applicability)*
Warranty of title	The buyer will get good title; the title transfer was rightful; the goods are free of any encumbrances or liens of which the buyer was unaware.	All sellers, unless the seller uses specific language or the circumstances are such that the seller does not claim to have title *or* that the seller is only conveying such title as he may have.
Warranty against infringement	The buyer will receive goods free of the rightful claims of any third party by way of infringement or the like, but a buyer who furnishes specifications to the seller must hold the seller harmless (indemnify the seller for any losses) against any claims arising from compliance with the specifications.	A seller who is a merchant who regularly deals in goods of the kind being sold; any buyer who provides specifications to the seller for the production of goods.
Merchantability	The buyer will receive goods that are merchantable: the goods must be able to pass without objection in the trade under the contract description; the goods are fit for their normal and intended use; are adequately contained, packaged, and labeled; conform to the promises or affirmations made on the label, if any; and run within the variations permitted by the agreement.	Merchant sellers—sellers who regularly deal in goods of this kind *or* sellers who by their occupation hold themselves out as having knowledge or skills peculiar to the goods or practices involved *or* who employ agents or brokers who possesses such knowledge or skills.
Fitness for a particular purpose	The buyer will receive goods that are suitable for a particular, as opposed to a "normal," purpose *if* at the time of the contract the seller had reason to know the particular purpose the buyer intended and that the buyer is relying on the seller's skill or judgment to select or furnish suitable goods.	Any seller who knows of the circumstances, the reliance by the buyer, and the particular purpose, unless the seller excludes or modifies this warranty.

modify any of the implied warranties. He may, however, limit the time during which any implied warranties will apply *if he gives a limited warranty.* Thus, an entrepreneur who is selling consumer goods (goods intended for personal or household use) should choose to give a limited warranty, limiting the availability of the implied warranties to the same time period as the express warranties given in the contract.

The entrepreneur can exclude or limit warranty coverage of his products, and in so doing he will be limiting the potential liability that arises from a breach of warranty, but he will not be able to avoid all potential product liability claims through manipulation of warranty terms and provisions. Product liability can also be based on negligence or strict liability in tort. Remedies under these theories may well be broader, they often last longer, and they frequently lead to larger judgments for injured parties. Entrepreneurs need to be aware of the potential liability they face for injuries caused by their goods beyond the liabilities imposed under warranty law.

NEGLIGENCE

A business can be found liable to an injured consumer of its goods on the basis of negligence if the injured consumer can establish that the business was negligent in the construction or manufacturing of the product, in the design of the product, *or* in their failure to warn of known dangers or defects in the product. The entrepreneur should also realize that the law no longer requires privity of contract in order to establish that the seller has a duty to the buyer. This means that a negligence claim can be lodged by a remote party, one who may have purchased the goods from the original customer with whom the entrepreneur dealt, or even one who may have acquired the goods from someone more removed from the initial purchaser. The entrepreneur is required to provide goods that are reasonably safe for their intended use, and this requirement extends to users beyond the purchaser.

STRICT LIABILITY

Another possible source of liability facing the entrepreneur involves allegations of strict liability, also known as strict liability in tort. Under §402(A) of the *Restatement of Torts*, Second, strict liability is applied when a merchant sells a good that causes harm to a consumer or user, and the consumer is able to establish all of the following:

1. the product was sold in a defective condition
2. the product reached the user or consumer without a substantial change in its condition
3. the product was unreasonably dangerous to the user or consumer because of its defective condition

It is important to note that §402(A) applies only to "merchant sellers" and does not apply to "casual sellers" of goods. A merchant seller is a seller who "regularly deals" in goods of the kind involved in the transaction, and who can therefore be viewed as an expert in these goods. Thus, an individual who sells an item through an online auction site such as eBay is probably not subject to the provisions of §402(A), but an entrepreneur who sells his merchandise on such a site would potentially be subject to liability under §402(A), despite the venue used in making the sale. It is also important to remember that a merchant seller can be held liable despite the fact that he exercised due care in the manufacturing or production of the product, and he can be held liable even if the injured party did not purchase the product directly from the merchant seller.[21]

(1) Liability under §402(A) will attach only to a merchant seller, which the entrepreneur will be; (2) and only if he sells a "defective" product that is "unreasonably" dangerous to the consumer; and (3) the product reaches the consumer without any substantial change in its condition. If the consumer is injured using the product, and these three criteria are satisfied, the entrepreneur can be held liable even though he used all possible care in the production of the product, and even though there is no allegation or proof of negligence.

This basis for liability imposes a substantial potential burden on the manufacturer. The "defective condition unreasonably dangerous to the user or consumer," referred to in § 402(A) is often measured at the time the injury occurs and not at the time the product was produced. Thus, an entrepreneur who produces a product with a long useful life may face liability in the future due to technological advances in the industry after production of the product but before the product is removed from service. The entrepreneur can also be found liable under this section for defects in design or construction, or for failing to warn the consumer of a known danger commonly faced when using the product.

Liability in this area is, or can be, limited by the state's *statute of repose*, which operates in somewhat the same manner as a statute of limitations. In the product liability area, a statute of repose establishes a time limit for how long a manufacturer faces potential liability for a product. For example, if the state has a 10-year statute of repose, a manufacturer—including an entrepreneur involved in manufacturing—can only be sued under product liability for injuries that occur within 10 years after the product is sold or installed. If a state has a longer period in its statute of repose, obviously the manufacturer faces potential liability for a longer period. If a state's statute of repose does not address product liability, there are no statutory guidelines for the length of time during which the manufacturer may be held liable.

CONCLUSIONS

A firm's reputation is a key factor in the firm's success. For an entrepreneur who is launching an enterprise, it is extremely important to build a good reputation in order to give the venture its best chance of success. Obviously, the goods or services the venture provides must be of sufficient quality that customers will want to purchase them, and they must be priced in a manner that is consistent with their quality and their niche in the market. Assuming that the entrepreneur has exercised reasonable diligence (met his "due diligence"[22] obligations) and that his venture is providing goods or services of adequate quality and appropriate price, he needs to take steps to secure a positive reputation and to provide a structure for preserving that reputation.

In 1998 the Reputation Institute and Harris Interactive conducted extensive research while developing a standardized instrument for measuring perceptions of companies across industries, and also with different stakeholders.[23] They found that people base their perceptions of businesses on one or more of 20 attributes, which can be sorted into six dimensions. These dimensions and attributes are set out in Table 10.3. One result of this research was a finding that there is a hidden cost associated with a lower reputation. Firms with lower reputations not only tend to have fewer customers, but they also have difficulty attracting investors, both of which lead to a lower market value. Entrepreneurs need to treat the reputation of the venture as a key component of the business and take steps to protect and enhance that reputation as an integral part of the overall operation of the enterprise.

If the entrepreneur follows the guidelines set out by the Reputation Institute, he has an excellent chance of developing a good reputation. He will then need to be concerned about protecting that reputation, which can best be accomplished by acting in a professional manner and by exercising reasonable diligence in watching the enterprise and its competition. He will need to be aware of any efforts to defame his name and reputation, or to disparage the venture's goods or services. The entrepreneur will also need to be alert to any attempts by a competitor to palm off its (probably inferior) goods as being produced by the

TABLE 10.3 Six Dimensions of Reputation	
Dimension	*Attributes*
Emotional Appeal	Perception of the business: how much the business is liked, admired, and respected.
Products and Services	Perception of the quality, innovation, value, and reliability of the firm's goods and services.
Financial Performance	Perception of the firm's profitability, prospects, and risks.
Vision and Leadership	Perception of the clarity of the firm's vision and the strength of its leadership.
Workplace Environment	Perception of how well the firm is managed, the quality of its employees, and the work environment of the firm.
Social Responsibility	Perception of the firm's ethics and "good citizenship" based on the perception of its dealings with the community, the environment, and how its employees are perceived.

Source: Fombrun, Charles J., and Christopher B. Foss, "The Reputation Quotient, Part 1: Developing a Reputation Quotient," *The Gauge*, Vol. 14, No. 3 (May 14, 2001).

entrepreneur's business, or to resell the venture's goods, claiming that the competitor was the producer of those goods.

If the venture is selling consumer goods, the entrepreneur should provide "limited warranties" for its products, and in the limited warranties he should restrict the coverage and protections of the implied warranties to the same time period as he is willing to give for his express warranties. If he does not so limit the coverage of the implied warranties, the warranty of merchantability will continue to apply for a "reasonable time," which is likely to be determined by an arbitrator or a jury.

The entrepreneur will also want to include warning labels on any products that the venture produces if there are any known dangers, as well as warning against known misuses of the product. Despite any and every precaution the entrepreneur and his venture may take in producing and marketing the product, there will be consumers who will find some "use" not anticipated for the product that may well cause damage to the product and harm to the consumer. Labels containing warnings about known dangers, including known misuses, or abuses of the product, lessen the likelihood of the entrepreneur being held liable in these situations.

In protecting his reputation and that of his venture, the entrepreneur should consider the application questions set out in the box below:

Application Questions

1. Is the entrepreneur at risk that his competitors will "palm off" his goods? What can he do to minimize the likelihood that "palming off" will occur?

2. What steps can the entrepreneur take to assure the quality of his goods or services?

3. Is the entrepreneur selling consumer goods? If so, what can he do to avoid strict liability?

4. What type of label or warnings will help the entrepreneur reduce his liability?

Summary

The development and protection of a good reputation is extremely important for any business enterprise, but especially for an entrepreneurial venture. A good reputation can help to generate profits, make it easier to raise funds, and enhance customer loyalty. An entrepreneur should dedicate a significant amount of time and energy to building and preserving his reputation and that of his venture.

The reputation of an entrepreneur or his venture can be harmed by verbal "attacks" on him as an individual or by attacks on the venture. Defamation involves communication to one or more third persons of false and injurious information about a person that holds the victim up to ridicule or harms his good name. Defamation that takes an enduring or continuing form, such as a writing, a picture, or an audio recording, is libel. An oral communication that defames a person is called *slander.* Both libel and slander are intentional torts, and the victim of either may file suit seeking damages as well as any other appropriate remedies.

Disparagement is also a tort, based on the communication of false and injurious information about the goods or services provided by a business. Disparagement is more difficult to prove because the entrepreneur will need to show that the false communication was made, that it harmed the reputation of the business, that the business suffered a financial loss due to the communication of the false information, and that the communication was done with malice toward the business and/or the entrepreneur.

Palming off occurs when another person provides goods or services that are claimed to be provided by the entrepreneur's firm when, in fact, they are provided by another firm. This other firm is attempting to benefit from the name and reputation of the entrepreneur's venture, while providing goods or services that are likely to be inferior. Palming off can also occur when another firm purchases the goods of the entrepreneur's enterprise and then resells those goods in the name of the purchasing, or second, firm, creating a belief that the second firm produced the goods when, in reality, it merely purchased them from the entrepreneur's firm and repackaged them.

Product liability arises when a good sold by the enterprise causes harm to the buyer of the good or the enterprises breaches a warranty connected to the sale. There are two types of warranties: express warranties, which are given by the seller in the contract, and implied warranties, which are given by operation of law when certain conditions exist in the sale of the goods.

An entrepreneur can also face potential product liability due to negligence in packaging, design, or manufacture of the goods; or he can be found strictly liable for selling a consumer good containing a defect which makes it unreasonably dangerous as produced and causes harm to a consumer when used.

Key Terms

defamation	limited warranty
disparagement	palming off
express warranty	Reputation Institute
full warranty	reputation quotient
implied warranty	slander
libel	

End-of-Chapter Questions

1. What is the difference between defamation and disparagement? If a false and injurious statement about an entrepreneur and his venture is communicated to others, is the communication more likely to be treated as a defamation or as a disparagement? Why?

2. How does the creation of an image for a venture through the development of a message relate to the establishment of a reputation? How does the message affect the "reputation quotient" of the venture?
3. Is the sale of a product by a retailer who purchased goods from the wholesaler/entrepreneur and then resold them to consumers a "palming off" of the product? Explain your answer.
4. Why would an entrepreneur be well advised to offer limited warranties on consumer goods he is selling to consumers rather than full warranties? Why should he bother to distinguish between a full warranty and a limited warranty?
5. What is an express warranty? How do opinions expressed by the seller during contract negotiations affect the existence of express warranties in that contract?
6. What must an injured consumer be able to prove in order to successfully initiate a claim against an enterprise, seeking damages for harm suffered based on strict liability?
7. What should an entrepreneur do to develop and protect the reputation of the enterprise he has launched?

Suggested Activities

1. Visit the Web site of the Reputation Institute and look at the information about the reputation quotient. Then determine how and to what extent the six dimensions of reputation relate to the development of an RQ.
2. Using a legal resource, such as Lexis or Westlaw, locate a product liability case involving a product similar to your own. Read the case. How does it inform your decisions about manufacturing and labeling your product? (If you are providing a service, look for a case about a product you will use in your venture.)

Notes

1. Lord Jeffrey, found at http://www.brainyquote.com/quotes/authors/l/lord_ jeffrey.html
2. "Companies in Crisis—What to do when it all goes wrong," Corporate Social Responsibility News and Resources, found at http://www.mallenbaker.net/ csr/CSRfiles/ crisis02.html
3. McCutchen, Phil, "Three Steps to Improve Company RQ (Reputation Quotient) for Better Profitability," SearchWarp.com, found at http://searchwarp.com/ swa8074.htm
4. *Black's Law Dictionary*, 7th edition (1999).
5. McCutchen, "Three Steps to Improve Company RQ."
6. *Black's Law Dictionary*, 7th edition (1999).
7. In the landmark case of *New York Times Co. v. Sullivan*, 376 U.S. 254 (1964), the court ruled that there must be a showing of malice before a public figure could recover damages for an alleged libel. Malice has a special meaning as defined by this case and its progeny.
8. Founded in 1997 by Dr. Charles Fombrun, Professor Emeritus of the Stern School at New York University, The Reputation Institute conducts research

and offers advice to firms seeking better reputations. Additional information can be found at http://www.reputationinstitute.com/index

9. McCutchen, "Three Steps to Improve Company RQ."

10. *Id.*

11. *Id.*

12. See, e.g., *Sears, Roebuck & Co. v. Stiffel Co.*, 376 U.S. 225 (1964), in which Sears produced a pole lamp that was virtually identical to a lamp sold by Stiffel and then sold the lamp for substantially less than a Stiffel lamp. The court found that since Sears did not claim that the lamps it sold were Stiffel lamps, Sears was not guilty of palming off.

13. "Passing off," IP/IT-Update (March 5, 2004), found at http:// www.ipit-update.com/passingoff.htm. "Passing off" in the United Kingdom is the same as "palming off" in the United States.

14. "Nestle Milk Products Are Recalled in Taiwan," *Quality News Today*, International Herald-Tribune (October 3, 2008), found at http://www.asq.org/qualitynews/qnt/execute/displaySetup?newsID=4787

15. "Mattel Recalls More Toys Due to Lead Hazard," FindLaw, found at http://commonlaw.findlaw.com/2007/09/mattel-recalls-.html

16. "Fisher-Price Toys Recalled Due to Lead Hazard," FindLaw, found at http://commonlaw.findlaw.com/2007/08/fisher-price-to.html

17. UCC §2-318.

18. 948 P.2d 1123 (Idaho 1997)

19. Walker farms purchased an herbicide to use on its grain crops after being assured that the herbicide would not harm the potato crops that Walker would be planting later, in his normal crop rotation. An American Cyanamid representative said that it was okay to use the herbicide on potatoes, and the label on the product stated that potatoes could be planted in rotation after spraying with the herbicide. However, the label contained a warranty exclusion and disclaimer that, among other things, limited damages to direct damages (the cost of the herbicide) and attempted to exclude the warranties of fitness and of merchantability. The court upheld liability for the manufacturer.

20. 15 U.S.C. §2301 et seq.

21. *Restatement* (Second) *of Torts*, §402(A).

22. "Due diligence" is the measure of prudence, activity, or care that is expected from a reasonable and prudent person under the circumstances. This term is often associated with the duties of directors of a corporation in carrying out their duties, or in reference to a stock broker. Reasonable diligence or due care have basically the same meaning without the possible confusion with the conduct of directors or brokers.

23. Fombrun, Charles J., and Christopher B. Foss, "The Reputation Quotient, Part 1: Developing a Reputation Quotient," *The Gauge*, 14, (3) (May 14, 2001).

CHAPTER 11

PROTECTING WHAT MAKES THE VENTURE UNIQUE

The road to business success is paved by those who continually strive to produce better products or services. It does not have to be a great technological product like television. Ray Kroc of McDonald's fame did it with a simple hamburger.[1]

INTRODUCTION

A successful entrepreneur is often the one who sees a need for goods or services that is not being satisfied, or who sees a better way to provide the goods and services offered by her competitors. An entrepreneur needs to develop a "hook," something that makes her venture unique, and thus attracts—and helps to retain—customers. Once she has developed this hook, she needs to make certain that she takes steps to protect it from competitors. While imitation may be the sincerest form of flattery, when that imitation is undertaken by a competing firm it may lead to a loss of customers, especially if the competing firm is a larger and better-known enterprise. Thus, it becomes imperative for the entrepreneur not only to develop a hook, but also to devise ways to protect her unique product or method from usurpation by her competition. Fortunately, there are various methods of protection available, including statutory provisions at the state and federal levels, as well as a number of protections provided by treaties in the international environment. Many of these protections apply to the **intellectual property** of the entrepreneur.

INTELLECTUAL PROPERTY

"Intellectual property refers to creations of the mind: inventions, literary and artistic works, and symbols, names, images, and designs used in commerce."[2] There are two broad types of intellectual property: industrial property, which includes **patents**, **trademarks**, **service marks**, designs, and inventions; and **copyright**, which includes literary and artistic works. The importance of intellectual property is reflected by the fact that the U.S. Constitution contains specific reference to the need for formal protection of such property: "Congress shall have Power . . . To promote the Progress of Science and the useful Arts, by securing for limited Times to Authors and Inventors the exclusive Right to their respective Writings and Discoveries."[3] Congress has, in fact, exercised this power by regularly enacting federal statutes governing the various areas included under the umbrella of "intellectual property," as well as by ratifying various treaties that provide international recognition and protection of these areas. In addition to these federal statutory protections, numerous areas of state law also provide protection for intellectual property. Palming off, discussed in Chapter 10, is a violation of state law, and often involves a patent or trademark **infringement**. **Trade secrets** are protected under state law both directly and indirectly: directly by statutes addressing industrial espionage and indirectly by upholding contracts that include non-disclosure clauses and restrictive covenants. (Contracts will be discussed in more detail in Chapter 12.)

Intellectual property, properly managed, can help make a venture unique; it can provide legal protection for the venture if a competitor infringes on the intellectual property. If the intellectual property is not properly managed, a competitor may be able to infringe with impunity. As a result, another firm may be able to "poach" the ideas or inventions the entrepreneur has developed, without the expenditure of capital, and then exploit the market, to the financial detriment of the entrepreneur. This makes proper management of intellectual property a priority for the entrepreneur. There are various types of intellectual property, each with its own unique rules and protections. The most important of these intellectual property areas are briefly described in Table 11.1.

PATENTS

A patent is a federally granted proprietary right given to the inventor for the fruits of her invention. Patents can be either *utility* patents or *design* patents. Utility patents, the more common type, cover the functional parts of machines or processes or the software used to drive machines; design patents are more cosmetic in nature, covering the appearance of articles, for example, a chair. The patent holder has the exclusive right to make, use, or sell the invention for a period of 20 years for utility patents, or 14 years for design patents, from the date of the patent application. (Since utility patents are much more common, the rest of the patent discussion will only deal with utility patents, unless otherwise noted.) A patent gives the patent owner the right to *exclude* others from making, using, or

TABLE 11.1   Types of Intellectual Property

Intellectual Property	Who Is Protected	Length of Protection
Patent	The person who files for and receives the patent from the U.S. Patent and Trademark Office; licensees of the patent holder	20 years for a utility patent, 14 years for a design patent Non-renewable
Trademark or Service Mark	The person registering the mark; licensees of the holder of the registered mark	10 years for the initial registration and 10 years for each renewal period. Unlimited renewals are possible
Trade Secret	The person who develops the trade secret	Undefined. So long as the secret remains a secret no one else can use it
Copyright	The author of an original work unless the author produced the original work as a "work for hire" The person who hired the author in a work for hire	If the author created the original work for himself or herself, the life of the author plus 70 year; if the work was produced as a "work for hire," the employer for whom the work was prepared owns the protection for the lesser of 95 years from its first publication or 120 years from its creation
Internet Domain Name	The person who registers the name or the person to whom he or she assigns it	Registration of a domain name is from 1 to 10 years, at the option of the registrant; registration is renewable at the expiration of the registration period; there is no limit in the number of renewals

Source: Courtesy of Daniel V. Davidson, © Daniel V. Davidson, 2009.

selling the invention for the entire 20-year patent period. Thus, a person who acquires a patent is granted a legal monopoly on the invention for 20 years in exchange for providing the Patent and Trademark Office (PTO) a full disclosure of the invention, how it is made, and what it does. After that 20-year period, the previously protected rights move into the **public domain**, becoming available to anyone and allowing competitors to copy it without any legal liability. However, the 20-year legal monopoly gives the entrepreneur/inventor an opportunity to exploit the market, building a brand name and establishing her niche in the field. In order to be patentable, an invention must satisfy certain criteria, as set out in Table 11.2.

The entrepreneur needs to apply for a patent within one year of her initial invention. Once she has applied, she can label her product as "patent pending," thereby giving notice to competitors that she has filed her application and that copying the invention may result in liability for infringement of the patent once it is issued. Once a patent has been issued, the entrepreneur needs to label her

TABLE 11.2 Criteria for Patenting an Invention	
The invention must fit within one of five classifications	1. Process type 2. Machine 3. Article of manufacture 4. Composition of matter 5. A new and useful improvement of one of the first four classifications
The invention must be new	The invention cannot be something that is already known or used by others; it cannot have been made, written about, or used by others anywhere in the world before the inventor invented it, and the patent must be applied for within one year of the invention.
The invention must be useful	There must be some utility for the invention, whether as a process, a machine, an article of manufacture, or a composition of matter.
The invention must be non-obvious	The invention must be something that a person of ordinary skill in the area would not have envisioned. (This is an extremely subjective criterion, which the PTO assesses after the fact—what others in the field or industry would have or could have envisioned before the inventor actually envisioned and built it.)

Source: Courtesy of Daniel V. Davidson, © Daniel V. Davidson, 2009.

product with the word "Patent" followed by the patent number. By doing so, she retains the right to sue infringers and, possibly, recover damages. Without providing such notice, she may not be able to recover damages from any infringers.

The PTO also provides for a provisional patent application (PPA), an intermediate step meant to provide some protection to the small enterprise or private inventor who invents something: It creates a one-year "grace period" before formally filing for a patent. The PPA allows the inventor to file what is basically a notification of *intent* to apply for a non-provisional patent; this allows the inventor to (a) label the product with "patent pending" and (b) take up to 12 months to file for the non-provisional patent. This 12-month period provides the entrepreneur/inventor an opportunity to test-market the product or explore the product's potential before undertaking the higher burden of formally filing for a patent; it also extends the entrepreneur's/inventor's patent protection for another year.[4] (A provisional patent application is available only for a utility patent: It cannot be used for a design patent.)

The PTO also issues patents for business methods, treating such business methods as new, useful, and non-obvious processes that are entitled to the same protection as would be afforded for the invention of a new piece of equipment. One of the earliest of these business methods patents was issued to Priceline.com for its "reverse auction" for airline tickets. While there is still a great deal of controversy over the issue of whether a business method should even be patentable, at this time the PTO *will* issue a patent for a business method if it meets the criteria. The courts have held that a business method can be patented, provided it "produces a 'useful, concrete, and tangible result.' . . . This renders it 'statutory subject matter,' meaning that it is eligible for patent protection as a business process even if the useful result is expressed in numbers, such as price, profit, percentage, cost, or loss."[5] Thus, an entrepreneur/inventor who develops a "new and improved" method of doing business may be able to obtain a patent on that method and then exclude others from emulating that method unless royalties are paid or a license is negotiated for her benefit.

It is important to remember that while a patent grants rights to the patent holder, it also imposes the burden of enforcing those rights on her. The PTO will not police the commercial world, looking for possible infringements, nor will it provide any technical or legal support if or when a patent case goes to trial. The entrepreneur/inventor must remain vigilant, and if she sees something that she believes infringes on her patent, she must take action to stop the infringement. The normal course of conduct is to seek an injunction to stop the infringing conduct, and also to seek damages from the infringing party. Another option is to obtain an injunction until such time as a licensing agreement can be reached, under which the patent owner collects royalties from the other party in exchange for the other party gaining the right to produce, use, and/or sell the patented item or process.

Key Point.   It is important to know how to get a patent. One excellent source is "How to get a Patent," from the USPTO, and found at http://www. uspto.gov/web/patents/howtopat.htm The USPTO also maintains a list of lawyers registered to practice before them at www.uspto.gov The entrepreneur should be wary since there are scam artists who prey on inventors.

One source indicated that a patent can cost anywhere from $4,000 to $8,000 but that the entrepreneur's attorney may be willing to work out a payment plan for her. For help in deciding whether to seek a patent, the entrepreneur should visit "Why Patent an Idea?" found at http://www.morebusiness.com/running_ your_business/marketing/d1007343402.brc

---

TRADEMARKS AND SERVICE MARKS

A trademark is a symbol, word, or design used to identify a business or a product.[6] A service mark "identifies and distinguishes a [business's] services and is given the same protections as a trademark."[7] (Since the legal protections afforded to the possessor of a trademark and a service mark are essentially identical, the discussion below will simply refer to trademarks.) Many trademarks have an intrinsic value since the reputation of the product and the brand loyalty that has been established by the business are reflected by the trademark, giving customers a sense of confidence and trust in products carrying the symbol. While an entrepreneur should be concerned first and foremost with developing a quality product and establishing her market position, she would be well advised to also give some thought to developing an appropriate trademark, preferably one that catches the eye and creates a positive reaction in customers. If the entrepreneur is not comfortable in designing her own trademark, there are numerous businesses that will design one for a fee.

Although registration is not legally required, the entrepreneur will also want to register her trademark with the PTO in order to have the greatest possible protection for her trademark. If she is already using the trademark, she can register it by filing a "use application." She can also file an "intent-to-use" application if she has designed a trademark but has not yet used it commercially. By registering the trademark the entrepreneur gains "ownership" of it, and the right to use it in the United States, and the right to prevent others from using the same trademark or one that is deceptively similar to the one she registered. If she does not register her trademark, and another firm is using a trademark that is the same or deceptively similar, she will have to resort to a lawsuit, and the court will have to determine which firm has superior rights to the trademark in question. The registration of a trademark is valid for 10 years, but the registration is renewable, and there is no maximum number of times it can be renewed. However, after the fifth renewal, but before the sixth, the entrepreneur will need to file an affidavit verifying that the trademark is still in use, otherwise the registration will expire.

Even if a trademark is registered, it can be lost under certain circumstances, that is, abandonment, improper licensing, assignment, and genericity.[8] A trademark is deemed to be abandoned if its use is discontinued by the owner, who does not intend to "resurrect" it. It will also be abandoned if the venture does not use the trademark for three consecutive years. If the entrepreneur allows another party to use the trademark through a license, as in a franchise agreement, and then she fails to provide proper supervision or require proper quality control, she may lose the trademark. Even if the trademark is not lost in this situation, the harm to the intrinsic value of the trademark may be substantial. Should the owner of the trademark assign the rights to the trademark to another party without a corresponding sale of assets, the trademark will be cancelled. Ironically, a trademark can also be lost when it is so effective that it becomes generically identified with a category of goods rather than with the particular good for which it was coined. When the trademarked name of a good becomes the generic name of the good in the minds of a majority of the public, the trademark is lost due to genericity. Examples of this include "Kleenex," now a generic name for facial tissue; "Aspirin," now a generic name for a type of pain reliever; and "Xerox," now a generic name for photocopy machines—although Xerox is fighting back by advertising, reminding people that Xerox is a trade name and that other manufacturers only produce photocopying machines. The entrepreneur needs to remain vigilant if she intends to preserve and protect her trademark. She needs to register it with the PTO, and she needs to take prompt action against any other businesses that use a deceptively similar trademark to identify their goods. She also needs to use the trademark as an adjective that describes her *specific* product rather than as a generic noun that describes a type of product! If the entrepreneur believes that her trademark is being infringed upon, she can seek legal remedies. Injunctive relief is available, and she can recover any damages that she can show, all profits the infringing party generated while infringing on the trademark, and her attorneys' fees and court costs.

TRADE SECRETS

An entrepreneur may develop a system or a method that may not be patentable, or for which she would prefer not to seek a patent. In these situations, the entrepreneur may choose to treat the system or method as a trade secret, opting not to make the information available to the public—even if there could be a valid patent and the right to exclusive use for 20 years. Customer lists are trade secrets if the information is not publicly available and the entrepreneur properly protects the information. Trade secrets are often an important component of a venture's intellectual property, and the entrepreneur will have the burden of protecting these secrets in order to preserve them and take advantage of the benefits that they provide.

Trade secrets can be protected by the entrepreneur using carefully drafted contracts, which include having non-disclosure clauses, and by treating the trade secrets as confidential within the operation of the enterprise. Both strategies should be used in order to have the greatest possible protection. A non-disclosure agreement is a clause in a contract in which the employee or contracting party agrees not to disclose confidential or privileged information, in exchange for some consideration received from the entrepreneur. (Consideration and other aspects of contract law will be discussed in Chapter 12.) The entrepreneur should not restrict the use of such an agreement to employees; rather, she should ask anyone with whom she discusses the protected material to sign a non-disclosure agreement. This includes friends and family! In order for the agreement to be legally enforceable, the entrepreneur must enter into a contract with the other party, which means that the other party will have to receive consideration, something of value, in exchange for the promise not to disclose the information. For friends and family a payment of some small amount of money (one dollar and other "good and valuable consideration") is likely to suffice. For an employee the consideration is that he will have a job if he agrees to sign the contract containing the clause. For a member of the board of directors (if or when there is a board of directors) the consideration is that he is receiving a seat on the board. For customers the consideration is the opportunity to do business with the venture. But regardless of the status of the other person, the entrepreneur will need to *give* something in order to *get* something, that being the right to enforce the contract and its clause.

The entrepreneur should also take steps to treat the information as confidential, thus showing the importance of the trade secret and her efforts to protect it and prevent disclosure to others. This can be done by, for example, dividing the production process so that no one person or department can access the entire procedure. Suppose that the venture involves a restaurant that is known for some secret recipes the entrepreneur brought into the restaurant. She may want to premix the herbs and spices before delivering them to the cooks in order to prevent the cooks from learning the combination of herbs and spices that have made the recipes so popular. Formulas should be treated as confidential and valuable assets; they should not be widely copied and distributed, and they should be kept under lock and key with limited access. Similarly, a new process should be guarded from "outside eyes," perhaps by denying tours of the facilities. A trade secret checklist is set out in Table 11.3.

The entrepreneur should work with her attorney to establish an effective trade secret protection program.

Trade secrets are also now protected by statute at both the federal and state levels. Federally the statutory protection is found in the Economic Espionage Act of 1996.[9] This act is intended to provide protection to the owners of trade secrets from the effect of industrial espionage. In order to qualify as a trade secret entitled to protection under this law, the owner must:

1. Take reasonable measures to keep the information secret.
2. The information must derive economic benefit, whether actual or potential, from not being generally known by or available to the public.[10]

Anyone convicted of a violation of the act can be imprisoned for up to 15 years, or can be fined up to $500,000, or both. Organizations found to have violated the act can be fined an amount of up to $5 million for a domestic organization and up to $10 million for a foreign organization. In addition, if a violation is proven in court, the court can order the forfeiture of any proceeds generated from the violation as well as any property used in committing the violation, thus taking away the proceeds and the property from the person found in violation.

TABLE 11.3   A Trade Secret Checklist
Does the venture have a trade secret?
If so, who within the enterprise needs to have access to this secret?
How can access be restricted to only those persons who need to have access?
What should the venture do to remind all of its employees that these areas are secret and must be treated confidentially?
Should a non-disclosure agreement (confidentiality agreement) by required of all employees?
What else can/should the venture do to protect its trade secrets?

These sanctions will be imposed criminally. The victim of the theft or misappropriation of the trade secret will usually be entitled to damages in a second suit, a civil suit, for the misappropriation, and all the damages suffered as a result.

The Uniform Trade Secrets Act (USTA) has been adopted by 46 states, the U.S. Virgin Islands, and the District of Columbia. (At this time, Massachusetts, North Carolina, New Jersey, and Texas have not adopted the act.[11]) This act provides a uniform definition of a trade secret, "as well as clarifying other aspects of the law, including how a trade secret is misappropriated and what remedies are available for violation of another's trade secret."[12] Whereas the federal statute is concerned primarily with criminal sanctions for the theft of trade secrets, the USTA is primarily concerned with providing civil remedies for the victims of such theft or misappropriation. Under the USTA, a trade secret is defined as:

> Information . . . that derives independent economic value, actual or potential, from not being generally well known to, and not being readily ascertainable by, other persons who can obtain economic value from its disclosure or use and which is the subject of efforts that are reasonable under the circumstances to maintain its secrecy.[13]

The remedies provided by the USTA include injunctive relief to stop the further exploitation of the trade secret by the person who misappropriated the information, and monetary damages awarded to the victim, either lost profits or the other party's unjust enrichment. As an alternative form of compensation, the victim may seek to charge the perpetrator a reasonable royalty rate for use of the trade secret. If the entrepreneur has not treated the alleged trade secret in a confidential manner or she has been lax in maintaining security, she will not be able to prove that there has been a misappropriation. Similarly, if the other person acquired the information by means of legal reverse engineering, he will not be found in violation of either the federal or state statutes, and the entrepreneur will not be entitled to any remedies.

COPYRIGHTS

Copyrights provide the broadest, most flexible, and probably least understood coverage in the area of intellectual property. Many people know that copyrights protect artworks and artists in areas such as music, poetry, books, plays, and movies. What a great many people do not realize is that copyrights protect *any* original work of authorship—a letter, a memo, an email, and so forth—as soon as this "original work of authorship" is put into tangible form, and that the author does not need to register the copyright in order to have protection. However, registration with the U.S. Copyright Office provides better protection for the author than an unregistered copyright, so registration is important if the material has significant value or the author does not want others to exploit her "artistic work." In order to file an infringement suit the copyright holder must register the copyright. Registration gives notice to "the world" (at least within the United States) that the material is protected by copyright, and this greatly increases the author's rights in court. Even if the material is not registered, the person claiming copyright can give notice to others that she is claiming rights in the work by appending the copyright symbol © and her name to the work. Under current U.S. law, a copyright gives the author the exclusive rights to reproduce, distribute, display, or perform the work for the life of the author plus 70 years. By contrast, a "work for hire" is protected by copyright for the lesser of 95 years from the date of publication or 120 years from the date of creation. A work for hire is any work produced by an employee in the course of his employment, or a work that is specially ordered or commissioned and produced by an independent contractor.[14] However, the entrepreneur should include express statements in her employment contracts with employees and independent contractors that she will own the works. This will remove any ambiguity and reduce the likelihood of litigation. One area of copyright law that has produced some controversy involves computer software. A computer program (software) can be copyrighted. An entrepreneur who produces a new type of software will want to copyright the software and register the copyright in order to be protected from competitors who otherwise could simply buy a copy of the program and then reproduce it under the competitor's name. While it is possible that a competitor will attempt to duplicate the program through reverse engineering, he will not be able to just reproduce it to the detriment of the entrepreneur. If the entrepreneur can establish that an infringement did, in fact, occur, she is entitled to injunctive relief, the impounding of any infringing materials, damages, and court costs plus attorneys' fees.[15]

It is important to remember that *any* "artistic work" is automatically covered by copyright, and that the reproduction or other unauthorized use of such works is a copyright infringement. To avoid accusations of copyright infringement, as well as the bad publicity and harm to reputation that a charge of infringing will bring, the entrepreneur should *assume* that anything and everything she comes across in fixed and tangible form is protected by copyright. Therefore, she should not just take that information and use it in a proprietary manner. It should also be noted that copyright registration is significantly less expensive than patent registration and that it is protected for a longer period of time.

Copyright protections are broad. There is a common perception that copyright protection is available only for formal writings that have been commercially published. In fact the law only requires a work to meet three basic requirements in order to be protected under copyright law:

1. The work must be fixed in a tangible medium of expression.
2. The work must be original.
3. The work must contain some amount of creativity.

The amount of creativity required is relatively low, and as a result most writing prepared for a venture would qualify, including product labels and advertisements.

THE INTERNET

The Internet is a wonderful tool, and an entrepreneur can use it to her advantage in developing and growing her venture. However, it can also pose threats to the entrepreneur and the venture, whether through negative Web sites (also known as anti-brand sites), disparaging comments, or through unauthorized use of intellectual property or the dissemination of information concerning intellectual property. An entrepreneur may be able to reach a much broader customer base by using the Internet, especially in sales, and she will be able to customize her advertising and her communications with those customers much easier in the cyber-marketplace than she would in the more traditional marketplace. She may also be able to establish links on the Net that allow her to reach customers that might initially have been beyond her reach. An entrepreneur should at least examine the opportunities presented by utilizing the Internet in an effort to develop a cyber-business "footprint" and tap a potential source of significant growth and development for her venture. Her Internet presence may make her appear much larger and more global than her physical presence would indicate.

DOMAIN NAMES

Domain names are like phone books for the Internet. When a person enters a domain name in an Internet search engine, he or she is transferred to the Internet site related to that domain name. A number of companies have registered their Internet domain names as trademarks, or have applied for a domain name that includes their trademarks plus "dot com" in an effort to use the Internet to reach new customers. Any entrepreneur who is considering doing business on the Internet should give some thought to an appropriate domain name, coupled with an examination of the Net for domain names already in use that might mislead potential customers or even cause harm to the entrepreneur or her venture. Domain names must be registered, and the registration is "first come, first served" to a great extent. A junior high school social studies teacher who recommends that his students visit the White House Internet site, for example, will need to emphasize that they visit "whitehouse.gov." "White House" is not a registered trademark; also, for a while the Web site "whitehouse.com" contained some adult—some would say pornographic—material.[16] Students who would visit such a site would, at the very least, come away with a different view of the White House and its occupants, a view that would not be flattering. YouTube and "utube" is another good example. Utube is the Web site of Universal Tube and Rollform Equipment Corporation. When YouTube arrived on the scene, it caused Universal Tube's site to crash because of the number of hits. Universal Tube also received nasty emails from people who were trying to reach YouTube but reached "utube" instead.

> For example, in *Universal Tube v. YouTube, Inc.*,[17] Universal Tube and Rollform Equipment Corporation initiated a suit against YouTube. Universal's website is www.utube.com and it contends that YouTube's

site at www.youtube.com has created numerous problems. Some of the causes of action have been dismissed, but the suit is going forward on the claims of unfair competition, dilution under Ohio law, and deceptive trade practices.[18]

Another example is that of 17-year-old Mike Rowe who took the domain name MikeRowesoft. Microsoft was not amused. After offering to purchase the domain name from Mr. Rowe for $10 and issuing a cease and desist letter to him, Microsoft was able to reach an out-of-court settlement, and Mr. Rowe transferred his domain name to Microsoft.[19]

Cybersquatters are known to "poach" domain names that are not protected by trademark. Despite the passage of anti-cybersquatting legislation, the threat posed by such poachers continues to grow. The number of dot com domain names has more than doubled since 2003,[20] and the number of disputes filed with the World Intellectual Property Organization (WIPO) increased by 25% from 2005 to 2006.[21] There is a movement afoot to seek legislation that will provide additional protection to businesses and famous people by providing greater statutory damage awards to victims of **cybersquatting** and closing the loopholes that permit such conduct, but no such protections exist yet. In the interim, the entrepreneur will need to register her desired domain name as quickly as possible. If she learns that her desired name has already been registered, she will need to either select a new domain name, negotiate with the owner of the desired name to purchase it and have it transferred, or file an appeal with the WIPO seeking to have the name transferred to her on the basis of misuse or abuse of the name by the person who registered it. (It is estimated that cybersquatting costs businesses over $1 billion per year because of a combination of misdirected customers and diverted sales, loss of goodwill, and the cost of combating fraud.[22])

COPYRIGHT ISSUES

Using the Internet is generally viewed as quick, easy, and relatively safe — computer viruses notwithstanding. However, using the Internet can also result in potential legal problems for an entrepreneur. Employees may send emails that allegedly infringe someone's copyright or trademark, often the employee is not aware that he or she has done anything improper. Hackers may be able to access the entrepreneur's Web site to steal trade secrets or other confidential information. Employees can download software or data on drives that are easily hidden, or can simply send such information to an off-site account for later access, to the detriment of the venture. Although the potential problems are serious, the entrepreneur should not shun the Internet; however, she should institute appropriate safeguards. An entrepreneur should have a policy in her workplace addressing Internet issues, with special attention being paid to restricting access to confidential information. The venture should have established policies regarding permissible access to the Net by employees, and these policies need to be spelled out in an employee handbook. The venture should have adequate firewalls, virus protection, and possibly even encryption software to provide adequate protection from hackers, malware, and other threats.

Entrepreneurs whose ventures will sponsor servers and allow customers to post materials should consult with their attorneys because they are exposed to a number of additional copyright problems in addition to the potential problems listed above.

The entrepreneur should also create a number of "signatures" for use with emails to protect herself and the venture from inadvertently making a contract offer or acceptance in what she thought was a simple communication. The solution is to have different email signatures and then append the appropriate one to each email sent. For example, a signature on an email to a person or firm with whom the venture is negotiating a contract might include a phrase such as: "No offer or acceptance can be implied from this email. All contractual offers or acceptance may be shown only by [name of entrepreneur]." The entrepreneur should check with her attorney regarding the form and style of these various email signatures and then take care to ensure that the proper signature is attached to each email as it is sent. She should also mandate the type and style of email signature that can be used by employees in emails sent from any of the venture's computers. Perhaps the standard should be modified to reflect the position of the employee within the venture's structure.

In applying the information in this chapter, the entrepreneur should consider the application questions set out in the box below:

Application Questions

1. What intellectual property does the entrepreneur own?

2. If the entrepreneur owns the intellectual property, is it going to be part of her capital contribution to the venture or is she going to sell or license it to the venture?

3. What intellectual property does the entrepreneur plan to develop? Who will be involved in the development? The entrepreneur should enter into appropriate contracts to minimize subsequent disputes about ownership.

4. How will the entrepreneur make money with her intellectual property? Will she sell the intellectual property, sell goods that use the intellectual property, or license the intellectual property?

5. What steps should the entrepreneur take to protect her intellectual property?

6. Who will develop the trademark and/or service mark?

7. What names should be used for the company, its products, and its Web site?

8. If these names or similar names are currently being used, can the venture purchase them at a reasonable price?

9. Is there a risk that the venture's trademark will become the generic label for the product? If so, what should the entrepreneur do to reduce the risk?

10. Should the entrepreneur obtain a patent or treat the intellectual property as a trade secret? What are the advantages and disadvantages of these two options?

11. Is there a risk that the entrepreneur and/or her employees will misuse the intellectual property of other people? What should the entrepreneur do to reduce the risk?

12. What signature lines should be used by the entrepreneur? What lines would be appropriate for her employees? Remember that signature lines can be image builders and marketing tools.

Summary

There is an old adage that says, "build a better mousetrap and the world will beat a path to your door."[23] However, this saying should also carry a caveat: protect the method of building the mousetrap, or the idea will be copied by your competition, and your competition will make every effort to capitalize on *your* idea to *its* benefit! An entrepreneur needs to be aware of intellectual property issues, and the potential protections that intellectual property can provide for a venture, as well as the potential liabilities it can create if the venture infringes on the intellectual property of others.

Utility patents provide the holder with a government-protected monopoly for 20 years. When the entrepreneur holds the patent, she can exploit and/or protect it for the statutory period. On the other hand, if she infringes the patent of another, she can expect to face injunctive relief and the imposition of damages for her conduct. Patents are only issued for new, useful, and non-obvious inventions.

Trademarks and service marks are registered with the Patent and Trademark Office, and provide the owner with the exclusive right to use that mark in selling, promoting, or otherwise exploiting the product or service to which the mark is attached. If another person or firm infringes on the registered mark, the entrepreneur can seek injunctive relief and sue for damages: if the entrepreneur infringes the mark of another, even if the infringement is inadvertent, she will face the same sanctions.

Trade secrets are methods of production or operation that are treated in a confidential manner by the owner of these secrets rather than registered with the government for statutory protection. As a result, trade secrets have fewer protections, and the entrepreneur who relies on a trade secret will have a more difficult time if someone acquires the information and competes with the venture. In order to avail herself of any viable protection, the entrepreneur must ensure that the information is treated confidentially. She will need to take appropriate actions to maintain secrecy, and thus security. She will also want to have every person who has access to the information sign a non-disclosure agreement (also called a confidentiality agreement). Copyright law provides the broadest area of coverage and the longest statutory time period for which protection is available. Copyrights exist automatically upon the placement of any "original work of authorship" into tangible form. However, the holder of the copyright will need to register her claim before seeking damages from alleged infringers. Copyright infringements occur even when the infringer has no conscious knowledge of the infringement, and the person who has infringed faces potential legal repercussions for such conduct even if there was no intent to violate the rights of the copyright holder.

The Internet is a wonderful tool, but it also is frequently the access point for obtaining trade secrets, copyrights, trademarks, and service marks. Entrepreneurs need to have policies and procedures in place to regulate and control Internet access and usage at the work site, and also adequate Internet security in place to prevent hackers and unauthorized access.

Emails may also present legal issues since electronic communications are now deemed to be "writings" for purposes of contract law. An entrepreneur is well advised to develop specialized email "signatures" to use with different types of emails in order to minimize the potential legal implications of emails that are sent without such specialized signatures.

Key Terms

copyright
cybersquatting
domain name
infringement
intellectual property

patent
public domain
service mark
trademark
trade secret

End-of-Chapter Questions

1. Suppose that an entrepreneur develops a new, useful, and non-obvious product or production method. Should she seek patent protection in order to ensure a 20-year government-protected monopoly, or should she choose to treat this development as a trade secret? Why?
2. What are the benefits of a patent when compared to a trade secret? What are the benefits of a trade secret when compared to a patent?
3. What is a trademark, and how does the possession of a trademark help a venture to gain or maintain market share?
4. How does a trademark differ from a service mark?
5. What does copyright law protect? How does a person acquire a copyright? What must a person do in order to recover damages if someone infringes her copyright?
6. What is a domain name? Can/should an entrepreneur attempt to acquire a domain name for a trademark? Why?
7. What is cybersquatting, and how does cybersquatting affect a business trying to do business via the Internet?

8. Why should an entrepreneur have policies and procedures regulating Internet access and its use at work? What possible drawbacks might such policies and procedures engender?
9. Develop three specialized email signatures. When would you use each one?

Suggested Activities

1. Determine a (hypothetical) domain name for a planned venture, and then examine whether that domain name is already registered. Also examine how one registers a domain name. Discuss the problems that you discover from your research. [One potential site to visit is Getting It Write, Inc. Domains, http://GIWIDomains.com]
2. Find a Web site with click art and/or stock photos. Read the user agreement for the site. Can you use the art or photos to create advertising materials for your venture? If so, is there a charge for this use? (Some possible sites to visit are flickr and Stock.xchng.)

Resources

1. Charmasson, Henri (2004), *Patents, Copyrights & Trademarks for Dummies* Indianapolis, IN: Wiley Publishing, Inc., Copyright 2004 by H. Charmasson.
2. Stim, Richard (2007), *Patent, Copyright & Trademark, an Intellectual Property Desk Reference*, 9th edition Berkeley, CA: Nolo, Copyright 2007 by Nolo and Richard Stim.

Notes

1. G. Kingsley Ward, as quoted in *And I Quote (Revised ed.)* by Applewhite, Evans, and Frothingham, St. Martin's Press, New York, NY, 2003, p. 31.
2. "What Is Intellectual Property," World Intellectual Property Organization, found at http://www.wipo.int/about-ip/en/
3. Article 1, §8.
4. "Understanding Provisional Patent Applications," Inventors, About.com, found at http://inventors.about.com/od/provisionalpatent/a/Provisional_Pat.htm
5. *State Street Bank & Trust Co. v. Signature Financial Group, Inc.*, 149 F.3d 1368; 47 U.S.P.Q.2d (BNA) 1596 (1998).
6. Kathleen Allen (2001), *Entrepreneurship for Dummies*, Wiley Publishing, Inc., Hoboken, NJ, (2001) p. 112.
7. William Francis Galvin, "About Trademarks and Service Marks," Secretary of the Commonwealth (of Massachusetts), Corporations Division, found at http://www.sec.state.ma.us/cor/corpweb/cortmsm/tmsminf.htm
8. "Overview of Trademark Law," found at http://cyber.law.harvard.edu/metaschool/fisher/domain/tm.htm
9. 18 U.S.C. §1831 et seq. (1996).
10. "Economic Espionage Act of 1996," found at http://www.ntc.doe.gov/cita/CI_Awareness_Guide/T1threat/Legal.htm

11. An up-to-date list is available on the NCCUSL Web site, found at http://www.nccusl.org/)

12. Radnack, David V., "The Uniform Trade Secrets Act," TMS Online, found at http://www.tms.org/pubs/journals/JOM/matters/matters-0601.html

13. USTA §1 (4).

14. The Cornell Copyright Information Center contains a great deal of information on copyright laws. It can be found at http://www.copyright.cornell.edu/resources/index.htm#select

15. Copyright Law—Chapter 5, 17 U.S.C. §§501–505, can also be found at http://www.copyright.gov/title17/92chap5.html

16. Pelline, Jeff, "Whitehouse.com goes to porn," CNET News (September 5, 1997), found at http://news.cnet.com/2100-1023-202985.html (This domain name was sold in 2004 and is now the home of a political commentary site).

17. 2007 U.S. Dist. LEXIS 40395 (N.D. Ohio 2007).

18. Kemp, Deborah J., and Lynn M. Forsythe, "YouTube as the Great Communicator and Copyright Infringer", 18 *S. L. J.* 207–222 (Fall 2008).

19. "MikeRoweSoft settles for an Xbox," CNET News (January 26, 2004), found at http://news.cnet.com/2100-1014-5147374.html

20. Sinrod, Eric J., "Perspective: Waging War against Cybersquatting," CNET News (August 15, 2007). This article can be found at http://news.cnet.com/Waging-war-against-cybersquatting/2010-1030_3-6202597.html

21. *Id.*

22. *Id.*

23. Ralph Waldo Emerson, found at http://www.brainyquote.com/quotes/quotes/r/ralphwaldo136905.html

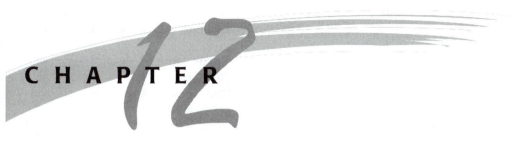

MINIMIZING AND SHIFTING RISKS THROUGH CONTRACTS

Business without profit is not business any more than a pickle is candy.[1]

INTRODUCTION

The overwhelming majority of people will enter into literally thousands of **contracts** in their lifetimes, yet if asked how many contracts they have made, most people will answer with a very low number. Some will even claim to never have entered into a contract. In a similar vein, many people believe that a contact must be in writing to be valid and enforceable. These people seem to accept the quote of Louis B. Mayer, "A verbal contract isn't worth the paper it's written on,"[2] as an accurate statement of contract law. Both of these seemingly basic beliefs are wrong. Contracts are part and parcel of everyday life in the United States, and everyone should have some basic understanding of contract law. For an entrepreneur, understanding the basic principles of contract law and knowing how to use contracts carefully and wisely can contribute significantly to the success of the venture.

A contract is "a promissory agreement between two or more persons that creates, modifies, or destroys a legal relation."[3] Every business, whether a business that provides goods or services or one that deals in real estate, is inextricably tied to contracts and thus to contract law. Contracts provide the "riverbed" through which the business's cash will "flow." Virtually every transaction the business makes will be made by means of a contract. Some of these contracts will be complicated and may well require the services of the firm's attorneys. Some of the contracts will be simple: they will often be entered into and performed without utilizing the services of those same attorneys. In fact, even the agreement to hire the attorneys will be based on a contract!

Contract law may well be the foundation upon which all businesses are built. Its importance can be seen from the development of contract law down through the years. Early in Anglo-American law, contracts were not deemed to be of overriding importance. In an agrarian society and economy, and in a feudal era with class distinctions, rights, and obligations, property law was much more important than contract law. As a merchant class began to develop, and as it became clear that the **common law** as it then existed was not adequate for protecting the rights or interests of merchants, the merchants themselves decided to act. These traders and craftsmen established their own "legal" system, the "Law Merchant."[4] Under the original "Law Merchant," merchants heard disputes between merchants and customers and settled them under the rules and regulations that had been developed by the merchants themselves. This system seemed to work very well—so well, in fact, that Parliament adopted the Law Merchant as part of the common law, providing one of the first examples of statutory regulation of a particular area of trade or commerce in English legal history.

When the United States was formed, the states adhered to their English heritage and continued to follow the common law, including the Law Merchant. Eventually, trade and the merchant class became so prevalent that it outgrew its common law coverage. With changes in technology, and with businesses becoming more regional or even national in scope, the variations of contract law across the states became problematic and a more uniform coverage was needed. This need was addressed by a variety of uniform acts dealing with specific areas of commercial law. By the early 20th century we had the Uniform Sales Act dealing with contracts for the sale of goods (adopted in 37 jurisdictions by 1950), the Uniform Negotiable Instruments Act (adopted in all 48 states, the District of Columbia, Hawaii, Alaska, the Philippines, and Puerto Rico by 1950), and the Uniform Bills of Lading Act (adopted in 32 jurisdictions). Each of these uniform acts was a significant improvement over the prior coverage provided by the common law, but by 1950 technology had advanced so quickly that each of these uniform laws was out of date, and serious modernizing was needed.

In 1954 the National Conference of Commissioners on Uniform State Laws proposed a new **Uniform Commercial Code** (UCC), an updated, modernized codification of a number of the previous uniform laws that had been adopted piecemeal. The UCC provided coverage of sales of goods, negotiable instruments, bank–customer relations, letters of credit, bulk sales, documents of title, investment securities, and secured transactions. Later additions to the UCC provided coverage of leases of goods and funds transfers. The UCC has been adopted, in whole or in part, in all 50 states, plus the District of Columbia, and its provisions are of tremendous importance to all businesses and business persons, including entrepreneurs.

The UCC, despite its importance, is domestic law: its application is basically limited to the United States. Many businesses today are involved in international trade. While there is no uniform commercial code for international trade, there are the United Nations Convention on **Contracts for the International Sale of Goods** (CISG) and the Lex Mercatoria, the Law Merchant as applied by the International Chamber of Commerce, to settle disputes among merchants in an international environment. The evolution of contract law is set out in Table 12.1.

In the following discussion we will look at how these different statutes affect the entrepreneur in his business operation, and the impact of these statutory or traditional rules and regulations on contract formation.

TABLE 12.1 The Evolution of Contract Law	
Type of Law	*Primary Coverage*
Common law of contracts	Primary emphasis on real estate; geared to an agrarian society
The Law Merchant	Initially, not really *law*, but rather the rules merchants used for self-regulation; eventually adopted by the British Parliament and made a part of the common law. Dealt with contracts between merchants and customers, especially consumers.
Uniform acts—various areas of coverage • Uniform Sales Act • Uniform Negotiable Instruments Act • Uniform Bills of Lading Act • Others	Covered specific areas of U.S. commercial law, without necessarily correlating with other related topics.
Uniform Commercial Code (UCC)	Successor to the various uniform acts, this was the first compilation of the most significant areas of commercial law into a comprehensive code that also cross-referenced and correlated coverage of the different areas. Only applies within the United States, but every state has adopted at least some parts of the UCC, if not the entire code.
United Nations Convention on Contracts for the International Sale of Goods (CISG)	An international treaty that addresses the sale of goods *between merchants* across national borders. Has many similarities to Article 2 of the UCC (the Law of Sales), but also has several significant differences. Businesses involved in international trade need to be aware of the coverage of this Convention.

CONTRACT FORMATION

Contracts are voluntary arrangements between parties in which the parties (1) reach an agreement and (2) exchange value in support of the agreement. The agreement involves an **offer** and an **acceptance**. At common law this offer and acceptance had to be "mirror images" of one another. The offeree (the person to whom the offer was made) had to accept the offer exactly as it was communicated by the offeror (the person making the offer). Any variation, deviation, or change was treated by the law as a counteroffer. This legally meant that the original offer was rejected and a new offer replaced it.

The UCC has greatly relaxed the rules for reaching an agreement, especially in Article 2, the Sale of Goods. Under the code, an offer can be accepted in any reasonable manner. No longer is the mirror image rule applied to contracts for the sale of goods. The code also says that if the parties act like they have a contract, the law will presume that they do have a contract. Because of these changes, contract formation is much less rigid or difficult than it was at common law, at least in the area of selling goods. Entrepreneurs need to be aware of these relaxed rules, otherwise the court may conclude that the entrepreneur entered into a contract when he did not believe that he had.

Consideration is the "quid pro quo" of the contract, the exchange or promised exchange of something of value that elevates a promise or moral obligation to a legal obligation, enforceable by the courts in the event of a lawsuit for breach of contract. Consideration is an agreement to assume a duty that did not previously exist, or surrender a right that did previously exist: it is given in exchange for the other party's agreement to also assume a duty or surrender a right. The value of the consideration is seldom considered. In other words, courts do not look at the adequacy of consideration, at least if adequacy is the only issue, since the parties are deemed to be capable of setting their own value for the goods, services, etc. being exchanged.

So, with contract formation being simplified and made easier, and with the relative "fairness" of the exchange not likely to be an issue, what is a person to do? How can a person protect his interests and ensure that he has not entered into a contract accidentally or carelessly? To many people the answer is obvious. There cannot be a contract unless there is a written agreement. This solution is simple, it is easy, but *it is wrong!* With some exceptions, oral contracts are perfectly valid and enforceable. They may present problems in establishing that a contract was made (the he said/she said conundrum), but if the proof is presented, the oral contract can and will be upheld unless it falls within a statutory exception that requires a writing.

Contracts that fall within the coverage of the Statute of Frauds must be in writing in order to be enforced; contracts for the sale of an interest in land must be in writing in order to be enforced; a few other contracts under certain state laws may also need to be in writing in order to be enforced. But except for these, a contract does not have to be in writing. It is quite possible that it *should* be in writing, but a written agreement is not mandatory. This means that an entrepreneur needs to be very careful in his communications and conduct with potential customers. What might be intended as a start to negotiations by one party might be deemed to be an offer by the other. The other party then accepts, and a contract exists where only a preliminary negotiation was intended.

The entrepreneur also needs to be aware that electronic communications such as emails or text messages are deemed to be writings under the law, and that an email or a text message that contains the essential elements of a contract can be considered to be a written contract that falls within the requirements of the Statute of Frauds. No longer is the traditional requirement of "reduction to a tangible form" needed for a communication to be viewed as "a writing." Under current law, electronic communications are now considered to be "written," thus satisfying any statutory need for a contract to be in writing *except* for negotiable instruments. People who are unaware of this may be careless while writing an email or sending a text message to another person, and the careless communication may well lead to the possible formation of a contract. The message could be viewed as the acceptance of an offer previously made by the other party, or it could be viewed as an offer that the other person decides to accept. In either case, a contract would now exist; it would be "in writing," providing stronger evidence than an oral agreement; and it would be in the words of the entrepreneur and "signed" by him.

WHAT CAN HAPPEN WITH AN OFFER?

When a person communicates an offer to the offeree, one of four things can happen. The offeree can *accept* the offer, creating an agreement. (If that agreement is supported by consideration, a contract would now exist, with all the rights and obligations that a contract entails.) The offeree can *reject* the offer. A **rejection** is a decision not to accept, and the offer is terminated. The offeror can *revoke* the offer. A **revocation** is a retraction of the offer, terminating it and ending the possibility of a contract based on that offer. And the offer can **lapse**; it can expire after the passage of a reasonable time without an acceptance, rejection, or revocation. Table 12.2 shows the various things that will terminate an offer.

One interesting aspect of American contract law is that an offer can be revoked by the offeror at any time prior to acceptance, even if the offeror has promised to keep it open for a given time period in order to allow the offeree time to consider the offer. Thus, if a seller offers to sell a product to a buyer for $300, and tells the buyer that she has "until next Monday to decide," the offeror could call the potential buyer the very next hour and revoke the offer, and the potential buyer would no longer be able to accept. The promise to keep the offer open "until next Monday" might be a moral obligation, but it is not a legal obligation.

Suppose the promise to keep the offer open until next Monday is in writing. Can the offeror still revoke the offer prior to acceptance, and prior to next Monday? At common law, yes he can. The writing of the promise did not make

TABLE 12.2 Termination of an Offer	
Acceptance by the Offeree	Shows consent to the proposed terms; indicates an agreement which, if supported by consideration, a contract makes.
Rejection by the Offeree	Shows an unwillingness to proceed on the terms proposed by the offeror, an unwillingness to enter into a contract on those terms. A counteroffer is deemed to be a rejection of the original offer.
Revocation by the Offeror	The offeror has the legal right to revoke his offer at any time prior to acceptance by the offeree. This right exists even if the offeror has promised to keep the offer open for some time period, although there are a few exceptions to this right.
Lapse	Offers have limited lives, and if the offeree has not accepted the offer within that limited life span, the offer will expire due to the lapse of time.

Source: Courtesy of Daniel V. Davidson, © Daniel V. Davidson 2009.

the offer irrevocable at common law. However, under the UCC if a merchant makes a promise *in writing* to keep an offer open for a stated period, he is legally obligated to keep the offer open for the stated period. (In most situations an entrepreneur is going to be deemed to be a merchant.) In addition, if the promise to keep the offer open does not have a stated expiration date, the offer is irrevocable for a "reasonable time" not to exceed three months. This is called a *firm offer*, and a firm offer is irrevocable.

Remember also that this firm offer rule is found in the UCC and applies to a merchant who sells goods under U.S. law. That same merchant negotiating a deal in an international sale of goods will be subject to the CISG. The CISG provides that *any* offer that the offeror promises to keep open for a stated time period is irrevocable, whether oral or written. It also provides that an offer that the offeree *reasonably* believed would be kept open for a stated time is irrevocable. Under the CISG, no writing is necessary. Rather than a "firm offer," as found in the UCC, the CISG simply considers these offers irrevocable.

Key Point. Entrepreneurs need to be very careful in promising to keep an offer open, especially if the other party is in another country. The rules governing firm offers under the UCC and those providing for irrevocable offers under the CISG may lock the entrepreneur into a position he would rather not occupy. If the entrepreneur considers committing to give the other party a time period in which to accept or reject, he needs to be certain he is willing to honor that time commitment.

Contracts can be used for more than simply buying or selling property or for hiring or providing services. An entrepreneur can use contracts to provide valuable protection for his venture or to either shift or minimize the risk in providing his venture's goods or services. Carefully crafted contracts can be a powerful tool in many disputes, and may even deter some disputes since the contract may well ensure that the entrepreneur will prevail if the matter goes to arbitration or litigation. Poorly crafted contracts, on the other hand, may encourage others to try to take advantage of the entrepreneur and to obtain advantages that should never have been available had the contract been prepared more carefully.

SPECIAL TERMS AND CLAUSES

Contracts can be structured to cover a myriad of issues, and the entrepreneur can use special terms and clauses to protect his business secrets or methods, to protect the venture against competitors who are using his ideas against his venture to his detriment, or to preserve the basic structure of a contract that may have one or more flaws. Some of the more important of these special terms or clauses are discussed below, and are also illustrated in Table 12.3.

TABLE 12.3   Special Terms and Clauses in a Contract

Term or Clause	*Purpose*	*Limitations*
Non-disclosure agreement	Protects trade secrets, unique business methods, or other confidential information	It may not provide the desired protection if it is used too broadly (i.e., *all* employees required to sign) or too narrowly (not everyone privy to such information is required to sign). Only applies to confidential information or unique practices. Does not protect against reverse engineering.
Non-compete clause	Protects against an employee leaving the firm and then either opening her own competing business or going to work for a competitor and sharing information or expertise gained in the employ of the entrepreneur	The competition restriction must be reasonable in (1) time, (2) geographic scope, and (3) its definition of competitors. Six months to two years is *normally* a reasonable time, but courts are likely to look at the industry in making a decision. Information technology areas are likely to have a very short time limit requirement.
Saving clause	Preserves the gist of a contract when a portion of the contract is deemed invalid for some reason or a part of the contract is breached or a party is in default	Needs to be carefully worded so that the entire contract will not necessarily fail due to a defective or invalid portion. May want to provide that the entire contract will fail if the deleted portion makes the balance of the contract unreasonable.

NON-DISCLOSURE AGREEMENTS

There is an old adage stating that "knowledge is power." This may be more accurate today than at any prior time in history. We live in an "information age," and information is probably more available today than it has ever been before. There are also technological methods for accessing information—methods that have not previously existed. Because of the breadth and depth of information available, and because of the methods available to gaining access to information, it is more important than ever for a business to protect its confidential information and trade secrets. Since it is virtually impossible to keep anything totally secret, the next best thing for an entrepreneur to do is use non-disclosure agreements (NDAs), either within his contracts or separately. While not foolproof, a well-designed NDA affords advance notice to the other party of the seriousness with which the information is guarded, and also provides legal protection in the event the other person discloses the information despite the agreement.

An NDA can be used to protect trade secrets as well as confidential information or methods used in a business. It can be used as a clause in a contract or as the basis for a separate contract. For example, an entrepreneur may want to add an NDA in an employment contract as one of its clauses to protect trades secrets or help ensure that confidential venture matters remain confidential. This clause will inform employees that the information is confidential and that failing to respect that confidentiality may result in legal liability. Similarly, the entrepreneur may include the same NDA clause in contracts with customers (rarely) or suppliers (more often).

Stated as simply as possible, an NDA is a contract or contract clause in which one party agrees not to reveal any proprietary or confidential information to anyone outside the firm with whom the contract was signed. The entrepreneur should consider having any and every person who is likely to have access to such proprietary and/or confidential information sign such a contract. This would include investors who may have access, employees, suppliers, and even independent contractors who may have access to such information while performing the tasks for which they were hired.

NDAs are especially prevalent in high-tech industries and in firms that are computer or Internet based. For example, "Sabeer Bhatia, founder of Hotmail, made sure that everyone who knew about his start-up company signed a non-disclosure agreement. Over a two-year period he collected over 400 NDAs from employees, friends and roommates. He believes that his secrecy efforts gave him a crucial six-month lead on the competition. He eventually sold Hotmail to Microsoft for a reported $400 million in stock."[5]

It is important to have people sign these contracts—and the entrepreneur will want to have these contracts in writing and signed—before they are given access to the information. Once a person has access to the information it may become more expensive to get him or her to sign an NDA, and the fact that he or she gained access makes it more difficult to show that the information was treated in a confidential manner that deserves protection. There also must be consideration to support the NDA. Without consideration there is no contract, and with no contract there is no legal protection. Obviously, an NDA in an employment contract is supported by consideration. The employee is receiving employment in exchange for her commitment to (1) do the job and (2) not disclose confidential information. But an NDA standing alone as a contract, rather than as part of a larger contractual agreement, must be supported by consideration. The entrepreneur will need to give the other party something of value, some consideration, for the agreement to reach the level of a contract.

Key Point. The NDA should only be used for confidential information, and it must be supported by consideration. A mere promise not to disclose confidential information is not legally binding; an NDA that is overly broad or attempts to cover every aspect of the entrepreneur's venture may be viewed as too vague to be valid or enforced.

One example of an NDA can be found (and downloaded) at http://www.how-to.com/Operations/NDAform.html.[6] Of course, the entrepreneur should have his attorney either prepare the NDA he will be using or, at least, review and approve any form he plans to use.

COVENANTS NOT TO COMPETE

An entrepreneur is likely to have a number of employees, and even some friends or relatives, who are in a position to observe and to learn what the entrepreneur is doing or plans to do, as well as learning the entrepreneur's methods or even his secrets. These employees, friends, or relatives would then be in a position to take the information gained and use that knowledge to compete with the entrepreneur, probably to his detriment. In order to avoid this risk, the entrepreneur would be well advised to have key employees and others with access to such information sign contracts containing a covenant not to compete.

Properly drafted, a covenant not to compete is legally binding in most states and will allow the entrepreneur to get an injunction against anyone who has signed such an agreement and then attempts to violate the covenant by entering into competition with the entrepreneur. However, if the covenant is drafted improperly, usually because it is too broad in its restrictions on competing, it may be declared void by a court and thrown out. This, in turn, will allow the person who had previously agreed not to compete with the entrepreneur to engage in such competition, siphoning off customers or otherwise causing harm to the venture.

Since these covenants are either a part of the contract or the entire agreement, they must be supported by consideration. Also, given the nature of these covenants, the agreement needs to be in writing and signed by the party against whom it will be enforced—the employee, friend, relative, or whomever. For an employee the consideration will be the employment that she will obtain upon signing the contract. For a director, partner, or associate, it will be the opportunity to hold the position within the venture. For friends or relatives the entrepreneur will need to include a statement of the consideration given, and will also need to actually deliver that consideration to the other party, showing his performance and thus binding the other party to the contract to also perform. The statement of consideration can be as simple as, for example, "for one dollar ($1.00) and other 'good and valuable' consideration . . . ", followed by the payment of the one dollar called for in the contract. (Payment by check is advisable so that the entrepreneur can show the cancelled check as evidence of the payment.) While this "nominal consideration" may not reflect the benefit derived by the entrepreneur from entering the contract, courts historically do not evaluate the adequacy of any consideration, being satisfied with the presence of consideration that was agreed to by each party to the contract.

Courts will not enforce a covenant not to compete that is overly broad, since such a covenant is considered to violate public policy, or even to be unconscionable. The party who is agreeing not to compete should not be precluded from ever competing; rather, she should be prevented from competing only for a reasonable time and within a reasonable geographic area, to allow the other party—the entrepreneur in this example—to establish his business free from her competition. A time limit of from six months up to two years is quite likely to be viewed as reasonable, whereas time limits of longer duration are likely to be more closely scrutinized, and may well be viewed as too broad and thus not valid.[7] Similarly, if a business only operated within a radius of 50 miles from its location, a geographic limit of 50 miles would most often be upheld, but a geographic restriction of 500 miles would be too broad and would not be upheld by the court. Both the time limit and geographic scope must be reasonable if the covenant is to be upheld by the courts.

Even if the entrepreneur selects a time limit that would generally be deemed to be reasonable, there is a chance that the courts will overturn the agreement because of time limit. For example, in *Earthweb Inc. v. Schlack*[8] the court ruled that a one-year restriction on employment with a competing firm was too long. Stating that "a one-year hiatus from the work force is 'several generations, if not an eternity,' " the court ruled that "the one-year employment ban specified in the contract's so-called 'non-compete' clause was just too long a period to apply to an Internet professional, 'given the dynamic nature of this industry' and its 'lack of geographical borders.' "[9]

One example of a non-compete agreement (NCA) can be found (and downloaded) at http://www.ilrg.com/forms/nocompet.html.[10] Of course, the entrepreneur should have his attorney either prepare the NCA he will be using or at least review and approve any form he plans to use.

> **Key Point.** The entrepreneur and his attorney need to "tighten" the non-compete agreement or **non-compete clause**. The time period stated in the agreement should be reasonable for the venture and its competitors, which may mean a shorter time frame than is normally used. The geographic scope should be limited to the area in which the venture operates. Overreaching will probably result in the court negating the agreement. Define carefully the "competition" for whom the other person must not work. Again, an overly broad "definition" is likely to result in the rejection of the agreement by the court.

Saving Clauses

A **saving clause**, also called a severability clause, is designed to protect the gist of a contract if one part of the contract fails for some reason. For example, if a contract has multiple parts, a saving clause will allow the parties to fulfill the balance of the contract if one part is breached or one party defaults on one part of the contract. Similarly, if one part of the contract is found to be illegal and thus void, the balance of the contract will remain in effect and will be fully enforceable. Should a court decide that one part of the contract as written is invalid, the court will allow the parties to rewrite that part in order to make it comply with the original intentions of the parties and the requirements of the court.

There are many examples of saving clauses available online, so finding one that fulfills the needs—and the style—of the entrepreneur is relatively simple. A few very good examples can be found on the Yale University library page,[11] including the following two examples:

> If any provision or provisions of this Agreement shall be held to be invalid, illegal, unenforceable or in conflict with the law of any jurisdiction, the validity, legality and enforceability of the remaining provisions shall not in any way be affected or impaired thereby.

> In the event that any one or more of the provisions contained herein shall, for any reason, be held to be invalid, illegal or unenforceable in any respect, such invalidity, illegality or unenforceability shall not affect any other provisions of this agreement, but this agreement shall be construed as if such invalid, illegal or unenforceable provisions had never been contained herein, unless the deletion of such provision or provisions would result in such a material change so as to cause completion of the transactions contemplated herein to be unreasonable.

The first example is a type that is commonly used in licensing agreements and only reflects the desire to maintain the gist of the contract. The second example is similar, but includes a statement that would have the saving clause apply only if doing so would not result in a material change in the obligations of the parties. Owing to this further provision, a clause similar to the second example would be better for most entrepreneurs.

ARBITRATION CLAUSE

Many businesses have begun including an **arbitration clause** in their employment contracts, mandating that any employee who has a dispute with the employer will resolve the dispute through arbitration rather than litigation. Ventures are also including arbitration clauses in many contracts with suppliers or customers. By including an arbitration clause the entrepreneur will be attempting to avoid the time and expense of a lawsuit, the publicity of information that ensues when a lawsuit is filed, and the potential for hard feelings and animosity after a public adversarial proceeding. In contrast to a trial, arbitration is normally quicker, less expensive, more private, and less adversarial. An arbitration clause is likely to be upheld by the courts if it provides for an arbitration that is, and appears to be, a fair and unbiased proceeding that ensures each party due process. However, if the clause appears to be one-sided in favor of the entrepreneur, as in a clause that allows the entrepreneur to select the arbitrator with no input from the other party, the courts are likely to allow the other party to litigate the matter.

There are many examples of arbitration clauses available in form books and on the Internet, and the entrepreneur should consult with his attorney before selecting a template for the clause he would like to use. One such clause is set out below:

> In the event a dispute shall arise between the parties to this [contract, lease, etc.], it is hereby agreed that the dispute shall be referred to [one of the following choices: (1) designate a specific USA&M office or alternate service by agreement of the parties; (2) provide a method of selecting the arbitrator and situs of the hearing, such as "from the county wherein the manufacturing plant is located"; or for multi-jurisdictional disputes (3) insert "a USA&M office to be designated by USA&M National Headquarters"] for arbitration in accordance with the applicable United States Arbitration and Mediation Rules of Arbitration. The arbitrator's decision shall be final and legally binding and judgment may be entered thereon.
>
> Each party shall be responsible for its share of the arbitration fees in accordance with the applicable Rules of Arbitration. In the event a party fails to proceed with arbitration, unsuccessfully challenges the arbitrator's award, or fails to comply with the arbitrator's award, the other party is entitled to costs of suit, including a reasonable attorney's fee for having to compel arbitration or defend or enforce the award.[12]

If an entrepreneur decides that he would prefer to use arbitration (or mediation) rather than litigation, he should be certain that such a clause in included in most, if not all, contracts entered into by the venture, and he should also familiarize himself with the policies and procedures of at least one of the major arbitration providers, such as the American Arbitration Association, to ensure that his conduct prior to the arbitration is appropriate under the circumstances.

FORCE MAJEURE **CLAUSE**

An entrepreneur should consider including a ***force majeure*** clause in contracts that call for future performance, when such a clause would be appropriate. *Force majeure* literally means "greater force," and a *force majeure* clause excuses performance in a contract if some unforeseen event — some greater force — beyond the control of the parties occurs, preventing performance of the contract obligation. Most commonly, these unforeseen events will involve a natural disaster, war, any "acts of God," or the failure of a third party to perform her duty to one of the parties to the entrepreneur's contact. A *force majeure* clause is intended to excuse a party from performance only if the failure could not be avoided by the exercise of due care by that party.

It is important to make sure that any *force majeure* clause applies to each party in the contract, and not just to the entrepreneur. The contract should also include some examples of events that will trigger the application of the clause, although the examples should explicitly be examples and not a complete list of covered events.[13]

BATTLE OF THE FORMS

An entrepreneur will be placing orders for goods from other businesses, and will also be receiving orders for goods to be provided by his venture. In both cases, it is quite likely that the prospective buyer has submitted his order on a **purchase order**, a form prepared by and for the benefit of the buyer. In accepting the proposed purchase, the seller is likely to reply with an "acknowledgement form," a form prepared by and for the benefit of the seller. When the parties exchange these forms, they act as if they have formed a contract in which the seller agrees to sell the quantity ordered at the price agreed upon, and with corresponding other terms. Unfortunately, they are also likely to discover that each party has included some terms on his or her form that do not correspond with the form provided by the other party. In fact, these terms will often directly contradict the terms in the other party's form. If or when such a situation arises, several questions spring to mind:

1. Do the parties have a contract?

2. If there is a contract, what are the terms of the contract?

3. How should the differences in the two forms be reconciled?

Common law required a mirror image before a contract existed, consequently there would be no contract if the acceptance did not mirror the offer in every particular. However, modern business does not tend to act in a manner consistent with common law, and in the area of sale of goods Article 2 of the UCC supersedes common law, recognizing the existence of a contract and providing a method for determining what the parties "agreed" to do in this contract.[14]

While the parties have exchanged forms that contain terms and conditions, (terms and conditions under which each party expects to perform and upon which each party relies in defining the contract), it is likely that neither party has actually read the other party's form carefully or in its entirety, and it is also likely that neither party has agreed to—or objected to—any terms or conditions contained in the other form. Under the UCC, this "non-agreement" will not defeat the existence of a contract. The UCC holds that the parties to a sales contract will be found to have a contract *if* they act as if they have a contract,[15] and the acts of shipping the goods (by the seller) and accepting the goods (by the buyer) show that each party is acting as if he or she has a contract. If the terms included in the two forms are not in total agreement—and they will not be—the code provides that the contract consists of "those terms on which the writings of the parties agree, together with any supplementary terms incorporated under any other provisions of the UCC."[16]

Since the buyer normally initiates the contract formation by submitting a purchase order, the terms in the purchase order are likely to control *unless* the seller specifically negates any terms he finds unacceptable in his acceptance/acknowledgement form. If the buyer has included terms that are not specifically negated, those terms will be part of the final contract. For example, if the purchase order includes a clause allowing for the collection of consequential (indirect or secondary) damages in the event of a breach by the seller, and the seller does not address the issue of consequential damages in his acceptance, the terms of the contract will include, and thus authorize, the collection of such damages if the seller happens to breach. Similarly, if the seller includes in his acceptance a limitation on warranty coverage, and there was no such provision in the purchase order, the limitation on warranty coverage will become part of the contract *unless the buyer objects upon receipt of the acknowledgement form.* These "battles of the forms" can lead to expensive litigation and negative results for an entrepreneur who is unaware of the potential for problems, or who does not take the time to read the terms proposed by the other party.

One way to avoid such problems is to insist that the parties negotiate a contract directly rather than relying on the exchange of forms to provide the framework for the contract. Following the negotiation, the entrepreneur should insist that the agreement be reduced to written form and signed by both parties. In so doing, the potential hazards of a battle of the forms can be avoided. Of course, such negotiations will take time, and will slow the commercial process, while the parties negotiate, discuss, and finally reach agreement on mutually acceptable terms; the slowing of the commercial transactions may have a negative effect on the entrepreneur's cash flow.

An excellent summary of the issues raised in a battle of the forms can be found at The Entrepreneur's Help Page.[17]

> **Key Point.** The UCC provides for a laxity in forming contracts that encourage commerce, but discourages the careful deliberations in contract formation that were commonplace at common law. The entrepreneur needs to ensure that he is aware of the contract terms to which he is agreeing, and should take steps to avoid agreeing to unacceptable terms, even if it entails slowing the process, or even losing the occasional contract.

In applying the information in this chapter, the entrepreneur should consider the application questions set out in the box below:

Application Questions

1. What steps should the entrepreneur take so that the venture does not "enter" into contracts accidentally?
2. What should the entrepreneur do if he does not have time to prepare a full blown contract?
3. Should the entrepreneur enter into non-disclosure agreements? If so, with whom?
4. What contract clauses should be included in the entrepreneur's contracts with his employees?
5. What contract clauses should be included in contracts with customers and suppliers?
6. Will the venture primarily be involved with the sale of goods under Article 2 of the UCC and/or CISG?
7. When the venture receives an order form, what should it do with the form? Who should be assigned the responsibility to read it thoroughly?
8. How can an entrepreneur select a law to govern his agreements?
9. Will the entrepreneur be involved in international contracts? If so, what provisions should he include in his international contracts?

Summary

Contracts are an essential component of any successful business venture. As a result, entrepreneurs need to understand what contracts are, how they are formed, and how they can be used to protect the entrepreneur and his venture. The rules governing contract formation are particularly important since these will oftentimes determine whether a contract even exists. Contracts are much more easily formed under the UCC than they are at common law. Under the UCC if the parties act *as if* they have a contract for the sale of goods, the court will find that they *do* have a contract. At common law there are very rigid requirements to be satisfied before the court will find that a contract exists.

An offer can be accepted, creating a contract (assuming consideration is present), or it can be rejected by the offeree, revoked by the offeror, or it can lapse. The right of the offeror to revoke an offer at any time before it is accepted is virtually unlimited at common law. Under the UCC, the right may well be tempered by the "firm offer" rule.

An entrepreneur should be aware of—and make appropriate use of—"special" terms and clauses in his contracts. **Non-disclosure clauses** should be used to protect trade secrets, business methods, and unique practices within the venture. All personnel with access to any of these should be required to sign a contract with such a clause (employees) or a separate contract (friends, family, directors, etc.). Non-compete clauses should be used to protect the entrepreneur from employees who take the information learned in the venture and either use it to start their own business in competition with the entrepreneur or who accept employment with a competitor, providing that competitor with information that would be harmful to the venture. A saving clause is used to protect a multi-part contract, or a contract with a number of clauses, from failing completely if one of the parts or clauses is invalid for any reason. The saving clause specifies that the balance of the contract is still valid and can be fulfilled, even if there are problems with some parts of the contract. Arbitration clauses are used to avoid litigation by agreeing to submit disputes and controversies to arbitration. The arbitration clause needs to be worded in a manner that shows a desire to provide a method of dispute resolution that is fair to both sides *and* also appears fair to third persons who may observe the situation from outside. A *force majeure* clause is used to excuse non-performance due to unforeseen external factors that make performance impossible or unduly burdensome. These clauses cover natural disasters, acts of God, and war among the things that will excuse performance without liability.

The battle of the forms arise when a buyer uses a purchase order and a seller uses an invoice or acknowledgement form and the forms do not agree on all of their terms. Courts applying the UCC will hold that a contract exists, and will then proceed to interpret what is included in that contract on the basis of UCC guidelines and rules. Entrepreneurs are well advised to avoid this potential problem whenever possible by negotiating a contract that both parties agree to and each party signs.

Key Terms

acceptance	non-compete clause
arbitration clause	non-disclosure clause
common law	offer
contract	purchase order
Contracts for the International Sale of Goods (CISG)	rejection
	revocation
force majeure	saving clause
lapse	Uniform Commercial Code

End-of-Chapter Questions

1. What is a contract? What distinguishes a contract from other forms of agreement or other exchanges of promises?
2. When docs a contract have to be in writing in order to be enforceable? How would a party prove that an oral contract had been entered into by the parties without the presence of a written document proving the agreement?
3. What is a non-disclosure agreement? When should an entrepreneur insist that his employees and/or acquaintances sign such an agreement? What protections will he have if he does have such agreements signed by these parties?
4. What is a non-compete agreement? When should an entrepreneur insist that his employees sign such an agreement? What must the entrepreneur do in structuring the agreement to give the greatest assurance that the courts will enforce the agreement?
5. What is a saving clause? Why would an entrepreneur want to include a saving clause in a contract with a customer?
6. What is an arbitration clause? Why would an entrepreneur want to use such a clause in an employment contract? Why would he want to use such a clause in a contract with a supplier or a customer?
7. What is meant by a battle of the forms? What will instigate such a battle? How do the courts resolve these battles under the provisions of the UCC?

Suggested Activities

1. Contact a local business or use a form book to get a copy of a purchase order and a copy of an acknowledgement form. Compare the terms the buyer would like to have included from the purchase order and the terms the seller would like to have included from the acknowledgment form. Using the rules set out in UCC §2-207, what provisions would be included in a contract based on these two competing forms?
2. Look up the case of *Dale v. Comcast Corp.*, 498 F.3d 1216 (11th Cir., 2007). Decide whether you agree with the court's opinion, and also what lessons an entrepreneur could/should learn from a review of this case about using an arbitration clause in a contract.

Notes

1. Charles F. Abbott, *And I Quote* by Applewhite, Evans, and Frothingham, Thomas Dunne Books, St. Martins Press, 2003, p. 229.
2. *Id.*, p. 71.
3. *Black's Law Dictionary* (1997).
4. According to *Black's Law Dictionary* (1997), "The system of rules, customs, and usages generally recognized and adopted by merchants and traders, and which, either in its simplicity or as modified by common law or statute, constitutes the law for the regulation of their transactions and the solution of their controversies."

5. Richard Stim, "Protect Your Trade Secrets with a Nondisclosure Agreement," Score, found at http://www.score.org/protect_your_trade_secrets.html

6. Provided by the How-To Network, found at http://www.how-to.com/Operations/legal-form-nda.htm

7. "Noncompete Agreements," NOLO, found at http://www.nolo.com/article.cfm/.

8. 71 F.Supp.2d 299 (S.D.N.Y. 1999), aff'd in part, 2000 WL 232057 (2nd Cir., 2000).

9. Carl S. Kaplan, "In Internet Time, A Year Is Much Too Long, Judge Finds," *CyberLaw Journal* (November 5, 1999), found at http://partners.nytimes.com/library/tech/99/11/cyber/cyberlaw/05law.html

10. "Employee Non-compete Agreement," found at publiclegalforms.com.

11. http://www.library.yale.edu/~llicense/sevcls.shtml

12. "Arbitration Clause," United States Arbitration & Mediation (USA&M), found at http://www.usam.com/services/arb_clause.shtml

13. *Force Majeure*, found at http://www.library.yale.edu/~llicense/forcegen.shtml

14. UCC §2-207.

15. UCC §2-204.

16. UCC §2-207(3).

17. "Battle of the Forms, Legal Aspects of Selling," The Entrepreneur's Help Page, TannedFeet.com, found at http://www.tannedfeet.com/battle_of_the_forms.htm

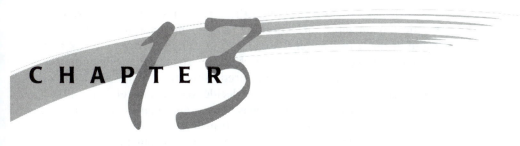

CHAPTER 13

OBTAINING INSURANCE TO PROTECT THE ENTERPRISE FROM RISKS

Facts are, insurance ratings are really dependent on the notion that some people are higher risk than others.[1]

INTRODUCTION

The entrepreneur should engage in risk assessment. She should determine what her risks are and what she should do about them. This will require a critical analysis of all the aspects of her business, including the people, property, and conditions necessary to a successful business operation. The entrepreneur should consider:

- safety issues
- the risk of crimes against the business
- the potential for fire or other disasters
- potential liability to others
- the financial condition of her venture, including its borrowing power and the costs of temporary closures[2]
- her personal financial position

It would be wise to discuss her list with her advisors in case she has overlooked some risks. She should prioritize the potential losses on the basis of their severity and likelihood. There are four basic ways to handle risks: eliminate them, reduce them, retain them, and transfer them. When the entrepreneur decides to eliminate the risk, she decides to stop providing the goods or services. For example, a pharmaceutical manufacturer may decide to stop manufacturing a particular vaccine because of the risks. The entrepreneur can decide to reduce the risk and/or severity of a loss. She can establish practices and procedures that will minimize the likelihood that her employees will be injured in the factory and file a worker's compensation claim. The entrepreneur can decide to accept or retain the risk. The costs of changing the business or of purchasing insurance may be more than she is willing to accept. Another alternative is to transfer the risk. In some cases the entrepreneur may be able to transfer the risk to her customers with a carefully drafted contract. For example, the skydiving instructor may require her customers to attend a safety class, view a video describing skydiving, and sign a waiver indicating that the customers are aware of the risks and they assume the risk of injury. When the entrepreneur purchases insurance, she is also transferring the risk. In this situation she is transferring the risk to the insurance company. The entrepreneur will not necessarily choose just one of these, she may combine the techniques to reduce risk. Often an entrepreneur who transfers risk to an insurance company will also try to reduce risks. Even when a loss is covered by an insurance policy, the loss will be disruptive to the enterprise. It can "cost" the entrepreneur time, energy, money and, sometimes, customers and reputation. The resulting "legal wake" will distract the entrepreneur and her employees from the primary task of growing the enterprise, even if the actual cost of legal defense and settlement are paid by the insurance company.

Insurance "protects" an asset or life, or it provides funds if the venture is liable. For example, the entrepreneur provides vehicles for herself and key employees. On the way to a business meeting with a potential angel investor, the entrepreneur has an accident driving the company car. The venture may be liable for the accident and, hopefully, it will have purchased insurance to provide protection for that liability. Although some business forms, like corporations, provide some protection for the entrepreneur's personal assets, they are not a substitute for being adequately insured. The venture itself may be liable, and the entrepreneur herself may be liable. In the prior example, the entrepreneur would be liable if she were negligent while operating the motor vehicle.

Insurance also protects the insured named on the policy.[3] This may be confusing to an entrepreneur who is operating multiple business entities. Assume an entrepreneur owns and operates a bowling alley. In her bowling alley, she also operates a coffee shop, and she has a store that sells bowling balls and accessories. She has formed all of these businesses as separate business entities. She should be careful that each entity has appropriate insurance. If the insurance policy insures only the bowling alley, her other two ventures will not be covered if a fire destroys the building and all three businesses.

The entrepreneur can protect her venture(s) from a number of different types of disasters and occurrences because there is a wide range of types of insurance, from automobile insurance to executive kidnapping insurance. This chapter will focus on insurance that the entrepreneur may want to purchase either through her venture or as an individual to protect herself and her assets. Writers often refer to this as "business insurance;" however, the insurance companies may not use this label. Insurance companies will generally refer to the specific types of insurance instead. Specific types of insurance will be discussed in this chapter and its tables.

Most insurance **premiums** will be tax deductible as a necessary business expense. Even so, insurance can be expensive. Insurance is one of the items the entrepreneur will generally be required to pay for in advance; In other words she cannot have a year's insurance and pay for it after the fact.[4] However, the entrepreneur may be able to pay for the insurance in quarterly or monthly installments. Also, the entrepreneur will not require all types of insurance. The type(s) of insurance she will need depends on the type of venture and the risks she decides to transfer in this manner. For example, she does not need product liability insurance if she is not manufacturing and selling products. The entrepreneur will be exposed to different types of risks depending on the type of venture. For example, a small consulting business with 8 clients will not be exposed to the same risks as a manufacturing operation with 25 employees who are exposed to combustible chemicals and dust.[5] The risks will also vary with the venture's stage of development: A beginning venture may not need **business interruption insurance** yet because it does not have much business. As discussed later, the entrepreneur can start with the most essential insurance for her venture and add insurance as her needs, income, and assets grow.

Although the law provides special rules for insurance policies, it is important to remember that insurance policies are also special types of contracts. The rules about contracts discussed in Chapter 12 apply. Much of the litigation surrounding insurance policies focuses on the meaning of contract terms in the policy and whether the particular event was covered by the language of the policy. The entrepreneur should document her conversations with the insurance representatives, and she should keep everything she receives from the insurance company and its representatives, including, copies of her application for insurance and sales brochures from the company. She may need these later to help prove that she reasonably believed the loss would be covered by her insurance policy.

The entrepreneur may be required to purchase insurance because of state or federal law, or because of contracts she has entered into. The state may require the entrepreneur to purchase worker's compensation insurance. Mortgages and leases commonly specify a minimum amount of insurance that the leasee must purchase on the property.

Insurance is primarily regulated by the states under the McCarran-Ferguson Act.[6] Many states license and regulate insurance companies operating in the state through the office of the State Insurance Commissioner. In addition to the state regulation, state law will influence both how the courts interpret the language of the insurance policy and when the entrepreneur will be legally liable for injury to others.

According to the U.S. Small Business Administration (SBA), "Buying business insurance is among the best ways to prepare for the unexpected. Without proper protection, misfortunes such as the death of a partner or key employee, embezzlement, a lawsuit, or a natural disaster could spell the end of a thriving operation."[7] There are a number of different types of insurance including property insurance, liability insurance, and business interruption insurance. There is no one standard package that will suit the needs of all entrepreneurs. Insurance companies do offer packages and the entrepreneur should evaluate these packages to determine if they meet her needs because the packages often offer a discounted price. Some small businesses will begin with a Business Owners Policy (BOP), which provides both protection for the venture's property and protection from liability. Some businesses start with a Commercial General Liability (CGL) policy, which protects only against liability. Other businesses put together the coverage they need "*a la carte.*" Generally, the entrepreneur will receive especially helpful advice from an insurance specialist who is knowledgeable about her particular type of business and can understand the unique risks related to it. Some insurance companies offer special packages that are tailored to particular industries. For example, an insurance company may offer a "producer's package policy" developed especially for filmmakers.[8]

The entrepreneur may wish to provide certain types of insurance as fringe benefits to employees and their families. This will also provide insurance coverage for her family. Health insurance, dental insurance, life insurance, long-term care insurance, and vision insurance are in this group.

INSURANCE VOCABULARY

Insurance, like many other areas, has its own specialized vocabulary. The entrepreneur will need to comprehend the terms in Table 13.1 in order to understand the policy and to communicate effectively with the insurance agent, insurance broker, or employee of the insurance company. An insurance agent is authorized by an insurance company to sell its products. In contrast, an insurance broker sells insurance products but does not have an exclusive relationship with a particular company, in other words, he can sell the products of multiple companies. Insurance company employees, like the employees discussed in Chapter 8, actually work as common law employees for an individual insurance company. The entrepreneur should be aware that the type of person with whom she deals may affect the products he offers. His compensation package may also affect his recommendations; for example, if there is a promotion on a product he may encourage her to purchase it if he is on commission, because he will receive a bonus. Regardless of whom the entrepreneur is dealing with, she should make sure that she understands the insurance being offered: She should not rely on the other person's representation that the insurance will cover her business needs.[9]

INSURABLE RISKS AND EVENTS

The law in most states requires that a person or business have an insurable interest before they can purchase insurance. The purpose of this rule is to prevent wagering. In fact, if the person who buys the insurance has no insurable interest, the policy itself is called a wager policy. Generally, the entrepreneur cannot purchase life insurance on the life of a sitting U.S. president. She does not have an insurable interest in the president's life. However, an entrepreneur who is producing a movie would have insurable interests in the life and health of key actors in the film. It would be expensive to replace the leading man after the filming has begun. Fireman's Fund Insurance Company insured the making of the *Iron Man* film with Robert Downey, Jr.[10]

In many states, including California, the entrepreneur cannot purchase insurance to cover intentional acts. She can only purchase it to cover negligent acts. Insurance policies often use the term "accident" to refer to negligent acts. Generally, punitive damages are not covered by insurance policies. An entrepreneur cannot purchase insurance to protect herself from regular business debts.[11]

PURCHASING INSURANCE POLICIES

SELECTING AN INSURANCE COMPANY

Insurance companies vary in the types of policies they sell, the states in which they are licensed, and the provisions (and language) in their policies. The cost of the insurance will also vary depending on the company. Although there are variations among insurance companies, insurance companies generally select one of the following three basic methods for establishing the rates, or premiums, they charge. They either:

- Calculate a class rate, where the insurance company places the entrepreneur in a class of homogeneous clients and charges the clients in the class the same rate.

- Use a schedule system, where the insurance company starts with a base amount, and the actual rate is determined by the current positive and negative features of the entrepreneur. For example, how far is the nearest fire department and fire hydrant from the entrepreneur's business premises?

- Use experience rating, or merit rating, where the insurance company uses the loss experience the entrepreneur has had in the past rather than current positive and negative features. For example, how many automobile accidents has the entrepreneur had during the last five years, and how much damage was caused by these accidents?

The entrepreneur may select from a stock insurance company, a mutual insurance company,[12] or a Lloyd's of London-type of association. (Lloyd's of

TABLE 13.1 Insurance Vocabulary

Term	Definition
Additional insured	This is an additional person or business that will also be protected on the insurance policy. Often the landlord may ask to be an additional insured on his tenant's policy. The additional insured can be insured for his or her own property interests, liability, or both.
Adjuster (Claim representative)	This is a representative of the insurance company who determines the cause and amount of a loss. The representative commonly makes a decision about the company's liability under the policy, that is, whether the loss is covered by the policy. Adjusters may be employees of the insurance company or independent contractors.
Carrier	This is another label for insurance company. The insurance company may also be called the second party.
Claim	This is a notification to the insurance company that a policy holder or some other person is making a claim under the terms of the policy. Some policies may require a written and timely notice. Many policies specify a time period in which the claim must occur.*
Commission	This is a fee or percentage paid to an insurance agent or broker. It is commonly paid by the insurance company.
Deductible	This is the amount that the entrepreneur will have to pay herself for a covered loss. If the loss exceeds the amount of the deductible, the insurance company will subtract the deductible amount from the amount that it will pay. If the loss is less than the deductible amount, the entrepreneur will have to pay for the loss herself. The deductible can be a dollar amount or a percentage, depending on the policy. Thus, if the venture has a $500 deductible on its automobile policy, it will have to pay $500 of the damages to the company car. The policy may specify different deductibles for different types of losses, such as vehicular accidents, theft, and vandalism. As a general rule, the higher the deductible (the more of the risk the entrepreneur is willing to accept), the lower the premium.
Endorsement	These are amendments to the policy or provisions that change or clarify the terms of the insurance policy.
Exclusions	These are losses or perils that the insurance policy does not cover. Life insurance policies generally exclude cases of suicide during the first two years of the policy.
First party coverage (Property coverage)	This is coverage for the insured's physical possessions and real property such as coverage for theft damage to the entrepreneur's business personal property.
Floater	This is a provision that covers personal property† that can be removed from the premises or high-value personal property that is not adequately covered by the regular policy limits.

(continued)

TABLE 13.1 *(continued)*	
Term	*Definition*
Inflation coverage	This is a provision in a policy covering property, under which the amount of coverage automatically increases when a certain index rises. The index used varies by insurance company. Most inflation coverage increases *and* decreases as the index rises and falls.
Insured	The person or business entity that is protected by an insurance policy.
Policy	The written contract between the insurance company and the person or business being insured. An insurance policy normally has two parts: the declarations page and the policy itself. The declaration page actually customizes the policy to the entrepreneur's business. It lists the named insured, location of the covered premises, policy period, limits of insurance by type of coverage, and deductibles. The policy covers the insuring agreement, definitions, what type of losses are insured and what type are not covered, special limitations, optional coverages, deductibles, conditions, and duties after loss. The policy would also normally include any endorsements.
Premium	The payment made to the insurance company to keep the insurance in force. Payments may be made annually or on some regular interval such as monthly or quarterly. The entrepreneur will probably prefer monthly payments unless there is a significant service charge for paying monthly.
Rider	This is a special provision which attaches to a policy. It changes the policy by increasing or decreasing coverage.
Third party coverage (Casualty coverage)	This is coverage for the insured's potential legal liability to another for a covered offense; as when, the entrepreneur is sued when someone slips in her retail store and claims that the slip is due to the entrepreneur's negligence. It covers both the legal liability to the third party and the cost of her legal defense.[‡] Common types of third party coverage are summarized in Table 13.3.
Underwriter	This is the company or person that evaluates what types of insurance and how much insurance the entrepreneur is allowed to purchase.

*The insurance company wants notice as soon as practical so that they can try to settle the claim and avoid a lawsuit. Most policies permit the insurance company to settle the claim: they do not need the permission of the insured. Once there is a claim the insured will have some duties; for example, she will have the duty to assist in the investigation and help protect the property from further loss.

[†]This Legal Companion uses the term personal property in the legal sense of the term. In the U.S. legal system, property is divided into real property and personal property. Real property is land and things that are permanently affixed to the land, such as buildings, hot water heaters, sheds, etc. (In Louisiana, real property is called immovables.) All other property is personal property. (In Louisiana, personal property is called movables.)

[‡]In many situations the cost of the legal defense greatly exceeds the amount of the legal liability to the third party.

London[13] quotes rates and provides insurance on a variety of unusual risks.) Lloyd's of London-types of associations are rare in the United States, so the discussion here will focus on the other two main types of insurance providers. Stock insurance companies, like other stock companies, sell shares of stock and the shareholders become the owners of the company, elect directors, and share in the net profits of the company. In a mutual insurance company, each policyholder (insured) becomes a member of the firm. Policyholders are entitled to vote on the firm's directors or managers, and they share in the firm's net profit either in the form of dividends or rebates on premiums *or* reductions in future premiums.[14] If the mutual insurance company is an assessment mutual company, policyholders *may* be liable if the company's losses exceed its assets. If it is a legal reserve mutual insurance company, the company establishes a reserve, and policyholders are not assessed. In selecting a company, the entrepreneur may wish to consider who is going to profit from the company's financial success. However, the range of products and the actual price of the coverage may be more important criteria for her.

Insurance companies are rated by A. M. Best, Fitch Ratings, Moody's Investor Services, and Standard and Poor's for their financial strength and/or credit rating.[15] The financial position of an insurance company is particularly important in an unsettled economy. Obviously, the entrepreneur will be disadvantaged if she purchases insurance from a company that fails after she has paid the premiums. Depending on the situation, she may also have difficulty obtaining a new policy from a different carrier.

Some insurance companies have a better reputation and higher customer (policyholder) satisfaction. (The same is, obviously, also true for insurance agents and insurance brokers.) It is more difficult to locate information about customer satisfaction, but organizations such as Consumers Union do rate customer satisfaction for some types of insurance companies.

COMMISSIONS

Commissions have an important place in the world of business; however, the entrepreneur should be wary when they are being used. The advantage of commissions is that they provide an incentive for an employee or independent contractor to work diligently. On the negative side, however, an insurance agent working on commission may select an insurance product or company on the basis of what the agent will receive and not on what is beneficial to the entrepreneur. Hence, individuals who promote themselves as "independent" insurance agents may not be so independent after all. (These potential risks also apply to insurance company employees who receive commissions.) In fact, the insurance commission system has led to unsavory practices, such as convincing the owners of life insurance policies to trade them in and purchase replacement policies in their place, thereby increasing the agent's commissions. This often operates to the detriment of the insured owner of the policy.

HOMEOWNERS INSURANCE VERSUS BUSINESS INSURANCE

An entrepreneur might think that her homeowners insurance will provide adequate insurance protection, especially if she is operating her business from her home office. Generally, a homeowner's policy will not cover home-based business losses. It may cover business property located in the home up to a certain dollar amount. It generally will not cover professional liability, loss of business data, and loss of business income. It also may not cover situations where a client slips and falls in the entrepreneur's home office. The average homeowners policy provides very little or no coverage for business personal property off premises, such as the entrepreneur's laptop computer she takes to an appointment. If the entrepreneur is operating her business from her home, she may be able to upgrade her homeowner's policy to obtain the insurance that she needs.

TECHNIQUES TO REDUCE INSURANCE PREMIUMS

There are a number of ways an entrepreneur can attempt to reduce insurance premiums. Some of them are specific to certain types of insurance. Other techniques may reduce premiums across multiple types of policies. Some of the latter include:

- Establish risk management and business continuity plans. These plans provide evidence that the venture has expertise in these areas and is committed to minimizing problems.
- Prepare reliable, accurate financial statements.
- Maintain accurate records of assets owned by the venture.
- Comply with the Sarbanes-Oxley Act (SOX) and best business practices.
- Show that the venture intends to manage risks and reduce the costs of insurance.
- Consider whether the location of the business will affect insurance premiums. The preferred location may be market driven, but for many ventures it is not. Is the business in an industrial location or a remote area? Is it in a part of the city subject to high crime rates?
- Record the loss history of the business. When there has been a loss, what has the venture done to reduce the risk of similar losses in the future? How does the venture manage risks of loss? For example, after a factory fire the entrepreneur may decide to install a sprinkler system, and to store flammable chemicals in a separate building away from the main facility.

Be aware that the reputation and problems of the venture's vendors reflect on the venture. If a large client of the venture is accused of deceptive billing, it may also reflect on the venture.

There are a couple major types of insurance, including property insurance and liability insurance. The entrepreneur is probably familiar with both of these coverages. Automobile insurance policies generally protect the entrepreneur's vehicle and provide liability protection in case she is sued by another driver. Property coverage will be addressed first.

PROPERTY INSURANCE

When an entrepreneur purchases property insurance, the insurance company will pay her for the covered damage to or loss of her property. Many policies include insurance coverage on both real and personal property, or, using insurance jargon, "property and contents." For example, the policy may include the factory the entrepreneur built, and the computers, electronic media, fax machines, and manufacturing equipment that she uses there. The property that is actually insured will vary widely because what the entrepreneur actually owns varies widely from venture to venture. In the previous example, the entrepreneur owned the factory and the equipment in it. In another situation, the entrepreneur may not own the building: she may have started a service business, where she rents her office and does not have expensive equipment. She may decide to forgo tenant's insurance until she becomes profitable or acquires expensive business assets.

Normally, the most basic policy available to the entrepreneur just covers fire. If the entrepreneur desires more coverage, she can generally purchase a property insurance package that would provide coverage for losses by fire, civil riot and commotion, smoke, hail, wind, aircraft damage, vehicle damage, explosion, and vandalism. As an alternative, the entrepreneur may purchase an "all risk" policy, which would be the most expensive package.[16] An all risk policy provides considerably more coverage; however, it will still have limitations and exclusions. In other words, it does not cover everything despite the title of all risk. Most packages do not cover losses due to theft: theft coverage would have to be purchased as an additional type of coverage.[17] The entrepreneur could purchase a "named peril" package that covers a list of perils she chooses, such as fire, wind, and hail.

There are a number of events that are excluded from most policies, regardless of whether they are all risk or named peril policies. Common examples include earthquake, earth movement, flood,[18] nuclear accident, and war. The entrepreneur may be able to purchase these coverages as **riders** or separate policies. For some of these perils, insurance may be available from a government entity. Even if these insurances are available, often the entrepreneur will choose to skip the insurance and retain the risk because the cost is prohibitive.

Property insurance policies have sections entitled "Property Not Covered" and "Property Subject to Limitations." The entrepreneur should read these sections carefully, and if she has high exposure to risk in these areas, she should ask about the cost of buying additional insurance by endorsements or **inland marine coverage**. (Inland marine coverage will be addressed in Table 13.5.) In considering whether the entrepreneur has a high exposure to risk, she should consider both the likelihood of the occurrence and the value of the property she is insuring.

The entrepreneur may be able to reduce her premiums for property insurance and reduce the likelihood of loss or the amount of loss by:

- installing a fire alarm and/or sprinkler system
- installing smoke detectors and adding fire extinguishers
- using safe procedures to handle and store dangerous or flammable materials
- installing a burglar alarm system
- improving the lighting in and around the building
- installing quality locks and deadbolts
- buying a secure safe
- hiring a security service to patrol the property

The entrepreneur can ask her insurance company if they have a safety inspector who can examine the property and offer suggestions. In many locales, law enforcement departments also inspect business properties and homes and provide suggestions for how to reduce the risk of break-ins and theft.

REPLACEMENT COST, ACTUAL CASH VALUE, OR POLICY LIMITS INSURANCE

Most property policies will compensate the entrepreneur for damage caused to the insured property by a covered loss. As with other types of policies, there may be deductibles and upper limits on the amount of coverage. The policy will also cover the total loss of items caused by a covered event, so the entrepreneur will need to decide how much the item is worth and make a decision about the type of coverage to purchase. Table 13.2 illustrates the payment options available for total loss coverage. The entrepreneur may choose different options for different assets. For example, if the venture has a two-year-old computer work station, replacement cost coverage may make more sense. The actual cash value of a two-year-old computer is relatively low because of obsolescence. If it is destroyed, the entrepreneur would not want to purchase another two-year-old computer, she would want to purchase a new one, which will probably be faster, have more memory, a new operating system, and new features.

LIABILITY INSURANCE

Liability insurance will protect the entrepreneur when a person or business makes a claim that her venture or her employees committed a tort. Risk management can reduce the likelihood that a tort will occur, but it cannot eliminate the risk. The entrepreneur or her employees can make a mistake, causing an injury to a "customer, client, competitor, or member of the general public."[19] Liability insurance provides two important coverages: it pays those sums the insured becomes legally obligated to pay as damages (if covered), and it pays for the cost

TABLE 13.2 Payment Options for Settling a Covered Loss	
Name	*Amount of Payment*
Actual cash value (ACV)	The entrepreneur will be paid the value of the item at the time it was destroyed. In most states, this is based on the cost of purchasing a new item at the time of the loss minus depreciation. This depreciation is not the same as the depreciation carried on the company books or tax return, but it is a factor of age, condition, use, and obsolescence at the time of the loss. In other words, the entrepreneur will be paid the actual value of the old item at the time of loss.*
Replacement cost	The entrepreneur will be paid the current cost of replacing the destroyed item *if* she actually replaces it.† She will be paid to "replace" the old item with a new one.
Valued policy (also called agreed amount or policy limits)	The entrepreneur will be paid the stated policy limits for the item destroyed if there is a total loss.

*This would not be the value of the item as carried on the financial records of the business.

†If the entrepreneur chooses not to replace the item, she will be paid the actual cash value.

of a legal defense. Many entrepreneurs will purchase a general liability policy and an umbrella liability policy[20] to protect against these claims. One source recommends that the entrepreneur buy sufficient liability coverage to cover at least twice her net worth.[21] Under liability insurance, the entrepreneur can buy protection for a number of different types of losses. See Table 13.3 for a description of some of the common types of coverage.

The importance of liability insurance cannot be overestimated. For example, in one case a disgruntled employee downloaded malicious computer code onto the networks of the company that employed him, its clients, and its vendors. The code sent confidential information into the public domain and destroyed some computer applications. It resulted in more than $10 million in liability claims against the firm.[22] While this type of claim is, hopefully, rare, the importance of coverage for such conduct by a disgruntled employee is obvious.

The insurance company is obligated to pay for the legal defense and the amounts the insured becomes legally liable to pay because of a covered loss. Consequently, in most states the insurance company is entitled to select the law firm that represents the entrepreneur. If the entrepreneur has legal interests that may be opposed to that of the insurance company, she may desire to hire her own legal counsel in addition to that retained by the insurance company. An example would be if the claimant is asking for an amount significantly in excess of the policy limits. If there was a settlement or a judgment in excess of the policy limits, the entrepreneur would be required to pay the excess amount.

TABLE 13.3 Types of Coverage in Liability Policies (Third Party Coverage)	
Name of Coverage	*Description*
Advertising injury	This coverage would pay if the venture *inadvertently* infringed the trademark of another business entity. Depending on the policy language, it may also cover liability for misappropriation of advertising ideas and disparagement of a person or entity's goods, products, or services.
Bodily injury	This coverage pays for physical damage or injury to a person's body, including any resulting emotional distress.
Medical payment coverage	This coverage does not require a showing of liability or fault. For example, if a customer falls in the entrepreneur's restaurant, it would pay for the customer's medical bills without a showing of fault. It does not include payment for pain and suffering or emotional distress.* It does not provide coverage for the entrepreneur or her workers.
Personal injury	This coverage would pay if someone claims the venture is responsible for false imprisonment, invasion of privacy, libel, or slander.
Property damage	This coverage would pay for the damage to the property of others, including the property of customers and suppliers that was in the care, custody, and control of the insured.

*It is generally believed that people are less likely to sue if they receive prompt payments to cover the medical costs of their injuries. This coverage provides money to them without their having to file a lawsuit or go to court.

PRODUCT LIABILITY INSURANCE

Entrepreneurs who manufacture, distribute, or sell products at the wholesale or retail level are potentially liable for their products based on a number of legal theories, including negligence, breach of express or implied warranty, defective products, defective warnings or instructions, and an unreasonably dangerous product. These entrepreneurs should consider purchasing product liability insurance. Product liability insurance does not reimburse the entrepreneur for the costs of repairing the defective product. It does pay for injury the product causes to the purchaser or user, or damage to his or her property.

WORKER'S COMPENSATION INSURANCE

Worker's compensation, discussed in Chapter 9, is funded by insurance policies in many states. The cost of a basic worker's compensation policy will be very low if the entrepreneur has no employees. The entrepreneur may wonder why she should purchase worker's compensation coverage if she has no employees. The insurance provides protection when she begins having employees; if it is determined that she is liable for someone else's employees who are injured on her premises; or if she believes that she has hired independent contractors but the court does not agree. As discussed in Chapter 8, the distinction between independent contractors and employees is not always clear.

Worker's compensation policies will be based on the category of the business, with different rates for different categories. It will also be based on the number of employees or amount of payroll. The insurance company may audit the books quarterly to compute the amount of premium the entrepreneur owes.

AUTOMOBILE INSURANCE

Most entrepreneurs are already familiar with automobile insurance policies. Most automobile insurance policies provide liability insurance, protection for assets (the vehicles), and coverage for injury to the driver and passengers. The standard auto policy provisions are summarized in Table 13.4. The entrepreneur should consider also purchasing uninsured and underinsured coverage. These coverages may be offered separately, or they may be combined. They reimburse the entrepreneur for her losses if the accident was caused by a motorist who either has no insurance (uninsured) or who has insurance with a low limit of coverage (underinsured). Unfortunately, state laws that require auto insurance do not eliminate the need for these coverages. In some communities, there are a high number of uninsured motorists and accidents involving these drivers.

TABLE 13.4 Standard Types of Automobile Insurance	
Type of Coverage	*Description*
Collision	This provides coverage for damages to the entrepreneur's vehicle arising out of a collision with another vehicle or object. This part of the auto policy tends to be the most expensive.
Comprehensive	This provides coverage for other types of damage to the entrepreneur's vehicle, such as fire, theft, wind, hail, or vandalism.
Liability coverage*	This provides coverage for the insured's liability to other people for bodily injury and loss to their property, such as bodily injury to the other driver and damage to his vehicle.
Medical payments	This provides coverage for medical payments to the insured and other people in the insured's vehicle.

*Automobile liability coverage is required in all states, except Mississippi, New Hampshire, Tennessee, and Wisconsin. If the entrepreneur or her employees are going to be driving on company business, she should purchase this insurance even if it is not required. See Nolo, "Small Business Insurance," found at http://www.nolo.com/article.cfm/objectId/C15734F6-12A4-4B4C-86B64DC607949877/111/182/ART/

As with other types of policies, there are techniques to reduce the amount of the premium as well as the likelihood of a claim. At a minimum the entrepreneur should consider:

- authorizing only certain employees to drive company vehicles based in part on their driving records (She may need to consider driving records while making decisions about hiring and promoting if she wants employees to drive company vehicles as part of their job performance.)
- offering defensive driving courses to employees
- equipping vehicles with safety equipment, such as seat belts in busses and vans
- promoting and encouraging vehicle safety

INTELLECTUAL PROPERTY INSURANCE

An American Intellectual Property Law Association survey found that the average cost to litigate a patent infringement case was over $1 million.[23] These costs place a beginning venture at a distinct disadvantage in litigation against a large, financially sound adversary. Intellectual property insurance can provide two basic types of coverage—loss to the entrepreneur's intellectual property, for example, copyright, patent, or trademark, and liability for damage to someone else's intellectual property.[24] Some policies insure for multiple types of intellectual property, and some insure only for one type, such as, patents, or even a particular patent. The entrepreneur can consider either or both types of coverage. The first can be called a "pursuit" policy, "offensive" policy, "enforcement" coverage, or "infringement abatement insurance," and it pays for the legal expenses incurred in suing someone who has allegedly infringed on the entrepreneur's intellectual property.[25] It is less common than the liability coverage and tends to be expensive. For example, Litigation Risk Management (LRM) charges $25,000 to perform an evaluation prior to issuing a patent policy, and the premium on the policy begins at about $25,000 per year for a policy with a $1 million limit.[26]

The liability coverage pays for infringement claims that are filed against the entrepreneur for actions of her venture. It can cover the acts of the company and its subsidiaries, and acts of officers, directors, and employees within the scope of their employment.[27] Often, it will also cover volunteer workers (gratuitous employees). It will pay for the defense of claims and for any resulting judgment up to the limits of the policy. It may be labeled "Defense and Indemnity" coverage. As with other insurance, this coverage will not protect the entrepreneur if she knowingly infringes on someone's patent. Generally, the policy will not protect the entrepreneur if she knows about the infringement or violation when she purchases the insurance. Prior to purchasing the insurance, the entrepreneur will be required to prove that she has filed for the registration of her copyright, patent, service mark, or trademark and has completed an appropriate intellectual property search.[28] In one case, where the coverage would have been helpful, an online insurance broker created "deep links" on its Web site, through which it sent users to the Web pages of various insurance companies, "creating a seamless navigational experience." In other words, it appeared to the user that the user was still at the broker's Web site. The insurance companies sued the online insurance broker for violating their copyrights and trademarks.[29]

BUSINESS INTERRUPTION INSURANCE

The entrepreneur should engage in business continuity planning (BCP), which involves developing strategies to prevent unnecessary long-term interruption to the venture's operations[30] and developing procedures to resume essential operations as quickly as possible. Creating a plan and taking the steps necessary to implement the plan may not be sufficient. The entrepreneur may also consider insurance. Business interruption insurance covers the entrepreneur and her venture for losses that require the business to shut down for a period of time due to a covered peril, such as a natural disaster, fire, or other catastrophe. A covered peril must cause the interruption in the business. A good set of records, especially those held at another location, will assist the entrepreneur in proving what she lost. The policy may cover:

- loss of earnings during the interruption. This would be the net loss caused, in other words, gross earnings prior to the loss less expenses prior to the loss.
- extra expenses incurred during the interruption. The entrepreneur can continue to operate her venture if she has additional funds. Examples would include the costs of moving to a new location, renting additional space, or renting equipment to use.
- loss of rents during the interruption.

An example of the latter would be if the entrepreneur owned an office building: Her venture operated from an office in the building, but she also rented out offices to other businesses. Because of a fire in the building, four of her tenants were unable to occupy their offices and, consequently, stopped paying rent until they were able to use their offices again. The insurance would compensate her for the lost rent.

SPECIAL TYPES OF COVERAGE

The entrepreneur should consider the special types of insurance described in Table 13.5 to shift the risks inherent in her business. The information in the description box indicates what type of property or activity is covered. The entrepreneur can use that information to determine if the coverage would be helpful to her venture. Most policies will have a limit on how much coverage the policy provides. For simplicity, the table refers to the coverage as a policy; however, it could be an endorsement or rider to another policy the entrepreneur is purchasing.

TABLE 13.5 Special Types of Insurance Coverage	
Name of Coverage	*Description*
Boiler and machinery	This policy would cover damage to boilers and other machines, including the pipes in the machinery.
Cargo	This coverage pays for damage to freight while it is in transit from one location to another.
Commercial liability umbrella policy	This policy provides excess coverage above the entrepreneur's limits on her other policies.
Completed operations	This policy protects the entrepreneur if she builds things such as homes and office buildings. It does not cover her for her mistakes during the construction. It will protect her from any *resulting* damage/injury should her building fail after she has turned the completed structure over to her customer. The policy covers the damage that occurs because of the entrepreneur's error. For example, if she did not put enough steel in a building and it collapses killing three people, the policy will cover the liability for the deaths. It will not cover the costs of correcting the building by inserting the correct amount of steel. Completed operations coverage is not limited to buildings. It can be purchased for other things the entrepreneur builds for her customers, such as furnaces or boilers.
Course of construction	This is a policy used when the entrepreneur is building or remodeling a property to suit her needs. It provides coverage for the period of construction. When the business is fully operational at the location it will require more coverage than during the construction or remodeling stage.
Crime	This policy protects the entrepreneur from theft, malicious damage, and embezzlement. It does not cover crimes in which she participates. This protection may be part of a packaged policy, or it may be specifically added to a policy.
Director's and officer's liability (D&O insurance or D&O liability)	This policy indemnifies corporate officers and directors for payments they make arising from business-related suits, including shareholder law suits.*
Electronic media	This policy protects the entrepreneur's computer programs and data.
Employer's non-owned auto	This policy protects the entrepreneur for liability arising from the use of automobiles not owned by her venture; for example, an employee uses his personal car for a business trip and collides with another vehicle.
Employment practices liability insurance	This policy protects the entrepreneur for her employment practices, such as defamation, discrimination, sexual harassment, and wrongful termination. It does not include worker's compensation claims. In many states, it does not cover intentional acts. It also may be called employers' liability insurance. However, that term is also used to describe insurance that indemnifies an employer when she has to pay for an employee's negligence under *respondeat superior*.

(*continued*)

TABLE 13.5 *(continued)*	
Name of Coverage	*Description*
Exterior signs	This policy protects the entrepreneur's signs that are outdoors.
Fidelity	This policy protects the entrepreneur from the lack of integrity or honesty of her employees or of a person holding a position of trust. The entrepreneur may choose employee dishonesty insurance instead, which is similar to fidelity coverage but covers more types of occurrences.
Floater	This coverage pays for a loss to movable property. It generally specifies a territory, and the property must be within the territory for the coverage to be in force.
Host liquor (liquor liability)	This liability insurance protects the entrepreneur for liability associated with the serving of alcoholic beverages.
Inland marine	This policy protects the entrepreneur's movable property.[†] It is, typically, property that is either actually in transit, held by a bailee, an instrument of transportation, *or* a movable type of property. It covers the specific property listed on the policy. It could be used to cover construction equipment that is moved from site to site, a traveling art exhibit, or a digital camera. The entrepreneur should compare this to floater insurance and select the one that best meets her needs.
Livery	This policy protects an entrepreneur who is transporting passengers, such as a taxi cab company or van service.
Malpractice (Professional liability coverage or errors and omissions liability coverage)	This policy protects the entrepreneur if she or her employees engage in a profession that is commonly sued for professional negligence. Common examples include dentists, doctors, lawyers, opticians, optometrists, real estate agents, and veterinarians. It pays for bodily injury, medical expenses, and property damage caused by the professional negligence, and the costs of defending the entrepreneur in litigation.
Products	This policy insures the entrepreneur if she manufactures products and a purchaser or user of the product is injured. The policy does not cover correcting the product, but it does cover the damage that occurs because of the entrepreneur's error. It is similar to completed operations coverage.
Property of others	This policy protects the entrepreneur for losses to the property of others when she is responsible to the owners of the property. For example, she may operate an automobile repair shop and may be responsible to her customers if their vehicles are stolen or burn while they are in her possession.
Sprinkler leakage	This policy protects the entrepreneur from damage from her sprinkler system.

(continued)

TABLE 13.5 (*continued*)	
Name of Coverage	*Description*
Tenant's improvements and betterments	This policy protects the entrepreneur if the business rents its business location instead of buying it. It generally covers improvements she made or acquired to the leased premises and cannot legally remove.
Trees, plants, and shrubs	This policy pays for the damage or destruction of the entrepreneur's landscaping, including trees, plants, and shrubs.
Web	This policy protects the entrepreneur's Web site against copyright infringement, damage caused by hackers and viruses, theft, and service interruption.

*Insurance companies consider a business' compliance with Sarbanes-Oxley (SOX) in establishing rates for director's and officer's liability insurance and other polices related to SOX exposure. (SOX was introduced in Chapter 4.)

†Inland marine insurance began as an outgrowth of ocean marine insurance, and it covered losses while goods were being transported on inland waterways such as canals, lakes, and rivers. It has been extended to cover property that is mobile, that is related to transportation or communication, or that otherwise requires special insurance.

In addition to the coverages on Table 13.5, the entrepreneur also can insure her accounts receivable, money and securities, and valuable papers and records.

MAKE A CLAIM TIMELY

Most insurance policies include a section entitled "Duties After Loss" which obligates the entrepreneur to take certain actions when there is a loss. The entrepreneur may not want to file a claim for every little issue; however, she needs to be cognizant of the deadline to file a claim specified in the policy. For their own protection most insurance companies specify a relatively short claim period. They too want to manage their exposure to risk. In addition, the insurance company may need to work quickly to obtain and protect evidence about liability and the amount of injury.

INSURANCE AS AN EMPLOYEE BENEFIT

Insurance can also be viewed as an employee benefit. Group health insurance for employees and their families is a coveted benefit. The entrepreneur herself may need health insurance. She may have left a full-time position, or may have been a full-time student with health benefits. She may find herself in a position where she does not have health coverage. Group health insurance can be a way for the entrepreneur to provide for herself and her family, and her employees and their families. In fact, her own needs for health insurance coverage may be her primary incentive for purchasing group health insurance. Providing free or discounted life insurance for employees' families is also a desired employee benefit helping her recruit employees.

The rates for both health insurance and life insurance may be affected by the lifestyles of the persons who are insured. In one case, an entrepreneur did not renew the group health insurance because the insurance company wanted her to lose a significant amount of weight and stop smoking cigarettes. The insurance company threatened to raise the rates significantly or stop coverage. The entrepreneur decided to stop coverage, thereby leaving herself, her family, and her employees' families uninsured.

Since lifestyles and current medical conditions may be an issue, the entrepreneur may be tempted to ask probing questions about employees' and applicants' medical conditions and family situations. The entrepreneur must use care not to cross the line and ask for information that is protected by law. For example, the entrepreneur may not ask whether the applicant is married, whether the applicant has children, and whether the applicant is taking any prescription medication.

The entrepreneur has to provide workers age 40 and older the same health care coverage offered to younger workers. If the plan is optional, older workers can be required to pay more in order to participate as long as the higher price is substantiated by actuarial charts.[31]

In the future, federal or state law changes may require entrepreneurs to provide health insurance for employees and their families. Entrepreneurs should stay current on the requirements. For information, entrepreneurs often rely on:

- insurance agents, brokers, or insurance company employees
- professional and trade associations, and their publications
- government agencies
- peers and mentors
- the Chamber of Commerce and/or Small Business Development Centers (SBDCs)
- the media
- legal counsel

The entrepreneurs who wishes or is required to provide health insurance should consider:

- a health insurance provider that uses managed care, such as requiring a second opinion before surgery and approval before expensive diagnostic procedures
- a monthly charge to employees who participate in the insurance, thereby transferring some of the expense to the employees
- a co-payment to be made by employees to encourage them to be reasonable about whether to seek medical care
- a health maintenance organization (HMO) or preferred provider organization (PPO). HMOs and PPOs *may* provide more health care coverage at a

lower cost than reimbursement coverage. The patient billing procedures *may* also be more streamlined.

- a Health Savings Account (HSA) to help employees set aside funds to pay for medical bills including high deductibles for health care
- a specialist to help analyze the insurance options

Cost will not be the only issue since the entrepreneur and her family will be users of the insurance plan.

The entrepreneur can also reduce health expenses by:

- providing healthy foods in the lunchroom and vending machines
- offering smoking cessation programs through work
- offering weight loss programs through work
- installing exercise equipment and/or offering exercise programs at work
- encouraging employees to have regular physical exams, flu shots, and other preventative care
- discouraging "presenteeism," which is when employees come to work when they are ill and contagious

When the entrepreneur pays part or all of the health insurance premiums for employees, she will generally receive a deduction for the venture's payment for both income and payroll taxes.[32]

LIFE INSURANCE ON FOUNDERS AND KEY PERSONNEL

"Life insurance is the only game you win when you die" or someone else dies.[33]

The venture should have a **business continuation plan** for how the venture will maintain operations if a key person dies, becomes ill or incapacitated, or decides to leave the company. The venture's plan may vary depending on which key person is being discussed. The venture may want to purchase key person life insurance that names the venture as the beneficiary if an essential person in the business dies, or disability insurance if one of the key parties becomes disabled and is no longer able to work. The purpose of this insurance is to compensate the venture for the loss of the key person and her knowledge, skill, vision, and effort, and to help the venture make the transition. Before purchasing the insurance, the entrepreneur should assure herself that the key person is really important to the operation of the venture and agrees to the purchase of the insurance. This is particularly important with the purchase of life insurance. One large bank decided to purchase life insurance on key employees in the middle- to upper-management levels. It revealed the fact that it was purchasing the insurance, and the managers were required to sign paperwork agreeing to it. However, the bank would not inform the employees how much insurance it was purchasing on their lives. Some of the employees were very uncomfortable with the bank's purchase. Life insurance is an especially sensitive topic in some countries, cultures, and religions. Some people believe that if something is stated it will become true. Obviously, the entrepreneur needs to be sensitive to the feelings and concerns of her employees, especially her key employees. While it may be a compliment to some that the firm needs to insure against their death, others may see it as crass and "dehumanizing."

If the venture is owned by more than one entrepreneur because it is a closely held corporation, partnership, limited liability company, or a limited partnership, the joint owners may decide to enter into a **buy–sell agreement** as part of their exit strategy. A full discussion of buy–sell agreements is outside the scope of this Legal Companion, and the entrepreneur should consult with a knowledgeable lawyer before entering into a buy–sell agreement. However, there are two general types of buy–sell agreements. In one type, called an entity-purchase agreement, the entity purchases the interest of the exiting owner. In the second type, called a cross-purchase buy–sell agreement, the remaining owners purchase the interest of the exiting owner. One issue with buy–sell agreements is how will the interest be valued, and another issue is what will be the source of funds for the purchase. If one owner exits because of his or her death, the purchaser(s) will need a quick source of funds for the payment. Life insurance policies can provide the necessary funds for whoever is making the purchase.

HOW TO SAVE MONEY ON INSURANCE

The entrepreneur should analyze her insurance needs and purchase wisely. She should consider the mix of premiums, deductibles,[34] and amount of coverage. The entrepreneur should:

- Prioritize her insurance needs, and purchase the insurance that she is required to purchase first. Then she should purchase other insurance in the order of priority. For example, if she is renting the business property, the lease will probably require tenants insurance. On the other hand, if she has a mortgage on the business property, the mortgage company will generally require insurance on the buildings and other structures.

- Consider the reputation of the company and the satisfaction level of its customers. For example, Consumers Reports rates different insurance companies and policies.[35] The entrepreneur can also contact the state department of insurance for information. Most insurance departments will provide data on the number of complaints filed against an insurance company and how many of the complaints the department considers to be valid.

- Consider purchasing more than one policy from the same company. Many companies offer "multiple line discounts."

- See if insurance is offered through business or trade associations. A group price may be available through them.

- Compare the prices of insurance companies owned by shareholders and mutual insurance companies. Mutual insurance companies often pay annual dividends to their policy holders and not to shareholders. However, some only offer limited types of insurance. Some business and trade associations have formed their own mutual insurance companies.

Price is not everything in insurance. The entrepreneur should consider the company issuing the policy. Is it reputable? Is it creditworthy? How reasonable is it to work with? Does it operate with multiple levels of agents and brokers who all receive commissions?

The entrepreneur should also consider how her actions and decisions affect insurance premiums. She can take actions that will reduce the likelihood of a loss, insured or otherwise. She should also be aware that her credit rating, the location of the business, and her claims history will influence whether the insurance company is willing to provide insurance to her, and the price for that insurance. The entrepreneur should examine a checklist, such as the one by Gregory Boop, on what type of information she should collect before she begins to shop for insurance.[36]

The entrepreneur should consider the application questions set out in the box below while selecting insurance for her venture:

Application Questions

1. What are the risks inherent in the entrepreneur's business? Is she going to eliminate, reduce, retain, or transfer the risks or some combination of them?

2. For all types of insurance, what is the cost to the venture, and does the cost make good business sense?

3. Is the venture legally required to purchase insurance under state or federal law?

4. Does anyone else require the entrepreneur to purchase insurance, such as landlords, lenders, or venture capitalists?

5. What liabilities are associated with the venture? Is insurance a reasonable way to protect against these risks?

6. How much insurance does the venture need to protect its assets, such as buildings, equipment, and inventory?

7. How much insurance does the entrepreneur need to protect her individual assets?

8. Does the entrepreneur have access to affordable health insurance through other sources, including her employer, a family member's employer, or an association?

9. Would offering health insurance enable the venture to attract and retain employees?

10. For health insurance, how much of the premium should the venture pay and what portion should the individual employee pay?

11. Does the venture have enough employees to enable it to obtain a volume discount?

12. Should the venture purchase life insurance on key executives and employees for its benefit? Would the venture suffer from the untimely death of any key executive or employee? How much would the venture suffer?

13. Is life insurance necessary to fund any buy–sell agreements?

14. Should the venture provide life insurance as a benefit to its employees? Should the venture pay for the policy, or should the cost be split between the venture and the employees?

15. Should the venture purchase director's and officer's liability insurance as a means of attracting directors and officers into the venture?

Summary

Insurance policies are a special type of contract with a special type of vocabulary. In making a purchase decision, an entrepreneur should consider the individual needs of her business, the exposure to risk, and the needs of her family and employees. She can take action to reduce the amount of premiums and the risk of loss. The entrepreneur should consider potential areas of risk and try to eliminate or minimize losses. Even though the loss may be covered by insurance, it will still be disruptive to the business enterprise. The entrepreneur does not want to pay any more than necessary to purchase quality insurance policies.

Key Terms

business continuation plan
business interruption insurance
buy–sell agreement
first party coverage

inland marine coverage
rider
premium
third party coverage

End-of-Chapter Questions

1. Why is it important to consider more than price in selecting an insurance company?

2. Distinguish among actual cash value, valued policy, and replacement cost insurance.

3. What are the differences between liability insurance and property insurance?
4. What types of ventures should consider insuring the property of others? Why?
5. What should the entrepreneur do to protect her electronic media?
6. Would business interruption insurance be more important to a nascent enterprise or a more established one? Why?
7. What types of ventures should consider intellectual property insurance? Why?

Suggested Activities

1. Obtain a business insurance policy from an insurance agent, broker, or insurance company employee. Analyze the policy. Summarize the policy by making two lists—what is included and what is excluded from the policy coverage. Are there any surprises? If so, what are they?
2. Locate the Web site of the state insurance commissioner or other state insurance regulatory body where the venture will be located. What type of information is provided on the Web site?
3. Assume that you are about to purchase a particular small business. Make a list of the types of insurance you think are necessary. Compare your answer with the information at one of these Web sites—the U.S. Small Business Administration, www.sba.gov (type business risk into the site's search box), or Insure.com, http://info.insure.com/business (use the Small Business Liability Tool under the Small Business Insurance button).
4. Locate another rating of insurance companies in addition to the ones mentioned in this chapter. How helpful is the information contained in the ratings? Why?
5. Assume that you are about to meet with your prospective insurance agent, broker, or insurance company representative for the first time. Make a list of questions to ask him.
6. Do most businesses purchase worker's compensation insurance in the state of operation? If so, what are the categories and rate structure used by the insurance companies?

Notes

1. Patrick J. Kennedy, found at http://www.brainyquote.com/quotes/quotes/p/patrickjk 292639.html
2. This would include how much loss the venture can absorb on its own.
3. It is unlikely in the following situation that all three businesses will be insured on the same policy. There are some types of policies, however, that cover additional insureds.
4. There are some types of insurance where the entrepreneur will initially pay a certain minimum amount and then she will be required to pay additional amounts based on audits by the insurance company. An example of this would be a Worker's Compensation policy which is based in part on the entrepreneur's payroll.

5. Or as one article put it, a business that manufactures power tools is at greater risk than a business that manufactures towels. Insurance Information Institute (iii), "Small Business Liability Insurance," found at http://www.iii.org/smallbusiness/liability/?printerfriendly=yes

6. 15 U.S.C. §§1011–1015. The Act returned most regulation of the insurance industry to the states. For a more detailed discussion of the Act, see the Insurance Information Institute (iii) Web site article, "The McCarran-Ferguson Act: What it Is, What it Isn't and Consequences of Repeal of the Insurance Industry's Limited Antitrust Exemption" found at http://www.iii.org/media/research/mcf/. For additional information about the proposed repeal of the Act and H.B. 1583, see Automotive Body Repair News (ABNR), "Repeal of McCarran- Ferguson Act Proposed," found at http://abrn.search-autoparts.com/abrn/article/articleDetail.jsp?id=589655, dated March 26, 2009.

7. Small Business Administration (SBA), "Get Insurance," at http://www.sba.gov/smallbusinessplanner/manage/getinsurance/SERV_INSURANCE.html.

8. Nolo, "Small Business Insurance," found at http://www.nolo.com/article.cfm/objectId/C15734F6-12A4-4B4C-86B64DC607949877/111/182/ART/

9. The insurance person may not truly understand the entrepreneur's venture and the risks inherent in it. In addition, some entrepreneurs are not willing to accept as much risk (i.e., go without insurance) as others. Some entrepreneurs have very few assets outside the venture and others have acquired significant assets that they are unwilling to risk.

10. "Assessing Multiple 'Iron Man' Hazards, Protecting Carrie Bradshaw's Bling—All in a Day's Work for Film Insurers; Unique Risks Covered by Fireman's Fund Insurance Company in This Summer's Blockbusters," *Business Wire*, (May 22, 2008), available on LexisNexis.

11. Nolo, "Small Business Insurance."

12. Reciprocal insurance companies (reciprocal exchanges) are similar to mutual insurance companies but they are outside the scope of this book.

13. Lloyd's of London is "a London insurance mart where individual underwriters gather to quote rates and write insurance." Bryan A. Garner (1999), Editor in Chief, *Black's Law Dictionary*, 7th edition, West Group, St. Paul, MN, p. 946. Lloyd's web page is found at http://www.lloyds.com/. The individual underwriters in Lloyd's act for a group of investors who pool their money to provide the insurance. Christine Ammer and Dean S. Ammer (1984), *Dictionary of Business and Economics*, Revised and Expanded Edition, The Free Press, A Division of Macmillan, Inc., New York, p. 234.

14. Benjamin Franklin and others chartered the first mutual insurance company in the United States in 1752. Ammer and Ammer, *Dictionary of Business and Economics*, p. 234.

15. More information is available at the companies' Web sites: A. M. Best is found at http://www.ambest.com/, Fitch Ratings is found at http://www.fitchratings.com/, Moody's Investor Services is found at http://v2.moodys.com/cust/default.asp, and Standard and Poor's is found at http://www.net

advantage.standardpoor.com/NASApp/NetAdvantage/servlet/login?url=/NASApp/NetAdvantage/index.do

16. The common package may be called the "basic" form and a more inclusive package may be called the "broad" or "special" form.

17. If theft coverage is important to the entrepreneur, she should make sure that it is included or added.

18. Information about flood insurance is available at the National Flood Insurance Program Web site found at http://www.floodsmart.gov/floodsmart/

19. Insurance Information Institute (iii), "Small Business." The cost of a lawsuit could bankrupt the enterpreneur's venture. Even if the venture is ultimately determined not to be liable, the litigation could be expensive and time consuming.

20. An umbrella policy (excess liability insurance) provides additional protection for events or occurrences that exceed the policy limits on the underlying liability policies. The underlying or primary policies are listed on the application along with their policy limits. As with other insurance, the umbrella policy will not cover all types of occurrences.

21. Eric Tyson and Jim Schell (2008), *Small Business for Dummies*, 3rd edition, Wiley Publishing, Inc., Indianapolis, IN, p. 164.

22. InsureCast, "Claim Scenarios: Internet Liability, Cybercrimes, and Ebusiness Interruptions," found at http://www.insurecast.com/html/cyberspace_loss_scenarios.asp

23. The survey was reported in Ronald C. Wanglin, Bolton & Company Web site, "A Primer on Intellectual Property Insurance," found at http://www.boltonco.com/boltonco/hotTopics/intellectualPropInsurance.asp

24. Automobile policies similarly offer these two basic types of coverage.

25. InsureCast, "What is Intellectual Property Insurance?" found at http://www.insurecast.com/html/intellectualproperty_insurance.asp. InsureCast sells (1) patent insurance which protects entrepreneurs from patent infringement; (2) patent infringement liability insurance for entrepreneurs who manufacture; use or sell things that may infringe someone's patent; (3) and intellectual property insurance which will help the entrepreneur enforce her rights to her patents; computer software design; copyrights; and trademarks.

26. Wanglin, Bolton & Company Web site, "A Primer on Intellectual Property Insurance."

27. *Id.*

28. During the application process the insurance company will inquire about the entrepreneur's prior intellectual property litigation, the entrepreneur's risk management practices, and the insurance company will require a patent search of the product or product line being insured. Wanglin, Bolton & Company Web site, "A Primer on Intellectual."

29. InsureCast, "Claim Scenarios."

30. For example, the entrepreneur may consider off site back-up systems to preserve company records.

31. Fred S. Steingold (2007), *The Employer's Legal Handbook*, 8th edition, Nolo, Berkeley, CA, p. 91.

32. See Internal Revenue Code §162 (1). Initially the tax deduction was not available to self-employed individuals on their tax returns. Effective in 2003, self-employed individuals can fully deduct health insurance premiums. Tami Gurley-Calvez (2006), *Health Insurance Deductibility and Entrepreneurial Survival*, Released April 2006, p. 4. This is a research study commissioned by the SBA Office of Advocacy and is found at http://www.sba.gov/advo/research/rs273tot.pdf Gurley-Calvez discusses the positive impact the change has had on the survival of entrepreneurships.

33. Ashton Applewhite, William R. Evans, III, and Andrew Frothingham (1992), *And I Quote, The Definitive Collection of Quotes, Sayings, and Jokes for the Contemporary Speechmaker*, A Thomas-Dunne Book, St. Martin's Press, New York, p. 228. "Saying" not attributed to anyone.

34. The entrepreneur can decrease the premium if she increases the deductibles. However, she should make sure that she can afford to pay the deductible that she selects.

35. "Weighing Your Health Plan Choices", Consumer Reports, 70(9) (September 2005), pp. 44–47. Partial information is found at their Web site in an article entitled "Weighing Your Health Plan Choices" found at http://www.consumer reports.org/cro/money/insurance/health/hmos-vs-ppos-905/overview/index.htm Additional ratings information is found at Consumer Reports (September 2007), p. 21 and there are articles on Flood Insurance, Consumer Reports (June 2008), p. 47 and Health Coverage, Consumer Reports (November 2008), p. 5.

36. Gregory Boop, "Business Insurance Purchase Checklist," available on the About.com Web site found at http://businessinsure.about.com/od/insuringyour business/tp/purchcheck.htm?p=1

IDENTIFYING LEGAL RISKS BEFORE *THEY* BECOME LEGAL PROBLEMS

First weigh the considerations, then take the risks.[1]

INTRODUCTION

"Most average entrepreneurs have trained themselves to react quickly to anything that happens, maintain their emotional state and take action. The excellent entrepreneurs, however, have the advantage of anticipating things before they happen and taking preventive measures."[2]

Every entrepreneur faces challenges, not just in the start-up period but throughout the life of the venture. A number of these challenges will be legal challenges or will involve situations with a legal component. When the entrepreneur is trying to brainstorm and analyze solutions, the potential legal repercussions will be instrumental in helping him select from among the possible solutions. Some solutions may initially seem feasible, but their implementation may be illegal or fraught with legal complications. Knowledge is an important part of decision making. The success of the entrepreneur's venture depends on his ability to deal with and resolve the problems that arise, including the legal problems. He can minimize the expenditure of funds and time by being cognizant of the law.

This book focuses on **preventative law**. Preventative law involves taking actions that prevent legal problems before they arise rather than dealing with them after the fact (i.e., remedial law). There are two key components to preventative law: considering the legal consequences of a given action *before* taking the action, and creating (and keeping) a paper trail. Both components are essential.

Practicing preventative law will help keep the entrepreneur out of court, allowing him to spend his time, energy, and money on the core business of the venture rather than sitting in a courtroom over the course of a trial and worrying about the consequences to his venture. In the unfortunate event that the entrepreneur does end up in court, the maintenance of a paper trail may provide evidence of the care he took in making and implementing the decision, and may allow the entrepreneur to avoid the imposition of liability or lessen the severity of any sanctions imposed. It is rare that litigants in court *truly* feel that they have "won" once they have paid all the court costs, expenses, and legal fees. Lawyers refer to the hazards of litigation, which means that either side can win the litigation. Very few court cases are a sure thing. If they were truly a sure thing, the side that is going to lose would be very motivated to settle out of court.

The entrepreneur cannot avoid legal problems unless he is aware that the potential for such problems exist. Entrepreneurs commonly talk about assembling "a toolkit" for their ventures. Knowledge of the law is an important part of the entrepreneur's toolkit. Legal problems rarely resolve themselves on their own. If a legal problem arises, the entrepreneur will need to consult with his lawyer, and maybe his insurance company, to discuss his options. These consultations may provide advice on how to resolve the problem, or they may encourage the entrepreneur to seek a settlement in order to minimize any potential loss or liability. Often it will be to the entrepreneur's advantage to resolve the problem quickly and with the minimum amount of publicity. Consequently, he will want to consider alternatives to the court system, such as negotiation, mediation, and arbitration. At other times it may be in the entrepreneur's best interests to allow the matter to go to court, relying on the judicial system to provide a resolution, which will also provide a precedent that may protect him and other entrepreneurs in the future should a similar issue arise. Such important decisions should *not* be made without seeking advice and counsel from his attorney and insurer. Some of the legal issues the authors have examined in this text are summarized in Table 14.1.

TABLE 14.1   How to Prevent Legal Problems

The entrepreneur should:

- Hire a competent lawyer appropriate for his needs and use the lawyer effectively. He should not be reluctant to have a quick discussion with his lawyer about potential concerns. *Chapter 1.*
- Remember that legal problems can and should be managed. He should try to avoid the problems that he can. When this is not possible, he should consider using negotiation, mediation, and/or arbitration. *Chapter 2.*

(continued)

TABLE 14.1 *(continued)*

- Select the appropriate business form for his venture at this point in time. In making this decision, the entrepreneur should consider the costs of establishing the form, the formalities that he needs to follow, the potential for personal liability, and the tax consequences of using the form. With most forms, it is critical to recognize that the venture is a separate legal entity from the entrepreneur. *Chapter 3.*

- Surround himself with formal and informal advisors and listen to them. This includes structuring his board of directors and/or mentors so that he will hear conflicting views. He should encourage the expression of varying views. The board should not be filled with individuals who always say "yes" or who are beholden to the entrepreneur. *Chapter 4.*

- Appoint or hire agents who can further the enterprise's goals. The entrepreneur should consider the type(s) of authority he is creating in his agents and the type of contractual liability that will result. The entrepreneur should also consider the type(s) of authority that he may have to act on behalf of the venture. *Chapter 5.*

- Analyze how much money the entrepreneur will need to launch his venture and to grow it. The entrepreneur should consider the potential sources of capital at various stages of growth. How plentiful or scarce are these funds? How much can he raise using these sources, and what will he have to give up in terms of return on investment and control? *Chapter 6.*

- Consider the types of torts that may be common in his type of venture and how to reduce the likelihood that these work-related torts will occur. He should remember that it is preferable to minimize the occurrence of torts, because any tort and the resulting publicity will tend to harm the venture's reputation. *Chapter 7.*

- Decide the work the entrepreneur will complete himself and the work that agents, employees, and independent contractors will complete. The entrepreneur should use care in selecting his agents, employees, and independent contractors. He should also use techniques to minimize the likelihood that he will be held legally liable for the acts of the workers he selects. *Chapter 8.*

- Be aware that local, state, and federal laws will place limitations on his employment practices, including hiring and promotion decisions, employee compensation, and other work conditions. *Chapter 9.*

- Be cautious to protect his reputation. It can take a long time to rebuild his reputation once it is damaged and the damage done may extend into his personal life and may thwart future opportunities to enter into business. *Chapter 10.*

- Protect his intellectual property, including copyrights, patents, trade secrets, trademarks, and service marks. When he deals with others, including employees and consultants, he should remind them of the need to protect his proprietary information. *Chapter 11.*

- Understand common contract terms and select terms that will aid him in reducing the risks of the transaction. Most business relationships, from hiring attorneys and independent contractors to leasing equipment and premises to selling his products, are based on contracts. *Chapter 12.*

- Consider his insurance needs so that he can protect his personal and business assets and his venture. Some types of insurance, like health insurance, can also improve the lives and health of the entrepreneur, his employees, and their families. *Chapter 13.*

- Read about potential legal problems and changes as the law develops. *Chapter 14.*

WORKERS, A POTENTIAL SOURCE OF LIABILITY

As the venture grows, the entrepreneur will need to hire employees, **agents**, and **independent contractors**. He cannot be everywhere and do everything himself, nor does he really want to do it all. He will hire employees to perform physical tasks for the venture. If an employee is engaged in a business-related task and is involved in an accident the entrepreneur may be liable to the third party under the theory of *respondeat superior,* that is, if the employee was in the course and scope of employment when the accident occurred.

The entrepreneur will hire agents to enter into contracts on his behalf, from sales agents to the chief financial officer (CFO). A worker can be both an employee and an agent, depending on her duties and job description. Many of his workers will be both. The entrepreneur should choose his agents carefully because the business' reputation is in the hands of these agents; he will probably be liable for the contracts they enter into based on the common types of authority, for example, express or apparent authority. In addition, if his agents are not honest and violate their fiduciary duties, they can injure the venture by their self-dealing.

An enterprise's agents generally work to further the interests of the venture, but there are occasions when an agent will overstep her bounds. The entrepreneur needs to make every effort to exert the proper amount of control over the conduct of his agents. This should include carefully drafted contracts that specify the scope of the agent's duties; an indemnification clause for wrongdoing or overreaching by the agent that results in liability for the entrepreneur; and the ramifications, including loss of employment, for any agent who does not adhere to the terms of the contract. The entrepreneur should also be very careful in discussions with any third persons with whom an agent is interacting, since the conduct of the entrepreneur may create apparent authority in the agent and, consequently, potential liability for the entrepreneur on any contract.

The entrepreneur may also hire independent contractors to perform physical tasks and/or enter into contracts. Independent contractors can be helpful, especially when the entrepreneur is starting out and does not have enough work to keep an employee busy. The entrepreneur can hire an independent contractor for the job when he has work. However, that flexibility also works for the independent contractor, and the independent contractor may not be available when the entrepreneur wants her. There is no *respondeat superior* for the acts of the independent contractor: however, the entrepreneur *may* be liable for the **torts** of an independent contractor on other legal grounds. When the independent contractor is entering into contracts for the entrepreneur, she is acting as an agent, and the normal rules pertaining to agents will apply.

CONTRACTS, THE FIRST LINE OF PREVENTION

Business operates by means of contracts. Careful contract formation is an essential element in the entrepreneur's efforts to effectively practice preventative law. A careful entrepreneur will consult with his attorney often when entering into a contract. The entrepreneur will want to determine if there are any terms the other party wants included that he is not willing to accept. For example, an **acceleration of payment clause** in a loan agreement may seem innocuous at the time of loan negotiation, but its implications may cause dire consequences. The entrepreneur will need to decide whether the funding being sought is so crucial that he is willing to accept the possible consequences of an acceleration of payment if the triggering event(s) should occur, and the likelihood of the occurrence of the triggering event(s).

The entrepreneur needs to be certain that he includes a **non-compete clause** and a **non-disclosure clause** in the contracts he will make with a number of his key employees and investors. This may well include family members and close friends. Some people may feel that including such clauses is an insult and shows a lack of trust in these relatives or friends, and, consequently, may decide not to include the clauses in order to avoid insulting these people. In doing so, the entrepreneur is risking more than friendship; he is risking his venture by relying on the good faith of these people. Is that a risk worth taking, especially for the entrepreneur who has put most, if not all, of his personal assets at risk in launching the venture? A discussion with his attorney about the advisability of such clauses should help him to make the correct decision. This discussion will also allow the entrepreneur to point out to his family members and friends that the inclusion of such clauses is not "personal," but rather a standard business practice and the clauses are being included "on advice of counsel."

The entrepreneur is going to produce goods or provide services for his customers, and when he enters into a contract to do so he undoubtedly has every intention of providing the goods or services in a timely manner, as specified in the contract. However, sometimes situations arise that make performance difficult or impossible. While the law provides some possible relief in such situations, the entrepreneur can obtain additional relief by including a *force majeure* **clause** in the contract. Such a clause excuses performance in the event that an unforeseen external factor hinders his ability to perform.

In hiring employees, including managerial employees, the entrepreneur should have an employee handbook that spells out the rights and obligations of the employees and the employer. In effect, this handbook will become part of the employment contract. The entrepreneur may want to include a mandatory binding arbitration clause, in which each side agrees to submit any claim or controversy to arbitration rather than going to court.

IDENTIFYING LEGAL PROBLEMS

Legal problems do not come pre-packaged, with red warning labels attached. Rather, they often crop up unexpectedly. Some such problems cannot be foreseen or prevented in advance, and others can be minimized by taking proactive steps. In these situations the entrepreneur needs to practice preventative law by taking steps to avoid, or at least minimize, the legal issues that can be anticipated. Some situations will not be so obvious, and the entrepreneur may be uncertain whether there are potential negative legal implications. In these situations, the entrepreneur should check with his lawyer to get an idea of the potential risks and their likelihood. An excellent rule of thumb for the entrepreneur is, "when in doubt check with your attorney" about potential legal issues or problems. He will find that the dollars spent on preventative law will provide an excellent "return on his investment."

KNOWLEDGE IS POWER

There is an old adage that says "ignorance is bliss." Bliss is defined as utter joy or contentment. While this adage is often cited, and provides a catchy "excuse" for a person's failure to take advantage of opportunities to learn, it is not the roadmap to entrepreneurial success. Any entrepreneur who desires success in his venture would be well advised to acquire as much knowledge as he possibly can. He needs to seek information and knowledge about the industry he plans to enter, the competition he will be facing, the demand—and the anticipated demand—for his product or service, and the direction the industry is likely to go in the foreseeable future. He needs to consult with his attorney about the legal issues that he *will* face, that he *might* face, and that he should make every effort *never* to face.

The entrepreneur needs to know the different business organization options available, and then he needs to select the organization type that is most advantageous for his venture at this point in time. He will need to know about employment law—including discrimination law, **agency** law, sales law, and taxation. He will need to make inquiries into the cost of capital as well as potential sources of capital. He should learn about export opportunities and potential export problems if his venture has the potential for international sales, as well as import rules and regulations if he expects to import goods or compete with manufacturers from other countries.

The entrepreneur will need to familiarize himself with **intellectual property** law, and he will need to recognize which types of intellectual property he will be using and what protections are available for them. He will need to know the difference between a trademark and a copyright, as well as the difference between a patent and trade dress. He will need to identify when developing a trade secret might be a better option than seeking a patent, and he will need to know how to ensure that a trade secret is properly handled to maximize its protection.

Francis Bacon once said "Knowledge itself is power."[3] According to Samuel Johnson, "Knowledge is of two kinds. We know a subject ourselves, or we know where we can find information on it."[4] The entrepreneur should have knowledge of the subject, the venture, before embarking into the field. He should also know where to find information for those areas in which he lacks personal knowledge. If he does these things, and if he follows the advice of those from whom he seeks this information, he increases the likelihood of success. He might also want to consider the advice of Dr. David M. Burns who said "Aim for success, not perfection. Never give up your right to be wrong, because then you will lose the ability to learn new things and move forward with your life."[5]

An entrepreneur must also remember that "Nothing will ever be attempted, if all possible objections must first be overcome."[6]

In applying this chapter and the material in this book, the entrepreneur should consider the application questions set out in the box below:

Application Questions

1. What areas of the law apply to the particular controversy at issue?
2. Can the entrepreneur's legal counsel help prevent the problem? If not, can legal counsel reduce the damage after it has occurred?
3. Should the entrepreneur consult with a specialist in a particular area of the law?
4. How much could the problem potentially cost the entrepreneur compared to the potential legal fees?
5. Are there any government agencies that can provide information and advice?
6. Are there any private organizations or reference works that can provide information and advice?
7. Can this problem be turned around into an opportunity? If so, how?

Summary

The entrepreneur needs knowledge about a number of things including recognizing and evaluating opportunities. He also needs to know about the law and where to obtain more information about the law. His lawyer is one excellent source, but there are others. The law evolves and changes, sometimes "at glacial speed," and sometimes seemingly overnight. While scanning the business environment for opportunities and threats, the entrepreneur should simultaneously scan the legal environment in which his venture operates or in which he plans to expand. The legal environment can "open" new opportunities, and it can close opportunities. The sooner the entrepreneur becomes aware of potential changes, the easier it will be to make adjustments when and if such changes occur.

Key Terms

acceleration of payment clause
agency
agents
force majeure clause
independent contractor

intellectual property
non-compete clause
non-disclosure clause
preventative law
torts

End-of-Chapter Questions

1. What is preventative law and how does it differ from remedial law?
2. What is meant by the hazards of litigation?
3. What is the difference between an agent and an independent contractor? Why would an entrepreneur want to have certain employees classified as independent contractors rather than as agents?
4. Why is the use of specialized contract clauses, such as a non-compete clause or a *force majeure* clause, advisable for an entrepreneur? What risks are posed by using such clauses in a contract?
5. What proactive steps might an entrepreneur want to take in order to identify legal problems, and why are such steps important for the entrepreneur?

Resources for the Future

Rather than include any suggested activities in this chapter, the authors have chosen to provide the reader with certain *Resources for the Future*.

One of the purposes of this text is to guide the entrepreneur as he moves forward with his venture. It is not a treatise on each topic covered. The law changes and sometimes the changes are swift and dramatic. The authors have collected some reliable Web sites the entrepreneur can use for additional current information on the topics covered by this guide. (The authors and publisher have made every effort to assure that the Web addresses are correct at the time of printing. However, Web sites do change and/or stop operating.) Many of these sites also provide free email newsletters which may be of interest to the entrepreneur. Only Web sites that allow free access have been included. Web sites such as Lexis and Westlaw are reliable, but will be a little expensive for the occasional research question.

- About.com   http://entrepreneurs.about.com
  This Web site has information on a number of topics for entrepreneurs. It includes information on Business Legal Organizational Structures and a "How To" Library.
- AFL-CIO (AFL-CIO is a federation of U.S. labor unions)   http://www.aflcio.org/yourjobeconomy/safety/wc/upload/comptable.pdf
  This Web site has a chart comparing state worker's compensation statutes at this address.
- All Business   www.allbusiness.com
  This Web site has useful legal information including checklists.
- American Arbitration Association (AAA)   http://www.adr.org
  The AAA home page provides information about its services.
- American Express Business Resources   http://www133.americanexpress.com/osbn/Landing/informyourdecisions.asp?us_nu=subtab
  This Web site includes information on a number of entrepreneurship topics including insurance.

- Beginner's Guide http://beginnersguide.com/accounting/sarbanesoxley/
  This Web site discusses Sarbanes-Oxley.
- BenefitsLink.com, Inc. http://benefitslink.com/index.html
  This Web site caters to the employee and benefits professional. It has a Web page that provides a way to search for specific provisions of ERISA at www.benefitslink.com/erisa/index.shtml.
- BFI Business Filings, Inc. www.bizfilings.com
  This Web site contains information about choosing a business form and the requirements. It also includes information about selecting an attorney.
- Business.gov www.business.gov
  This official government site includes information about hiring a lawyer, laws and regulations, and workplace issues.
- Business Owner's Toolkit by Commerce Clearinghouse http://toolkit.cch.com
  This Web site includes sample form contracts, tax information, and other information of interest to the entrepreneur.
- *BusinessWeek* Online www.businessweek.com/smallbiz
  This Web site has a legal solutions section. It includes a section on how to form a corporation.
- Candela Solutions www.candelasolutions.com
  Candela Solutions is an accounting firm that focuses on working with boards of directors and management. Their Web site provides information about Sarbanes-Oxley.
- CEO Business Express www.ceoexpress.com/default.asp
  This Web site is "the Executive's Internet" and provides links to business news sources, including newspapers and business magazines.
- Committee of Sponsoring Organizations of the Treadway Commission (COSO) www.coso.org
  This voluntary organization developed the COSO internal control standards, which are currently the only standards recognized by the SEC for compliance with Sarbanes-Oxley. The entrepreneur can obtain a free set of the COSO standards and information about how to interpret them from the Web site.
- Cornell Library http://www.library.cornell.edu/
  Cornell has its Copyright Information Center at www.copyright.cornell.edu/.
  The Cornell Copyright Information Center includes a detailed chart showing the effective dates of various copyrights in the United States. It is listed on the Web page under Resources and is called the "Public Domain Chart." It was revised January 1, 2009, and is found at http://www.copyright.cornell.edu/ public_domain/
  The site has a number of other copyright resources.

- *Directors & Boards Journal* http://www.directorsandboards.com/
  Directors & Boards Journal is a quarterly journal on serving as director or CEO. It posts selected articles from the journal on its Web site.

- Entrepreneur.com http://www.entrepreneur.com/
  This Web site includes articles and videos on a number of topics of interest to entrepreneurs. Two articles of particular interest are "Hiring and Orienting a New Employee" found at www.entrepreneur.com/humanresources/hiring/article 80126.html and "Establish a Workplace Safety Policy" found at www.entrepreneur.com/humanresources/employmentlaw/article80144.html

- Entrepreneurs' Help Page www.tannedfeet.com
  This Web page includes information on law and legal forms. It has information about forming an LLC, a corporation, a partnership, and a sole proprietorship.

- Saint Louis University John Cook School of Business Entrepreneurship Program EWeb http://eweb.slu.edu
  This Web page has information and advice for entrepreneurs.

- Financial Executives International www.fei.org
  This is an organization of CFOs, vice-presidents of finance, treasurers, and audit committee members. The organization posts the current issue of its magazine on the site. Sarbanes-Oxley is a common theme in the organization's publication.

- FindLaw Small Business Center www.Smallbusiness.findLaw.com
  This Web site has information about employment, intellectual property, and "Ten Things to Think About—Picking a Business Form." The general FindLaw Web site found at http://public.findlaw.com/?DCMP=KWC-G-PUBLIC is also helpful.

- Home Biz Tools www.homebiztools.com
  This Web site specializes in information for home based businesses.

- *Inc.com* www.inc.com/guides/start_biz
  Inc. Magazine has an article entitled "Tort Claims Business Owners Should Watch Out For," which discusses intentional torts at http://www.inc.com/articles/legal/gen_biz_law/defamation/15379.html.

- Independent Contractor Report http://www.workerstatus.com/
  This Web site has updates on rulings and other issues important for entrepreneurs who hire independent contractors.

- Inside Sarbanes-Oxley www.insidesarbanesoxley.com
  This Inside Sarbanes-Oxley Web site contains articles, blogs, book lists, and discussion groups.

- Insurance Information Institute www.iii.org
  This Web site includes information about interpreting insurance policies and responding to natural disasters.

- Insure.com http://info.insure.com/business

  This Web site has a Small Business Liability Tool under Small Business Insurance, which lists common types of businesses and the insurance they should purchase.

- International Chamber of Commerce http://www.iccwbo.org/

  This Web site has information about doing business internationally.

- InterNIC.com www.internic.com

  This Web site provides information about registering Internet domain names under the Internet Corporation for Assigned Names and Numbers (ICANN). More detailed information is available from ICANN at www.icann.org

- JAMS (formerly known as Judicial Arbitration and Mediation Service) www.jamsadr.com/employment_guide-2003.asp

  JAMS handles a number of types of arbitration, including arbitration in employment matters. This Web page has its rules and procedures for employment arbitration.

- Job Accomodation Network (JAN) http://www.jan.wvu.edu/links/adalinks.htm

  The JAN Web site has numerous resources on the Americans with Disabilities Act, including recent amendments to the statute.

- Jill Gilbert Welytok www.abtechlaw.com

  Welytok has a Web site with information about Sarbanes-Oxley. She is the author of *Sarbanes-Oxley for Dummies* referenced in prior chapters.

- JoeAnt.com http://www.joeant.com/DIR/info/get/3831/52587

  JoeAnt has a business owner's toolkit at www.toolkit.com, which offers a number of resources including a detailed guidebook, business checklists, business forms, human resource help, and a place to ask questions.

- Ewing Marion Kaufmann Foundation http://www.entrepreneurship.org/

  The Kaufmann Foundation's goal is to foster entrepreneurship and entrepreneurship education. Its Web site includes information of interest to entrepreneurs.

- Lambda Legal Defense and Education Fund www.lambdalegal.org

  This Web site maintains an updated list of state and local laws that prohibit workplace discrimination based on sexual orientation.

- LearnAboutLaw www.learnaboutlaw.com

  Under its Reference button, this Web site has links to state statutes for all 50 states at http://www.learnaboutlaw.com/state-statutes-for-all-50-states. The entrepreneur clicks on the state in which he is interested and then selects the type of code he wants to research. It also has links to the secretary of states offices at http://www.learnaboutlaw.com/secretary-of-states-office-links

- Martindale.com http://www.martindale.com/

  This is the Web site of Martindale-Hubbell that publishes legal directories. It includes some information about the law and searchable data bases for lawyers and law firms.

- National Association for the Self-Employed (NASE) www.nase.org

  This Web site has information on a number of topics ranging from health care to taxes. The entrepreneur can also obtain individualized advice from the consultants.

- National Center for State Courts http://www.ncsc.org/

  This Web site contains information about alternate dispute resolution and the state courts, including information about the court structures in the states.

- National Conference of Commissioners on Uniform State Laws (NCCUSL) http://www.nccusl.org/nccusl/default.asp/

  The NCCUSL provides fact sheets and information about its efforts to encourage states to adopt uniform acts. The University of Pennsylvania, in conjunction with NCCUSL, posts drafts and final versions of some of the uniform acts at http://www.lawupenn.edu/bll/ulc/ulc.htm

- Nolo Press www.nolo.com

  Nolo Press has a number of free articles and a free online legal encyclopedia at its Web site.

- SCORE, Counselors to America's Small Business www.score.org

  SCORE has articles and podcasts on a number of topics of concern to entrepreneurs. The entrepreneur can also ask questions or locate a local SCORE office.

- Small Business Advisor www.isquare.com

  This Web site has articles for the entrepreneur addressing questions, such as "should I incorporate in Delaware?"

- United Nations Commission on International Trade Laws http://www.uncitral.org/

  This Web site has information about the Commission's initiatives.

- United States Chamber of Commerce www.uschamber.org

  This Web site includes topics of interest to small business owners. It also discusses the agenda of the Chamber of Commerce.

- United States Congress http://thomas.loc.gov

  Thomas is Congress's Web site for information on federal legislation.

- United States Copyright Office http://www.copyright.gov

  This Web site includes information about copyrights.

- United States Department of Commerce www.doc.gov

  This Web site provides information for various types of businesses. Its Bureau of Economic Analysis has a Web site at www.polisci.com/exec/commerce/01529.htm, which includes economic data for different industries.

- United States Department of Justice http://www.usdoj.gov/a-z-index.html

  This is the main index page for the Department of Justice.

- United States Department of Justice Computer Crime & Intellectual Property Section http://www.cybercrime.gov/

  This Web site includes information about how to report cybercrime and intellectual property crime.

- United States Department of Labor (DOL)

  U.S. Department of Labor's *Occupational Outlook Handbook* is available at www.bls.gov/oco/home.htm. DOL's Web page on retirement plans is available at www.dol.gov/dol/topic/retirement/erisa.htm. DOL's index for programs under the jurisdiction of the DOL's Wage and Hour Division is available at www.dol.gov/esa/aboutesa/main.htm. The federal minimum wage laws are administered by the regional offices of the Wage and Hour Division of the DOL. Contact information for the regional offices is available at www.dol.gov/esa/contacts/whd/america2.htm. DOL's list of addresses for state labor departments and other state labor resources is www.dol.gov/dol/location.htm. State minimum wage laws are at www.dol.gov/esa/minwage/America.htm

- United States Environmental Protection Agency (EPA) www.epa.gov/smallbusiness

  The EPA Web site has information on environmental issues and how to do business with the EPA.

- United States Equal Employment Opportunity Commission (EEOC) www.eeoc.gov

  This Web site has an extensive collection of information on the ADA, including publications. One publication that is especially good is *The Americans with Disabilities Act: A Primer for Small Businesses*, which can be downloaded or read online.

- United States Government Printing Office http://www.gpoaccess.gov

  This Web site includes many federal documents and links to federal agencies.

- United States Internal Revenue Service (IRS) www.irs.ustreas.gov

  The IRS Web site has IRS forms, instructions, and booklets. Many of the forms can be filled out online and printed. Information about employees, independent contractors, and statutory employees is also available. It has a section for business tax issues at http://www.irs.gov/businesses/.

- United States National Labor Relations Board (NLRB) www.nlrb.gov

  This Web site includes information about the National Labor Relations Act, how cases are handled, and the rights of employers.

- United States Occupational Safety and Health Administration (OSHA) http://www.osha.gov/index.html

  This Web site provides links to the state OSHA Web sites.

- United States Patent and Trademark Office http://portal.uspto.gov

  This Web site includes information about patents and trademarks. There is a searchable data base. "How To Get a Patent" is available at http://www.uspto.gov/web/patents/howtopat.htm. A list of lawyers registered to practice before the USPTO is at www.uspto.gov

- United States Securities and Exchange Commission (SEC) http://www.sec.gov

  The SEC provides free access to SEC electronic filings at http://www.freeedgar.com. It also has a Web page that discusses SOX at http://www.sec.gov/about/laws.shtml#sox2002

- United States Small Business Administration (SBA) www.sba.gov

  The user can type in search terms at this Web site at www.sba.gov/tools/resourcelibrary/index.html

- United State Supreme Court www.supremecourtus.gov

  This official Web site posts Supreme Court opinions. Generally, opinions will be posted within a day or two after the decision is announced.

- United States Tax Court www.ustaxcourt.gov

  This Web page provides information on tax cases, tax court procedures, and a video about the tax court.

- University of Chicago http://adminet.uchicago.edu/admincompt/icug/icintro.shtml

  This Web page addresses the distinctions between employees and independent contractors and it has advice for people who hire independent contractors.

- *Wall Street Journal* Center for Entrepreneurs www.startupjournal.com/

  The Wall Street Journal provides information about small businesses at this Web page.

Notes

1. Helmuth von Motke, found at http://www.quotationspage.com/search.php3?homesearch=risk&startsearch=Search
2. Alex McMillan, *Teach Yourself Entrepreneurship*, p. 74, © 2006 Alex McMillan, Hodder Headline, published in the United States by McGraw-Hill Companies.
3. Francis Bacon, as quoted in *And I Quote* by Applewhite, Evans and Andrew (2003).
4. Samuel Johnson, as quoted in *And I Quote* by Applewhite, Evans, and Frothingam (2003).
5. http://www.quotationspage.com/subjects/success/
6. Johnson, Note 4, *Supra*.

INDEX